pencil markings
noted 6-4-2020

Peace and War on the Anglo-Cherokee Frontier, 1756–63

Peace and War on the Anglo-Cherokee Frontier 1756–63

John Oliphant

Louisiana State University Press
Baton Rouge

Published in the United States of America 2001 by
Louisiana State University Press

Published in Great Britain 2001 by
Palgrave Publishers Ltd

ISBN 0–8071–2637–3

10   09   08   07   06   05   04   03   02   01
5   4   3   2   1

The paper in this book meets the guidelines for permanence and durability of the
Committee on Production Guidelines for Book Longevity of the Council on Library
Resources. ∞

For Pippa, Tim, Rolly and Ruth

Contents

List of Maps

Preface

The starting point for any serious research into Anglo-Cherokee relations during the Seven Years War is the mass of official correspondence to be found at the Public Record Office at Kew. Class CO 5 contains the reports of governors to Secretaries of State and the Board of Trade, along with voluminous enclosures and the Sessional Papers of the colonial assemblies. Of these the papers relating to South Carolina have been by far the most useful, while those relating to Virginia, North Carolina and Georgia have been of subsidiary, but significant, interest.

The writing of Chapters 2 and 3 depended quite heavily upon the dispatches written by William Henry Lyttelton, governor of South Carolina 1756–60, to the Board of Trade. Lyttelton enclosed with these letters numerous copies of letters received from the frontiers, particularly from Forts Prince George and Loudoun in the Cherokee country. Some of these enclosures can be found in the Lyttelton Papers in the William L. Clements Library, alongside a truly vast assemblage of letters never forwarded at all. A few of these were laid before the Commons House of Assembly and so found their way into the so-called 'Indian Books', published as *Colonial Records of South Carolina. Series 2. Documents Relating to Indian Affairs 1754–1765* (University of South Carolina Press, for the South Carolina Department of Archives and History, Columbia, 1970). These collections together reveal how the governor's view of Cherokee relations was built up; and it must be said that it was constructed of materials often misleading and too often mendacious.

The role of Virginia's Indian recruiting and of Brigadier-General John Forbes was approached partly through the Virginian papers in CO 5; but also, and much more fruitfully, through Forbes's headquarters papers in the possession of the University of Virginia. These were supplemented with the Forbes Papers in the Dalhousie Muniments, located in the National Register of Archives (Scotland) at GD 45/2. A. P. James collected a mass of Forbes's out-letters, including many in neither of the above collections, published as *The Writings of General John Forbes Relating to his Service in North America* (Collegiate Press, Menasha, Wisconsin, 1938). These sources also contain valuable material relating to William Byrd's recruiting expedition, as do some original documents in the 'Virginia Papers' (Series ZZ) in the Draper

Collection owned by the State Historical Society of Wisconsin. Further evidence of Byrd's work as recruiting agent, as well as his later role in the Cherokee war, can be found in the second volume of a published selection of the Byrd family's correspondence edited by Marion Tinling, *The Correspondence of the Three William Byrds of Westover, Virginia 1685–1776* (University of Virginia Press for the Virginia Historical Society, Charlottesville, 1977). The editor has been particularly careful to cite the location of the original document (where known) and of any copies (in CO 5 or WO 34, for example), making verification of many of the transcripts fairly straightforward. This suggests that other transcripts taken from less accessible archives can be relied upon.

An awe-inspiring number of original letters by Forbes, Lyttelton, Atkin, Sir William Johnson and may others can be found in the Loudoun and Abercromby papers, at the Henry E. Huntington Library, San Marino, California. A significant number of these have been published in the Forbes, Bouquet and Johnson collections, but many have not, and they supply important detail for the period 1756–8.

A second important PRO class is WO 34, the Amherst Papers, volumes 47 and 48 of which contain the commander-in-chief's correspondence with officers and governors in South Carolina. The large part of these volumes is given over to the letters which passed between Major-General Sir Jeffrey Amherst, Abercromby's successor as commander-in-chief in North America, and Colonel James Grant, commander of the 1761 expedition against the Cherokees. Historians have long acknowledged Grant's humanity and the reluctance with which he pursued his orders to inflict heavy losses upon his foes before allowing them to make peace. It has also been long recognized that Grant allowed the Cherokees a peace significantly easier than that expected in South Carolina; and that he was rewarded with execration in the colony because of it. David H. Corkran's *The Cherokee Frontier: Conflict and Survival 1740–1762* (University of Oklahoma Press, Norman, 1962) and J. R. Alden's *John Stuart and the Southern Colonial Frontier* (University of Michigan Press, Ann Arbor, 1944) are both magisterial books of their kind. Densely detailed, judicious, broadly sympathetic to Grant, and rightly admiring of the Cherokee statesman Attakullakulla, they are still the best histories of Anglo-Cherokee relations in the period. But both authors took the correspondence at face value and assumed that Grant's behaviour could be explained largely by military and logistical difficulties. In Tom Hatley's more recent work, *Dividing Paths*, an ideological desire to portray the Cherokees as victims of unrestrained aggression – as in large part they certainly were – causes the humane Grant to disappear altogether. It cannot be denied that Grant could be ruthless when he chose, but that was a less important side of his character than the sympathy and even fellowship he felt for the Cherokees. A careful reading of his letters to Amherst reveals that he intended to conclude a moderate peace from the start, and that his commander-in-chief's inflexible attitude compelled him to evade his orders in order to do so.

This interpretation is confirmed by other sources, all of which have been used by other historians, but rarely in conjunction. The most important of these is the vast collection of Grant Papers, known as the Ballindalloch Muniments, at Ballindalloch Castle in Banffshire. Here are letters which were unknown to Corkran and Alden, and which Hatley did not use at all. The owners, Mr and Mrs O. M. Russell, kindly lent me working space and personally produced the bundles I needed. Unfortunately Bundle 772, Grant's letter book for the 1761 campaign, is now missing, even though it was cited (and quoted from) in Paul David Nelson's recent biography, *General James Grant: Scottish Soldier and Royal Governor of East Florida* (University Press of Florida, Gainesville, 1993).

The Library of Congress possesses the fascinating journal kept by Christopher French, a light infantry captain who liked to record each day's events in some detail. As we shall see in Chapter 5, French's record contains vital clues to the negotiations between Grant and Attakullakulla at the end of May 1761. Corkran made extensive use of French but failed to notice, because he was not looking for it, that he actually mentions the secret conference held before the public talks.

French's account of events up to 5 June can be checked against a much shorter and balder diary kept by Major Alexander Monypenny, Grant's second in command. Monypenny also reveals the marked conviction in the British camp that peace was about to be secured. Corkran did not use Monypenny, which may account for his failure to notice the private negotiations, but I was able to obtain typed transcripts of the major's journal and order book from the Gilcrease Museum in Tulsa, Oklahoma.

French is also a lively source of the general mood in the British camp – at least among the officers – during the successful negotiations of July to September 1761, and he suggests openly what the official record itself seems to suggest: namely that Grant had no intention of allowing the retributive executions demanded by South Carolina, even had the Cherokees accepted them. Other British officials shared Grant's sympathy, if not his freedom of action. The preference of Governor Henry Ellis of Georgia for a compromise settlement is well brought out in Cashin's *Governor Henry Ellis and the Transformation of British North America* (University of Georgia Press, Athens and London, 1994).

But the behaviour of the lieutenant-governor of South Carolina, William Bull, was far more ambivalent. Bull had to answer to his Council and Assembly, and the record clearly shows that he disliked and evaded conflicts, sometimes at the expense of principle. The evidence on this point is so unambiguous that I have readily followed Eugene Sirmans's suggestion in *Colonial South Carolina: A Political History* (University of North Carolina Press, Chapel Hill, 1966) that during the difficult negotiations of 1761 he twice caught a 'diplomatic illness'. For this reason J. Kinloch Bull's somewhat eulogistic, sometimes apologetic biography, *The Oligarchs in Colonial and Revolutionary Charleston: Lieutenant-Governor William Bull and his Family* (University of South Carolina Press, Columbia, 1991), should be approached with caution.

Clearly one has to end somewhere and the details of the Anglo-Cherokee frontier were never finally settled. The discussions at Augusta in 1763, the plan of 1764, the survey and marking of the boundary in 1765, to say nothing of the subsequent revisions prior to the American Revolution, all have valid claims, yet to include them would have extended the thesis well beyond its word limit, and perhaps without making a proportionate contribution to the subject. For present purposes the 1761 Treaty of Charleston, which decided that there should be a formal boundary, and one reasonably favourable to the Cherokees, is a better terminal point than any of these. But in that case the consequent realignment of Cherokee diplomacy and politics between Charleston and the Congress of Augusta in 1763 becomes an essential epilogue to the story. Thus in the final chapter it was necessary to reach out towards 1763 and Augusta. This Epilogue, intended to balance the introductory survey of Anglo-Cherokee relations, does not pretend to break new ground and relies substantially on secondary materials. There are, however, exceptions. The section on the Cherokee visit to London in 1762 relies heavily upon the Burney Collection of newspapers in the British Library, where they can be consulted on microfilm. There are also interesting accounts in the *Royal Magazine* and *Gentleman's Magazine* which can be consulted in their original form. By using a wide range of London journals a detailed narrative of the Cherokee embassy can be constructed, just as Carolyn Thomas Foreman did many years ago in *Indians Abroad 1493–1938* (University of Oklahoma Press, Norman, 1943). However, the press was often seeking to entertain rather than to inform, and to take the newspapers too literally – as Foreman sometimes does – is to invite embarrassing errors. To some extent the papers can be checked against each other, but we are fortunate in having other published sources. *The Memoirs of Lieutenant Henry Timberlake* (London, 1765), also used by Foreman, are by far the most important. A work not available to Foreman, *The History of Parliament*, reveals a curious ambiguity about the identity of the Lord Eglintoun who presented the Cherokees to George III. Unfortunately present biographies of Timberlake's companion, Thomas Sumter, are not at all helpful, while the so-called 'Sumter Papers' in the Draper Collection are in fact transcripts from the London newspapers! For the Augusta Congress I have made considerable use of the papers in CO 5/65, as well as a number of microfilmed letters in the Amherst Papers in the Clements Library.

Some manuscript collections were out of reach. The Henry Ellis Papers in Georgia, the James Glen Papers at the University of Virginia and Lyttelton's out-letters at the Clements Library were all unmicrofilmed at the time of writing. Henry Ellis's interventions in Cherokee affairs were neither direct (he deferred to South Carolina) nor substantial, and evidence about these initiatives crops up elsewhere. Glen's governorship of South Carolina came to an end in 1756, although he tried his hand as an Indian agent in 1758; a recent biography casts little new light on the later episode beyond that available from other sources.

However other very substantial collections have been filmed or otherwise copied. The Tracey W. McGregor Library at the University of Virginia not only lent the three reels of Forbes Papers free of charge, but threw in a very useful calendar as well. The Library of Congress sold me the film of Christopher French's journals; Yale University Library made me copies of their files of the *Maryland Gazette*; and the Gilcrease Museum supplied a copy of their typed transcripts of Monypenny's journal and order book. The William L. Clements Library lent films of their Lyttelton, Amherst and Gage collections at a modest cost. The vast Draper Collection, though fully filmed, is marketed as a commercial project and very expensive; however, I was able to purchase the Virginia Papers series, which contains some original materials, through the Cambridge-based firm of Chadwick Healey.

Few of these items would have been affordable had it not been for the generosity of the History Department at Queen Mary and Westfield College and of the Central Research Fund of the University of London.

The College supported my preliminary visit to Ballindalloch and made it possible for me to see the French, Lyttelton and Monypenny documents. The Central Research Fund made two grants which allowed me to make a second visit to Ballindalloch and Edinburgh, and to obtain the remaining microform materials. A visiting fellowship allowed me to spend a month at the Huntington in the summer of 1999, principally among the Loudoun and Abercromby Papers.

My thanks are due to the many archivists and librarians who provided invaluable assistance, often well beyond the call of duty. The Huntington preserves an intimate and friendly atmosphere making it a delightful place in which to work. From the Clements Library Dr Robert S. Cox wrote me long, cheerful letters, and his colleague, Susan Swasta, saw that I received the right films. The Early American specialist at the Library of Congress suggested a number of manuscript locations. In the United Kingdom the reference staff at Eastbourne Central Library bore my demands for use of the microfilm readers, and for arcane interlibrary loans, with fortitude and patience. The University of Sussex likewise allowed me use of their microfilm readers and their large and convenient collection of secondary works. Susan Richardson of Interlibrary Loans at QMW was indefatigable in her efforts to obtain the most obscure and elusive items. In Edinburgh the staff at General Register House gladly helped me find my way through the guides to the sources I needed.

On a more personal note, my former colleagues Roger Whitmore and John Berryman gave up valuable time to assist in the preparation of the maps and to proofread the PhD thesis which later became this book. My wife and children have helped in these and innumerable other ways over the years, with immense and generally cheerful forbearance.

Finally I must thank the Imperial History seminar at the Institute of Historical Research for listening patiently to early versions of the chapters on Grant and to an expanded account of Ostenaca's visit to London. It would be invidious to single out individuals, but Emeritus Professor P. J. Marshall knows how much I owe him in terms of friendship and support. Above all I must express my immense gratitude to my former doctoral supervisor, Emeritus Professor Glyndwr Williams. His patient and encouraging guidance over a decade of part-time work has made the following chapters much better than they might otherwise have been. Whatever shortcomings remain are my responsibility, not his.

Acknowledgements

I am grateful to the following for permission to use the illustrations in this book: Map 1 is based on Betty Anderson Smith, 'Distribution of Eighteenth Century Cherokee Settlements', in Peter H. Wood et al. (eds), *Powhatan's Mantle: Indians in the Colonial Southeast*, published by the University of Nebraska Press, 1989; Maps 2 and 4 are adapted from R.C. Simmons, *The American Colonies*, © R.C. Simmons 1976, with the permission of PFD on behalf of R.C. Simmons; Maps 3 and 8 are adapted from *The Indian Boundary in the Southern Colonies, 1763–1775* by Louis De Vorsey, Jr., copyright © 1966 by the University of North Carolina Press, used by permission of the publisher; Map 9 is reproduced from *Memoirs of Lieutenant Henry Timberlake* (London, 1765), by permission of the British Library (shelfmarks 1418.h.2, 279.f.29, G.14547).

1

Long Canes Creek: Anglo-Cherokee Relations to 1756

The Cherokee nation inhabited some sixty towns[1] scattered across the southern tip of the great Appalachian range, from the Tennessee, or Cherokee, River in the west, to the edge of the Carolina piedmont in the east. Most of the region was mountainous, wild and formidable, giving the Cherokee far greater security than would have been available in the piedmont or tidewater regions. Yet it also gave the nation great strategic importance, giving its warriors access to two river systems, those of the Savannah and its tributaries in the east and the mighty Ohio–Mississippi system to the west. The whole region was perhaps a hundred miles from east to west, and about fifty miles wide.

The Cherokees' importance also derived from their numbers. Their relatively isolated mountain dwellings afforded them considerable protection, not only against the direct impact of white settlement, but against the Old World pathogens which devastated the piedmont and tidewater peoples. Though far from immune to the ravages of smallpox, measles, typhus, influenza and whooping cough, the Cherokees and other inland peoples were able to partially rebuild their numbers between epidemics. In time they learned to abandon traditional treatments, such as sweating followed by cold baths, which only encouraged the smallpox and brought on secondary respiratory complaints. Thus in the first half of the eighteenth century their numbers dwindled relatively slowly. In 1685, possibly over a century after the first appearance of smallpox in their towns, there were over 32 000 Cherokees. Although this number was halved by the great epidemic of 1696–9, by the early eighteenth century there may have been as many as 20 000 of them, 6000 of whom were active warriors.[2] By contrast the white population of South Carolina, the colony nearest to the nation and most concerned with its affairs, was only 12 000 in

1720 and still no more than 15 000 by 1740.[3] In 1738 a terrible smallpox epidemic carried off about half the Cherokee nation, reducing them to between 9000 and 11 000 people, and about 3000 warriors.[4] But they were still almost as strong as the Creeks, and much more numerous than the Chickasaws, with about 500 warriors. The Catawbas had only 300, reduced by smallpox to about 50 in 1758. Of all the southeastern nations only the distant Choctaws, with 5000 gunmen, were appreciably more powerful.[5]

By 1750 the numbers of South Carolinian whites had risen to 25 000;[6] while the Cherokees, beset by Creek raids, could do no more than hold their own. But South Carolina also had a potential fifth column in the shape of 39 000 black slaves[7] who might rise in rebellion at any moment. North Carolina and Virginia, with far larger white populations, had their own slaves and were not much interested in the Cherokees. Georgia, with only 4200 whites, was continually terrified of annihilation by the Creeks,[8] the French, the Spaniards, or a combination of all three. As we shall see, the nightmare of a general slave rebellion, perhaps combined with a general Indian war, consistently deterred South Carolina from deploying its full strength on the frontiers. Under these conditions even the reduced numbers of the Cherokees could appear very formidable indeed.

The valleys and mountains divided the nation into four or five discernible regions. The names usually given to them, if not the regions themselves, may well be of European origin, reflecting as they do the geographical view from South Carolina. Yet the European classifications were based at least to some extent on Cherokee reality, for in diplomacy and war each tended to follow its own interests. There is some archaeological evidence that they represent distinct chronological cultural phases from about AD 1000, the Overhill region (Maps 1 and 9) being the most recent. Nevertheless, as Dorothy Jones argues, these differences concealed an underlying consensus as to the general goals of the nation.[9] These goals included the security of the nation's hunting grounds, obtaining a sufficient supply of reasonably priced trade goods, and sustaining the nation's independence.

The Lower Towns or Settlements were those at the foot of the Appalachians along the Keowee River, with one or two towns on the Tugaloo. It was these towns which were most exposed to Creek attacks from the south, and, far more inexorably and dangerously, the steady advance of British settlement from the east. The Middle Settlements, over the first passes from the Lower Towns, were built along the upper Little Tennessee River and its tributaries. Northeast of the Middle

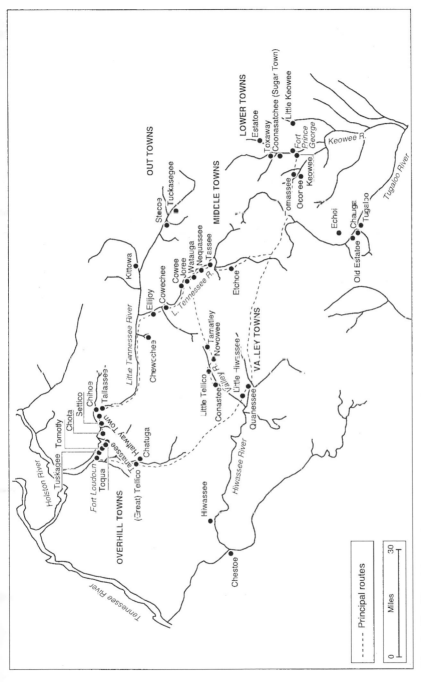

Map 1 The Cherokee country

Towns, sheltering under the wall of the Great Smokies, lay the Out Towns, a small isolated group of settlements centred on Stecoe. The Valley Towns, on the banks of the upper Hiwassee River and of its tributary the Valley, may have been home to half the Cherokee population, and reputedly had the best hunting. The Overhill Towns, on the lower Little Tennessee and separated from the Valley Settlements by the Unaka Mountains, were the most distant from Carolina, and included Chota, the 'mother town' of the nation.[10] Exposed to the raids of Iroquois, Shawnee and other northern Indians, and lying uncomfortably close to Fort Toulouse in the Creek country (Map 2), the Overhills were very sensitive to the problem of relations with the French. As early as 1746 they asked South Carolina for a fort to protect their homes and families from raids, but they also took care to keep open their communications with Louisiana.[11]

Though the Cherokees had probably been settled in that region for some 300 years, their language was an island of Iroquoian dialects in a Muskogean sea,[12] suggesting an earlier migration from the north. Indeed, Cherokee tradition spoke of just such a migration.[13] But Cherokee was not a closely knit language. The isolation of the valleys bred linguistic diversity into at least three related dialects. *Elati*, spoken only in the Lower Towns, and therefore most exposed to the white advance, is now extinct. *Kithuwa* was the speech of the Middle Settlements, some of whose inhabitants escaped Removal in the 1830s, and is still spoken in North Carolina. *Atali*, the dialect of the Valley and Overhill Towns, survives among the descendants of the removed Cherokees in Oklahoma.[14]

But even within a region united by a common dialect individual towns had considerable independence. Because the Cherokee economy, like that of all eastern woodland nations, was semi-agricultural, permanent settlements were made wherever the rich valley bottom soils were sufficiently level to support gardens. A settlement might consist of as few as two or three households, say a dozen people, to over 500 men, women and children. These groups of quite substantial log and daub houses, sometimes two storeys high, were grouped into organizational units known as 'towns' of 350–600 inhabitants, each with its 'town house' or assembly hall. The town house was always a massive structure, built to seat the entire population on circular tiers of benches around a central fireplace. Built of logs and roofed over with earth, a town house looked like a small sugar-loaf mountain rising from the centre of a town. Probably the need to get everyone into the town house for council meetings, together with the limited space for gardens, tended to determine the size of towns. Yet there were anomalies. The buildings of Great Tellico and Chatuga were intermingled, but the two towns had separate town houses. But while Chota and Tomassee were physically distinct, they shared one town house and one council.[15]

In the council the seats nearest the fire were reserved for the town dignitaries. The most senior in time of peace was the headman, usually a priest, together with other elders or 'beloved men'. These were older men who, somewhere between the ages of fifty and sixty, had ceased to join war parties. Next was the war leader, or Warrior. Others included, in roughly descending order of status, the Outacité or Mankiller, the Raven and the Slave Catcher. Behind them sat the 'young men', active warriors who had set up their own households and thus ceased to be 'boys', and the adult women. Everyone sat with his or her clan, and each of the seven clans – to say nothing of individuals – might have its own view. No headman was able to impose decisions by his own authority; rather he was supposed to follow the consensus of the council, a consensus which was naturally difficult to achieve.[16]

Decisions for or against war, for example, were usually taken at the council which marked the turning of the Cherokee year in September, an event marked by the ceremony of ritual renewal called the Green Corn Dance, and which every Cherokee at home would attend. On these occasions alone all the war officials – priest, leader, speaker, surgeon – would speak and were listened to very carefully. But not until the whole council, with all its contrasting elements, had decided for war could plans be laid and war parties assembled. Even then there was no means of conscripting warriors and no military discipline in the western sense. Even after a war party set out an individual warrior could refuse to fight or return home without formal penalty – though it might be hard to face his peers afterwards. Individual war leaders had to rely on volunteers and enthusiasm, and once the war bands set out the warriors were beyond the control of the elders at home.[17]

With the elders almost devoid of coercive power, war was as hard to prevent as to plan and direct. For in some ways individual Cherokees were under stronger legal obligations to their clan than to the wider community. The most dramatic, and fatal, of these obligations fell under the law of blood vengeance. Should a Cherokee murder a member of another clan, it was the duty of the victim's clansmen to settle the account by killing him. If the killer had the sense to flee another member of his own clan would have to pay the price instead, unless the murderer himself went to war and returned with a scalp for the victim's clan. But once retributive blood was shed, that was the end of the matter; retaliation by the murderer's clan was not tolerated, as it could have rapidly divided the nation in a destructive civil war.[18]

However, should the killer be a foreigner any member of that man's nation would suffice as a scapegoat, and the blood feud could be open ended. To guard against this danger the duty of revenge did not operate against aliens living in the nation. Other Indians living among the Cherokees had no clan to avenge them if they were killed; consequently no Cherokee was obliged to take revenge upon them. White residents, usually traders, had to be treated even more circumspectly, as killing one could lead to an embargo – as in 1734, 1746 and 1751 – or even war. But that did not remove the individual's *right* to take revenge if he so chose, and Cherokee deaths outside the nation certainly imposed an obligation to do so. Thus it was quite possible for individual young men to plunge the whole nation into war.[19] As we shall see it was this fatal mechanism which dragged the nation into conflict with South Carolina in 1759, against the will of the vast majority of headmen. In Estatoe in the Lower Towns, for example, the Old Warrior who favoured peace was totally unable to restrain Seroweh (or Saluey), the Young Warrior who favoured all-out war.

With such anarchy even at the town level, it is hardly surprising that towns could and did act independently within their regions. Yet the same forces of clan loyalty which made control by the headmen so difficult could and did produce regional cooperation. Delegates from the towns would assemble in the town house of the district's 'beloved town': Keowee in the Lower Settlements, Hiwassee in the Valley, Chota in the Overhills. But with little or no coercive power against wayward towns, regional decisions could not be made binding. Whatever was said at Keowee, Estatoe went its own way, while among the Overhills, Tellico and Settico led the way to war. Nor was there any real central authority for the nation as a whole. Chota, the 'mother town' and the home of the priestly Uku or Fire King, had a traditional moral primacy. But by 1730 Chota was being overshadowed by the rivalry of the warrior faction led by Moitoi, the war leader of Great Tellico.

Such decentralization was a disadvantage even when the nation's main enemies were Creeks and northern Indians. But the creeping advance of white settlement in the early eighteenth century and the growing dependence of the nation upon British trade goods made a stronger centralized authority more attractive. On their side the British were looking for a recognizable government with which to do business. So when Sir Alexander Cuming went into the nation in search of trade in 1730, and demanded that the Cherokees submit to George II, the Tellico alliance saw a chance to use the outsiders to reinforce their own position. In return for yielding an undefined suzerainty to the Crown, Moitoi of Tellico was recognized as 'emperor' of the Cherokees: a totally unprecedented constitutional invention.

A great meeting of warriors in the town house at Nequassee had apparently agreed to yield the nation's lands to the Crown, and the seven-strong delegation which subsequently accompanied Cuming to London had solemnly ratified that decision. Alexander Hewatt, who had lived in South Carolina, and who wrote in 1779 when the treaty was within living memory, certainly took that view. The Nequassee meeting, representing as he thought the consent of all the Cherokees, 'had laid the crown of their nation' at the feet of George II. But neither the warriors at Nequassee, nor the London delegation, had any such intention, and even if they had their cession would have had no legal standing in Cherokee eyes. Though Sirmans refers to the seven as 'chiefs', only two of the party were headmen and they certainly did not reflect the will of the nation. One man, who had only joined the delegation en route to Charleston, did not sign at all; another, the future Cherokee statesman Attakullakulla, was only fifteen. Even the wording devised by the Board of Trade was hardly an assertion of absolute title: the Crown graciously gave the Cherokees 'the privilege of living where they pleased', a very sensibly vague formula in view of that nation's still considerable military strength and remoteness. The problem of blood vengeance was mitigated by a British undertaking to deal with whites who killed Cherokees, while the Cherokees promised to hand over any warrior who killed an Englishman.[20] There was no attempt to attach the Cherokee country to an existing colony such as South Carolina[21] or to appoint resident officials. In practice British officials continued to treat the Cherokees as a sovereign people. By recognizing Moitoi as emperor the British had invented a completely new constitutional role, and backed the Tellico–Hiwassee alliance against the claims of Chota. Thus Moitoi (1730–41) and his successor Amouskositte (1741–c.53) were tolerated only because they could threaten and punish wayward towns and warriors.

Gearing argues that this warrior state was far too weak to fulfil its functions. For example, in 1734, when a trader was robbed and South Carolina imposed an embargo, the subsequent negotiations were conducted by the Lower towns, not the emperor. Trade was cut off again in 1746 when, at a time when South Carolina was frightened by French overtures to the Cherokees, a trader was murdered. As this would have left the nation open to Shawnee and Creek attacks, Amouskositte promptly threatened to destroy the town concerned if the killer was not surrendered or executed. The man's fellow townsmen took the point and shot him. But this was the only case of such action before 1753. From 1742 Amouskositte was undermined by Chota's overtures to the French. Though pressed by South Carolina, he could not take decisive action against French agents without provoking a destructive civil war. A third embargo in 1751, though resolved by the emperor, demonstrated the need for a stronger 'state', and caused his displacement by the Uku of Chota, Connecorte, by July 1753.[22] Over the next five years, so Gearing argues, Connecorte built up a far more centralized 'priestly state', with significantly more freedom to discipline the unruly, and a new system to recall the Overhill hunters to Chota should they be needed. Connecorte's 'second man', Attakullakulla or the Little Carpenter, was sent on diplomatic missions, and as early as 1753 told James Glen, the governor of South Carolina, that he spoke in the name of Old Hop, 'the great beloved wise man of the nation'. The war leader of Chota, Occonostota, was now Great Warrior of the whole nation and could sometimes exercise central direction over war parties.[23]

But the Uku was not an absolute monarch. He had to govern by consensus, and Occonostota, Attakullakulla and others could and did challenge his policies. Connecorte was strong because he understood how to manage the most important innovation of the so-called priestly state: the enlarged Chota council. According to Gearing this body met at least once a year, during the Green Corn Dance festival, and more often in times of crisis. It consisted of the beloved men and clan sections of Chota, with delegations from each of the towns. These would be made up of the town headman, his second man, a messenger or runner to convey the news homewards, and any members of the town council who wished to come. On the whole the young men did not dispute the beloved men's right to determine policy, although they might ignore it when they chose. But because membership was so comprehensive, and regional and local differences so great, obtaining the necessary consensus among the elders was extremely difficult. Only a leader of great prestige and political acumen could have obtained the large measure of agreement evident amongst the Cherokees from 1756 to 1759.[24]

The issues underlying the Anglo-Cherokee war were complex and deep rooted. First, and most fundamentally, the inexorable advance of the white settlements and growing British commercial and military power in the region raised the question of Cherokee independence. Could the nation survive as an independent entity, with full sovereignty over its own lands? Or would survival mean some kind of vassalage, under which the Cherokees would lose their political independence but preserve their identity and their lands? Or would the nation go the way of the Natchez and the tribes of the Carolina tidewater – to annihilation? Second, if the nation was not to be dispossessed, where would the boundary of white settlement be? Who would define it and how could it be enforced? Third, the nation's growing dependence upon European trade goods had put the Cherokees in a vulnerable position. How could the skin trade be made fair and honest, and an abundance of vital items guaranteed? How could South Carolina be restrained from using its near monopoly of the Cherokee trade as an oppressive diplomatic weapon? Fourth, could some of these problems be alleviated by finding alternative partners to South Carolina – Virginia or the Louisiana French for example? Fifth, could the French even provide sufficient support to sustain the Cherokees in war? Sixth, and finally, could South Carolina and other colonies be restrained by a benevolent imperial government working through its servants in America? Even if the means could be found, would British ministers have the persistence and determination to carry such a policy through?

There was no question of British sovereignty over the Cherokee country, even though the Cherokees were steadily moving towards some kind of political dependency. Before 1755 diplomatic relations with Britain had apparently been based on the 1730 treaty which, as we have seen, did not significantly reduce Cherokee independence. From 1732 until 1739 the Tellico–Hiwassee alliance underlined their freedom of action by adopting Christian Gottlieb Priber, a Saxon exile and enthusiast for political experiments based on natural law. His plans for a highly centralized state attracted Moitoi, while many other Cherokees liked his emphasis on the nation's independent diplomatic role. This last factor alarmed British traders and the South Carolina authorities, who thought he was a French agent.[25]

In 1739 the War of Jenkins' Ear had aroused fears of a Spanish descent upon South Carolina and Georgia,[26] and of French intervention under the Family Compact.[27] The outbreak of the War of the Austrian Succession deflected the French government from that particular project, but only exacerbated colonial fears of their meddling with the southern Indians. In 1742 the long-feared Spanish attack on Georgia finally came; and, though it failed, exposed the weakness of

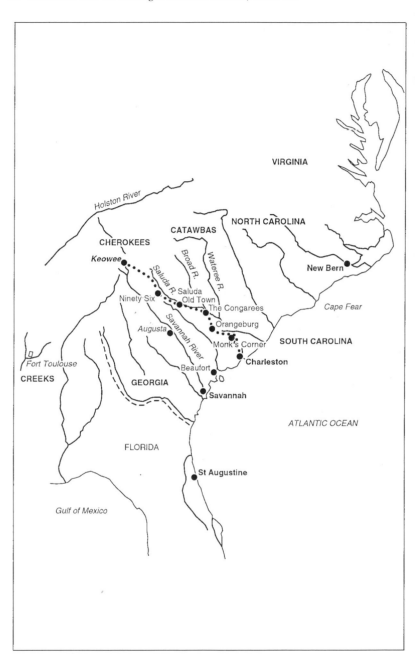

Map 2   The Carolinas and Georgia

Britain's southernmost colonies.[28] The beginning of a formal Anglo-French war in 1744 made the question of Indian allegiances all the more critical. With no garrison to speak of, and with twice as many negro slaves as white settlers, South Carolina was peculiarly vulnerable to external attack. Indeed, one of the principal reasons for fearing Spaniards in Georgia was the possibility that they might incite slave revolts. The Indians' initial responses to requests for help were friendly, if non-committal, but by May 1746 the traders were sending alarming reports of a French mission offering the Cherokees peace and a fort to protect them against the raids of the Iroquois and Creeks.[29]

The news sent the expansionist governor of South Carolina, James Glen, on a great tour through the Carolina back country in order to counter French influence amongst the Cherokees, Chickasaws and Creeks.[30] At Ninety Six, he met Amouskositte who, representing the Tellico–Hiwassee alliance, agreed to drive out the French emissaries and northern Indians. In return, Glen raised the possibility of building a Carolinian fort to protect the exposed Overhill towns against enemy raids. '[B]ut', as Glen put it, 'as they are pretty jealous of their Liberty they did not readily agree to it'.[31] In fact neither side was able to keep its promises. Amouskositte, of course, could not have thrown out the foreign Indians and French agents protected by Chota. Glen had no royal authority to promise a fort, and could not persuade the Commons House of Assembly to vote the necessary funds, although members were willing to pay for a fort nearer home, amongst the Lower Cherokees.[32] In 1748 the Peace of Aix La Chapelle prevented further action, although the Cherokee–Creek war and the consequent danger to traders kept the project alive. There was no question now of subverting Cherokee independence through direct military assistance.

Even Glen, when it suited him, could make a point of the Cherokees' sovereignty. Writing in 1749 to M. Vaudreuille, the governor of Louisiana, about the return of prisoners of war, he refused to discuss which European nation should have which Indians.

Many of the Indian Nations are free and Independent, the Natives and Original possessors and Proprietors of the Lands and Countries they Inhabit and have never been Conquered by any Crowned head whatsoever, and no doubt have a right by the Law of Nature, and of Nations to make Treaties of Peace and Commerce, with whom they please, so far I presume you will readily Agree with me, and to say more may be a matter of to Delicate a Nature for me at present too enter upon ...[33]

It followed, though Glen carefully did not say so, that such Indians might yield their sovereignty, fully or in part, to whomsoever they chose. He hoped that sooner or later, through the Overhill fort scheme, that the Cherokees and other neighbouring Indians would give up their freedom to the British. The fort would at first, he thought, 'prove a bridle in the Mouths of our Indians', and in due course turn them into 'Tributaries, by obliging each town in every Nation to pay an Annual acknowledgement of a few Skins for this Protection ...'[34] But for the time being that independence was an established fact, and the starting point for all frontier diplomacy. Like many a British official, Glen expressed his ideas in the prevailing language of the Enlightenment, with its emphasis upon the natural right to freedom of at least those peoples who already possessed it. Indeed, it is significant that Glen – like William Bull, Archibald Montgomery and James Grant[35] later on – never questioned the servitude of black slaves, yet could be extremely sensitive to the existing liberty of these children of Nature.

From 1751 the defensive, but apparently aggressive, moves by the French of Canada to secure a position on the Ohio brought the question of a Cherokee fort to the fore again. A war crisis between South Carolina and the Lower Cherokees in that year gave Glen a specific opportunity to resurrect it. By now Chota had abandoned its French connection, in order to outbid the failing Tellico–Hiwassee faction as a location for the Overhill fort, and although he had for some time avoided giving a specific commitment, he saw that support for Chota might give more leverage for British interests than the waning star of the Young Emperor.

On 13–14 March 1752 the Commons house again gave its approval for a fort amongst the Lower Cherokees. Members voted £3000 for the project, on condition that as much as possible of the land between Ninety Six and Keowee was bought from the Cherokees.[36] If carried out this proviso would have deprived the Lower Towns of so much hunting land that they would have become permanently dependent upon South Carolina. This fell far short of Glen's schemes of undermining the independence of the whole nation, but it was a start. The final settlement negotiated between Glen himself and the Lower Cherokee headmen led by the Raven of Toxaway gave South Carolina a patch of land on the Keowee river directly opposite the town, and a strip the width of the fort (200 feet) from the site to Ninety Six to serve as a road. Glen later represented this to the Board of Trade as the cession of *all* the Cherokee lands up to Keowee, including 'many thousand acres of valuable soil'.[37] But there was no cession: the agreement gave South Carolina the *use* of the land specified in the treaty, but not sovereignty over it. In fact the agreement put the frontier where it had been in theory since 1747, at Long Canes Creek, about 60 miles from Keowee. Even the presence of a garrison at Fort Prince George, as the new post was called, was less of a curb than Glen had hoped, for it was not easy to supply and was overlooked by high wooded ground well within musket range.[38] Apart from South Carolina's extraterritorial rights on the lands appertaining to the fort, Cherokee sovereignty was not compromised. *(Building of Fort Did Compromise Cherokee sovereignty.)*

Glen therefore made a further effort to obtain Cherokee submission in 1754. The clashes on the Virginia frontier inspired him to shift the focus of action to his own sphere by proposing a thrust westward, at least to the confluence of the Tennessee and Ohio rivers, to cut Louisiana off from New France. This would require at least one regiment of regulars from Britain and, even more importantly, the cooperation of the Cherokees, through whose territory the expedition would pass. Glen therefore proposed that a delegation of seven headmen, including Attakullakulla and Ostenaca, should go to London to sign a formal cession of sovereignty to the Crown, in return for a fort to protect the Overhill towns. In the course of 1754 the idea of a Cherokee fort won the approval of the Lords of Trade, who could see the immense advantages of friendship with a powerful nation with access to the riverine communications of the west.[39] *(we clashes with France on the)*

But the scheme foundered on a maze of shoals. Most importantly the Cherokee leadership were not blind to Glen's real aims. Although a few headmen supported the plan they rapidly withdrew when Connecorte voiced his disapproval. The promised fort could not be paid for as Sir Thomas Robinson, Secretary of State for the Southern Department, had entrusted all of the £10 000 available to the southern colonies to Governor Robert Dinwiddie of Virginia. Dinwiddie, himself an investor in the Ohio Company, was unwilling to let Glen deflect his own colony's expansionist thrust on the Ohio. Glen could get no more than £1000 out of him and the South Carolina Commons was not inclined to stump up the rest. Robinson also vetoed the idea of a Cherokee mission to London, and Glen was reduced to inviting Old Hop to Charleston to make a formal submission.[40] The Fire King, who was quite prepared to make conciliatory but vague promises along the lines of the 1730 treaty, declined to come himself. The journey was, he said, too long for a cripple.[41]

Old Hop's refusal was more than a diplomatic rejection of British sovereignty. It was an insistence upon negotiating upon equal terms.

When the Cherokee delegation led by Attakullakulla and Occonostota reached Charleston in May 1755 it brought Connecorte's offer to meet half-way between the colonial capital and Chota. After consulting his council and the Commons Glen agreed to go. On a blazing June day at Saluda Old Town (Map 2), under an arbour of poles and thatch, the Governor of South Carolina met the Uku of the Cherokees. Behind them stood Glen's retinue of Carolinian gentlemen, colonial militia and regulars from the Charleston garrison. Before them, in a vast crescent, sat five hundred Cherokees.[42]

The Treaty of Saluda, negotiated over seven days and concluded on 2 July, was without doubt a major event in Cherokee–British diplomacy. But it did not bring the unequivocal acknowledgement of British sovereignty which Glen so eagerly sought. Glen tried to make the sovereignty question the first item of business, but Attakullakulla insisted that the Cherokees were more interested in trade. Glen bowed to the Second Man's insistence and accepted a range of proposals favourable to the Cherokees: the licensing of more traders, a better scale of prices, the prohibition of rum. In return they ceded their lands to the Crown and allowed Carolina to build a fort in the Overhill country. On 2 July Attakullakulla formally laid a bag of earth at Glen's feet.[43]

Did the Cherokees really mean to give up their independence? To the Board of Trade, and perhaps in his own mind, Glen represented Saluda as the triumphant culmination of his policy: as an acknowledgement of British sovereignty. Glen's own secretary was personally convinced that the Indians had knowingly given up their independence,[44] and more than one historian has no doubt that the delegation led by Attakullakulla 'undoubtedly knew what they were doing and were properly authorised to do it'.[45] In fact the Cherokees had given up only an as yet unspecified piece of land for the fort (Glen's secretary was greatly impressed by the skill with which Attakullakulla selected possible sites from the map) and a vague suzerainty which could always be repudiated later. Tom Hatley has recently pointed out that the giving of the bag of earth meant not submission but 'a symbolic gesture of alliance'. Glen himself had his doubts and insisted upon token payment for the lands as evidence of a legal transfer; the Cherokees resisted this at first and agreed in the end 'only out of politeness'.[46] Even then the fort was not built at once because Glen could persuade neither Dinwiddie nor his own assembly to provide sufficient funds. Even an visit to Charleston by Attakullakulla in December produced no immediate action.[47] It fell to the next governor, William Henry Lyttelton, to find the money and begin work on Fort Loudoun near Tuskagee in the autumn of 1756 (Map 9). Even then the soldiers could be supplied only from Fort Prince George, by way of tortuous packhorse paths through the heart of the Cherokee mountains. Atkin suspected that should relations deteriorate the unfortunate garrison would find themselves hostages.[48] Fort Loudoun was even less of a bridle on Cherokee independence than Fort Prince George.

Moreover Glen's grandiose claims were condemned by other imperial officials, like the governors of North Carolina and Virginia and George Croghan in Pennsylvania.[49] They feared that his apparent greed for territory and cynical use of presents would gravely damage British efforts to wean other Indian nations away from the French. The British government tacitly ignored the Treaty of Saluda: Edmond Atkin, the first Superintendent of Indian affairs in the south from 1756, was commissioned – and behaved – as an imperial ambassador rather than as a political resident.[50] Indeed, the Secretary of State was so unimpressed by Saluda that he sacked Glen for general incompetence. In practice even the South Carolina Commons House of Assembly, usually the voice of settler expansionism, continued to regard the Cherokees as an independent nation: when serious fighting broke out in 1759–60 the Commons spoke not of a rebellion but of a war. In 1761 their peace demands were not for outright annexation, but for pressing the frontier within 26 miles of Keowee.

Recognition of Cherokee independence made the fixing of the frontier the most critical issue of all (Map 3). Hewatt thought that a frontier cession, and consequently a boundary line, had been made as early as 1721.[51] But Wallace and Willis have since pointed out that there is little or no evidence for this agreement,[52] and as late as 1730, when Hewatt assumed a further cession had occurred,[53] the settlements were sufficiently far apart to make such measures unnecessary. However, the Carolina settlements had thrust outwards in the 1740s along the Saluda, Catawba–Wateree and Broad Rivers. An important nucleus was at Ninety Six on the Cherokee trading path, where the trader Robert Goudey had about two square miles of land. A population explosion, mainly fuelled by natural increase, was under way in South Carolina and its neighbours. In addition many Scots-Irish immigrants were arriving via Charleston or trekking overland from Pennsylvania via the inland valleys. The Indians faced the loss not only of a vital source of

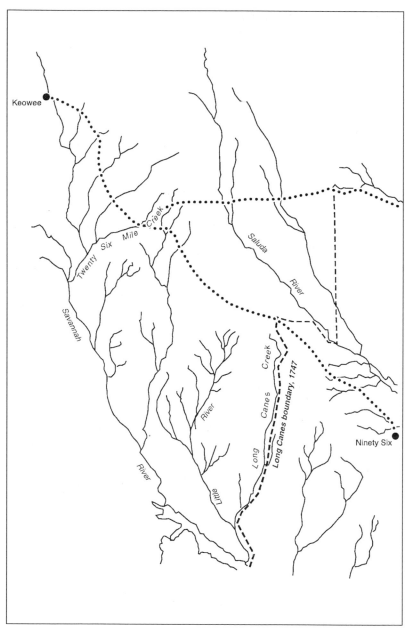

Map 3 The Cherokee–South Carolina boundary, 1747–61

food, but also the hides needed to exchange for the crucial trade goods. As the small farmers pressed into the fertile valley bottoms of Appalachian foothills, speculators manoeuvred to exploit the demand for land. This speculation was trivial compared with similar operations in Virginia and Maryland, but it was sufficient to bring about a significant cession of Cherokee land. In 1737 and 1741 John Hamilton's applications for 2000 acres around Ninety Six were refused by the Board of Trade. But in 1746 John Turk and Michael Taylor petitioned South Carolina for the purchase of Indian land on the north side of Coronaca Creek. By then the area had become so denuded of game, and clashes with the whites so commonplace, that the Lower Cherokees were probably glad to sell. Taking advantage of the friction, in 1747 Glen bought the whole left bank of Long Canes Creek, a tributary of the Savannah. The line was to run along the creek from its confluence with the Savannah to its source thence directly overland to the headwaters of the nearest tributary of the Saluda or Santee, and from there due north until it intersected the path leading from Keowee to the Catawba towns.[54]

This was a development of the utmost significance: at Saluda and as late as the Congress of Augusta in 1763 the Cherokees were to claim Long Canes as their fixed frontier. But to Glen it was no more than a temporary expedient. By 1751 Hamilton had at last obtained a 200 000 acre survey around Ninety Six, part of which sprawled across Long Canes. Hamilton appears to have made few sales, at least at first, but at about the same time Scots-Irish settlers were moving onto the lower Wateree. In 1755 over 300 families arrived from Pennsylvania, and more were on the way. By 1756 numbers of settlers, again encouraged by officially authorized surveys, had pushed into the fertile bottoms along the Little River. To disguise this violation the river was officially described as the north-west fork of Long Canes Creek.[55]

Further north (Maps 1 and 4) the frontiers were advancing, but for the time being the threats were much more distant than that of the Long Canes settlers. German and Scots-Irish settlers were appearing along the Yadkin and Catawba Rivers in North Carolina, next door to the embattled Catawbas, but nibbling at the edge of the Cherokees' hunting grounds. In Virginia speculators were taking up land grants along the Kanawha and New Rivers, again on the fringe of Cherokee territory. By 1751 the watershed between the New and Holston Rivers had been closely settled; four years later, when John Mitchell published his famous map, the whites were as far westward as Stalnaker's plantation on the upper Holston.[56] After the Anglo-Cherokee War the

Virginian movement downstream was to present a major threat to the Overhills. But by 1756 this danger was still far away compared with that from South Carolina, and indeed, west of Virginia the Cherokees were actually expanding into a vacuum created by the decline of the Iroquois.[57]

The incessant pressure on the South Carolina frontier was thus the key to Cherokee restlessness in the 1750s. As we shall see in the next chapter, by 1758 the Lower Towns were petitioning the governor of Georgia to obtain the removal of intrusive settlers who were ruining their hunting. In the same year a Presbyterian missionary, William Richardson, found both Lower Cherokees and Overhills incensed at the slaughter of game and the intrusion of unauthorized settlements up to fifty miles above Long Canes.[58] In 1762 the Virginian soldier-emissary, Henry Timberlake, found that the settlers' encroachments had been the chief cause of Cherokee attempts to reach an accommodation with the French.[59] More recently Robert M. Weir has reached the same conclusion.[60]

Second only to land in importance was trade. Weir sees the trade embargo which followed the failure of Lyttelton's expedition in the winter of 1759–60 as the immediate cause of the renewal of the war.[61] The embargo was provocative because the Cherokees, like most eastern nations, had become irrevocably dependent upon European trade goods and presents. The Cherokees grew maize and beans (and even exotic fruits such as peaches) in the summer. But after the autumn harvest they dispersed in family groups for the winter hunt, in which firearms were now almost essential tools. Guns, bought with deer hides from European traders, were no more accurate than bows and arrows. But a lead ball was far more lethal, giving the hunter a shorter chase after a mortally wounded whitetail deer. Meanwhile the European diseases tended to remove the older men, those whose role was to teach the old techniques of weapon making. Thus the arrival of the new technology, which Indians learned to use but not to emulate, coincided with the slow erosion of their native expertise.[62] Once dependent upon guns for killing game – and, for other purposes, steel hatchets, knives, fishing hooks and iron cooking pots – the Indians had to rely on outsiders for some of their most basic needs.

The result was the commercialization of the Indians' pursuit of the whitetail deer, valued by European and colonial leather workers as the finest material for gloves and book bindings. The southern beaver, although numerous, had a far less attractive pelt than its northern cousin and suffered rather less. Black bear furs were saleable but the market for them was insignificant compared to the demand for fine leather. Although commercial hunting eroded the once abundant deer populations, natural reproduction and interruptions to hunting caused by war saved them from extinction.[63] As neither Georgia nor the French could supply sufficient goods in exchange for these skins, and as Virginia was too distant, the Cherokee trade was dominated by South Carolina, and that colony was not slow to use this potent diplomatic weapon.

From 1742 the Carolina trade became literally a matter of life and death for the Lower Towns, which bore the brunt of a savage war against the Creeks. We have already seen how in 1746 the murder of a trader was followed by a cessation of trade which would have left the nation defenceless against Creek and Shawnee attacks. Trade was resumed but the Creek war went on, and the perils of Cherokee dependence upon South Carolina were again underlined in 1748. An episode almost identical to that of 1746 was followed by the capture of two British surveyors by a party of Senecas, probably based at Chota. The Senecas took their captives to Keowee where the Lower Cherokees, already incensed by violations of the Long Canes boundary, would not willingly return them to Carolina. When the traders in the Lower Towns gathered to attempt a rescue, Wawatchee of Coonasatchee threatened to kill all the white traders in the nation. Glen at once cut off trade and demanded the release of the surveyors, the surrender of Wawatchee, and the expulsion of the northern Indians. Once again shortage of ammunition forced the Cherokees to bow to what they understandably saw as outrageous demands, a humiliation which intensified the already strong anti-British feeling of the Lower Cherokees.[64] At the time only two of their towns were still inhabited, the rest having been burnt or emptied by Creek raiders using British muskets and powder.[65] Glen negotiated a Creek–Cherokee peace in 1749, promising to enforce it with the trade weapon, but Senecas continued to raid Creek towns, and in the autumn the Creeks again attacked the Cherokees. Glen refused to impose an embargo for fear of driving the Coweta Creeks into the arms of the French. On 14 April 1750 bands of British-armed Creeks destroyed the towns of Echoi and Estatoe, yet again Glen failed to act, this time because Georgia would not support trade sanctions. The Cherokees, furious at Glen's breach of faith, already angered by the Long Canes violations and encouraged by northern Indians, were on the brink of war with South Carolina.[66]

Early in 1751 the violence reached a crisis when two Carolina traders with a Creek war party were cut down by Cherokee warriors. South Carolina, this time supported by Georgia, once again cut off the Cherokee trade. The impact upon the Cherokee towns was intensified by a bad winter hunt – made worse by the interference of Creek marauders – and the traders' consequent refusal, prior to the embargo, to extend credit.[67] Had they the means the Lower Cherokees would probably have attacked the South Carolina frontier that spring. As things were Glen was able to negotiate a treaty reopening the trade and reorganizing the system of licensing traders. This agreement was reaffirmed in 1755 when Glen at last threatened the Creeks with sanctions and mediated another Cherokee–Creek peace.[68]

But the fundamental trade issues were not solved. The new system, by licensing traders only for particular villages, should have eased the problem of over-competition in a tightening market. Nevertheless, abuses by traders using false weights and measures became more common in the 1750s, as more and more Virginians appeared, and returns of skins dwindled in the face of overhunting and advancing settlement. The most serious offenders were John Elliot, licensed to trade at Chota, and Goudey of Great Tellico and Chatuga. But most traders, caught between the need to extend credit to their customers against the returns of the winter hunt, and the demands of their own creditors in Charleston, were sooner or later drawn into dishonest practices. The cheating by traders on the one hand, and their periodic failure to obtain sufficient goods from Charleston, kept Cherokee resentments and suspicions simmering.[69]

Thus the subsequent Anglo-Cherokee alliance was extremely fragile. The wonder is not that it collapsed in 1758–9, but that it lasted so long. Despite efforts at centralization going back as far as 1742, British Indian policy was fragmented between the various colonies, and although particular colonies might affect to take a lead with the nations on their doorstep – New York with the Iroquois, Pennsylvania with the Delawares, Virginia on the Ohio, South Carolina with the Cherokees – there were in effect 13 separate jurisdictions and policies. There was some greater cohesion in the north, where the great Iroquois confederation was still the dominant factor. The colony of New York had good relations with the Iroquois – especially with the neighbouring Mohawks, less so with the Senecas – who had been hostile to the French since the seventeenth century. Through this special relationship, known as the 'Covenant Chain' of friendship, New York could exercise influence over the many nations whom the Iroquois regarded as vassals. This indirect unity was certainly flawed – the Iroquois claims often outstripped reality – but not even this was available in the south. Here no people had ever accepted Iroquois supremacy, and where no one nation dominated, there was no single agency through which to coordinate relations with Choctaws, Creeks, Chickasaws, Cherokees and Catawbas.[70] Of these the Cherokees and Creeks were no more united internally than the Six Nations, thus further complicating the problem. On top of this South Carolina's primacy had begun to slip in the 1740s. As we have seen Georgia had more or less taken over Creek affairs – with uncomfortable results for the older colony's relations with the Cherokees – and in the 1750s Virginia began to undermine South Carolina's position with the Cherokees themselves.

From the Cherokee point of view, particularly that of the Overhills, the Virginian interest represented an opportunity to reduce the nation's dependence upon South Carolina. The appearance of Virginians near the Holston could mean an alternative source of trade; and Virginia's growing difficulties with the French in the Ohio Valley put the Cherokees in a position to bargain military assistance in return for commerce. As early as 1752 Amouskositte had travelled 700 miles to open negotiations with Dinwiddie, who by 1753 thought he could bring about a Catawba–Cherokee peace with the Iroquois.[71] In 1754 a Cherokee request to form a settlement on the Roanoke River to facilitate trade with Virginia was refused, on the ground that it would become a target for northern Indians.[72] But this was the year of Washington's defeat and the establishment of Fort Duquesne at the forks of the Ohio; and Virginia tried to buy Cherokee help with the tentative offer of an Overhill fort.[73]

The first results were meagre. Because their towns were still dangerously exposed, rather than because of Glen's active discouragement, only a handful of Cherokee scouts appeared to join the unfortunate Major-General Edward Braddock's advance on Fort Duquesne in 1755.[74] In February 1756 150 warriors took part in an expedition against the Shawnee town on the Great Sandy River; an operation suggested by Ostenaca, the Mankiller of Tomotly, in December. Unfortunately the raid collapsed when two Virginian supply canoes capsized and a number of white soldiers deserted.[75] But Glen's failure to meet his Saluda obligations ensured that the Virginian alliance was strengthened. In March the Treaty of Broad River bound the Cherokees to provide 400 warriors in return for arms, presents, and an Overhill fort.[76] Broad River was, argues Corkran, 'a major diplomatic triumph for the Little Carpenter'. The treaty quieted what he calls 'nativist' resentment of the concessions made at Saluda by having committed Virginia to the breaking of South Carolina's trade monopoly.[77] The Virginian fort would replace, or at least balance, the one promised by Glen at Saluda; the 400 warriors who were to go to Virginia would be given arms, ammunition and presents. Better still, the Virginians seemed at first to be eager to stand by their promises. Major Andrew Lewis began work on the fort, on the Little Tennessee opposite Chota, in June,[78] long before the appearance of the South Carolina expedition to build Fort Loudoun (Map 9). Finally – should relations deteriorate – the isolated garrison would become hostages for Virginia's honourable behaviour.

But Attakullakulla may not have been the main political beneficiary among the Cherokees. In April Ostenaca visited Williamsburg where, although he could not obtain sufficient presents for the Great Sandy veterans, he was treated like a king. Dinwiddie's carriage was placed at his disposal, and both coming and going he stayed with young Thomas Jefferson's family.[79] He returned to the Cherokee country as the champion of close relations with Virginia: relations which he meant to manage, so outflanking the Carpenter's primacy in Tomotly and in the nation in general. Like Attakullakulla, and many other Indian leaders at the time, Ostenaca grasped that a claim of particular influence with the Europeans was a big step towards prestige and power at home.

For all that many Overhills were still deeply suspicious of the British, be they from Virginia or Carolina. South Carolina was very slow to build her promised fort; Governor Sir Charles Hardy in distant New York and Halifax in London were appalled at the damage being done by the delay.[80] The Virginian fort turned out to be a fraud. For Dinwiddie, although very liberal with his promises, and quick to demand his Cherokee auxiliaries,[81] had never intended to provide a garrison. To appease Lyttelton, Loudoun and Halifax, he made a show of finding 150 men; but he refused to send them until 400 Cherokees arrived in Virginia. This and his other excuses – there was no money, Virginians would not enlist for such a service, the troops were needed elsewhere – were transparent but effective. Even Loudoun's direct order, and his appeal to South Carolina for additional troops,[82] came to nothing. The fort remained empty and quickly fell into ruin.

Thus the alliances concluded at Saluda and Broad River were bound to bring the Shawnees and other northern raiders down upon the

Cherokee towns, without providing compensating protection. Braddock's defeat, the Great Sandy fiasco and the loss of Fort Oswego did not augur success for a war against the French. Meanwhile Creeks, Shawnees and French agents argued that France would be the best guarantor of Cherokee security. French trade might replace that of the dangerous British, while raids by nations allied to the French – the Shawnees in particular – would cease. The few partisans of a French alliance were strongest at Tellico, Chota's defeated rival for national leadership. But Connecorte himself kept in touch with the French, and as trouble with South Carolina and Virginia grew he was to find the French option increasingly attractive.[83] Even the Carpenter, who by 1756 was committed to good relations with the British, probably wanted to preserve some connection with Louisiana.

Glen had tried to halt the slide as early as 1742 by taking up the suggestion of Lieutenant-Governor Clarke of New York to extend the 'Covenant Chain' southwards. The question had become urgent because the westward spread of British settlement had intersected the 'warrior's road' taken by war parties travelling between north and south through the Shenandoah Valley; and already there had been clashes between war parties and settlers in Virginia and South Carolina.[84] Clarke's idea was for British governors to broker treaties of friendship between all the nations friendly to Britain.[85] Since the Iroquois constantly raided – and were sometimes raided by – the Catawbas[86] and often the Cherokees[87] and Creeks, and since the Creeks were soon to be at war with the Cherokees, this policy was optimistic to say the least. South Carolina and Clarke had indeed arranged a Catawba–Cherokee peace in 1742, before Glen's arrival, but this was contingent upon the Overhill towns sheltering Iroquois parties moving against the Creeks.[88] Glen's attempt to support a pro-British revolution within the Choctaw nation failed miserably, and his attempts to adjudicate between Cherokees and Creeks were riddled with difficulties. Nevertheless this approach was attractive to ministers in London because it offered a unified Indian policy cheaply, and without offending the vested interests of particular colonies. The notion that quarrels between the friendly Indian nations were matters of prestige rather than of substance, and that all matters could therefore be resolved at a general conference, was misguided but powerfully attractive. As late as 1747 the Duke of Newcastle, then Secretary of State for the Southern Department, was studying a document containing exactly this kind of suggestion.[89]

But by that time it had become glaringly obvious that without a coordinated Indian policy the American colonies could never win the battle for Indian hearts and minds which was already being waged with the French. One possible solution was to require colonial governments to find a means of cooperating for defence and to co-ordinate their Indian policies. That in turn would mean a far more centralized, London-directed policy. When George Montagu-Dunk, Earl of Halifax, became President of the Board of Trade in 1748, the ministry began to move rapidly in this direction. Newcastle, Halifax's cousin, was Britain's leading official authority on American affairs and, as J. E. Stagg has shown, the two men worked well together.[90] Halifax also cooperated closely with the Duke of Bedford, who led a Paris commission concerned with the boundary of Nova Scotia, and had the accumulated expertise of the Board of Trade at his disposal. He also worked closely with the cartographer and geographer John Mitchell. Misled in his first years of office by the assurances of the Ohio Company and by governor Dinwiddie of Virginia, he quickly learned that leaving Indian policy to expansionist local interests could only lead to trouble. By 1752 Halifax had not only made himself an expert on American affairs, but had won for the Board the right to nominate colonial officials and to receive all routine correspondence.[91] Thus, as Stagg shows, the evolutionary process of policy-making which culminated in the Proclamation of 1763 had its origins in the War of the Austrian Succession, and arguably had roots going back much further still.[92]

By the summer of 1753 the French were rapidly winning the allegiance of the Ohio nations and were already building a chain of forts from Lake Erie to the headwaters of the Ohio itself.[93] The Board of Trade received news of these activities in August. Halifax warned Newcastle that urgent action was necessary and, at his cousin's suggestion, produced a discussion paper for circulation within the Cabinet. The result was a circular letter sent out by Holdernesse, Newcastle's successor at the Southern Department, warning governors to take care in their dealings with Indians and to act firmly against encroachments by the French. But soon after this letter went out in September the news reached London that the Mohawks, the Iroquois nation most threatened by British expansion, had broken off relations with New York.[94]

Halifax quickly persuaded the Board to draft orders for an inter-colonial conference with the Iroquois and other interested nations at Albany, in an effort to repair the damage. In particular, there were to be no more private land deals; in future cessions must be made to the Crown alone, and then by the consent of the whole nation concerned in open council. The Privy Council gave its approval and the instructions went out on 18 September. This, observes Stagg, was the first concrete expression of Halifax's conviction that only 'a more closely controlled state-dominated approach' could resolve the problems of Indian relations and counter the French threat.[95] In effect New York was being told to put its house in order[96] by removing Indian grievances, the first interference of its kind but far from being the last. Thus Halifax's initiative was far more than a pragmatic response to a diplomatic disaster: it was the government's first step towards the position that Indian nations had genuine rights, which it was the duty of the imperial authorities to protect. But the conference was poorly attended, even by the northern colonies, and was more significant for the shady land deals concluded on its fringes than as a landmark in Indian affairs. Far more important was a radical scheme drawn up by Halifax and submitted for discussion in April 1754.

This remarkable document called for a chain of forts, funded cooperatively by the colonies, from Mobile on the Gulf of Mexico to Nova Scotia. Not only would each fort have its agent to deal with Indian affairs – regulating trade, supervising conferences, seeing that the Indians gave their full consent to any land cessions – but there should be two districts divided by the Ohio, each in the charge of a 'Commissary General', or superintendent. These officials were to have charge of all civilian and military matters pertaining to Indian affairs within their respective districts, and would be supported as the occasion demanded with British regular troops.[97] This was the first general scheme to take in the colonies south of Virginia, and thus embracing Glen's efforts to tie down the Cherokees. But unlike Glen's plans, it specifically provided for the protection of the Indians against both expanding settlement and unscrupulous traders. It also proposed to put Indian affairs beyond the reach of ambitious and unreliable governors and grasping colonial assemblies by providing for direct imperial control. Moreover, it was the first suggestion that British rather than colonial forces might be made responsible for enforcement.

But as affairs on the Ohio went from bad to worse Halifax's scheme was subsumed into a plan providing for a royal commander-in-chief for the whole of British North America. When this plan went out to governors in October 1754 the idea of having two Indian superintendents was left out, because it had already been decided to place them under the broad supervision of the commander-in-chief. From 1754 the British commander-in-chief in North America was in charge of all troops and military operations there, including the recruitment and use of Indian mercenaries. Commanders-in-chief and their subordinates came to assume that their authority overrode, or ought to override, mere provincial governors in all things even vaguely military. Lord Loudoun believed that when Braddock was first commissioned the government had made no mention of local military powers of governors, 'not Conceiving that the Governors would interfere in this Point'. But as the result had been confusion, the government had framed Loudoun's own commission of 1756 so as 'to divest the civil Power of all Command over the Troops in this Country...' Loudoun not only wrote in these terms to governor Hardy: he circulated copies to his subordinate commanders, including the Swiss mercenary colonel Henry Bouquet, who was being sent on an expedition to South Carolina.[98] Bouquet's subsequent strident dispute with that colony's assembly over quartering may not be unconnected with this letter.[99] Brigadier-General John Forbes, commander of the 1758 Fort Duquesne expedition, was irritated by the obstruction of colonies which (he thought) fell under his own authority. 'My military business', he wrote, 'is nothing to the trouble I have with the governours and Assemblys of all these provinces who are all in a certain manner under my direction'.[100] Though actual treaties with Indian nations – Pennsylvania's with the Delawares at Easton, South Carolina's with the Cherokees at Charleston – were scrupulously left to the colonies concerned, commanders-in-chief necessarily came to have a formidable influence over Indian affairs.

But Halifax, Robinson and Newcastle had not forgotten the idea of having two superintendents of Indian affairs; indeed this was the most important surviving feature of Halifax's scheme. In 1755 the Board of Trade accepted the suggestion of Edmond Atkin, a South Carolina councillor with an obsession with Indian affairs, to divide North America into a southern and a northern district, divided by the Ohio, and to appoint a civilian Superintendent of Indian Affairs in each.[101] Atkin, of course, became superintendent in the Southern Department. In the north the post went to the redoubtable William Johnson, friend and exploiter of the Mohawks, who had been urging a structure like this for some time. But neither Atkin nor Johnson had the power to override provincial governors, and their operations were paid for through the commander-in-chief. Thus while useful diplomatic agents – and even the slow moving and clumsy Atkin did good work among the Creeks – the superintendents were continually obstructed by governors like Glen, Lyttelton and William Bull, and hamstrung by the parsimony and distrust of military commanders. Loudoun, rightly expecting Atkin to be dilatory in recruiting Cherokees for Forbes, corresponded directly with Lyttelton himself, and appointed his own recruiting agent, William Byrd of Virginia.[102] On 21 March 1758 Byrd reported to Forbes from South Carolina that Atkin was ill at Cape Fear, 'so no Difficulties will arise from him ...'[103] Thus even after 1756 the direction of Indian affairs was still dangerously fragmented between governors, superintendents and soldiers.

In such conditions a strong personality could often take action which might be decisive. A colonial governor, possibly eager for military glory, certainly driven by a misguided sense of duty and almost wholly insensitive to the complaints of Indians, could set a whole frontier aflame. This, as we shall see, was the case when Lyttelton launched South Carolina into an unnecessary official war against the Cherokees in 1759. Lyttelton failed because, while insisting on total capitulation by the Cherokees, he lacked the military force with which to bring them to their knees. Certain regular commanders of detachments, however, including those sent to save South Carolina from Lyttelton's folly, had other ideas. Far from their hard-line commander-in-chief and backed by the only army capable of ending the war, such men could act independently and justify themselves later. Jack P. Susin has rightly made much of the activities of Colonel Henry Bouquet in this sphere.

Bouquet, when commander at Fort Pitt, formerly Fort Duquesne, took it upon himself to interpret the wider implications of the 1758 Treaty of Easton. It is perfectly true, as Richard White and James Merrell show, that the Ohio nations expected the British to withdraw after the expulsion of the French, and that Bouquet, deceived by his interpreters, too easily assumed that he had persuaded them otherwise. But Bouquet used the British military presence to protect the native inhabitants, not to exploit, rob or coerce them. On 4 December 1759 at a conference of Ohio nations he promised in the King's name that the British did not intend to take their lands. He declined the Ohio Company's offer of 25 000 acres in return for recruiting French and German settlers, on the grounds that Easton forbade all settlement beyond the mountains, and that it bound Virginia and Maryland as well as Pennsylvania. Two years later he was forcibly to remove Virginian and Maryland settlers, and in October 1761 issued a proclamation banning all settlements not authorized by the commander-in-chief or a colonial governor. Subsequently more senior officers felt constrained to take the same line. At Fort Pitt

on 12 August 1760 Brigadier-General Robert Monckton, now commander of British forces in the south, repeated Bouquet's promise to an
audience of Iroquois, Miamis, Shawnees, Wyandots and Potawatamis.
Even the commander-in-chief, Sir Jeffrey Amherst, who loathed Indians
and whose insensitive behaviour was to provoke Pontiac's War in 1763,
saw the sense of promising not to take land.[104]
   Sosin argues that such initiatives were partly leading, partly antici-
pating, and partly responding to the Board of Trade's evolving
boundary line policy. According to Sosin the notion of a continuous
boundary between Indian and white settlements reached its
culmination in 1763 after a long process of evolution during the
Seven Years War, and that an important part of that evolutionary
process was the Treaty of Easton. When the Lords of Trade pressed
the Pennsylvania proprietors into negotiation, they had really
intended to ban all settlement west of the mountains. In 1760 they
set out to temper victory with restraint. In 1760 the Board warned
New York to respect Indian rights when the colony opened its northern frontier to settlers, and next year condemned New York for
ignoring its recommendation. All settlement beyond the
Appalachian watershed was banned in 1760 pending a firm decision
by the British government. Early in 1761 Virginia was told not to
encourage the reoccupation of the land grants held by the
Greenbrier and Kanawha companies before the war, but abandoned
under Indian attack. Finally in November 1761, a month after
Bouquet had taken unilateral action, an Order-in-Council forbade
grants of Indian lands by royal colonies without reference to the
Board. The circular letter instructing the governors of Nova Scotia,
New Hampshire, New York, Virginia, North Carolina, South Carolina
and Georgia went out on 3 December.[105]
   Sosin has placed beyond doubt the evolutionary nature of the British
boundary policy, and shown clearly how individual officers like
Bouquet could have a crucial impact. Thanks to him it is no longer
possible to imagine, as Alvord did, that the policy of 1763 was predom-
inantly the outcome of the domestic rivalries of British political
factions. His thesis is of course too sweeping to be conclusive; even
now it will take a great deal of work to decide whether he was right
about Easton, for example. Yet, paradoxically, in two directions it is
not sweeping enough. First, as we have seen, the period of evolution
was much longer than Sosin thought: it went back at least to the War
of the Austrian Succession. Second, Sosin deliberately limited himself
to the colonies adjacent to or north of the Ohio, on the rather curious

grounds that the southern colonies had been thoroughly studied already. Stagg confined himself to the same area. But had they looked closely at the Anglo-Cherokee War they would have found Bouquet's former subordinates, Archibald Montgomery and James Grant, behaving very much like their old commander in the north. While Bouquet was proclaiming and enforcing a boundary on the Ohio, Grant and Montgomery were striving to impose upon South Carolina a peace as favourable to the Cherokees as they could make it. Grant in particular was convinced that checking white expansion was the key to a settlement, and in 1761 deprived South Carolina of much of the land it had hoped to annex. Moreover, his peace-making activities attracted the personal attention of the Secretary of State, Lord Egremont, and so formed part of the mosaic of evidence leading to the Proclamation of 1763. Neither Alden nor Corkran noticed that Grant was committed to a compromise peace from the start, and that he formed part of a small but discernible group of field officers who felt far more sympathy for Indians than for white settlers.

The year 1756 was thus a watershed and a paradox: it saw both a modest beginning to benevolent imperial intervention and the start of the slide to war. The superintendencies were finally established, marking a significant step on the road to a unified policy. The army acquired overall responsibility for their activities, and Loudoun, with his high-flown ideas of his office, arrived in America. The conflict with France was going badly and the outbreak of war in Europe made conciliation of the Native Americans more urgent than ever. But on the Anglo-Cherokee frontier the 'middle ground' required to sustain fruitful relationships did not yet exist. There was no cultural meeting point where, as in White's *pays d'en haut*, both sides had reached 'a common conception of suitable ways of a acting'.[106] Indeed, as Dowd has shown, the closer their relations became, the more Cherokees and whites distrusted each other. The treaties of Saluda and Broad River created alliances, but each side had radically different ideas about the nature and goals of these relationships.[107] The Cherokees wanted to safeguard their territory and autonomy, while Glen and the Long Canes settlers were bent on their subjugation and expropriation. The Cherokees saw themselves as equal allies whose sacrifices deserved presents and cheap trade goods: rewards sufficient to compensate their families for their lost hunting. Dinwiddie saw them as mere mercenaries: useful but contemptible auxiliaries, whose aid should be purchased as cheaply as possible, and if necessary by deceit. Consequently British presents seemed to the Cherokees mean and insulting, while Cherokee complaints looked like greed, ingratitude and lack of proper deference. When the Indians rewarded themselves by theft or force, they provoked counter-violence, anger and distrust. The Sandy River shambles thus began a spiral of resentment capable of bringing down the alliance altogether. The arrival of Lyttelton, with his very one-sided view of the obligations set out in the 1730 and Saluda treaties, and his insistence upon the continuing primacy of South Carolina in Cherokee affairs, ushered in a period of extreme tension – and ultimately war.✓

2

'Two Brothers Falling Out': the Slide to War, 1756–59

In the autumn of 1758 a series of savage combats broke out in the back settlements of Virginia. White settlers, exasperated by the robberies and violence of warriors en route to or from the defence of the frontier, ambushed Cherokee parties without distinction. Cherokees, frightened of British intentions, short of trade goods, cheated of their presents for courageous service and out to avenge fallen comrades, struck back in implacable fury. Britain and the Cherokee nation were on the brink of a conflict neither side wanted, and which could only assist their enemies. The crisis was largely the outcome of chronic British mismanage ment of Cherokee affairs over the preceding two years. French intrigue had fanned suspicions raised by the failure of both South Carolina and Virginia to honour the pledges of Saluda and Broad River. Lyttelton blankly ignored the most sinister danger of all – the creeping advance of white settlement beyond Long Canes. When the Cherokees marched north in 1757 and 1758 they were already wary of their allies. But service in Virginia – the Cherokees' side of the bargain – might be the only means of securing the trade and protection they needed. With generous and tactful treatment the British might still have restored the Cherokees' trust and defused a very dangerous situation. Yet the clumsiness of the superintendency system, the rivalries between superintendent, colonies and military commanders, ensured chaos, confusion and, ultimately, violence. Had Loudoun and Abercromby been less busy and blinkered, had John Forbes been more healthy and less harried, perhaps the generals would have taken unilateral action. Their failure to do so left Anglo-Cherokee relations teetering on the precipice of open war.

Saluda and Broad River did not end the resentful manoeuvres of the defeated Tellico–Hiwassee faction, and these resentments were vigorously exploited by French agents. The most important of these was the Chevalier Louis de Lantagnac, a French officer who had been captured in 1745, turned his coat, and spent years as a Cherokee trader with a South Carolina licence. But in 1755, with war about to erupt, he had defected to Fort Toulouse where he was employed by Louis de Kelérec, the Governor of Louisiana, to direct French propaganda amongst the Cherokees. By 1756 he had two subordinates in the field: Pierre Chartier, a half-Shawnee known as Savannah Tom, and a Canadian whom the British called French John, supposedly Connecorte's slave.[1] French John's status gave him immunity from arrest by the British soldiers who arrived to build Fort Loudoun, and his and Chartier's insinuations were supported by visiting Shawnees and by anti-British factions amongst the Creeks. In the late spring of 1757 Kelérec was able to reinforce this effort by building a base on the Lower Ohio, eleven miles below the mouth of the Tennessee (Cherokee) River. Besides checking Cherokee raids against the Mississippi River traffic, Fort de l'Ascension, or Massac as it came to be known, could be used to build French credit within the nation.[2] By the autumn these moves, exploiting the failure of the British colonies to provide an adequate trade, Virginia's failure to man her fort, South Carolina's delay in building hers and British military reverses, were bearing fruit.

In October 1756 the Mankiller of Tellico led a 24-strong delegation to Fort Toulouse. There he, the Shawnees and the French officers tried unsuccessfully to commit a Creek embassy to a joint attack on the British. Afterwards the Mankiller went home, but Lantagnac took five of his companions to Mobile and thence to New Orleans.[3] In November these five, claiming to represent the whole nation, signed a preliminary treaty with Kelérec. The Cherokees undertook an alliance against the British in return for promises of copious quantities of trade goods and presents. Shortly afterwards the merchantman *Revanche*, homeward-bound with Kelérec's report and a copy of the draft treaty, met HM sloop *Jamaica*, and the papers fell into British hands. Coming at a time of failure in the north and conspicuous weakness in the south, the news of the Franco-Cherokee alliance caused a mild panic. Loudoun, understandably mistaking the Cherokees' motives, thought it demonstrated the folly of giving Indians ammunition before they had proved their willingness to fight the enemy.[4]

In fact the treaty was a dead letter. The Cherokees who agreed to it did not represent the whole nation, even though – as Captains Raymond Demeré and John Stuart at Fort Loudoun suspected – Connecorte and Attakullakulla had given the embassy their approval.[5]

Nor could they get their goods until the governor of Canada had agreed, and they had actually taken British scalps. Kelérec could not in the end produce the vital flow of goods; for nearly three years he received nothing from France, and much of what arrived in 1758 and 1759 had been ruined at sea. But at the time the Tellico move had sinister implications. By November it had produced rumours of an imminent French invasion of Georgia and South Carolina, and as late as May 1757 Henry Ellis in Georgia attributed to it the reported dispatch of a French fleet for the Mississippi.[6] It was not the only straw in the wind.

Meanwhile, Lantagnac had persuaded the Mankiller of Tellico that Kelérec would build a fort at Hiwassee, or at the junction of the Hiwassee and Tennessee Rivers. If in return the people of Tellico and Chatuga would move to Hiwassee and take a British scalp, he would send them a hundred horse loads of presents, including ammunition.[7] This was well beyond Louisiana's resources, and although the Mankiller seems to have presuaded some Tellicos to move, he soon changed his mind and brought them back.[8] This second agreement was therefore as empty as the first. But it inevitably aroused fears that Connecorte and Attakullakulla were privy to the whole business. Moreover, by inciting Tellico to active hostility it threatened to sever one of the two principal paths connecting Fort Loudoun to Carolina.

When Raymond Demeré found out about it the prospect of being marooned in the heart of the Cherokee country filled him with alarm. He was even more frightened by attempts to take that vital British scalp. Two Tellico traders fled for their lives, and on 2 January a warrior tried to stab a third; meanwhile the Mankiller had posted an ambush on the Tellico–Chota path. Demeré sent an urgent message to Cornelius Doherty, the trader at Little Hiwassee, to divert anyone coming from Keowee onto another path through the mountains. When the Mankiller approached the fort with a gang of warriors, ostensibly for a conference, the commandant prepared for an attack, and remained on his guard despite the Mankiller's subsequent pleas of fealty.[9] In March three of the five Tellicos who had visited New Orleans came home to tell Connecorte of the French promises. But all they had actually been given was a French flag which they brought home and flew over the Tellico town house. Shortly thereafter the Mankiller of Tellico took a war party to Virginia. Rumour had it that he went not to defend the settlers, but to steal their horses.[10]

Under these circumstances the appearance of a Shawnee delegation at Tellico and Chatuga was bound to provoke violent measures. Thomas Smith, the Chatuga trader, took the news to Demeré at Fort

Loudoun on 6 June. He in turn consulted the newly returned Captain John Stuart and Lyttelton's recruiting agent, Lieutenant-Colonel Howarth. Howarth and Stuart wanted to kill the Shawnees, but saw the importance of making the Cherokees accessories after the fact. The officers called in Connecorte, Kanagatucko (commonly called Standing Turkey) and 'the Settico Warrior called the Small Pox Conjuror', the only important leaders neither hunting nor at war. Invited to act against the Shawnee enemies of the British, Old Hop 'Evaded [a] direct Answer'. War, he said, was not his business. Standing Turkey pointed out that it was 'not their Custom to Strike People who Came to their Towns in a peaceable and Friendly way', meaning the British themselves as much as the Shawnees or the French. But the officers then threatened to keep the two older headmen at the fort until the Cherokees did as they were asked. At that the Small Pox Conjuror abruptly gave in and promised to arrange the assassination of the Shawnees. In the end, however, it was a detachment from the garrison led by Lieutenant James Adamson and Ensign Richard Coytmore which ambushed the enemy on 9 June. Three were killed, and a woman was taken, but two men and a woman escaped, 'our people being but awkward at this sort of war'. Significantly even the Tellicos, warned at the last minute not to accompany the Shawnee party, had stood aside. Not long afterwards the Tellico and Chatuga headmen offered to go to Virginia in return for a supply of British ammunition.[11]

Thus even Tellico was divided, and the hostile faction there as yet had no wish to become openly embroiled with the British. They knew well that many Cherokees, Old Hop included, had been frightened by their town's harbouring the nation's enemies and had urged Demeré to step up the completion of Fort Loudoun.[12] Besides Stuart and Demeré were holding their new prisoner hostage for the 'Prince' of Chatuga's son, then with the band of Shawnees living amongst the Creeks.[13] Any further Cherokee collaboration with the southern Shawnees would invite unpleasant consequences. Moreover, it was soon reported that the Creeks were about to expel the Shawnees, or at least force them to disperse amongst their towns. Demeré, seeing that a little courting might do much under these conditions, made a great fuss of the Tellico Mankiller when he returned in June with only one scalp.[14]

But at the same time, Demeré knew that his high-handed actions had only driven Tellico's resentment underground, and had probably intensified it. A new French overture, accompanied by liberal offers of goods, might swing them round to active hostility again. By the end of June there were rumours of a plan to surprise his fort, and such talk was still being heard at the end of July.[15] Late in July Chartier and French John appeared openly at Tellico, where the headmen refused to hand them over to Demeré. But when Chartier killed a soldier's wife Demeré sent a party after them and they fled.[16] At about the same time Attakullakulla returned from a raid towards the Mississippi, where he had discovered Fort Massac.[17] Consequently Demeré was on his guard against an attack, 'for', as he uncharitably put it, 'Savages are but Savages at last and are easily obtain'd by Luker of gain'.[18] Demeré may have been unsubtle in his analysis of motive, but he was not far wrong about the consequences of not supplying an adequate trade.

Demeré had long since realized that trade goods were one of the keys to the problem. Not only did Tellico feel slighted by not having received British presents, but, as John Stuart had recognized, resented the shortage of British traders and trade goods. Even if the Cherokees who had already gone to Virginia should return with scalps and presents aplenty, others would find there was no one able or willing to fit them out. Stuart depicted illicit traders short of goods and terrified of imprisonment for debt: 'there is not one in the nation who has a licence or dares go to Charles Town for one and the Indians will now Expect to be more regularly Supplyed.'[19] In fact a number were licensed but by July 1757 even Elliot of Chota was in serious financial straits. The supply of skins with which to pay their Charleston creditors had been failing for some time as the whitetail herds were depleted at the rate of 150 000 a year.[20] The expeditions to Virginia had already made things worse, for in the autumn of 1756 'none of the Indians went to their proper hunting ground'. Consequently very few skins were taken, the Indians failed to pay their debts to the traders, and the storemasters at Ninety Six and Augusta, finding themselves unpaid by the traders, refused to supply more goods on credit. The Indians thus found the trade from South Carolina drying up, not improving as promised at Saluda, and Stuart predicted 'very bad consequences'.[21] By July Old Hop, following a Talk by visiting Creeks, was 'murmuring about the Traders that had been so long promised from Carolina, and saw none came ...'.[22]

More and more, traders resorted to fraud. At Fort Prince George the officers requested a larger set of scales 'for the use of the Publick', apparently to provide an independent check.[23] When at Fort Loudoun the Cherokees complained about Elliot's false weights and inflated prices Demeré investigated. The Indians brought Elliot's 'Stillards' or scales, and found he was weighing 12 lb of hides at 10 lb. The Cherokees wanted them flung into the river, but on second thoughts agreed to let Demeré send them down to Lyttelton.[24] Elliot was furious.

[A]s no goods are come up for Elliot, he makes a great noise, and wants to know the reason of it, for which he will soon sett out for Charles Town, and carries some Indians with him. [T]he great warrior will go with him as he says, I should advise him not to Carry Indians with him on that Account, perhaps he might Repent of so Doing, he does not spare the little Carpenter with his Tongue and wants to do this or that to him & to take all his horses, he being the Occasion of all this, as he Says, he says that Some Officers have made themselves very Bussy, more than they can Answer for, that is meaning my Self, and says that he will buy & Sell as he pleases in his own house and no body shall interfer in it.[25]

But having brought Elliot to the point of ruin the Overhills realized that a dishonest trader was better than no trader at all. They had little ammunition, and absolutely no reason to believe that new traders were coming. On 18 July some packhorsemen sent by Elliot to buy more goods returned without loads. 'Elliot's horses coming back empty is enough to over Sett every thing that has been done', commented Demeré. Elliot managed to swing Occonostota, who had been one of his accusers, onto his side by giving him presents, and on 18 July Old Hop, Occonostota, and other headmen held 'a great Caball and Consultation' at Elliot's house. Demeré feared that relations would deteriorate further if something was not done quickly. The whole affair was undermining Attakullakulla, who was blamed for the Saluda agreement and for encouraging the complaints against Elliot. By 23 July rumours were flying about that the British, having deliberately stripped the Cherokees of ammunition, were sending up a large force to destroy them. As Stuart pointed out, to save the situation Lyttelton would have to send up the ammunition 'necessary to fitt them for their hunting grounds'.[26] Lyttelton did so, but he could not force merchants to give the traders further credit, nor could he force reluctant traders to go to the Cherokee towns. In mid-August he wrote to Old Hop and the Overhills admitting as much. When on 25 August Demeré tried to read his Talk there was uproar.

I had scarce read half of it, and finding that Traders were not coming among them they stop'd me and Said That they had a Great Many Young Men in their Towns, and that they had Guns but wanted very much Powder and Bullits, that the late Governour Promised them two Years ago, that he would send Traders Among [them] and that they Shou'd be Supply'd with every thing, that they had Many Letters to that Purpose, but that they where nothing but Lyes, and expected when you came they should be provided Better, & that You had Promised them when they were in Town that You would send them Traders, that they had waited a long while and have never seen one Yett, that you had told them lyes ... They said Further that they thought King George chose for Governours those men that could tell Lyes best.[27]

Their mood was not softened when Demeré pointed out that it was Elliot who had failed to bring them goods. When he told them that the ammunition was already on the road 'they said they should believe it when they should see it'. Attakullakulla poured oil on the troubled waters, assuring Demeré – with his tongue lodged firmly in his cheek – that they only wanted ammunition to defend his fort against the hordes of enemy Indians about to descend upon it. Demeré promised to provide powder and ball, and the immediate crisis was past.[28]

Ostenaca, the Mankiller of Tomotly, had meanwhile pinned his hopes upon the pledges made at Broad River. In May 1757 he had set off 'to Sollicit a Garrison for the Virginia Fort and a trade from that Province ...'[29] Ostenaca, of course, was anxious to sustain a diplomatic connection which had given him so much importance. Stuart saw at once that Lyttelton must not hamper this overture by ill-timed insistence on South Carolina's commercial and diplomatic primacy. 'A Well Regulated Trade no Matter from which Province will do Good, but the Least Appearance of rivalship between the provinces cannot fail of doing harm.'[30] Ostenaca's mission was not a mere appendix to a scalp-hunting trip to the Ohio; it was his main business. 'Judges friend goes through the Catawba Nation and the back Settlements direct to Williamsburg', observed Stuart, 'which has more the air of a peaceful than a Warlike Expedition'.[31] On 27 June he met Atkin at Winchester, and showed him copies of the letters from Virginia.[32] But Dinwiddie, though he could see the connection between the empty fort and the unruly behaviour of his Cherokee auxiliaries, continued to prevaricate and make excuses for doing nothing.[33] He did obtain a law from his assembly enabling him to sell Indian goods below cost, so undercutting the French, but, as he admitted to Lyttelton, this was a cost-cutting measure meant to replace present-giving.[34] On 23 August the Chota council sent Dinwiddie one last Talk – which they stipulated John Watts should read to Ostenaca – and summoned the Mankiller home.[35] When Ostenaca returned in October he brought several horse loads of presents, a Talk from Atkin, and news of 'how Friendly he had been use'd' in Virginia, and a White Man to wait on him'. But he was very ill,[36] there was no trade to speak of, and still no garrison for the fort.

There was also a great danger that the irruption of large Cherokee war parties into the Ohio region would offend the Iroquois and provoke a new war with the Six Nations. The Cherokee may also have suspected that they would be used to punish those Ohio nations, particularly the Delawares, already negotiating with the British for peace. There was, indeed, some reason for their fears: although Forbes himself wanted to keep the Cherokees away from the Delawares, Loudoun thought that a little scalp-taking would keep them happy while Forbes's army assembled. As it was the Cherokees were at war with Shawnees and Twightwees (Miamis), with the Creeks always an unknown quantity. The northern expeditions of 1757–8 took place against a background of intense Cherokee diplomacy, which led to non-aggression pacts with the Iroquois and a number of the Ohio nations.[37]

In such a tense atmosphere the presents which went with service in Virginia had a magnified importance. Their economic significance was, however, only part of the picture. To Cherokees, as to other Indians, gift-giving was part of the essential protocol of friendship and treaty making, symbols of ratification and good faith, as Dorothy Jones points out, in the context of the Augusta congress of 1763, 'a meaning which went beyond words'.[38] The Indians who went to Virginia in 1757 were in a suspicious mood, and only presents could give them full confidence in British honesty.

Of the 400 Indians who screened the Virginia frontier in the spring and summer of 1757, Corkran estimates that 250 – seven or eight bands of 13 to 60 warriors each – were Cherokees. But this was only a fraction of the nation's strength. Most of these were Lower Towns warriors under Wawatchee, and only one band came from the Overhills.[39] Virginia had prepared presents for their reception but unfortunately nearly all of them were delivered to Bedford Court House, on the Overhill route. This was nowhere near the Lower Towns' Path which lay further east. Worse, the trader employed to guide them on to Winchester was busy enjoying a Catawba girl. Thus when Wawatchee's warriors reached their rendezvous in Luneburg County, at the house of a magistrate called Clement Read, they found neither presents nor guide.[40] Virginia's promises, like South Carolina's, had been empty (Map 4).

Wawatchee thereupon allowed his warriors to take what they needed, 'following', as Corkran laconically notes, 'the usual Cherokee pattern in such instances'.[41] They terrorized Read's family, killed a Chickasaw who protested, and set off for Bedford. En route they plundered the plantations they passed and, if Read's account is to be believed, raped a 13 year-old girl.[42] Only with great difficulty were they persuaded to go on from Luneburg to Winchester for their presents. Dinwiddie had Wawatchee and the Swallow Warrior brought to Williamsburg, only to let them discover that there were no presents there either.[43] Already irritated by the dearth of trade and by the steady, ominous trickle of white settlers into their hunting grounds, they had undertaken a distant service for no gain at all. Worse, though the warriors probably did not appreciate it at the time, they had built up a dangerous head of resentment in the Virginia back settlements.

By mid-May there were 148 Cherokees, 124 Catawbas, and about 60 other Indians at Fort Loudoun near Winchester,[44] with no one to command or look after them. Atkin, whose job it might have been, had only just arrived in Williamsburg and was urgently wanted in South Carolina. As it was the Indians were all likely to go home at any moment. Their truculent demands forced the poor commandant to promise everything they asked for, 'and they made a List', observed Atkin, '[which] would make you laugh to see how they rack'd their Brains to make it out'. Dinwiddie and the Virginia council persuaded a reluctant Atkin to go up immediately to enquire into the Cherokees' crimes, and especially into the murder of the Chickasaw. But on 11 May the Catawba contingent arrived in Williamsburg, angry and unruly. Atkin pacified them in his usual effective but ponderous way, and two weeks had gone by before he was ready to leave. On 26 May he set out for Winchester 'to face the Freebooters', as he put it, but without any great hopes of success. 'If I succeed as well with them [as with the Catawbas]', he wrote, 'it must be by God's Grace, or a Miracle, as I am no Magician.'[45]

In fact he must have had some necromantic qualities, for he kept about two hundred of the Cherokees on the Virginian frontier throughout the summer. Though still 'under no manner of Command' and 'avaritios [sic] & greedy after Presents' – Dinwiddie at least completely failed to grasp the Cherokees' feelings on that point – they

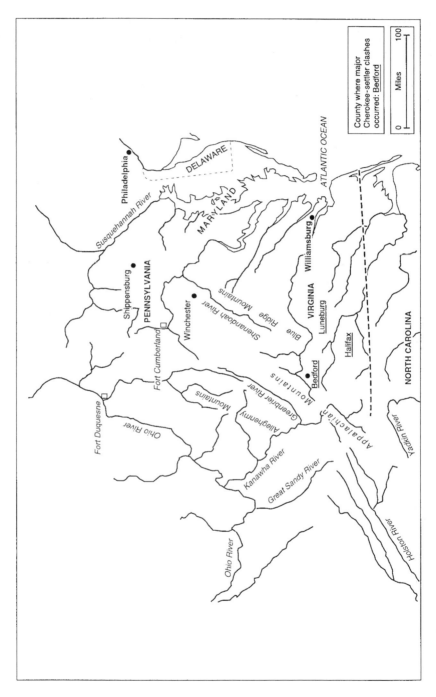

Map 4. Virginia and Pennsylvania

bravely defended the outlying settlements.[46] They even went on the offensive and took scalps within two miles of Fort Duquesne.[47] Not until the evening of 13 August did the last Cherokee leave Winchester for home, and by then the Superintendent had sent for a hundred Catawbas to replace them.[48] In June and August he had his interview with Ostenaca, listened to his complaints, discussed ways of rewarding distinguished warriors, and gave him the Talk for Connecorte.[49] Atkin, whom Dinwiddie had once thought reluctant to do his duty, had clearly 'been of much Service'. Unfortunately, he could not remain in Virginia. 'I expect him here [from Winchester] in a Week or ten Days', Dinwiddie told Lyttelton as early as 22 July, 'when I presume he will proceed for your Place ...'[50]

Behind the Cherokees' concern for presents and trade lay the wider issue of white encroachment of Cherokee lands. All along the Carolina frontier white settlers hunted either for preference or to supplement their farming,[51] while the ragged line of settlements crept ever further beyond the Long Canes line. Violence became frequent as Cherokees and settlers competed for the dwindling herds of whitetail deer. Early in 1756 Cherokees returning from the Broad River conference had attacked and beaten a settler. In the following months Cherokees had killed farm animals and invaded houses to such an extent that by June the Amelia district settlers were ready to abandon their homes.[52] Later that summer Cherokees, having 'given the planters Notice to quit their Settlements' committed 'several Robberies and Depredations' on the Broad and Catawba Rivers in North Carolina.[53] Toward the end of the year Indians, presumably Cherokees, had so threatened 'a Neighbourhood of People living on the southering Branch of Broad River' and 'some of the Inhabitants from the northernmost Branches of that Part of Santee called Great Saludy' that they abandoned their settlements. The empty houses were plundered and fired, spreading panic so much that 'almost the whole Place threatens to break up'. By January 1757 a government agent had begun to build 'a strong Fort for the Reception of the Inhabitants hereabouts in case of Emergency ...'[54] Early in 1757 ten Cherokees, responding to a French invitation, paid a visit to Fort Duquesne on the forks of the Ohio. The news was quickly relayed to Johnson by a Seneca informer, Silver Heels, who believed that the uncontrolled expansion of Carolina settlers onto Indian lands was to blame.[55]

In November the storm broke. Four Estatoe hunters, two men and two women, were shot in their camp near the Little Saluda River by a gang of Long Canes settlers. The killers scalped and mutilated the bodies, ripping one woman open, and leaving the remains for the wolves. Shortly afterwards they sold their victims' deerskins at Augusta. The local whites, as they probably always did in such cases, blamed Chickasaws, Catawbas and even four white outlaws from North Carolina. But this time there was a witness, a black living with the Savannah River Chickasaws, able to identify the killers: and it was Cherokee investigators, not white magistrates, who found him.[56]

Estatoe and the other Lower Towns were bitterly angry and sent Lyttelton that most sinister of messages: black beads mixed with white, to show that the path was now bloody. In the Cherokees' minds the murders were inextricably linked to the whole issue of the Long Canes trespassers. Yet, remembering the 1730 Treaty and the terms of Saluda, they postponed their own right to vengeance and asked Lyttelton for justice: if the black's evidence would not do, there must be whites who had seen the hides sold at Augusta.[57]

> Still we shall not kill any of the white People till we see wheather [sic] these People will be brought to Justice. As we have got forts built here we expect to live all as one as you may see by the Beads black and white mixed, but now the white People incroach two [sic] nigh upon our Lands and kill all our Deer so that we cannot find Meat for to eat, and we desire that you may order them away, and not allow them to come so nigh again. The string of white Beads is your own Talk formerly when the Path was white and clear, but the String [of] black Beads shew that the Path is foul and bloody; still we will do nothing to the white People til we hear whether these People are brought to Justice or not. We expect to hear soon what Resolution you intend to take about it.[58]

Lyttelton understood the Cherokee demand for revenge and explained that, because the victims had been scalped, at first he too had imagined the criminals to be enemy Indians. But he quite reasonably refused to punish anyone but the proven killers.[59]

> It is the Rule of our Law which I cannot depart from, that we are not to punish the innocent for the guilty, but if ever I can discover who they are who have done this Deed, I will immediately cause the Offenders to be punished with the greatest Rigour, and in the mean Time the Warriors at the fort shall give Presents to the Relations of the Deceased to wipe away their Tears and I hope you will consider the Path to be still as clear and open as ever it was. It sometimes

happens that a guilty Person among us runs away and makes his Escape and then we are forced to be satisfied.[60]

Probably Lyttelton was simply doing his best to defuse what he knew to be a very ugly situation. But his suggestion that 'white People are not used to scalp'[61] must have sounded disingenuous to Cherokee ears; after all, that had not prevented his frontier agents from accusing the gang from North Carolina. His refusal to yield life for life appeared to be a flagrant disregard for Cherokee law and the duty of clan vengeance. At best it looked like an attempt to screen the murderers. The Cherokees may well have suspected that Lyttelton's 'beloved Men who act as Judges of the People in those parts'[62] – notably James Francis at Ninety Six – were implicated themselves. Worst of all, he had ignored the fundamental issue, that of creeping invasion across the Long Canes frontier. No Cherokee could see an equitable reason – as opposed to reasons of discretion and diplomacy – why they should not seek their own satisfaction, perhaps expelling the settlers themselves. Alden reduces this incident to the status of a footnote. But Milling, though he misses the significance of the complaint about encroachment, rightly sees it as a milestone on the road to war.[63]

When two Virginians were murdered in part settlement of the account in March 1758 it was by a party from Estatoe. The Estatoe people admitted as much, though they tried to shuffle the blame first onto the Raven of Toxaway and then onto an unnamed Overhill who, they alleged, had led the party.[64] The Raven, with this or another party, may have slain as many as five more whites.[65] Revenge was certainly not the only motive. Lachlan McIntosh at Fort Prince George thought horse stealing was behind this later violence. Dissatisfaction with presents, heavy-handed commanders, and Virginian incompetence may have played some part, but as Milling points out, the perpetrators may well have been going to, not leaving, Virginia.[66] The main reasons were undoubtedly the Long Canes encroachments and the unrequited blood of November, and whites in the Cherokee country might well be the next victims. When the Cherokees welcomed some Shawnees flaunting three white scalps, the trader Jerome Courtonne fled to Charleston in panic.[67] As we have seen, at the end of the year the Presbyterian missionary William Richardson found that even at Chota the boundary issue was the most important cause of hostility.

War might have been avoided had a means been found to resolve the chaos in the management of Cherokee policy, and in the management of Virginia's Cherokee recruits in particular. Tragically the events of 1757 made the various authorities more competitive and determined to pursue their parochial aims than before. Neither Lyttelton nor Dinwiddie was prepared to back Atkin to the hilt. Dinwiddie wanted only his Indians, and if that meant appointing his own agents so be it. Lyttelton, on the other hand, wanted to get rid of a potential rival and to sustain South Carolina's primacy in Cherokee affairs.

Lyttelton, ambitious and with influence at home, was determined to sustain the South Carolina governor's role as director of Indian policy in the south. In August 1757 at Beaufort near the South Carolina–Georgia boundary he held a conference with Henry Ellis, the newly arrived governor of Georgia, and with Colonel Henry Bouquet of the Royal American Regiment, commander of the regulars sent to defend the southern colonies. Here Lyttelton made it quite clear that it was he who was in overall charge of all Indian affairs south of the Ohio, not Georgia, and certainly not the army. He insisted upon a tough policy to keep the Cherokees in order.[68] This was hardly surprising given the reports he had been receiving from the Cherokee country and Virginia: as far as he could see the Cherokees were useful allies, but also undisciplined savages liable to attack British settlers or even turn to the French.

Cashin observes that at Beaufort Henry Ellis readily deferred to Lyttelton's supremacy in Indian affairs. Although that did not stop him arranging his own conference with the Creeks soon afterwards, he explained himself to his colleague in the most respectful and apologetic terms.[69]

> I can assure You Dear Sir that I have no sort of ambition of being principal Negotiator with the Indians. I have neither the abilities, or the means to support that character effectually. What I am doing is merely to avoid the imputation of negligence in a matter of great concernment to this Province, & the discharge of what I take to be my duty.[70]

Cashin also suggests that Lyttelton's firm line was supported by Bouquet, who apparently declared himself astonished that importunate Cherokee delegations came so frequently to Charleston. Citing the Swiss mercenary's notorious remark that the Ohio Indians should be given smallpox-infected blankets, Cashin adds that Bouquet had no sympathy for Indians.[71] There is a sliver of truth in these observations –

perhaps rather more than a sliver – but there is another, more sympathetic, and possibly more important side to Bouquet as well. Whatever
he said at Beaufort, Bouquet clearly understood the importance of the
Cherokees, and of keeping their friendship. He ordered Paul Demeré,
who had succeeded his brother Raymond at Fort Loudoun, to cultivate
Attakullakulla and to send down all the Indian intelligence he could
gather.[72] By late August he was optimistic about Indian affairs. The
Cherokees, he told Loudoun, 'seem to be our sincere friends & have
made the path to the French bloody'. He was particulary impressed by
Attakullakulla's discovery of Fort Massac. He was contemptuous of
Virginia's attempt to buy such loyalty with their unmanned fort, 'a
meer bubble constructed to humour the Indians'.[73] On 10 September he
wrote to Demeré, expressing his hope that the latter would succeed in
sustaining the Cherokee alliance, and in persuading the warriors to go
to war. He also wanted him to obtain some reparation from the Tellicos,
'or discover the sentiments of the Nation on their account'. He would
need to know the town's exact location and strength in order to be able
to punish its people if they became 'troublesome'.[74]

This was certainly a strong policy, but it was directed solely against a
town guilty of collaboration with the French, harbouring enemy agents
and murder. A week later he wrote to Lieutenant Lachlan Shaw, now
commanding at decrepit Fort Prince George, where some warriors were
demanding presents with menaces. In that letter he suggested that the
Cherokee alliance was worth almost any concession short of submitting to open blackmail. 'As long as the Indians behave decently', he
wrote, 'I shall approve of all reasonable Measures taken to keep up the
Friendship with them ...' But he did not want to yield to any unreasonable demand 'when they ask it with Authority. We want to be
their friends and not their Slaves':[75] a sentiment he was to repeat, in
almost identical words, to George Croghan in 1759.[76] The demands he
had in mind in 1757 were very specific – involving threats against the
decrepit fort – and he was pleased when Shaw's repairs brought them
to an end.[77] He may not have shown much understanding of the
Cherokee position, but neither had other officials. At the time his
stance was moderate and friendly, and his troubles with white
Carolinians over quartering may well have caused him to think Indians
far less troublesome. We have already seen how in 1759–61 Bouquet
tried to screen the Ohio nations from settler encroachment.[78] Certainly
his former subordinates in South Carolina, Archibald Montgomery and
James Grant, were to show far more sympathy for the Cherokees than
for the white settlers they were supposed to protect.[79]

Even the apparently damning business of the infected blankets is less conclusive than it looks. Cashin, determined to make Bouquet the foil for Ellis's sensitive tolerance, cites no other source than Billington's *Westward Expansion*. Billington, in turn, gives no source at all.[80] It has been left to Richard White to point out that the idea of the blankets came from Amherst, and that Bouquet agreed, adding that they should copy the Spanish practice of hunting down Indian guerrillas with dogs.[81] But this was the summer of 1763, the height of Pontiac's War, a campaign so cruel that Algonquian headmen were denouncing the atrocities on their own side.[82] Anger and frustration may have driven Bouquet to agree to germ warfare, but there seems to be no concrete evidence that he ever carried it out. To argue backwards from this incident, to assert that he must have favoured harsh measures in 1757, is to build a pyramid on a very wobbly apex.

The question of Bouquet's position is far from trivial, for the role of the British army in Cherokee affairs was about to be greatly increased. The British strategy for 1758 called for a three-pronged attack on New France. The southernmost prong was to be an assault on Fort Duquesne under John Forbes, whose regulars, provincials and Indians were to rendezvous at Winchester in Virginia on 1 May. In the winter the fleet in the Gulf of St Lawrence and some of the troops were to be switched to the Gulf of Mexico for an attack on Louisiana, a project designed to remove one of the southern colonies' nightmares forever.[83] To Lyttelton's relief the pugnacious Bouquet – who had stirred up the conflict over quartering – was to go with his Royal Americans and Montgomery's Highlanders to assist Forbes.[84] This new offensive meant even greater efforts to recruit southern Indians, not only to defend the Virginian frontier, but to screen Forbes's advance through the very forests where Braddock had come to grief.

Yet who would coordinate this effort? Atkin, the obvious choice, was out of reach. He did not return to Williamsburg from Winchester until 5 October, and then became embroiled with Dinwiddie over primacy in Indian policy. Consequently he did not sail for the Carolinas until 10 November. His plan was to call at New Bern, quickly conclude some business with Dobbs, and in a few days set sail for Charleston.[85] But at Cape Fear he was laid low with a severe bout of gout, and in any case the Indian affairs of North Carolina were more complicated than he had thought. He became entangled in the question of the building of the protective fort, which the Catawba leaders were demanding in exchange for their services in the north. That question was in turn caught up in a complicated dispute about the boundary between the two Carolinas, and consequently which colony could claim jurisdiction over Catawba affairs. To muddle matters even more thoroughly the Catawbas were exploiting the situation to play one colony off against the other, and so obtain the best possible deal.[86] Atkin did not arrive in Charleston until 23 March.[87] By that time he had rivals in the field.

Atkin may have muddied the waters with his self-importance and grandiose claims for his office, and he may have been more methodical than swift. But his task was simply too vast for one man, even operating through deputies, let alone for one whose powers were so circumscribed. As he saw himself, either his commission must override all provincial authorities or it was nothing. Colonial governors and British generals on the whole preferred it to be nothing. Ellis opposed Atkin altogether, and Virginia was inclined to circumvent him.

Lyttelton supported Atkin but as an agent of his own authority, and then only as a temporary and unsatisfactory expedient. As late as April 1759, when Atkin appealed to South Carolina to help him control the Creek trade, Lyttelton and the Council would offer to make him 'a Provincial Agent, by Virtue of which he wd. be furnished with a power of requiring & commanding the attendance & obedience of traders ...'[88] But even as a provincial agent the Superintendent was both inefficient and dangerous. Lyttelton thought he must go.

In August 1758 Lyttelton submitted to the Board of Trade his views of how a more comprehensive and efficient system might be constructed. The two superintendents and their vast districts should be replaced with a series of Crown agents who would live 'constantly' with the nations to which they were assigned. In the south there should be one with the Creeks (perhaps also taking responsibility for the Chickasaws) and one for the Cherokees (who might also look after the Catawbas). At present the only resident agents were the military officers at the forts. But this was such a disagreeable duty that the commanders had to be regularly relieved, 'from which it will often happen that a very unfitt Man to manage Indian affairs will have the Command',[89] while the Superintendent, with his vast responsibilities, could not possibly reside anywhere for long himself. 'The Gentleman who has the honor to Act in that Station may probably think he does his duty if he sometimes makes a Visit to one or the other of these Indian Nations ...' Resident agents alone could supply the intimate knowledge and constant flow of intelligence essential to successful diplomacy.[90]

Trade, thought Lyttelton, should not be a matter of private profit, but managed and subsidized by the Crown to assure the Indians of a plentiful supply of cheap goods. If that meant loss rather than profit, so be it; the government should regard it in the same light as a subsidy to a European ally. The agents were to be empowered, either jointly or at least in conjunction with the governors, to issue and revoke trading licences. With that would go the right to adjudicate disputes and award compensation to Indians in cases of fraud.[91] Here, as he frankly admitted, he had one eye on the danger of 'rivalship' posed by the new Virginian trade law.[92]

But although these agents were to communicate directly with the Board of Trade, they should correspond 'also with the governors of the different Provinces when ever anything occur's [sic] which it was material they should be informed of'.[93] By that he meant any Indian matters affecting the traditional sphere of the colony concerned. For example, in the matter of the North Carolina border he had already insisted that any settlement must leave the Catawbas and Cherokees 'within this Province ...'[94]

Lyttelton recognized that the agents would be unable to keep the peace and discipline traders without military support. For this reason their position in nations where there were British forts would be far more tolerable than elsewhere.[95] But he did not want the agents to be a civil authority empowered to call for troops in a crisis, let alone give them the right to authorize their use. On the contrary, he wanted the agents to be under the direction of the commander-in-chief in all things military.[96]

Here he had touched on a truth which generals tried to ignore, but which James Grant was to pounce upon in 1761. It was that the commander-in-chief and his deputies, who alone possessed real supra-colonial authority as well as the means to enforce it, must ultimately take responsibility for a coordinated Indian policy. This had been partly recognized in London when the superintendents were placed under the commander-in-chief. Indeed, the Secretary of State, Henry Fox, had told Loudoun that he might ignore Atkin's warrant if he could find someone more suitable.[97] Consequently, although Atkin trailed him from London to New York to Albany to Philadelphia, Loudoun had been in no hurry to give him his instructions.[98] But the Earl did not appoint another superintendent, and had no alternative vision of an integrated Indian policy, only a profound distrust of Atkin and a determination to bypass him wherever possible.

Loudoun distrusted Atkin, his slowness, his gout and his claims to expertise in dealing with Indians, and expected him to be very late in his recruiting mission to the Cherokees. '... I am afraid Mr. Atkin will be dilatory in the Execution of that Affair', he warned Lyttelton, unless the South Carolina governor were to spur him on. Thus, as 'Mr Atkins has not informed me where he is, and as he is so often confined at this Season of the Year, by the Gout ...' Loudoun had appointed his own agent. This was William Byrd, member of the Virginia Council and former Broad River commissioner, 'a particular friend of mine' who was 'Zealous and Active for the Publick Service' and experienced in handling Indians. Just to underline the point he made Byrd his postman.[99] To make quite sure that Atkin could make no mistakes, Loudoun appointed interpreters of his own to go overland to the Overhills and tell them to attend the proposed great meeting at Keowee. With them he sent Captain Abraham Bosomworth, who had been asked for by Lyttelton, and who had convinced Loudoun that he had 'been much among the Cherokees'.[100]

To stop him objecting, Atkin was told that Byrd and Bosomworth would be his assistants.[101] But Byrd himself understood that the Superintendent was to be kept out of the picture as much as possible. After 21 days at sea 'in a continual storm' he reached Charleston to learn that Atkin was still laid up at Cape Fear. He had still not arrived ten days later, 'so', he told Forbes, 'no Difficulties will arise from him'.[102] To Loudoun he observed, 'I apprehend all difficulties in regard to him are removed by his absence & indisposition.'[103] From Cape Fear Atkin could neither assert his authority, nor make the expedition to Keowee wait until he was well enough to come.

It was true that the Superintendent had managed to throw one spanner into the works, by shipping all the Indian presents he had been supplied with in New York as private property. They were in his Charleston house already, awaiting his arrival, and until then legally beyond Byrd's reach. Lyttelton solved the problem by persuading the Council to apply part of the £20 000 sterling which the Commons had already voted for a provincial regiment. Byrd now had ample credit with which to buy presents – in theory enough to equip a thousand Indians – and prepared to start for the Cherokee country. Time was more important than ever, for reports were reaching Charleston that over 200 Cherokees had already left for Virginia. Realizing the trouble which might ensue from stray parties traversing the Virginian back settlements, Lyttelton sent his own agent, Howarth, to urge them to wait and meet Byrd at Keowee. Howarth was armed with a promise of goods worth 4 cwt of 'lather' (value £4285 14s. 3d.); and with Talks addressed to Connecorte, the Lower Towns' headmen, Ostenaca, and the Raven of Hiwassee. Although he found Lyttelton 'rather slow', Byrd expected to be at Winchester for the great rendezvous of 1 May.[104]

On the eve of his departure Byrd's satisfaction was briefly interrupted by Atkin's arrival. Byrd, Atkin and Lyttelton immediately conferred on what was to be done. Atkin gallantly offered to start for Keowee at once, but, to Byrd's relief, he was easily persuaded to send a letter instead. Next morning Byrd received a packet containing a letter of advice from Atkin (in case he had forgotten the gist of yesterday's meeting) in which the Superintendent stressed the danger of 'expence and disquietude to the inhabitants within our settlements' when the warriors marched north. Byrd should be very careful in choosing the Cherokees' 'conductors' in order 'to prevent irregularities if they pass through our settlements (out of which they should be kept as much as possible) ...' He went on to make a number of sensible suggestions for the journey. Byrd's 'conductors' should never lose sight of the Cherokees and should discourage straggling; misbehaviour should not be dealt with directly, but only through the warrior leading that party; rum, if allowed at all, must be strictly rationed and heavily watered. As an afterthought he nominated two reliable traders, Richard Smith of Keowee and John Watts of Chota, 'being sworn interpreters for the king's service & conductors', as the best people to translate his enclosed Talk for Connecorte. In that Talk he apologized for taking so long to arrive, having been delayed by 'the Great King's Business' and his own illness, and naming Byrd as his proxy.[105] Atkin was being as helpful as he could, though Byrd may well have felt that he was being taught how to suck eggs, the Superintendent's deep anxiety about the dangers stands out in every line. By letting Byrd do his job for him, Atkin had abdicated the coordinating role which should have been his, but the point may, however, be academic. Howarth and Byrd quickly discovered that the march they were supposed to oversee had already begun.

As early as January parties of Overhills had been setting out in search of scalps and presents. On 15 January Attakullakulla and Occonostota had returned from their Mississippi expedition with 12 scalps (half French, half Twightwee) and three prisoners (two Frenchmen, one Twightwee). Here were all the tokens of dramatic success, and although Demeré had too few goods to reward them properly, every warrior in the towns could see the new gun given to every man who had taken a scalp or a captive. Nor could they fail to notice the presents, including boots and paint, given to every member of the party. Within two days 20 Settico warriors set off to harry Fort Massac, stopping to get powder, ball, flints, knives, paint and a hatchet from Demeré as they passed. On 2 March the leader of another party asked for presents to fit out a raid on Fort Massac; Demeré told him he would rather he hunted down a band of Twightwees who were harassing the Overhills hunting grounds. But by mid-February several gangs had started for Virginia. Demeré and Attakullakulla (who had actively encouraged the raid on Fort Massac) tried to persuade them to wait for Atkin and his goods, but they were no match for the ardour of young men after renown, scalps, presents and plunder.[106] By 10 April, when Howarth reached Fort Loudoun, nearly all the Overhill warriors had gone, most of them down the Tennessee to harry Fort Massac.[107]

Unfortunately this warlike emigration did not mean that all the earlier Anglo-Cherokee tensions had been resolved. The dishonesty of the traders, including Elliot, was still a problem. As Paul Demeré complained, it had been a mistake not to take Elliot's licence away.

I am sory that i ever wrote to your Excellency concerning Elliot i am most sure that he dont use the Indians very well, they complain to me very much about him, when he sells them Rum it is half water, and his Goods very Dear, and short measures, i told them it was thich faults, and that your Excellency had sent Weights and Measures, that they should not be in posed upon. the Little Carpenter told me, that he would speak to you about it, therefore i begin first.[108]

Demeré had few goods left to give the war parties – gunpowder was urgently needed – and the bills he had given Cornelius Doherty for emergency supplies had not been honoured.[109] The previous summer's troubles over presents in Virginia and the November murders near Long Canes had not been forgotten, and it is likely that many of the young warriors moving north had their minds on revenge and plunder as well as presents. Attakullakulla, disappointed at not receiving a personal letter from Lyttelton, determined to take the trade issue to Charleston in person.[110] His discouragement of parties bound for Virginia – and his enthusiasm for expeditions to the Lower Ohio and the Mississippi[111] – was no doubt partly to undermine his rival, Ostenaca. But he was probably also frightened of the consequences of allowing unescorted war parties to trail through the North Carolina and Virginian settlements. No doubt with the Chota council's backing, he assembled 82 followers, eight of them women, and set off for

Charleston. At Ninety Six he met Howarth who begged him to wait for Byrd. But the little warrior was not to be deflected; he pushed on and on 30 March, at a settlement on the Little Saluda River, he encountered Byrd himself.[112]

Byrd made no impression at all on the Carpenter; indeed the Cherokee tried hard to persuade the Virginian that nearly all the warriors had left the nation and that his mission was useless. That afternoon Byrd tried again, delivering the Talks from Lyttelton, Loudoun and Atkin. These appeals to the Cherokees' duty to their allies, symbolized by the promise of presents, left some of the Cherokees 'very wavering', but did not move Attakullakulla. Next day he repeated the explanation he had already made to Demeré: he must go to Lyttelton because he had many complaints to make, and to be rewarded for his raid against the French. Byrd tried again to turn him back but without avail. Finally a compromise was struck: Attakullakulla would go on with one headman from every town represented in his party. The rest, 52 in number, would go back with Byrd, but the Carpenter warned them not to leave for Virginia until he returned with satisfactory answers from Lyttelton. Attakullakulla also promised that, if successful in Charleston, he would meet Byrd again at Chota in 26 days and march on to Winchester with all the men he could raise.[113] Thus, having placated Byrd without compromising his mission one iota, Attakullakulla took his depleted party on to Charleston.

Byrd pushed on to Keowee. Here he met Howarth, who reported that the Overhills had already gone to war and that the men of the Middle Towns had refused point-blank to go anywhere. He had not raised a single recruit. Byrd, still undeterred, summoned the sixty-odd remaining warriors in the Lower Towns to Keowee. After some discussion these men agreed to go to Virginia, provided that Byrd took them himself, 'by the lower path', and set out on 1 May. He then made a tour of the Middle Settlements.[114] Here he met so much passive opposition that he was obliged to enlist the aid of James Beamer and his *métis* son Thomas. Long serving traders like Beamer, who had spent almost thirty years at Estatoe, had a great deal of influence over the people with whom they lived.[115]

The Cherokees, as we have seen in the case of Elliot, understood their dependence on their traders, and would put up with almost anything to keep them. The traders, on the other hand, knew that expeditions to Virginia would ruin them. Beamer, for example, was owed quite considerable debts by the Indians, and if they lost their winter hunt again he would not be paid, 'yet he has laboured with all his skill to raise the most he could & they go down with me with his son'. As this would be 'to his utter ruin' Byrd gave Beamer an order for £2000 drawn on South Carolina, and asked Lyttelton to give him as much again,

> which does not amount to half his debts & as the Indians are going & gone to war they look on all their accounts as settled. This is a circumstance I could by no means avoid without spoiling my whole scheme, for I am well assur'd if Mr. Beamer had been inclined he could have prevented me from raising a single man out of his town.[116]

Indeed, he observed, all traders had a vested interest in preventing recruiting 'as they fear their creditors will seize their effects in their [the Cherokees'] absence, which they will not suffer when they are at home'. He therefore suggested that all the traders licensed by South Carolina should be given 'protections' against proceedings, at least until the end of the next winter hunt. 'I wish', he told Lyttelton, 'you may not think me both mad & unreasonable, but you know what sort of people I have to deal with'.[117]

Whatever the role of Beamer's influence, all the Middle Towns solemnly promised to go to Virginia with Attakullakulla.[118] But they would do so only if Lyttelton had promised more traders in their part of the nation, and if Lyttelton, by giving the Carpenter presents, seemed to undertake to reward them and cancel their debts. Byrd sent Talks to the Valley Towns and obtained a similar reply. From the Middle Settlements he sent another Talk to the Overhills. But they 'from superstition' would not come to Keowee, preferring instead the direct route from their towns to Virginia. A dream had warned them that danger awaited them on the lower path: they preferred not to be embroiled in the Lower Towns' quarrels with the Virginian settlers.

All Attakullakulla's warriors who had returned with Byrd went to join this party, which may have exceeded 200 men. Even then their departure was delayed: Attakullakulla returned to Keowee, extremely suspicious of Lyttelton's promise that his presents would follow by waggon, and determined not to move a step without them. Nor was he convinced that Lyttelton would replace Elliot; when the Chota trader himself appeared at Keowee full of promises and contrition, the Carpenter and Occonostota struck a bargain with him rather then be left with no trader at all. They wrote to Lyttelton and withdrew their complaints.[119]

The Carpenter's distrust of Elliot, the late arrival of Lyttelton's presents, and the perils on the path to Virginia made him anxious and irritable. If there were to be trouble with the settlers he wanted to be nowhere near it. He would not budge until the presents came; and if the Carpenter was being awkward, his rival Ostenaca had been openly obstructive.[120] Even the hospitality of Keowee women had its drawbacks. 'The Squaws are the only good things to be met with here', Byrd observed on 30 April, '& I cannot break them of anointing themselves with Bears Grease, & depriving themselves of the greatest Ornament of Nature.'[121] Next day he discovered that the Carpenter's example had reduced his party from an optimistically calculated 100 to less than 60.[122] Byrd remonstrated and there was a sharp, brief quarrel.

> That little savage was very insolent this morning [wrote Byrd], said we all told him lys & that neither he [n]or his men would go to Virginia, however he is now well pleased again, & has promiss'd to go as soon as his wagon comes up.[123]

Byrd had to march from Keowee on 1 May, the day he should have arrived at Winchester, with the 60-odd Cherokees. He left George Turner, a trader, at Keowee to accompany the Carpenter's party to Chota and thence on to Winchester. But Attakullakulla would not promise to arrive before 1 June, and in fact he was still waiting at the end of May.[124] Parties, including one from the Middle Settlements,[125] continued to leave throughout May, so that Byrd's 57 were only one of many parties trickling northward. By then some of the bands which had left in the winter were returning by the same paths.

Thus Atkin's and Byrd's nightmare was realized. Parties of armed Cherokees were strung out over the paths leading to and through Virginia, and the settlements which had been the scene of clashes in 1757. There was every prospect that the leading bands would arrive at Winchester before their presents, and then either go home or help themselves. Each of Byrd's own recruits expected goods to the value of 40 lb of leather to be waiting for him.[126] But the trouble broke out long before the first of his Cherokees reached Winchester. The deaths of the five Virginians in March, apparently in revenge for the November 1757 murders, may also have been over the horses which several parties appropriated on the path.[127] This was not necessarily always thieving. Hewatt, following Dr George Milligan, argues that there were many stray unbranded horses in the back country which were no man's property and which anyone could claim. 'As the horses in these parts ran wild in the woods it was customary, both among Indians and white people on the frontiers, to lay hold on them and appropriate them to their own purposes.' Thus many Cherokees returning from Virginia, 'having lost their own horses', took such strays 'never imagining that they belonged to any individual in the province'. Thus when the Virginians attacked 'the unsuspicious warriors' the Cherokees were outraged and flew to arms.[128]

This view is admirable in sentiment, but unfortunately ingenuous. Cherokees do not seem to have been too particular about whose horses they took, even on their outward journey, and after the troubles of the previous summer settler tempers were short. There were clashes and early in May the party guilty of the March killings was attacked on its return journey. Three warriors were killed, two captured and all the gang's goods were taken.[129] Byrd heard of it when he had marched no further than the Yadkin River settlements in North Carolina (Map 4), and his own Cherokees were barely restrained from seeking vengeance at once. He wrote at once to McIntosh, asking him to give presents to the assaulted group and pressed on with his own people to Winchester.[130] By the time they reached Winchester on 21 May, however, the Cherokees were seething with anger, and bent on taking revenge on their way home.[131] News of further bloodshed in Bedford and Halifax Counties did nothing to soothe their ire.[132] At Carlisle in Pennsylvania the overlong absence of a band already on forest patrol made the new arrivals very restless; at Shippensburg presents were taken by force. The Virginia Council and Major-General Jeffrey Amherst, then at Philadelphia en route to Halifax, were reduced to hoping that Byrd would somehow calm the Cherokees; in fact he could not even vouch for those he had escorted in person. Henry Bouquet more sensibly arranged a conference with all the headmen at Winchester, even before he could extract the necessary order from Forbes.[133]

The British Indian management system, if that is not too strong a word, had tottered into chaos. Everyone could see it but no one was willing to take the responsibility for definitive action. Forbes heard that Johnson was sending his deputy Croghan to 'adjust' the troubles with the Cherokees and thought he might take overall command. 'I wish he may arrive in Time to be of any Service, for all those affairs have somehow been cruelly neglected, and are at Present in the greatest Confusion.'[134] Meanwhile Forbes, who well understood that the Cherokees' demands would 'not admit of delay or temporising', found himself begging Pennsylvania for guns. The Pennsylvanians had refused to pay any part of the costs of bringing the Cherokees across North Carolina and Virginia, thus exacerbating the shortages there. Now they were even trying to deny him the 218 weapons kept in the provincial arsenal, on the grounds that they were not Crown property. He had ordered his quartermaster-general, Sir John St Clair, to buy up whatever was needed himself – blankets, matchcoats, deerskins, vermillion – to ensure that the promises made to the Cherokees were honoured.[135] Even this ran foul of administrative confusion and parochialism. Indian goods already earmarked by St Clair had been bought up by Johnson's agent, Ferrell Wade, for the benefit of the Ticonderoga campaign. Consequently the appearance of hundreds of Cherokees demanding presents had caught Forbes unprepared, and forced him to impose an embargo on all such goods remaining in Philadelphia, 'the whole being but scarcely sufficient to keep these people together and to Prevent their returning home'.[136]

Forbes should not have been lost for a solution. In April Abraham Bosomworth, still in Virginia for want of guides, had become the Virginian agent at Winchester.[137] Revealing a startling ambition, he had at once asked Abercromby, Loudoun's successor, for control of Atkin's local personnel and goods.[138] He had spent the rest of the month at Winchester, trying to keep the Cherokees and Catawbas together, and investigating the Cherokees' behaviour.[139] But the news of Forbes's arrival brought him to Philadelphia,[140] to urge his ideas of Indian management upon the general. He pointed out that there must be one person responsible for the Indians joining the army, with ample presents and adequate interpreters at his command. Bosomworth tactfully suggested that Christopher Gist, Atkin's deputy in Virginia, should have this responsibility, an opinion which Atkin, suspecting Bosomworth's ambition, naturally shared.[141] It was not long, however, before Bosomworth was suggesting himself. Bouquet, who had clearly been talking to Bosomworth, was soon suggesting that Forbes should cut through the Gordian knot of superintendents, deputies and agents altogether. In their place he should appoint his own man, either Gist or Bosomworth, to operate under military authority only.[142] Bouquet's suggestion was the only one which might have ended the chaos, for the army stood above provincial narrowness and rivalry, and had far more independence and authority than Atkin. Amherst, not entirely trusting Bosomworth and wishing to bypass Johnson, favoured Byrd with Bosomworth as his assistant.[143]

But it would have taken a courageous, even reckless man to deliberately clash with so many civilian authorities, especially when he needed the colonial assemblies' support for his expedition. Forbes, though relentlessly brave, was far from rash and he was very ill.[144] Abercromby, who would do nothing without Johnson's approval, provided only moral support. Indeed, Forbes's backing for Pennsylvania's direct negotiations with Delawares and Iroquois offended Johnson, who was promptly supported by the commander-in-chief.[145] Forbes therefore continued to shuffle the thorny crown of Indian management onto other, less wary, heads. In June his cousin James Glen, who had already offered his services from South Carolina, arrived with Montgomery.[146] Forbes had little faith in Glen's self-proclaimed expertise, but he let him go to Winchester partly as a 'last shift', partly to avoid hurting his feelings.[147] Forbes rather desperately hoped that Byrd and Glen would manage to cooperate, but they fell out when Byrd would not accept Glen's suggestions.[148] Meanwhile, he had ordered Bosomworth, already on his way to the back country, to prepare the ground for Bouquet's conference at Winchester.[149] None of these agents was ever given overall authority. Forbes continued to muddle along as best he could amongst all his other difficulties, and to complain when neither of the superintendents came to rescue him.[150]

The Cherokees, finding few presents or arms at Winchester, were disgusted by the news that Forbes was not yet ready to march. Forbes, who had earlier expected Byrd's recruits to be too late to help him, was initially sympathetic.[151] Reaching Philadelphia weeks before his regular battalions, he observed that 'necessity will turn me a Cherokee, and don't be surprised if I take F. du Quesne at the head of them; and them only ...'[152] He directed Halkett, his major of brigade, to see that officers did everything they could to please the Indians and to keep them with the embryonic army.[153] But Montgomery's Highlanders did not disembark in the Delaware until 6 June, and not until the end of the month did Forbes march west to Carlisle. Even then he continued to have trouble assembling sufficient waggons, pack saddles and supplies. Another factor was the choice of route. After some dithering Forbes decided to go by a shorter route from Pennsylvania, rather than use Braddock's longer but ready-made road from Virginia. His hesitation was understandable, as either choice was bound to offend one of the colonies competing for trade and lands on the Ohio. But it was 12 August before he had made up his mind and moved on to Shippensburg.[154] (Map 5) Long before then many Cherokees were to drifting homewards.

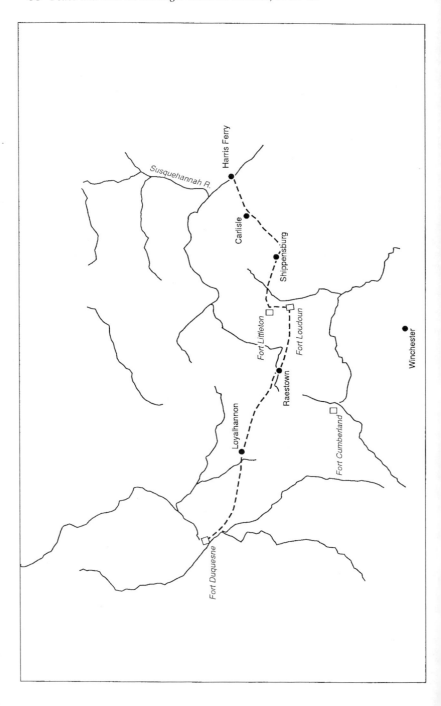

The Raven of Hiwassee and 30 warriors had left by the beginning of May.[155] Attakullakulla's brother Willinawaw, for example, had led a band from the Overhill country in March, joined forces with a warrior called Thick Legs, and made an abortive reconnaissance towards Fort Duquesne. But having seen no enemies and taken no scalps, and with some of their warriors fallen ill, the two leaders had turned for home. Other parties plundered houses, lifted 'great Gangs of Horses', and fought bloody skirmishes with their white pursuers.[156] At Fort Loudoun in Pennsylvania Captain William Thompson was struggling to keep those still assembled. The most prominent leader there was the turbulent Wawatchee, perpetrator of the 1757 outrages, and who had, as Bouquet put it, 'beaucoup de Credit parmi eux'.[157] On or just before 5 June an Indian called Anthony and another runner arrived from Carlisle; apparently they brought news of the clashes with the settlers. After a conference the Indians at the fort told William Trent, the commissary appointed to look after them there, that they were going home in three days. They wanted their presents at once, and would not wait for the conference with Bouquet. If they did not get them they would plunder every British house they passed on the way home, and might even join the French. Trent's position was all the more unenviable since he had never had a proper interpreter, and was now obliged to use 'this Scoundrel Anthony'. As Trent observed, had the Indians been told their exact terms of service at the outset, and agreed the presents they would receive in return, the trouble might have been ameliorated. Forbes ruefully admitted that he was right.[158] By 23 June all but the 57 Cherokees Byrd had brought to Winchester himself had gone home, plundering as they went. Armed Virginians had followed them, and Byrd expected to hear of combats and Cherokee deaths. Even those Cherokees remaining at Winchester were restless and he doubted they would stay long.[159] The trouble spluttered on into July,[160] and in August, just before Forbes reached Shippensburg, there was more friction at Fort Loudoun. Fifty Cherokees, turning back from Bouquet's advanced post at Raestown, were demanding the return of presents they had left there, and seemed to be threatening the fort.[161]

Forbes now turned to the man who, had either of them known it, might have been the ideal choice for a military superintendent of Indians. Major James Grant was 38 years old and second-in-command of Montgomery's regiment. Grant was a forceful character, and an able and ambitious officer; but he combined with this the less attractive habit of deliberately cultivating his superiors. During his service in South Carolina he had become Bouquet's close friend, and it would be strange indeed if Grant (and Montgomery for that matter) had not shared Bouquet's dislike of colonial parochialism and his awareness of the importance of befriending the Cherokees. Soon after his arrival in Pennsylvania in June his charm and abilities had seduced Forbes, who consulted and corresponded with him. When news of the Fort Loudoun crisis arrived, it was Grant who was sent forward to deal with it. Though allowed two companies of Highlanders, he was advised to use persuasion and to avoid the use of force.[162]

He and his men made a forced march to Fort Loudoun, arriving lame and footsore at dusk on 15 August. To Grant's surprise the Cherokees had been quiet and orderly, and did not even ask for the rum he had brought with him. But the warriors were very anxious to have their presents and be off home. Grant knew he must play for time, hoping to keep them until Forbes should arrive. Next morning he pretended to be too tired to see the Cherokees until the following day, when he would be at their disposal. But the Cherokees would not wait and he had finally to hand over the presents hoping to 'bring them into better temper'.[163] They were delighted and Grant arranged a conference with 'the Chief Men' for the morrow, and sent them an invitation to dine afterwards. Again the Cherokees did not take the bait. Now in possession of their presents, there was nothing to detain them, and they left 'without waiting either for Talk or Dinner'.[164] Grant had lost the game, but found he had enjoyed playing it. The Cherokees seemed to him reasonable, even amiable, fellows who had done no more harm than lifting a few horses. There was only one agitator, 'Anthony', whom Grant would have seized if he could, but not at the expense of alienating the others.[165] This liking for the Cherokees, his unforced willingness to see their point of view, his tolerance of their peccadilloes and – above all – his preference for parley over force, were to have a profound effect upon events in 1760 and 1761.

But Forbes, though sympathetic to grievances against traders and encroaching settlers,[166] lacked Grant's sensitivity towards Indians, and still insisted that Indian management was not his responsibility. Unable to detain his precious scouts, he turned his anger upon both the Cherokees and the Superintendents. 'The Cherokees', he told Lyttelton, 'have behaved most infamously to us, having met with every Civility and good usage as to presents ...' In return they had deserted the army and committed 'great outrages' during their return. This came on top of the news of Abercromby's disaster at Ticonderoga, which Forbes believed would allow the French to reinforce Fort Duquesne. There may have been errors made in handling them, he conceded, but Atkin and Johnson were solely answerable for that.[167]

> [A]nd I must say that it was astonishing to me, to see the greatest body of Indians ever assembled in our Service, totally neglected by the two Gentlemen employed by the Government for the management of the Indians.[168]

Johnson had pleaded that he was busy with the Six Nations, and Atkin had ignored Forbes's summons to Winchester. Gist, 'who stiles himself his deputy', had done little but spend money to no effect.[169] Forbes wrote as much to Atkin himself, asking petulantly why the Superintendent stayed a thousand miles from where he was most needed, and demanded his presence at the imminent conference with the Ohio nations at Easton.[170]

There was some justice in these complaints, Ohio affairs were certainly very important. But Forbes, like most theatre commanders, failed to see the significance of events far distant from his own operations. As we have seen, the many calls on Atkin's attention over such a vast area meant that he had little time for any of them. By November he was trying to pre-empt trouble with the Creeks.[171] Forbes' real recourse was to take independent action himself, just as Bouquet had suggested, especially as since 24 June the southern governors were required to correspond directly with him.[172] But when Forbes finally did act he moved with a soldier's faith in autocracy backed by force, and against the wrong target: the Little Carpenter.

Attakullakulla had been expecting trouble in Virginia, but he was no less horrified when the news of the May clashes reached Keowee. The spectre of war with the British, the greatest conceivable disaster, had risen before his eyes. At once he sent a Talk to Byrd, deploring the Cherokees' aggression, and begging Byrd to persuade his own party not to seek revenge.[173]

> I understand that we have both lost some of our people, and their blood was spilt upon the path, and I heard it was our own people's fault, which makes me very uneasy.
> The French I always lookt upon, as our greatest enemies, and they lie very near our Nation, likewise the Creeks, and Chickessaws is likely to brake war with us. I always desired our young fellows, not to hurt the wite people, nor kill any of our friend Indians, but now

they have done both, which makes me very unessy, for my people kils their friends, as well as their enemies; & I cant tell whitch way to turn myself ...I desire that you may tell all our people that is their, that on their return, they wont hurt aney witeman, or aney of their effects, that I may not hear eney bad talks after their return ...[174]

Four days later the presents arrived from South Carolina and the Carpenter's confidence was temporarily restored; now, too, he could assert his leadership through generosity to his men. On 4 June, after the goods had been distributed amongst the Carpenter's followers, they and Turner set out for 'over the Hills'.[175]

But by the time they arrived at Fort Loudoun on 12 June news of further clashes to the north had convinced Attakullakulla that he and his people must not go to Virginia. That meant breaking his word to Byrd and Turner, and a public declaration might bring on the conflict he dreaded. He therefore adopted that time honoured diplomatic weapon, prevarication. Every day when Turner visited him he had a different excuse. More than once the Carpenter and his friends were drunk (hardly surprising under the circumstances, if undignified) and begged time to recover.[176] A day was finally fixed for their departure. But the Cherokees made no preparations, and Occonostota and Standing Turkey announced that 'the Conjuror' must give his approval first. Sure enough on 21 June, the agreed departure day, Old Hop revealed that the conjuror had declared against them going until the fall. If they did, after two moons sickness would break out. The weather was too hot for marching and the Cherokee could not afford to lose young men, unlike the whites 'Who were like the Leaves of the Trees'. Turner and Demeré were annoyed, thinking the whole deception had been for the sake of the presents.[177]

For his part, Attakullakulla was angry at being called a liar, especially since Turner had brought no belt of wampum to prove that he was indeed sent by 'the Great Warrior of the North'. He was also frightened by the talk of vengeance which was sweeping through the Overhill towns. Just as with Byrd, for a brief revealing moment, the Carpenter lost his temper. Turner had to travel northwards on his own, making a detour through the Catawba country for safety.[178]

The Middle Settlements, angry over their losses in Virginia, were in an even more dangerous mood.[179] The Lower Towns were also seething. Early in July the headmen of Keowee, Tistoe and the Wolf, had to endure a reprimand from Lyttelton,[180] whom Fauquier,

Dinwiddie's successor, had asked to intervene. Their reply was dignified, measured, but bitter.

> ... two of our young Fellows dreamed that they heard their Oldest Brothers crying with the Hatchet in their heads, and they went out to Warr, and found them and took Revenge. This black wampum is the Path where the French go and come, to kill our brothers the English, and we went this Path, and took Revenge for our Brothers loss; now we are come home to where we have built a Town, where we, and he, shall sit down and eat and drink as Brothers. We found him always good and Civil, and at Winchester likewise we found the great and Dreadful Warriors there very good likewise, but on the Path between that and this place those that we thought to be our Brothers prov'd our Enemies. The Dreadful Warriors there and our Hd.men here conclude it is to be as two Brothers falling out and that one overthrew the other and we think no more of it, than if two of our Children had been playing togeather and one had hurt the other; and we hope you will think the same.[181]

After all they had brought back two enemy scalps, and had as a consequence of the war had no hunting since the previous autumn.[182] A month later they again assured Lyttelton that they and the Overhills wanted peace.[183] These were statesmanlike attempts by two responsible headmen to defuse the conflict before it could spread. But matters were rapidly passing beyond their control as each day came more reports of parties attacked by whites. Already the mercurial Wawatchee, just returned from the north, had gone 'over the Hills' to get support for a campaign of vengeance. By mid-August a trader was spreading the rumour that Georgia had bribed the Creeks to attack the Cherokees; other whites in the nation, whom McIntosh thought far more dangerous than the most intransigent Indians, were peddling ever more rum and spreading scare stories; and there was talk of surprising Forts Prince George and Loudoun. When Richard Smith and one Cromwell came to recruit for Forbes, they were lucky to get a mild refusal.[184]

In September the conciliatory headmen lost their grip on the Lower and Middle Towns. Smith's and Cromwell's recruiting had been ruined partly by the news of more Cherokee deaths in Virginia. In early September the Estatoe party recruited by Byrd and the Beamers was ambushed at Goose Creek in Bedford County and lost three dead. Only Thomas Beamer's energetic efforts, riding up and down between the opposing forces for two hours, prevented a pitched battle. Shortly afterwards a Middle Settlements party lost four killed at the same place, and immediately after that another band suffered four killed and five wounded. This was more than even Tistoe and the Wolf could bear. On 17 September the Lower Towns' warriors announced to McIntosh that they were off to Virginia for revenge. McIntosh persuaded them to wait 14 days to hear what satisfaction Lyttelton would offer, but there was no doubt as to what would happen if he offered none. Ohatchie [Wawatchee] and Seroweh, the young Warrior of Estatoe, summed up the militants' position succinctly: 'there is but six gone, but that is nothing in comparison with what will go, if we have not a favourable Answer from the Governor.' In fact 40 warriors had gone from the Middle Settlements and another 30 from two of the Lower Towns. At Estatoe even James Beamer was too frightened to speak openly against war; he asked Lyttelton to grant the indebted traders 'protections' from arrest, so that they might take refuge in South Carolina. McIntosh, with a weak garrison, an unreliable interpreter and expecting another shipment of rum, begged his chief to hurry.[185]

By the end of September, when Smith and Cromwell reached the Overhills, Attakullakulla knew that he must go to Virginia. To refuse again would destroy all his precious credit with the British; if he went he might be able to obtain sufficient satisfaction from Fauquier to stop the war. Old Hop and the Chota council agreed with him. Despite their diplomatic abjurations of revenge, they could barely restrain their own young men, and the Lower and Middle Settlements were out of control. Attakullakulla left with Cromwell and Smith on a fundamentally diplomatic mission, but perhaps thought it politic to leave the question of his military service open. Ostenaca and Occonostota separately provided that now commonplace diversion from the north: raids against Fort Massac.[186]

But while the Overhill leaders struggled to support the tottering peace, Lyttelton took action almost guaranteed to bring it down. His attitude is understandable. He had arrived in the colony in 1756 with a well-thumbed copy of the 1730 treaty in his pocket, from which he learned that murderers on both sides must be punished and compensation paid.[187] But as we saw from his reaction to the black beads sent to him after the November 1757 killings, he understood this clause in a purely legalistic sense. Those actually guilty should be dealt with if caught and properly convicted, but the innocent should not suffer for the wicked. Moreover, satisfaction was a matter for governments, not individuals; if the Cherokees wanted redress they must apply to the colonial authorities. The Cherokees, of course, believed in collective responsibility and direct retribution, but all Lyttelton's actions and utterances proclaim that if he understood this concept at all he rejected it as uncivilized and barbaric. Lyttelton had been receiving a white-oriented version of events which made the Indians out to be thieves and blackmailers, who extorted protection payments from settlers on their way to and from Virginia. Fauquier had written to him taking that position in June and had done so again now, his allegations apparently backed by written testimony. If the settlers had killed Cherokees it was primarily in defence of themselves, their families and their property.[188] As Lyttelton knew from the reports from Demeré and McIntosh, there was at least a grain of truth in these stories. Who was Lyttelton to believe? The lieutenant-governor of Virginia and the white settlers he was sworn to protect? Or heathen savages, as he saw them, who had more than once shown themselves unreliable, slippery and violent? In June he and the Council had been prepared to believe that the violence had been caused by 'the bad behaviour of Stragling Gangs of the Cherokees', and that the headmen need only be asked to keep their young men under proper control in future.[189] Even now he was, by his own lights, prepared to be patient and moderate in the face of murderous attacks.

But he was not about to be bullied by the Lower Towns' ultimatum. He had prepared his reply by 26 September but it was not delivered at Keowee until mid-October. In it he rebuked the Cherokees for not going to Fauquier for redress and asked them to recall the war parties. In return he would ask Fauquier to provide adequate compensation, and he himself would 'give Presents to the Relations of your People that have been slain, sufficient to hide the Bones of the dead Men and wipe away the Tears from the Eyes of their Friends'. But if they continued to seek blood for blood the British would stop their trade and turn all the might of their armies against them. The Cherokees, he added, had no right to wage war on Virginia because of the acts of a few individuals.[190]

All this revealed an appalling blindness to the Cherokee position, but it was neither foolish nor ruthless in conception. Indeed, it showed some insight into the ritual importance of gifts; though he failed to see that presents offered without unalloyed contrition were worthless.[191] Lyttelton's policy was perfectly consistent with the stand he had taken at Beaufort over a year before: as the ultimate director of Indian policy in the south he would tame these errant savages, as he saw them, with a restrained but firm hand. That he really was in charge of Cherokee affairs at least was beyond dispute. Atkin had abdicated his responsibility there by refusing to turn aside from Creek affairs, preferring instead to send a sealed letter to the headmen through Thomas Beamer.[192] The stage was clear for Lyttelton to appear as the peacemaking proconsul.

At first his performance seemed to carry the audience along. The Lower, Middle and Valley Settlements were far from anxious for a crippling trade embargo and a war with South Carolina. The headmen used the threat to bring the young men temporarily under control. James Beamer's private advice to the headmen of Estatoe, Thomas Beamer's carrying the Talk through the nation, and the deflating effect of a Creek raid on Little Estatoe – revealing that efforts to enlist Creek aid had failed dismally – all helped to tilt the balance. At Fort Prince George on 26 September a great meeting of delegates from fourteen towns, led by Wawatchee and Seroweh, delivered a conciliatory Talk and offered to send an embassy to Charleston.[193] On 8 November, by which time the war parties were being recalled, the deputies duly appeared in the Council chamber. Here they patiently heard Lyttelton repeat his September Talk, and accuse their nation of the first aggression. They then left for home believing that they had saved the peace.[194] On 10 January the headmen of New Hiwassee in the Valley Settlements paid a similar visit.[195]

In the Overhill Towns too, there was a slackening of tension. There was even some response to an appeal from Glen. Ostenaca, though he expected Cherokee reactions to be mixed, told McIntosh that 'You may depend upon me and my Gang.'[196] Thick Legs actually went towards Fort Massac.[197] But all was not as it seemed. Once again the winter hunt had been lost and the Cherokees were short of arms, ammunition and cloth. They had already heard that Attakullakulla had been badly treated by Forbes. Richardson, who reached Fort Loudoun about 10 December, found the Cherokees unwilling to hear him preach until Attakullakulla should return. Early in February 1759, sensing that he could expect little from the Carpenter, and frightened by the Overhills' truculence, he retreated hurriedly to Keowee.[198] In January Occonostota bluntly refused to serve the British cause again; and in February the rumour went round that the British were going to attack the defenceless Cherokees. The young Overhills held a night meeting at Tanassee, where some were in favour of killing the whites and cutting off Fort Loudoun. The Mortar appeared in the Overhill towns in March, reviving old fears of French agents. When three of Attakullakulla's people came home, confirming that their leader had been treated abominably by Glen and Forbes, Old Hop and Occonostota made a great fuss of them. Although Willinawaw, Ostenaca and Round O brought Demeré a wampum belt of friendship, he did not trust them.[199] Everyone was waiting for the Carpenter. When he came his attitude would decide between peace and war.

Alden was not far wrong when he asserted it was 'at least partly because of the influence of Attakullakulla that the Cherokees remained friendly in the fall of 1758'.[200] This was even more true of the winter and spring of 1759. After reaching Winchester he had yielded to Glen's and Forbes's insistence that he should accompany the army towards Fort Duquesne.[201] In mid-October he joined Forbes at Raestown, just as the camp was celebrating the repulse of a French attack on the advanced post at Loyalhannon. Forbes, by now so ill that he had to be carried in a litter, had lost all faith in Indians and all those connected with them, 'the most imposing Rogues that I ever had to deal with'. He was also anxious and upset over the capture of James Grant ('my only plight anchor and support') in a skirmish before Fort Duquesne a month before, and in no mood to tolerate Indians who preferred talk to war.[202]

Even now Attakullakulla did not make the diplomatic purpose of his mission sufficiently clear. He made four or five speeches warning Forbes of the storm which was about to break; but at the same time he demanded a high price for staying with the army. Forbes was bitterly angry, but he needed the Carpenter's scouts for the final push. He may also have wanted a hostage against further Cherokee depredations. Feigning indifference, he gave in, and the Carpenter's 40 warriors accompanied the expedition. On 24 November Forbes's men heard a gigantic explosion as the garrison blew up their magazine. Next day the British took possession of an empty, smoking ruin. But Attakullakulla had heard of the French preparations from local Indians six days earlier; when Forbes proved sceptical, he had immediately taken his men off towards Williamsburg. From the Cherokee perspective the Carpenter was exercising his right to leave a war party once his presence was no longer necessary. To the British this looked like the last in a long series of Indian desertions. Forbes, or possibly Glen, had them pursued, arrested, disarmed and stripped them of their presents and the beads they were taking to Fauquier. Forbes sent an account of the incident to Lyttelton, who had a Talk describing it read at Fort Prince George.[203] The Cherokees, who had gone with the army only to oblige Forbes, were being treated as common deserters.

However at Winchester Attakullakulla found a sympathetic ally in Christopher Gist, and was eventually allowed to go to Williamsburg.

Here, whatever his private feelings, he successfully convinced Fauquier that he repented of what the lieutenant-governor was pleased to called his 'scandalous Behaviour'. Fauquier, for his part, was sensible enough to part with the Carpenter on good terms. Thus when Attakullakulla reappeared at Keowee on the tense evening of 14 March 1759 he chose peace, not war. To the general relief he sent a Talk to Lyttelton, before setting off for Charleston to explain his version of the events in person.[204]

But here too he was careful to keep up the mask of contrition. The general impression in the colonial capital was that he had come to apologize.[205] Lyttelton and the Council, for their part, realized that the Carpenter was too important to be ignored, and that his timely return had defused a particularly nasty situation.[206] Lyttelton was therefore careful to combine his reprimand with conciliation; while the Carpenter, patiently but firmly, stated his side of the case. At the end of their long conference of 17, 18 and 21 April, Lyttelton believed that he had secured the friendship of the most influential man in the nation, and had bound him to prevent future hostilities. By providing Keowee with the trader of its choice he hoped that he had also defused any latent hostility amongst the Lower Cherokees and 'brightened the Chain of Friendship'.[207]

He was wrong: over this fragile friendship hung the shadow of the tomahawk. Even as the Carpenter turned for home it fell.

3

Lyttelton's Folly: How the Anglo-Cherokee War Began

In October 1759 Lyttelton declared war on the Cherokee nation. He did so in the face of a divided council, of Commons unwilling to vote sufficient funds and a Cherokee delegation patently bent on peace. He threw conciliation to the winds by abducting two sets of Cherokee deputies and marched on the Lower Towns with a quarter of the militia of the province. Yet this expedition was incapable of forcing the Cherokees to accept the will of South Carolina. Underfunded, under-manned, undersupplied and eventually ravaged by smallpox and desertion, it failed even to bring the Cherokees to action. Having concluded a treaty too humiliating for the undefeated nation to keep, he returned to Charleston in hollow triumph. There can be no doubt that Lyttelton's ill-considered war and the subsequent massacre of his hostages at Fort Prince George ensured savage reprisals against the South Carolina frontier, and went far to make peace unattainable for a further two years. The most anyone has found to say about this debacle is that South Carolina succeeded in spreading the cost![1]

Why did Lyttelton commit such a folly? No historian has found a satisfactory explanation. Sirmans, appalled by the ramshackle organization of the expedition, wondered if the chaos on the frontier had made the governor panic. But a glance at Lyttelton's record as a calm and deliberate executive made him reject that interpretation. It must have been the lure of military glory that spurred him on.[2] There is much to commend this explanation. Lyttelton, as both Sirmans and Weir observe, had wanted to lead a major British assault on Louisiana. His plan had reserved a major role for the South Carolina militia – and for himself – by including only about a hundred regulars from the local Independent Companies. When Pitt rejected the plan in favour of concentrating on the reduction of Canada, he looked for other fields for his martial ambition – and found the Anglo-Cherokee War. Robinson points out that he declared war without consulting any other colony except North Carolina (which was bound to play a subordinate role) and did not ask Amherst for troops.[3] But can we really believe that a hitherto cautious governor precipitated his colony unprepared into an unnecessary war for no better reason than personal ambition? To argue in this way diminishes both Lyttelton and the significance of the conflict he unleashed.

✳Lyttelton genuinely believed that war was both necessary and inevitable. His own in-letters, many of which appear in the South Carolina 'Indian Books', the South Carolina Council journals, and his reports to the Board of Trade, all show how his picture of the situation built up in his mind. He already thought that the Cherokees in Virginia had behaved with inexcusable savagery, that the headmen's plea that the young men were out of control was at best disingenuous, and that Attakullakulla's so-called desertion of Forbes was only one example of Cherokee slipperiness and unreliability. Moreover there were signs that some Creeks led by the Mortar were drawing the Cherokees into a French alliance. Clearly, he believed that he had no choice but to react strongly. Unfortunately he did not understand the diffused and consensual nature of Cherokee polity, or if he did, dismissed it as unacceptable. Not very surprisingly, he took much the same way to the Cherokee law of clan vengeance; if he grasped it at all, he regarded it as too barbaric to be countenanced. Consequently he did not regard the Cherokees as a free and independent people with a right to negotiate as equals. Thus his diplomacy took the form of hectoring and threats: the Cherokees must give 'satisfaction' for their depredations and give up all contact with the Creeks and French.

Such expectations became self-fulfilling. In the spring of 1759 the great majority of headmen were anxious to remain at peace with South Carolina. But by September his evident contempt and distrust had filled many of them with loathing and fear. Contacts with the Creeks and French intensified, largely out of fear of the Anglo-Creek alliance which the Cherokees believed was in the making. The Lower Cherokees and even the Overhills were incensed at the persistent encroachments of the Long Canes settlers, and the Lower Towns had good reason to detest the officers at Fort Prince George. Yet when intelligence of these grievances reached him from Fort Augusta, from Henry Ellis in Georgia or from the Cherokees themselves, he dismissed it. Lyttelton resented the advice and interventions of that perceptive and eccentric busybody Henry Ellis in a sphere which he regarded as his own. The analyses of well-meaning but suspicious Paul Demeré at Fort Loudoun, and downright delinquent Richard Coytmore at Fort Prince George, continued to confirm the mental picture they had already helped to form. Any news to the contrary must therefore be a red herring, meant by the Cherokees to distract the governor from the business of extracting justice for their crimes.

Lyttelton was under pressure from other directions as well. His Instructions bound him to 'roll back' the powers seized by the Commons House of Assembly over the previous half-century. Among these powers were the rights to scrutinize all the original documents concerning Indian policy, and to supervise, through its Indian Affairs Committee, the purchase and distribution of Indian gifts. Until 1761 Indian trade was overseen by a Commons-appointed commissioner, William Pinckney. These rights, of course, gave the members considerable influence over Indian diplomacy. On that subject Lyttelton's Instructions were quite explicit. He was 'to use all possible ways and means' to regain or sustain good relations, 'especially with the Cherokee Indians inhabiting the Mountains on the North West side of the said Province...'[4] The governor was expected to run Indian affairs himself.

But attacking the Commons' privileges too vigorously would produce political deadlock.[5] Similarly an Indian policy which strove to protect Indians, rather than to punish them for their depredations against white settlers, would invite crippling opposition. Such paralysis would be as displeasing to his patron Halifax as total inaction, and the ambitious Lyttelton could not afford to upset the President of the Board of Trade. Lyttelton's desire for the jewel of the Caribbean was well known; in October 1758 Forbes referred to him sarcastically as 'the Govr. of Jamaica'.[6] Although he was appointed to this post ten months later, and probably knew about it before declaring war on the Cherokees,[7] the pressure to sustain his reputation as a successful governor was strong.

Thus Lyttelton, in Indian affairs as in other matters, took a middle course. While successfully regaining a large measure of executive control, he stopped well short of provoking embarrassing trouble.[8] To do this he needed a Cherokee policy sufficiently tough to win general approval. This would go some way to explain his persistent dismissal of Cherokee grievances, his one-sided interpretation of the 1730 treaty, his obtuse insistence upon 'satisfaction' when peace could only be had without it, and his readiness to resort to force in October.

Moreover, this political need created a double motive for not inviting regular troops. First, South Carolina must be seen to be in charge of southern Indian policy. Governors, as Lyttelton had been careful to ascertain, were required in military matters to obey the directions of the commander-in-chief,[9] and that in turn would mean playing second fiddle to local commanders like Henry Bouquet. Second, the quartering dispute of 1756–7 had shown that the presence of regulars could lead to very serious conflict with the assembly. The governor as a royal official was bound to support the demands of the soldiers for adequate shelter, lighting and fuel, yet his Instructions obliged him to avoid giving the Commons any opportunity to assert its rights. As Jack P. Greene points out, such disputes could and did have very significant constitutional implications.[10] Thus for political reasons Lyttelton felt obliged to take a firm line and to enforce it with the resources of South Carolina alone.

That being the case Lyttelton had to look for Indian allies, and that placed him under pressure from a surprising quarter. The Catawbas, continually at war with the Iroquois and other northern Indians, wanted to bounce South Carolina into providing a protective fort on the Catawba River in return for a military alliance. To do so they tried to promote a Cherokee war, continually offering to pursue raiders, accusing the Cherokees of assaults on their own people, and crudely attempting to undermine Attakullakulla's efforts to promote peace. Once the Cherokees began to raid North Carolina settlements well within South Carolina's sphere of influence and very near to the Catawba towns, Lyttelton found it increasingly difficult to deflect their demands.

Thus, although Lyttelton's policy was fatally flawed, it was neither dominated by personal ambition, nor was it unconsidered. Lyttelton's folly was to accept uncritically intelligence which portrayed the Cherokees as bloodthirsty, disloyal and even treacherous. He not only failed to understand the Cherokee point of view, but rejected whatever alternative explanations of the nation's grievances came his way. *

On 25 and 26 April 1759 three gangs of 'Indians supposed to be the Cherrockees' struck at a string of settlements on the Yadkin and Catawba rivers, inside North Carolina. Three scalps were taken from two families on the Yadkin itself, and eight on a stream called Fourth Creek. On the south fork of the Catawba 'a Dutch Man', Conrad Mull, his wife and son were slaughtered and scalped. North of the river, at 'William Morrison's Settlement', the raiders murdered eight children of a settler called Hannah. On 3 May 25 marauders led by Moitoi of Settico reached the Overhill Towns with no less than ten scalps; nearly a week after that two more parties returned to Settico with the scalps of three white men. A fourth party, some 20 warriors strong, was rumoured to be still 'out against the settlements'. The news filtered back to Lyttelton from a number of sources: Samuel Wylie, who was South Carolina's agent amongst the Catawbas, Lieutenant James Adamson in pursuit of deserters, Coytmore at Fort Prince George.[11]

There can be no doubt that the majority of the Cherokee headmen were appalled. Moitoi had set out on his raid on the very day he had received a message from Attakullakulla via Tistoe. In this message the Carpenter had asked the Cherokees to wait quietly in their towns as he had already made up the quarrel with Virginia.[12] It looked as if Moitoi had deliberately tried to wreck the Carpenter's negotiations and spread the war to the Carolinas: only a distant observer could imagine that the raiders, 'being unacquainted with the Southernmost Bounds' of Virginia,[13] had made a terrible mistake. Occonostota, who had been travelling down the Little Tennessee when the news reached him,[14] was shocked and embarrassed. Only days before he had visited Demeré to promise to use his influence against Franco-Creek intrigues and to link his name with Attakullakulla's.

> It is true that these Sorts of Talks make often Impression on some of our People, and we have great many of bad Men amongst us, but now I have come...you will hear no more bad Talks, for I am friend to the English, and shall never make peace with the French. I [remember] when I was in Carolina last, I told the Governor that I should always be true, and I desire you to acquaint him that I am still the same, and that I shall never give him Room to think otherwise. I desire you...to write to the Little Carpenter and tell him not to be uneasy [and] that everything is quiet here.[15]

Now he at once returned to Fort Loudoun to complain of the Settico people's villainy and to protest that had he heard of the raids beforehand he would have stopped them. Demeré, sensibly divining that the leading headmen wanted peace, invited Occonostota to bring Connecorte and Standing Turkey to dinner on 12 May.[16]

At that meal all three Cherokees expressed regret for what had happened and contended that, as the raiders had pretended to be going hunting, there had been no opportunity to stop them. But, they reminded their host, the raids had been provoked by the Virginian settlers killing Cherokees.[17] In other words, they saw no reason why their legitimate quarrel with Virginia, even when pursued so far to the south, should involve South Carolina. When Demeré asked what he should tell Lyttelton and what satisfaction would be given, they were conciliatory but evasive. Occonostota asked Demeré to wait until Attakullakulla came and a general meeting of warriors could be held. 'For our own part you may be shure to live in Peace and Quietness.'[18]

In the Lower Towns Attakullakulla's brother and ally Willinawaw led a group of headmen to Fort Prince George to ask Coytmore to tell Lyttelton 'that the Lower towns were of quite a different Way of thinking from the others'.[19] Three days later, on 11 May, Wawatchee delivered a Talk addressed to Lyttelton on behalf of all the Lower Settlements, in which he insisted on their desire to remain at peace with South Carolina. But he too argued that the Cherokees' real quarrel was with Virginia. 'At Present there is a little stumbling Block lying in the Virginia Path, for there is Blood in the Way between us and Connustoogee.' Settico was only one town and had acted in a moment of madness; the people there had been drunk but were now sober. 'Though, there are great rogues amongst us, our Thoughts are good.' Wawatchee had personally urged his young men to remain quiet, just as Lyttelton had asked. He had also sent a message to Fauquier by way of the trader Richard Smith and hoped to have a reply soon.[20] Two days later Tistoe made his own approach on behalf of Keowee.

> We are now together with our brothers, the White People who live with us as if in one town...which we think well of: and shall always do ... [Y]ou told me and my People, to stay quiet at Home, which we have strictly [observed]. As for the Mischief that has been done, it was alone the Towns over the Hills, [especially?] Settico[.] [W]e are all quiet and think Well in these Parts...[21]

✳He added that the Middle Settlements also had 'good thoughts' and stressed the need for whites and Indians to live peacefully together.[22]

Next day, 14 May, Attakullakulla reached Keowee 'in a wavering condition and very dissatisfied' according to Coytmore,[23] and not surprisingly. Having had less than satisfactory treatment from Lyttelton, he was confronted with news that could ruin all his work in Williamsburg and Charleston. The most he could do was to limit the damage and quieten the warriors as Lyttelton had asked. He at once sent runners ahead to Old Hop and the Overhills urging them to stay in their towns until he arrived.[24] No doubt the same runners enjoined the young men of the Middle Towns to do likewise.

The Middle Settlements may have heard the news already, for as soon as Moitoi had appeared with his scalps Coytmore had sent a string of white beads to Round O of Stecoe.[25] Whatever the means the dreadful story spread rapidly. On 16 May the representatives of 13 towns met at Joree in the Middle Settlements to hear Lyttelton's Talk. Though this Talk mingled suspicion and threats with talk of peace, the headmen seized upon its conciliatory aspects. They were convinced, they said, of the falsehood of rumours spread 'by young Runnagadoc fellows from Town to Town',[26] meaning, as we shall see, stories that the British were about to combine with the Creeks to crush the Cherokees. They also fully believed in Lyttelton's 'Fatherly Love'. Taking up his metaphor they declared that the dark cloud had gone from the sky and all was now bright and clear. They too recalled the friendship urged upon them by George II in 1730, and promised that their leader, Tossitee of Stecoe, would visit the governor. Tossitee and the headmen from Joree, Watuga, Cowee and Nequassee put their marks to a pledge never to waver in their commitment to good relations with the British.[27] But they made it quite clear there could be no question of satisfaction on either side. 'what has been killed on both sides of these 13 Towns should be Utterly Buried in Obscurity and never more thought on...'[28] Like the Lower Towns the Middle Settlements were eager for a peace based on a mutual renunciation of retribution.

Once Attakullakulla had reached Fort Loudoun on 26 May the Overhills made their own gesture. Runners were sent through all the towns to summon the headmen to a great meeting at Chota which assembled three days later. Here the line taken at Keowee and Joree was repeated, the Cherokees would offer peace but not 'satisfaction'. Next day, Old Hop, Attakullakulla and a 'Great number' of Cherokees went to Fort Loudoun to report their deliberations to Demeré. They were not received graciously. Demeré accused Chota – and implicitly Connecorte – of receiving 'bad talks' while Attakullakulla had been away – in other words, of conspiring with the Creeks. Old Hop denied everything while the Carpenter retorted sharply against things done behind his back. Nothing like it, he insisted, would ever happen again, and he demanded that his Talk should be written down and sent to

Lyttelton. But, as Demeré observed, the sticking point was still the same: 'they are no way disposed to give Satisfaction for the Mischief they have done...'[29] Not understanding that neither Old Hop nor Attakullakulla could interfere with the Cherokee revenge law, Demeré put their reluctance down to fear of Tellico, the town believed responsible for depredations in Virginia. 'I believe' he wrote,'[they] dare not meddle with that town as it is very numerous.'[30]

But by now the full horror of the Yadkin massacres had filtered back to Charleston. For the first time the Cherokees had struck well within South Carolina's orbit. On 21 May the Council considered the letters from the frontiers and advised Lyttelton that Dobbs of North Carolina would probably 'consult' him over the affair – in other words, ask him to take action – and that Lyttelton should therefore take the lead in seeking 'satisfaction' at once.[31] Next day Lyttelton composed a Talk to Old Hop and Attakullakulla demanding the surrender or execution of the murderers. Adopting an injured tone, he reminded Attakullakulla how at their recent meeting in Charleston he had 'brightened the Chain of Friendship between the two Nations', and upbraided the Carpenter for failing to keep the nation quiet.[32] This was hardly fair, for Attakullakulla had not been in the nation when Moitoi had set out. But the governor made things worse by going on to insist that Attakullakulla had promised to give 'Satisfaction' for any future outrages against whites.[33]

Thus Lyttelton and his advisers, no doubt genuinely shocked by the savagery of the attacks, decided to assert South Carolina's traditional supremacy in Indian affairs and to pre-empt any accusation of tardiness in protecting settlers. They had refused to accept that the Cherokee headmen could not deliver up the murderers, just as the Cherokees failed to grasp that Lyttelton could not overlook the murder of children on the boundary of his own province. When these demands were read to Attakullakulla and Old Hop in the Fort Loudoun guard-house, they were given three days in which to consider their reply. But in the subsequent meetings in the crowded town house, the vast majority of the Chota council – led by Occonostota – refused to give up their kinsmen. Attakullakulla privately informed Demeré that to persist would only make matters worse. He could only recover eight of the Settico scalps for burial and obtain Settico's plea for forgiveness.[34] Lyttelton had affronted the Cherokees most anxious to remain on good terms with him; and the Cherokees had lent weight to Lyttelton's darkening suspicions.

A good deal of Lyttelton's distrust sprang from fears of growing French influence in the nation, and in particular that a number of Anglophobe Creeks led by the Mortar were urging them on to shed blood. As early as March the Council had discussed letters from two traders – James Beamer at Estatoe and Lachlan McGillivray in the Creek country – reporting rumours that the Creeks and French would attack Fort Loudoun in the spring. The rumours suggested that they might be supported by disaffected Cherokees. The alarm was sufficient for the board to order a reinforcement of 70 men 'and a proper number of Officers' from the provincial regiment to join Demeré. The soldiers were to take with them an assortment of presents and the victualling agents were told never to allow the fort to have less than six months' provisions in store.[35]

Even before he knew of the Yadkin River massacres, the hospitality afforded to the visiting Creeks had alarmed Demeré. On 27 April he had told Occonostota that 'Old Hop and Standing Turkey had given me Room to be on my Watch by receiving so kindly the Mortar and his Gang', even after having been warned of their machinations. Occonostota promised to raise the matter in the Chota town house that evening. When he did so Connecorte and Standing Turkey told him that the Mortar only wanted a patch of land, freedom to hunt for hides, and access to the relatively low prices and plentiful goods of the South Carolina traders.[36] What else may have been said is not recorded, but we may safely surmise that the Great Warrior knew better than to accept this tale at face value. Perhaps he and the others hoped that it would allay Demeré's suspicions. But when he solemnly repeated it to Demeré next day the captain was not impressed. He had information to the contrary, he said, and named the Cherokees who had provided it. The Great Warrior declared himself at a loss, and anxiously asked Demeré not to write to Lyttelton until he returned, and meanwhile to 'send for Willinawa and Judges friend'.[37]

Over the next few days Occonostota made some alarming discoveries. First, when he had first arrived in the Cherokee country the Mortar had said that the Spaniards of Florida and the French at Fort Toulouse were sorry that so many Cherokees had been killed in Virginia. More seriously, the night before Moitoi had set out on his raid the Mortar had been his guest, and the two of them had sat up talking until very late. On 2 May the Great Warrior brought Willinawaw and Ostenaca – Judge's Friend – to break the news to Demeré over dinner. As we have seen, it was on this occasion that Occonostota offered to prevent any further intrigues. A day or two later Moitoi appeared with his scalps and Occonostota and the other headmen hastened to dissociate themselves from him and from the Mortar's plots. But Connecorte and Standing Turkey still protected the Creeks from expulsion,[38] and Occonostota himself was careful not to burn his bridges to the Creek nation and the French.

There was by now some unease over the news that the Mortar, possibly in collaboration with the French, was building a settlement of some kind at the confluence of the Coosa and Coosawatchee Rivers. Cherokees from Hiwassee and other towns were said to be paying frequent visits.[39] Demeré at once began to incite the Overhills to destroy it, but without success. Coytmore, sure that the Valley and Overhill Cherokees had given their consent to the settlement, and deeply worried about the consequences of French influence so near, asked Round O to take action. The old warrior's reply worried him even more: the story was a lie, he said, and besides the Creeks were friends.[40] Thus on 29 May, on the occasion of reading Lyttelton's Talk, Coytmore put the same request to a meeting of the Lower Cherokees. To his dismay Wawatchee refused angrily: such 'Lyes' would not deceive him into attacking his Creek friends.[41] On 9 June two Cherokee messengers had left for the Creek country and Fort Toulouse. Although the British had yet to learn who had sent them, one was an ambassador from Connecorte and Standing Turkey, and the other a Chickasaw acting for Occonostota. As late as 11 June there were Creeks still in the Cherokee country, and Lyttelton's plea that they should not be allowed to settle at Estatoe Old Fields had been ignored.[42] Clearly even the friendliest headmen were not about to break with the Creeks just to please South Carolina. With these reports coming on top of the Mortar's activities and the Yadkin murders, even information which revealed a different side to the picture was capable of sinister interpretations.

At the very end of June 'young Malachi' or Togulki, 'King' of the Coweta Creeks, had arrived at Fort Augusta on the Georgia side of the Savannah. Togulki was the 'inexperienced and insecure' son of Malachi, the great leader of the Lower Creeks who had died in 1756, and whose brother Stumpe was Togulki's political mentor.[43] He told the commander, a South Carolina lieutenant by the extraordinary name of White Outerbridge, that the trip was a whim: while out hunting he had suddenly decided 'to ramble this way'. But Outerbridge's suspicions were aroused by the simultaneous appearance of Stumpe, Malachi's 'Uncle who is his Guardian from the Cherokees who I am informed [has] been there some time'. Stumpe told McGillivray that the Cherokees were terrified of a joint attack by the Creeks and British, 'to Cut them off Root and Branch'. This terror rested on nothing more substantial than a few words let slip by Thomas Beamer, who had been at Augusta with Atkin in the winter. Atkin, presumably referring to the clashes in Virginia, had remarked that the Cherokees had behaved badly towards their friends the British. So fragile had Cherokee confidence in the English become that it was at once deduced that Atkin's mission was to promote an Anglo-Creek alliance to punish the Cherokees. They had at once appealed to the Creeks of Stumpe's party for help, 'and press'd very hard upon them to Continue in their nation by way of Safeguard'[44] Such a fear, if general amongst the Cherokees, would go far to explain Connecorte's courting of the Mortar, the nation's failure to expel his party, and Round O's and Wawatchee's refusals to act against the Coosa settlement. Properly seized upon this story might have suggested a more conciliatory path for Lyttelton's policy. Unfortunately the rest of Outerbridge's story reeked of the dark plotting Demeré and Coytmore had been reporting for months.

Stumpe claimed that he had refused to involve his nation in Cherokee affairs, but the meeting with Togulki was clearly not accidental. This pair and 'several others' became very aggressive, demanding from Outerbridge 'provisions, ammunition, saddles, bridles, hatchets and other things', and were very angry when they did not get them. At about nine o'clock that evening they mounted and rode off towards the Cherokee country. But they were soaked by heavy rain and turned back for something to warm the inner man. They reached Fort Augusta in the dead of night 'Hooping and Hallowing' and demanding drink. A worried Outerbridge gave them some liquor, whereupon they vanished again. Outerbridge surmised, not unreasonably, that Togulki was in the pay of the French, and that he had gone to raise Cherokee fears to an even greater pitch.[45] In this way the story of Cherokee apprehensions of the British appeared as just another strand in the Franco-Creek campaign to suborn them.

Thus by mid-summer Lyttelton was becoming more and more firmly convinced that a significant number of Cherokee headmen were leaning towards the French side. His anxiety was all the greater after the discovery early in July of a planned slave rebellion: 'the Indians were to be sent to and they would come and assist in killing all the Buckraas.'[46] Although the plot turned out to be little more than an idea, the danger it represented was very real. What if a French-sponsored Creek–Cherokee attack coincided with a black uprising? Given these fears he had to take seriously the complaints of his only Indian allies, the Catawbas, who were busily undermining Cherokee influence in Charleston. This small nation, now a congeries of refugees from the broken coastal tribes, could muster little more than 150 warriors. They were almost continually at war with the Iroquois and other northern nations, and none too friendly to the Cherokees. Indeed, a Cherokee woman had just been murdered in one of their towns, and the Cherokees had taken satisfaction in kind. The Catawbas were thus irrevocably committed to friendship with the Carolinas. North Carolina, as we have seen, had undertaken to build a fort for their protection, but the Catawbas knew that they needed the support of Lyttelton's colony as well. As Atkin had observed as long ago as 1757, they were adept in playing the colonies off against each other to obtain the best possible bargain.[47] If obtaining that commitment meant promoting an Anglo-Cherokee War, so be it.

As early as April the Catawba leader had paid a visit to Charleston to counteract Attakullakulla's attempt to mend fences there, and Lyttelton had interrupted the talks with the Carpenter to hear him. Hagler first asserted, through his own interpreter 'Tommy', his nation's commitment to help the British drive away the French; and he gave Lyttelton a tomahawk to be sent to the King in token of this alliance. 'The Tuscaroras, Cherokees, Creeks & Chickasaws have taken fast hold of the English also, and promised to Assist in driving away the Enemy, I hope they will do so.' He then emphasized the superior loyalty of the Catawbas by recounting his warriors' deeds on the Fort Duquesne campaign. Finally, he brought up his quarrel with the Cherokees over the dead Catawba woman; although he had met the Carpenter since coming to Charleston, and receiving from him a string of white beads with three black ones attached, Attakullakulla had not even mentioned her. In other words, the Catawbas required vengeance upon the Cherokees just as the British did. The Cherokees had also been listening to 'bad talks' at Chota – meaning of course the Mortar's machinations – which he would investigate further.[48] In other words, the Catawbas and British now had another common enemy in the Cherokees. The fact that Catawba scouts would be invaluable in protecting the back settlements should war come remained unspoken.

At last Hagler came to his price. North Carolina had begun two buildings: a fort to protect the nation and a house for Hagler to live in. But work on the fort had soon been abandoned and the house left without a chimney. Nor was there a trader in the Catawba country, so the Catawbas were short of powder and ball. The Superintendent of Indian Affairs had likewise failed to fulfil his promises. 'Squire Atkin', he observed, 'promised me a long while ago, that he would send us some Goods, and would do many things for us, I have long hunted for those Goods, but never could find them, nor has he done any one thing for Us...' He then returned to his theme of loyal Catawba service on the Ohio, and promised similar steadfastness if South Carolina itself were attacked. 'The English & Catawbas have but one Heart, therefore when any Country attacks the English, I will go fast to their Assistance; & your Excellency will hear of my exploits.'[49] If South Carolina would provide protection, ammunition and trade then the Catawbas would protect the frontiers against the scheming Cherokees.

Lyttelton was quick to praise Hagler and his people for their loyalty. He promised to build the fort if the Catawbas would show Wylie the site they preferred, and artisans would be sent to complete Hagler's chimney. He promised them presents and approved of Hagler's proposal to send one of his headmen, Captain Heirs, as emissary to Chota. But he was careful not to fall into the trap of regarding the embassy as Hagler had represented it: as an intelligence gathering operation against the potential common enemy. Instead he hoped that Heirs would 'make every thing Straight with the Cherokees, for they are the Children of the Great King George likewise, and the Catawbas & them ought to know no Enemy but the French'. As for the murdered Catawba woman, she had been killed while Attakullakulla had been in Virginia, and he had just promised 'to make a particular Enquiry into that Affair', as well as into Chota's dealings with the Creeks. Moreover the governor knew that the woman had been killed in revenge for the Cherokee woman slain by the Catawbas. Going suddenly onto the offensive, he turned to the question of some harmless 'Settlement Indians' slain by Catawbas at Monk's Corner, a move which left Hagler scrabbling for excuses.[50] Lyttelton had made it plain that he would not be bounced into a Cherokee war to support the Catawbas, or at least not yet. For he was uncomfortably aware that should the Catawbas provoke a conflict, he would have to support them. Perhaps, if a war became likely, he should choose his own moment to begin it rather than wait to be dragged in by his allies.

He was not allowed to forget this lesson, for the Catawbas did not relent. For them the Yadkin River murders were a diplomatic gift. Wylie first heard of the killings from the Catawbas themselves, who at once offered to demonstrate their indispensability by going after the raiders. 'They seemed to be greatly incenced against the Cherrockees', reported Wylie, 'and declared their firm attachment to His Majesty.'[51] In the end while 22 Catawbas helped to bury the dead, 15 warriors joined several whites in a pursuit party led by one Matthew Tool.[52] Though the chase was carried deep into the mountains the pursuers at last lost the track and returned empty handed.[53] Nearly four weeks later, on 30 May, a 30-strong Catawba delegation led by 'Captain Johnny' came to Charleston to express their sorrow and to offer to slay the Cherokee murderers.[54] Once again their aim was to undermine whatever trust the Cherokees still enjoyed in South Carolina.

> The Catawbas go along the Path, and touch no Person, they have but one tongue, but other Indians come hither, who have two Tongues, they deliver good Talks here in purpose to get goods, and when they go away, they give out bad Talks.[55]

Once again Lyttelton avoided the trap. While he promised presents and praised the Catawbas' pursuit of the killers, he refused to loose them against the Cherokee towns. As the Cherokees had 'professed themselves children of the Great King George', he would first hear what they had to say. Later if necessary he would call the Catawbas to war and take satisfaction by force, but at present he wanted peace.[56] Thus in less than a month Lyttelton had been pressed from outright refusal to unleash the Catawbas to a conditional promise to do so.

On 11 June Hagler stepped up the pressure. In a Talk addressed to Lyttelton he bewailed the capture of seven Catawbas in a raid by northern Indians, and hinted that the Cherokees might have been involved. 'I have received a Hatchet in my people's heads as [soon?] as the white people', he declared, '& am sory for it.' As soon as he knew for certain that Cherokees had taken part he would inform Lyttelton by way of 'your Warrior Adamson my brother'. In 1758, he claimed, the Cherokees had joined with a band of Shawnees to attack whites. Now he claimed, Attakullakulla himself was trying to draw the Catawbas into a conflict with the British. The string of white beads 'which is mixed with Black beads' which the Carpenter had given (he now said 'shown') him in April, had turned out to be an incitement to war. 'I find it was a Talk to Join them against my Brothers the white people.'[57] It is possible that Attakullakulla did put out feelers while both leaders were in Charleston in April; he had good reason to detach from Lyttelton the only Indians eager to raid the Cherokees on his behalf. But to seriously pursue an anti-British alliance at the very moment when he was trying to settle the quarrel with South Carolina and Virginia would have been uncharacteristically foolish. The beads concerned were either given to Hagler to mark the unsettled dispute over the murdered women, or, more likely, Attakullakulla had shown the string given to him by Lyttelton on 21 April. If so, Attakullakulla had been frank about Lyttelton's distrust, and Hagler was now trying to exploit the Carpenter's confidences by misrepresenting him.

Hagler's crude tactics reflected his own increasingly desperate position. He went on to play on Lyttelton's and South Carolina's claim to primacy in southern Indian affairs in an attempt to speed up the building of the promised fort. He pressed for it to be built on the Yadkin, well inside North Carolina and in a position to guard both white and Catawba families – 'whilst we go to warr for our great father King George over the water'. Contradicting his own April admission that North Carolina had left him in the lurch, he claimed that the Catawbas had refused Dobbs's offer of a fort because they preferred to deal with South Carolina.[58] In fact the nation was frantic for adequate protection from any quarter. As John Evans later reported, North Carolina's desertion had left them 'under the Greatest Consternation Possible'. The kidnapping of the seven warriors had frightened them terribly and they expected to be raided again at any moment. Hagler's failure to resolve the crisis was undermining his position and tempting others to take direct action. One of his rivals, Colonel Eavs, privately volunteered to scout the Cherokee towns 'at this next new moon'.[59] There was also the danger of conflict with the nearby North Carolina settlers at Wraxaw Old Fields, from whom the Catawbas had to buy corn. Greedy settlers and dishonest traders had stripped the Indians of all their goods, including their ammunition. Whether this was literally true or not there was certainly a great deal of dangerous tension between the two communities.[60]

Lyttelton repeated his promise to build a fort as soon as Atkin returned from the Creeks; he sensed that a proposal to infringe North Carolina's claims would come better from the Superintendent than from him. But by September, with still no sign of Atkin, the Catawbas were no longer willing to wait. Sixty warriors were already fighting alongside the British in the north; the settlements were consequently denuded of defenders; and there was no ammunition. Atkin, as Evans observed, might well be too late.[61] Lyttelton, by this time confronted with a series of murders around Fort Loudoun, saw that he might soon have to choose between preserving the now tattered peace with the Cherokees, and supporting the only Indians willing and able to assist him. For many of the Cherokee headmen who had been so anxious to conciliate in May were now on the brink of war.

In the Lower Towns this alarming erosion of confidence in Carolina's good will was in part the long-term consequence of Lyttelton's arrogance and inflexibility. But the suddenness and violence of the change was due to the appalling behaviour of the young officers at Fort Prince George. Less than twenty years later the trader James Adair published his *History of the American Indians*, in which he accused the officers of twice raping Indian women while their men were away hunting, not to mention generally arrogant and provocative posturing.[62] Milling long ago pointed out that Adair's evidence combined with that of the documents in the Indian Books prove that their actions were decisive in a tense and unstable situation.[63] Indeed, most historians have simply accepted Adair's version.[64] This is understandable – the crime is so horrible that even to question its reality could seem indecent – but the historian in search of proof might not be convinced. Unhappily the additional evidence in Lyttelton's in-letters tends only to confirm Adair's story. There was, as Merrell reminds us, a fine line between the sexual liberty enjoyed by Indian women and the traditional hospitality they offered, and outright sexual assault, a line crossed all too often by whites on the southern frontier.[65] As the Cherokee allowed even married women particularly wide latitude, that line must have been especially fragile around Fort Prince George. It is perfectly clear that Lieutenant Coytmore, Ensign John Bell and an interpreter raped a woman at Estatoe, and it is probable that their generally aggressive and contemptuous behaviour was shared by Ensign Alexander Miln and others.

On or shortly after 22 June there was a furore at Fort Loudoun. Demeré discovered that Bell had been selling rum to the Cherokees, in direct disobedience of an order. When confronted Bell shut himself up in his room and, with the interpreter and the remains of six purloined kegs for company, proceeded to drink himself under the table. Though officer of the guard he stayed there all day and in the evening Lieutenant Maurice Anderson had to do 'the Parole' for him. Later Bell staggered to Demeré's quarters to accuse him of selling the rum himself. When Demeré ordered him back to his room the scene was suddenly elevated from the merely squalid to the squalidly spectacular. 'He Broke out upon me', as Demeré primly put it, 'with Reproachful and Provoking Speeches.' Demeré promptly ordered Ensign John Bogges, who had witnessed the exchange, to confine Bell to his room. Bell went quietly as far as his door, but then he suddenly attacked Bogges with his fists and screamed abuse at the soldiers who ran to help. With a drunkard's strength he broke away as far as the parade ground outside the gates. There he marched up and down for most of the night, shouting out that Demeré was a'French coward'. Next day he kept to his room 'pretty Decently' and on the day after that he wrote Demeré 'an Excusing...for his being Drunk'. Demeré answered 'by hand of Ensign Bogges' that he must make a public apology in front of the whole garrison. Bell complied and Demeré, indulgent to the last, merely exchanged him for another ensign at Fort Prince George. The whole question of discipline he left to Lyttelton.[66] Incredibly, Lyttelton did nothing. The incident was an alarming comment on conditions at Fort Loudoun, and the governor should have seen the dangers of leaving an insubordinate officer who sold rum to Indians in such a sensitive post as Keowee. Yet Bell remained there until Bull and Grant finally removed him in 1761.

Soon after Bell's arrival at Fort Prince George Coytmore was the victim of an attempted fraud, the grisly nature of which may well indicate the Cherokees' general opinion of him. On 30 June Scroweh, the Young Warrior of Estatoe, and his brother Half Breed Jemmy the Conjuror, came to Fort Prince George. Although Jemmy did the talking, the silent Seroweh was clearly the leader. Seroweh, said Jemmy, was prepared to take the hatchet and go against the Coosa settlement. Naturally, given the state of public opinion in the Lower Towns, he would have to pretend to be going hunting. What would Coytmore give him in return for taking such a risk? Coytmore promptly offered him presents worth 200 lb of leather for a prisoner, and 50 lb worth for each scalp. Seroweh seemed very pleased with this offer and promised to start in two days. But soon after this interview Coytmore heard that some young men had returned to Estatoe with three English scalps 'quite green', and that it was these that Seroweh would pass off to him as French.[67]

Lieutenant Coytmore was affronted. Next day, on 1 or 2 July, he went to Estatoe and told Seroweh that he had changed his mind and now wanted only prisoners. He did not mention the fresh scalps. But the following day he took the newly arrived Bell and the fort's interpreter to Estatoe to seize them. They found Half Breed Jemmy's wife home alone. According to Coytmore she was startled by his knowledge of the scalps and admitted that they were in the house. She was quite proud of them, pointing out that one of her relatives had recently been killed by whites. But when she went to fetch them they had gone, probably taken, she said, by Seroweh who had dropped in earlier on his way to Chota.[68] Neither Jemmy nor Seroweh were at home, and presumably the other Estatoe men were also away; the officers were angry at the attempted trick, and at being forestalled. It is not too fanciful to imagine that this was the occasion of one of the rapes reported by Adair. Even if it was not, the picture of three men brow-beating and bullying a woman in her own home at midnight (by Coytmore's own admission the party did not return to Fort Prince George until 3 a.m.)[69] is not a pretty one.

Nor need the case rest wholly on Adair's rumours and the damaging admissions made by Coytmore. Allegations made by the Cherokees themselves arc on record. When Tistoe of Keowee went down to Charleston with Occonostota's peace mission in October he specifically accused Coytmore of sexual impropriety, drunkenness and generally arrogant behaviour, and implicitly of withholding Lyttelton's Talks.

> Tho' I love my brethren of the Fort, yet I have found something bad about them, they have used us ill, and the officer says he is no affraid of us, their bad usage has occasioned our people to do what they have done, I am sory for it. The Officer gets drunk, he goes to our Houses & draws our Women from us, he paints himself and says he is a Warrior, but we are not Warriors, and has to do with our women at his own pleasure. The Gentleman that was at the Fort Before [Lachlan McIntosh] I loved, for he caused a Gun to be fired when any message came from Your Excellency, and alwise communicated it to us.[70]

The 'Officer' was plainly Coytmore, but Tistoe also mentioned Bell, though the Council clerk did not record it. One of the councillors present, Lieutenant-Governor William Bull, remembered hearing his name and told Montgomery and Grant about it six months later. But Lyttelton was not interested. Having formed his own picture, he regarded any such accusations or complaints as red herrings, designed to divert him from the main business of extracting 'satisfaction' from the slippery savages before him. It is hardly surprising that men of the Lower Towns took up the hatchet. Early in 1760, as we shall see, a gang of them led by Occonostota killed Coytmore, seriously wounded Bell and just missed the interpreter. Seroweh, who became the most implacable of the hostile headmen, claimed in 1761 that he had been driven to war by the affronts of Coytmore, Bell and Miln. Two of the prisoners taken by Montgomery in 1760 said the same.[71] On the British side the crimes of the Fort Prince George officers became notorious. In March 1761 McIntosh returned to Keowee, and Miln (Coytmore's successor), Bell and an officer called Wilkinson were all relieved of their duties.[72] In May James Grant placed Miln under arrest, and in September, as soon as the preliminary peace with the Cherokees was settled, he court-martialled him. Miln was charged with no less than eight breaches of the Articles of War during his tenure as commander between Coytmore's death in January 1760 till McIntosh's arrival in March 1761. In that time he had allegedly sold military stores to the Indians for private gain; leaked to the Cherokees news of an ammunition convoy; taken £10 for goods which were never supplied; played cards with the men (to encourage them, he said); stolen salt meant to be exchanged for food; put his own brand on horses belonging to John Elliot the trader; embezzled food stores; and censored officers' letters, presumably to ensure that his crimes were kept secret. The court of enquiry chaired by Grant's close friend and second-in-command, Alexander Monypenny, found Miln guilty.[73] Grant urged Amherst to quickly confirm the decision, and the commander-in-chief, though at first refusing to be rushed, eventually did so.

Taken together these were serious breaches of discipline and probity. But they were made long after Miln had been relieved of his command, and individual accusations, such as that of playing cards, bordered on the vindictive. Grant's real quarrel with Miln was over his treatment of the Cherokees, which he believed had lengthened the war by nearly two years. Locking up a Cherokee peace delegation in 1760, for example, was not a court martial offence; and had in any case been dismissed by Bull as a youthful excess of zeal. But the raping of Cherokee women and the taunting of their menfolk would have been equally beyond the scope of military law, especially with only Indian witnesses to rely on. Grant's malice becomes easier to understand if we infer that he was punishing crimes which went right back to 1759, and which could never be brought to trial. This interpretation is strengthened by the fact that the crimes committed in and near Fort Prince George were notorious throughout the back country long after the war. The itinerant Anglican priest, Rev. Charles Woodmason, preaching to a newly raised company of Rangers, admonished them not to behave as the Fort Prince George garrison had done: for their 'Ill conduct and

Licentiousness' had sparked off a bloody Indian war.[74] We must conclude that the crimes alleged by Adair and others are proved beyond any reasonable doubt, and must account for the hardening of Cherokee opinion in July 1759.

By 22 July Demeré was picking up sinister rumours about Tellico and Settico, both of which were in touch with the Coosa settlement and with the Creeks. Moreover, six young men had set out from Toxaway, apparently to raid either Virginia or North Carolina. This seemed to be only the tip of the iceberg, however, for news was increasingly hard to get as the Cherokees became more suspicious and less communicative. As Demeré put it, 'very little reliance can be placed upon the promises of these Savages'.[75] Even Attakullakulla could not restrain the young men who wanted war, and his influence among the headmen was ebbing away. The only way to preserve what was left of his position was to temporarily withdraw from the nation and dissociate himself from the demands for satisfaction emanating from the forts. He went to Demeré and told him that 'the Young People in his Gang' were insisting on a raid against the French. His real meaning was clear: he could no longer keep his promise to keep the Cherokees quiet, but he could stop Old Hop making a French peace. Three days later he set off with Willinawaw and 30 young warriors still loyal to him: at once there was trouble in the Overhill country.[76] Connecorte, always more ready than the Carpenter to look for allies to balance the British, sent messengers northward to seek assistance in case of war. Worse still, rumours were flying about of about 30 Creeks and a few French coming to help the Cherokees to cut off Fort Loudoun.[77]

In the Lower Towns even the hitherto cautious headmen were preparing to pick up the hatchet and welcome the Creeks and French. Unlike the Overhills they had the constant pressure of the Long Canes settlers to worry about; but they knew war with South Carolina would render themselves vulnerable to the inevitable trade embargo. At the very end of July their ambassadors brought four Creeks, two of them headmen of towns near Fort Toulouse, to meet representatives of all the Lower Towns at Keowee. Though the participants were sworn to secrecy, Coytmore had with difficulty managed to suborn one of the young warriors who attended. The Creeks delivered a few white and many black beads, claiming the French at Fort Toulouse, who had great respect for the Cherokees, had great quantities of trade goods. If the

Cherokees would join them, the French and Creeks, against the English these goods would be theirs. When the Cherokees cautiously replied that they must have two days to send 'over the Hills' before offering their reply, the Creeks answered that a similar embassy to theirs had already gone to Chota. When the meeting convened two days later Wawatchee, who had so recently refused to attack the Coosa settlement, spoke on behalf of 'all these lower towns'. The British, he said, had let down the Cherokees by supplying insufficient goods. Therefore the Cherokees, who trusted the Creeks, would join them in war against the English.[78] He meant, of course, that the Lower Towns could not even consider war until they had an alternative source of trade, and that the Cherokees would not accept the Creek assurances without guarantees. The Cherokees, he said, would only take up the hatchet when the Creeks had slaughtered all the British traders in their own country. The Creeks took this evidence of suspicion very calmly, and produced a red pipe and some tobacco sent, they said, by the French. Tistoe, hitherto the most moderate and cautious of the headmen, accepted them.[79]

Coytmore's spy claimed that it was agreed that the Creeks would massacre the traders in the fall. When the news reached their towns the Cherokees would approach Coytmore for ammunition with which to defend themselves and the fort against Creek raids. Once the powder and bullets were in their possession they would be used against the British. The news was confirmed by Beamer, who had his own contacts. There was confirmation, too, of another kind. Immediately after the meeting the headmen ceased to visit the fort, so that by 3 August Coytmore could write that 'not an Indian of the least Distinction' had entered the fort for days.[80]

This was Coytmore's version, which Lyttelton seems to have accepted whole. But in Georgia Henry Ellis heard a different story. According to his sources the Cherokees had complained not only about trade, and of their losses in Virginia, but raised their far more fundamental resentment of the settlers' encroachments. War was being considered, but far from plotting an alliance with the Creeks, the Lower Towns were afraid that the Creeks would join the British. Thus the meeting was to persuade the Creeks to 'stand Neuter' rather than to conclude an offensive alliance with them. In reply the Creeks had scornfully blamed the Cherokees for their own misfortunes 'in giving unbounded Liberty to the white people in regard to Lands and Forts'. They would not promise support should the Cherokees go to war, whereupon the Cherokees insisted that the Creeks should go home and convene a general meeting of their nation to decide their attitude to the British. Ellis concluded that the Creeks would not lightly begin a war, and if they did not the Lower Towns, properly handled, might stay quiet too.[81] Here was confirmation of Outerbridge's intelligence of early July.

The Lower Towns' hesitation brought Moitoi of Settico down from the Overhill country, where the other Creek embassy had already been received. Suspecting that Attakullakulla's influence lay behind their caution, he set about undermining the Carpenter's reputation as the unfaltering man of peace. At a meeting at Wawatchee's house in Sugar Town, he claimed that Attakullakulla had told Demeré that he was going hunting, but in fact had gone to see the French at Fort Toulouse. Old Hop and the other Overhill leaders, he said, were waiting only for the support of the Lower Settlements before going to war. By 23 August Moitoi had returned to Chota, but he left behind a group of headmen around Wawatchee who were ready to fight.[82] Even Wawatchee, however, was still willing to try for a peaceful settlement. Clearly such a settlement must include a fixed limit to white expansion above Long Canes, or, preferably, expel the settlers from all the lands wrongly occupied since 1747. Long experience, most notably the murders of November 1757, had shown that it was no use applying to Lyttelton. In mid-1759 he and the Council were still approving land grants on the 'north fork' of Long Canes Creek and in other sensitive frontier areas.[83] But Henry Ellis of Georgia might listen and intercede on the Cherokees' behalf.

On 13 August Wawatchee visited John Vann of Broad River and addressed to him a Talk for Ellis. Wawatchee denied that the Cherokees were in league with the Creeks – a statement at least technically true – and pointed out that the fundamental problem was that

> the People of South Carolina having made encroachments on their Lands and have Settled so near to their Nation, that it of course makes the Deer scarce, so that they are not able to support their Wives & Children with meat & Cloaths.[84]

He asked Ellis to plead the Cherokee case with Lyttelton and to arrange a meeting with him. Ellis, eager to seize a possible avenue to peace, passed the Talk on to Lyttelton without delay, urging him to take up the offer it contained. The Cherokees, he argued, clearly expected to be attacked from both South Carolina and Georgia, and by the Creeks, against whom they had been organizing their defences. They had no aggressive plans of their own. But the Creeks, irritated by Atkin's clumsy diplomacy, might well turn hostile unless deflected very quickly. Therefore, to avoid a Cherokee–Creek alliance, he and Lyttelton must immediately make a pact with the Cherokees 'upon the best terms we can, the overture they have made opens the way for it'.[85] But he knew Lyttelton well enough to fear that the necessary concessions would not be forthcoming; and the consequence of that, as he pointed out, might well be the destruction of Georgia.

I beg however that Your Excellency will not think too contemptuously of these Savages nor let this opportunity slip of setling the matter with them: for it is terrible to reflect upon the desolation an Indian War would occasion. This colony in its present exposed and defenceless State would run a great hazard of being totaly destroyed; the very bad condition of the Fort at Augusta and the large quantity of Indian goods in that Town are great temptations to such people ...[86]

So anxious was Ellis to secure an accommodation between South Carolina and the Cherokees that he offered to act as mediator, perhaps at a congress at Augusta, perhaps in the presence of Lyttelton's ambassador.[87]

But as soon as Coytmore heard of the Talk he rushed to denounce it as hypocrisy. This was hardly surprising for, as Ellis's earlier letter shows, Coytmore had already suppressed two cardinal points of the Keowee conference which did not fit the picture he wished to convey to Lyttelton. These were the Cherokees' ambivalence about their relations with the French, and the continuing importance of the boundary problem. Coytmore's relations with the Cherokees were now so poor – we do not have to accept his word that only Creek intrigues stopped the headmen coming to his fort – that his life was in real danger. There remained only two solutions: to ask to be relieved, which would be humiliating, or to promote an Anglo-Cherokee war in which the Indians would be defeated. Two years later James Grant, having already spent one whole campaign in the province, reached this same conclusion about Miln and Bell.

Coytmore need not have worried. Lyttelton and the South Carolina Council took his version of the Creek visit at face value, which of course suggested that both Fort Loudoun and Coytmore's post were about to be attacked. On 14 August they conducted an urgent investigation into the critically low supplies in both forts, and decided to send John Stuart up to Fort Prince George with supplies and 70 reinforcements.[88] John McQueen, a merchant who supplied the Indian traders, was called in and grilled to discover how much ammunition the Cherokees were likely to have. When McQueen revealed that since 1 June he had sold the traders over 2000 lb of powder and ball, he was abruptly ordered to supply no more until further notice.[89] The Cherokees had lost their vital ammunition supply on the eve of the autumn hunt. Nothing was more likely to confirm the Cherokee fear, long known to Lyttelton, that the British intended to destroy them. Moreover, McQueen had claimed that in recent months the Cherokees had been sent more general goods than ever before, which seemed to discredit the Cherokee claim that they had been poorly supplied.[90]

Nor would Lyttelton allow the Cherokees to outflank him by opening talks with Virginia. Fauquier, through the agency of Richard Smith, had continued the conciliatory diplomacy he had begun with the Carpenter in December 1758. In the spring, after the Yadkin River murders, he was reassured by the returning Presbyterian missionary, Rev. John Martin, and in June had offered to reopen trade.[91] But now that Lyttelton was taking a strong line with the Cherokees their reconciliation with Virginia had to be prevented at all costs. Lyttelton obtained the Council's backing for a letter to Fauquier, requesting him to take hostage a two-man Cherokee delegation which had gone to Williamsburg 'until the real intentions of the Cherokees are more fully known'.[92]

He was too late. By 12 August Fauquier had made a formal peace on terms which shocked Lyttelton. The Cherokees had apologized for Seroweh's raids into Virginia and promised to prevent it happening again; Fauquier had accepted that there was no way of preventing the Young Warrior exacting revenge, and admitted that the Bedford County settlers had frequently been guilty of shameful treachery. The delegates were on the way home with Smith, while at Salisbury in North Carolina Fauquier was assembling trade goods in anticipation of the nation's approval.[93] But because Fauquier put off writing,[94] Lyttelton was for some seven weeks under the illusion that Virginia would support his embargo. Conciliation was not on his agenda.

Nor was Lyttelton willing to take the boundary issue seriously, even though its importance to the Cherokees had now been reported to him from two different sources. The trouble was that in both cases the channel of communication had been Ellis. He and the Council took umbrage at Wawatchee having approached another government at all, seeing in it an attempt to subvert South Carolina's primacy in Indian affairs, an attempt which Ellis, in proposing his conference at Augusta, seemed all too anxious to further. In the words of the journal, 'Indians dependent upon and connected with this Government ought not to be encouraged in making Complaints about the Inhabitants of this Province to any other Government ...'[95] Lyttelton, supported by the Council, replied with a Talk taking the Cherokees to task for their impertinence, and complaining that none of the complaints made by Wawatchee had ever been addressed to him,[96] a less than subtle way of treating them as fiction. Moreover, 'this Government is able to transact the Business belonging to it, without the Intervention of any other Government'. The Cherokees should have sent a properly accredited delegation to Charleston if they had any just complaints, and he would give a safe conduct to such an embassy should the nation care to send one.[97] But, just to make absolutely clear whose stories he believed, Lyttelton insisted that he was doing this 'notwithstanding the Information he had received of the late bad behaviour and evil Intentions of some of their people against the white people'.[98] In short Lyttelton did not intend to address any grievances except his own, for in his mind the Cherokee complaints had no validity whatever. He had proposed the meeting, as he told the Board of Trade, rather to allow Stuart to get to Fort Prince George unmolested, than with any real hope of a lasting settlement.[99] As for Ellis, though he continued to plead for a settlement ('an event much to be desired') and to argue that the Cherokee–Creek threat had been exaggerated, he was firmly told that a conference was a matter for the future[100] – in other words, when the Cherokees had capitulated. With that earlier letter to Fauquier in view, we may wonder whether, somewhere at the back of Lyttelton's mind, the notion of taking the deputies hostage was already stirring.

Although the Council's decision to stop the ammunition was provocative, it should still have allowed a breathing space while the traders disposed of the supplies they had in hand. But as long ago as 22 May Lyttelton had ordered the forts' commanders to impound the traders' ammunition should the situation become dangerous. By the time Lyttelton was composing his answer to Wawatchee's Talk the mood at Keowee had become downright menacing. Coytmore and other officers were now threatened openly, wood cutting parties were taunted, and both Seroweh and Wawatchee admitted sending war parties against the settlements. Messengers sent from the fort to Old Hop were searched for letters. Coytmore, presumably having heard of the Council's order of a week before, acted on his earlier orders and seized all the ammunition, guns and flints 'that I could come at'.[101] Coytmore was understandably anxious to save his own skin, but his action suddenly brought open war very much closer.

The goods concerned belonged to Samuel Benn at Chota and Cornelius Doherty at the already warlike town of Tellico. Consequently when on 21 August the Overhills heard of the seizure there was uproar. Next day Corn Tassell, Demeré's friend and informant, came to him to ask why the ammunition had been stopped, and whether either he or Lyttelton had ordered it. He also pointed out that many Cherokee families would be going hunting after the Green Corn Dance, and would need that ammunition to secure hides and meat. Poor Demeré found himself having to explain away Coytmore's rash action as an act of self-defence against the Lower Towns; he denied that either Lyttelton or himself were involved and promised that the Overhills should have their ammunition 'when they pleased'. Corn Tassell replied that he was very glad to hear it because 'there is a great many begin to talk very indifferent about it; and I shall go to Night to the Town House and shall acquaint them with what you say'.[102]

Whatever was said in the town house did not satisfy the Chota council. Occonostota, whose good offices in keeping the Overhills quiet had been rewarded with distrust and treachery, was now prepared to threaten the British with force. The council instructed him to tell Demeré that if the ammunition was not delivered all the fort's supplies would be cut off. On 22 August the Great Warrior invited himself and the headmen of Tellico and Chatuga to dinner at Fort Loudoun and put the issue to him directly.

> You know very well that after the Little Carpenter was gone to Warr, you desired me to go no where but to stay at Chote to endeavour to stop all bad talks, I have been no where, and I have stay'd at Home on purpose to oblige you and every thing has been very quiet. I should be very glad to know if it was the governor's Orders, or yours, that our Hunting Ammunition has been stop'd, at Keowee.[103]

Demeré repeated the answer he had given to Corn Tassell. But Occonostota was not to be put off. With great dignity and firmness he reaffirmed his determination to prevent violence, and formally demanded the ammunition as an essential condition of peace.[104] Once again Demeré promised what was not in his power, to order Coytmore to release the ammunition. The Great Warrior undertook to transmit this answer to the Chota council that evening, but warned that time was short.

> These two last Winters I have been at Warr, and my people are almost Naked, therefore I intend to go a hunting, a little while after the Green Corn Dance that they may be Cloathed except you should prevent me by some unforseen Danger.[105]

The Overhills could not have been plainer. For some time it had been evident that the British intended to punish, or even destroy, the nation for the depredations of a minority. The steadily nibbling pressure of the frontier settlers, Lyttelton's insistence on satisfaction, Atkin's mission to the Creeks and – the last straw – the ammunition stoppage all pointed in the same direction. The nation would certainly go cold and hungry should the winter's hunt be lost and Chota had decided to play the highest card it had: to take Fort Loudoun hostage. Demeré had no more than 18 days' provisions left and little in the way of presents for those Cherokees still ready to display their loyalty by going to war, 'and if any thing shou'd happen, and the Path shou'd be stop'd, the Garrison wou'd be in great Danger'.[106] With the fort so vulnerable a blockade might just force the British to hand over the precious powder and ball; it was worth the risk, the almost certain risk, of war. Even now, however, headmen throughout the nation were prepared to accept Lyttelton's invitation to Charleston to make one last-ditch effort to secure peace.

But as far as Lyttelton could see the accumulating evidence overwhelmingly confirmed his own opinion of Cherokee perfidy. As early as spring settlers had begun leaving the frontier districts, and in June a Ranger had been killed and scalped while finding his horse.[107] On 1 August a Cherokee woman secretly told Demeré of the June embassies to Fort Toulouse.[108] From the Congarees John Stuart reported that bands of Creeks and Cherokees were hovering around the back settlements, and that two German settlers had left their homes on Twelve Mile Creek to avoid being scalped. A Catawba party brought similar news and by 29 August the whole area was in arms and parties were scouring the woods. Stuart was worried that his men (now only 60) would be infected with the panic.[109] At the end of August Seroweh admitted having lifted scalps in the Carolina settlements, and defied Coytmore to take them from him. By late September random acts of violence had driven settlers to the brink of mass flight, and the Creeks appeared to be stirring the Cherokees to exact a blood price for lands never paid for.[110] All this only confirmed Lyttelton's view that the boundary question was a spurious issue, whipped up by Franco-Creek machinations, and little more than a fig leaf for acts of gratuitous violence. News of attacks on packhorse men and traders also pointed in this direction. About 30 August one of the Lower Cherokees, a warrior called Big Canoe, fired at the trader Cornelius Brown from a thicket. The bullet whipped through Brown's clothes, just grazing his side, and he lived to tell the tale.[111] Peter Arnaud, a French packhorse man employed by James Beamer, was less fortunate. He was one of two men with a convoy taking flour up to Fort Loudoun. A party led by the Man Killer of Tellico ambushed it at a place where the track descended steeply through woods towards the Tellico River. Arnaud, who had the bad luck to be in the lead, was brought down by the first shots and his body rolled off the path.[112] A party from Great Tellico scoured the woods for his corpse but it was never found; in Beamer's opinion they had taken the scalp and thrown the body into the river. Beamer ended his letter to Lyttelton on a mysterious but ominous note. He had news, which he dared not commit to paper, but which he would convey to Lyttelton face to face, 'which If you was to know the truth of I am Certain you would make an alteration for the Security and Ease of the Whole Province and other Besides'.[113] Whatever Beamer meant, it could only have further alarmed a governor already convinced of the reality of a Creek–Cherokee conspiracy.

Nine days later four warriors from Settico took their first scalp outside Fort Loudoun. Gunninghame, a trader living in the town, was selling the Setticos ammunition which probably came from Georgia. Glad to be free of licensed competition, he tried to keep the South Carolina embargo going by urging the warriors to attack stragglers from the forts. It was the soldiers, he claimed, who were responsible for cutting off the ammunition and therefore deserved to die.[114] Thus on 7 September, the last day of the Green Corn Dance, the town sent the four young men 'to way lay this Fort ...' Their victim was Samuel Simmons who had gone out to gather wild grapes. The Settico men caught and scalped him under the horrified eyes of the sentries, 'within a hundred Yards of our Corn field'.[115] Two days later Demeré sent out a party to bring the cattle into the fort for safety. The men were followed by a large band of armed Cherokees, whom Demeré later heard had been sent by Ostenaca, the Mankiller of Tomotly, 'who is the Head of all this Mischief'.[116] The cattle party returned safely by another route,[117] but the implication of such an important figure from the Carpenter's own town was a sinister development. On 11 September the hostile warriors scalped William Veal, a trader 'that lives in Chittowee', thus winning, thought Maurice Anderson, the last of 'the three scalps they wanted' to obtain goods and ammunition from the French. At least four war parties were known to have gone out against the South Carolina back settlements, and the messenger who carried the warning to Long Canes and Ninety Six was lucky to get through alive. By now the roads across the mountains to Keowee were 'all blocked up' and the garrison, with only 14 days' flour, were killing and salting their cattle as fast as they could.[118]

When Stuart reached Fort Prince George on 22 September – escorted for the last 15 miles by warriors from Keowee – he found the track to Fort Loudoun cut and the traders from the Middle and Valley Settlements, warned by friendly Cherokees, streaming in for shelter. Bands of warriors were now almost constantly watching the fort and the 'Keowees' – Tistoe's people – had warned the garrison to allow only armed parties out. Having lost a further 18 men by desertion en route from the Congarees, and at a loss for packhorses, Stuart dared go no further. In his view war had practically broken out already. 'The powder and shot I have under my Convoy', he observed, 'would at this Juncture be a tempting Bait to the Enemy, I think I may call them so.' Worse, three Lower Creeks 'who have been long expected by Mr. Coytmore', arrived in Keowee on the night of 24–25 September on as yet unknown business. By this time Stuart feared that he would soon be unable to communicate with Charleston at all, as the roads behind him were 'blocked up' and passable only by 'strong escorts'. In short, not only could he not reach Demeré, but Fort Prince George itself was in danger. Under the circumstances he could do little but take charge of the fort's defence until reinforcements could arrive.[119] Stuart was neither a cold official, nor an arrogant young man with too much power. During his earlier tour of duty at Fort Loudoun he and the Cherokees had grown to know and like each other. If such an experienced observer asserted that war had broken out, Lyttelton could hardly be blamed for believing him.

Against this background the efforts of some headmen to defuse the crisis by negotiating the release of the ammunition looked like blackmail. The day after Simmons's murder a great delegation of Overhills, representing all the towns, visited Fort Loudoun to demand the release of Benn's and Doherty's property. When Demeré pointed out that they would have to ask Coytmore, Ostenaca and Occonostota were selected to go. Both refused to carry Demeré's letters, but the Great Warrior promised to give 'strong Talks' to all the towns as he went down, to take Benn and Doherty with him, and to escort Stuart safely over the mountains on his return. Demeré, cheered by this straw of hope, gave his letters to Benn, 'which I was obliged to put in the lining of his Saddle for fear of accident'.[120] No sooner were Occonostota and Ostenaca on their way than Connecorte sent for the headmen of Chota, Tanassee, Tomotly and another friendly town.[121] In an attempt to regain the diplomatic initiative from the Great Warrior, the ailing old Uku sent them to tell Demeré that only Tellico and Settico were guilty of killing whites. When Demeré replied that those towns could not be forgiven and must give satisfaction, the four sought another approach. Two days later, having consulted the Warriors of Tellico and Settico, they returned to repeat the old story that the young men of those towns were out of control. Old Hop could easily have the warriors responsible seized and handed over, but, as one of the headmen pointed out at once, that might well make matters even worse. Demeré replied in a manner worthy of Lyttelton himself: 'Do you think that you can shed the blood of his Majesty's Subjects whenever you please, and say after that you are sorry for it …[?]' Once again he insisted on satisfaction and sent a detailed account of the conferences to Lyttelton. He now pinned all his hopes on the Carpenter, whom the four headmen said would return very soon.[122]

Meanwhile Coytmore was approached by none other than Wawatchee, who had dared to complain of the Long Canes people through another government. The Cherokees, he argued, had no powder for hunting. Coytmore, adopting a self-righteous air, replied that if the Indians had not fired at Brown and Arnaud they could have had some at once; as things were, he must consult Lyttelton first.[123] Wawatchee, never as conciliatory as Tistoe, was not in a generous mood. His reply was menacing: 'It is true that they have fired at some of the white People and Perhaps may find a little yet for that Purpose.'[124] Relations did not mend next day when Wawatchee was presented with Lyttelton's contemptuous reply to his offer of peace talks. He told Coytmore that he had given Vann a good Talk, and had not claimed to be commissioned by the nation 'as mention'd in the Letter …'[125] On the afternoon of 25 September Ostenaca, Occonostota and 18 other Cherokees reached Keowee with Benn, Doherty and another trader called Cornelius Cockley. The two leaders immediately gave notice of their intentions, which Stuart feared would make war inevitable.

> This day [26 September] they are to make formal demand of Benn's Ammunition, which in the present Situation of Affairs must be denied them, and that the consequence will be an open and declared War, which will certainly happ[en] whether their demand be granted or not.[126]

Next day Stuart, as the senior officer present, met Occonostota and Ostenaca in open conference. They put to him the usual argument: Settico was the only town which 'was bad', whereas their own intentions were good; they only wanted to obtain the hunting ammunition and hoped that the past could be forgotten.[127] Stuart evaded the request in a manner which left the door to peace still open. Coytmore, he pointed out, had only acted on Lyttelton's instructions and could not release the ammunition without further orders. As for himself, he was only passing through en route to Fort Loudoun and had no authority to treat. Therefore, if they really wanted peace, the Cherokees would have to go to see Lyttelton himself in Charleston. The Indians asked for two days to consider their reply.[128] It cannot have escaped their notice that Lyttelton had not once offered to come up to treat with *them*, or even to meet them half-way, as Glen had done at Saluda. The trip to Charleston would thus suggest submission on their part. Moreover, with all the British officers sternly demanding 'satisfaction' on the governor's behalf, the journey could be dangerous. Nevertheless Occonostota and the others were willing to take the risk. On 28 September they told Stuart that they would go. Stuart left them under no illusions as to the reception they could expect. He insisted that only headmen properly authorized by their towns should go, 'and gave them to understand that they might Expect Satisfaction for the Murders Committed in their Nation would be Demanded'. Coytmore selected some Lower Towns headmen to go with them.[129] Soon after no less than 38 prominent Cherokees set off for the colonial capital. Although Ostenaca soon lost his nerve and turned back he did not molest Stuart on his way up to Fort Loudoun, as some of the British expected.[130] The others pushed on, their procession a notable tribute to the determination of the more responsible leaders of the nation to snatch peace from the jaws of war.

They were too late. Lyttelton was convinced that war had already begun. Fort Loudoun was cut off and Fort Prince George was practically under siege, in what Coytmore already called 'absolute open War',[131] despite the friendly gestures of the Keowees. From Charleston Occonostota's demand for ammunition seemed to echo the alleged Cherokee–Creek conspiracy earlier revealed by Coytmore, especially as Malachi and a band of Cherokees were reported to have passed through Augusta en route for Savannah.[132] That is, it looked like a plot to trick the British into parting with their powder before turning on them. Meanwhile, so it appeared, the peace loving Ellis was to be lulled into a false sense of security, and Coytmore's slurs on Wawatchee's sincerity and veracity continued to carry far more weight than his proposals. Already the Council had authorized Coytmore to stop warriors lurking under the walls 'at unseasonable hours', if necessary by force.[133]

On 30 September Lyttelton ordered the provincial militia to prepare for a general muster. The three-gun signal which boomed out from Fort Johnson was repeated from post to post throughout the province.[134] Next day, still not knowing the outcome of the Great Warrior's conference with Stuart, Lyttelton asked for and obtained the Council's advice to mobilize the inland halves of each of the three county militia regiments. Half of each of these mobilized companies were to be marched to a general rendezvous, ready for an offensive; the remainder were to mount patrols against possible slave rebellions. The Chickasaws and Catawbas, the latter getting their wish at last, were offered ammunition in return for fighting the Cherokees, while the 150 provincials and independents in Charleston, a tiny garrison for Fort Johnson excepted, were ordered to be ready to march. Lyttelton wrote to inform Ellis and Stanwix of his action, carefully avoiding any suggestion that the latter should provide troops. But he asked Dobbs and Fauquier for help, and asked Atkin to stir up the Savannah Chickasaws and Creeks. Virginia's aid, as he told the Board of Trade, would be crucial 'as it might be found extremely difficult for us, notwithstanding our utmost endeavours to open a Communication with that place [Fort Loudoun] from Keowee through the passes over the Mountains'.[135]

Thus the political and strategic parameters which would govern the war to its conclusion were laid down at the outset. The war was clearly intended to assert South Carolina's primacy in Indians affairs; and to assure the Commons that its forces would not be turned to wider imperial purposes. The appeals to North Carolina and Virginia were no more than invitations to place their forces at Lyttelton's disposal; indeed Ellis and Dobbs were asked to urge upon Fauquier the importance of relieving Fort Loudoun. Stanwix politely expressed confidence in Lyttelton's ability to deal with the crisis, though he was ready to send troops if asked.[136] Thus although Robinson was wrong to claim that only North Carolina was approached, he was correct as to Lyttelton's purpose.

Three days later Lyttelton announced to the Council that he would lead the expedition in person. He would immediately ask the Commons to provide arms, provisions and waggons for a new provincial regiment of 700 men and for the 1500 militia; and to save time he would send the House a message rather than make a speech. At this point the councillors became alarmed and warned Lyttelton that unless he called out more militia he would not have an army large enough to tackle the Cherokees.[137] Undaunted the governor sent his message to the Commons next day, 5 October.[138]

The Commons was not very cooperative. Though convinced that the Cherokees must be punished, members did not intend to write the governor a political and military blank cheque. As long ago as June Lyttelton had asked for a provincial regiment of 700 men and been granted only 300. Now the members wanted clarification of the numbers they were desired to support, and asked what had become of two 20-man Ranger companies raised in July. Lyttelton at once provided the information they wanted, but on 11 October the Commons asked him to postpone his declaration of war. Lyttelton, nettled, insisted on going ahead without a formal declaration, and on 12 October the Commons voted his funds – but less than he wanted, only until the 1 January, and only for operations inside the province.[139] Yet Lyttelton's war seems to have been popular. The *South Carolina Gazette*, presumably reflecting a wide band of public opinion, applauded 'our Excellent GOVERNOR' for taking the only course possible.[140]

It was not until 13 October that Lyttelton received word of Occonostota's approaching party, which was by then within three days' march of Charleston, and of Round O's not far behind.[141] On the 14th he informed the councillors, and next day he and the Council considered their reaction. Round O could be welcomed with all the usual formalities as his towns had never been associated with the violence. But Occonostota's far more representative embassy was coming on behalf of parts of the nation which had been deeply implicated in the hostilities. Thus although both parties should be given 'proper apartments', the Great Warrior's people 'should not be received with the usual Marks of Friendship'.[142] But, given what he knew of events at Fort Prince George, Lyttelton could not believe that either delegation came 'disposed to agree to such terms as may render an Accommodation with them practicable'.[143] Indeed there was to be no negotiation in the normal sense at all. Lyttelton was to insist on 'full and ample Satisfaction', failing which he was to tell them of the projected expedition – which would certainly extort the necessary submission.[144] He could then step up the pressure by revealing that although Virginia had agreed to open a trade with the Cherokees, it had been halted after the latest murders had occurred.

On 7 October Lyttelton and the Council had learned that Smith was assembling a 100-horse pack train laden with trade goods and ammunition. With the Council's support Lyttelton ordered the nearest militia colonel to intercept Smith in North Carolina and impound his goods.[145] The Cherokee ambassadors would thus be faced with an unbroken South Carolina embargo and the prospect of a disastrous winter hunt. In effect Occonostota and his fellow headmen were to be told in no uncertain terms that their sincerity was suspected, and that no terms short of abject surrender would suffice. Next day the Great Warrior's party arrived in Charleston.[146]

The conference took place on 18, 19 and 22 October and achieved nothing except to lead Lyttelton into his monumental error of judgement. When the Cherokees were called into the council chamber Occonostota, 'Spokesman for the other Indians', announced that he had come in response to Lyttelton's invitation which had reached him at Hiwassee while en route to Fort Prince George. Lyttelton answered scornfully that his reply to Wawatchee's Talk had left the responsibility to make proposals with the Cherokees.

> ... [B]ut I did not invite you to come, I only permitted you so to do in case you was desirous of it. Therefore you are to expect no Talk from me, till such time as I know what you have to say.[147]

Taken aback Occonostota and his companions asked for an adjournment until the next day to consider their reply.[148] Well might they be surprised. Lyttelton had not only offered them a meeting; he had promised them a safe conduct to and from Charleston. The Cherokees could hardly be blamed for construing this as an invitation, or for assuming that it meant that Lyttelton had something to propose. Next day, their composure recovered, the Cherokees played the only card they possessed: the familiar argument that since blood had been spilt on both sides the hatchet could now be buried without recriminations. Occonostota submitted that although the towns around Chota had been implicated in the killings, 'I was not the beginner of them'.[149] He then suggested that the trouble might be ended by raising the trade embargo. Laying a bundle of deerskins at the governor's feet he asked that past injuries should be forgotten in the interests of future friendship. 'Your Warriors have carried the Hatchet against us', he said, 'we have done the same against them, and both have acted like Boys ...' The hatchet should now be buried for good.[150]

But when Lyttelton refused to pick them up as a sign of his acceptance the atmosphere became more heated. Tistoe made his impassioned attack upon Coytmore and Bell. The Head Warrior of Estatoe pointed out that it was the young men of his town, not he, who had raided the white settlements, and the Black Dog of Hiwassee wanted to know whether his town should be punished for the misdeeds of others. But, despite Bull's objections,[151] their complaints were brushed aside. Lyttelton merely asked them if they were all in agreement with what had been said and dismissed them so that he could consult the Council. With the Indians safely outside, it was quickly decided that Occonostota's offer could be accepted only if the delegates had been properly authorized to treat 'concerning any Satisfaction', and then only if the Cherokees would agree to hand over a specific number of murderers for execution. If these conditions were fulfilled a peace might be concluded on the lines of the 1730 Treaty.[152]

But no one was deeply surprised when the Cherokees refused. Occonostota, of course, had originally been authorized only to demand the powder at Fort Prince George. It had not been until Lyttelton's invitation, or permission, had reached him en route at Hiwassee that the notion of going to Charleston had entered his head, and not until Stuart had refused to give up Benn's ammunition had he decided to act on it. Besides, he knew perfectly well that Chota would never accept such a peace. The Lower Towns' representatives seemed willing to treat, but any agreement they made would have to be ratified at home. The Cherokees could not and would not accept the justice of a bargain which punished one side only and failed to recognize their law of vengeance. Lyttelton and the Board, equally understandably, concluded that a treaty made under these conditions would be 'insecure and improper' because it would be impossible to keep the militia assembled until the nation decided whether to ratify it. Yet Milligan was right to observe that Lyttelton had thrown away a chance to obtain by agreement what he would later attempt to obtain by force.[153]

But there was less agreement as to what to do about it. Four of the councillors wanted to take at least some of the delegates hostage, so forcing the nation to give up the murderers and avoiding the need for a military expedition altogether. The other four present opposed the idea, not on the grounds that such treachery would make peace impossible, but because they believed that military action would be necessary anyway. Lyttelton himself rejected the notion of taking hostages because it would violate his safe-conduct, and decided to take the delegates with him on the march to Keowee. With the council still evenly divided the governor sent for the Indians and told them that they would have to accompany the soldiers so that the safe-conduct could be honoured.[154] Two days later the provincials and regulars from Charleston set out for the rendezvous at the Congarees. On 29 October the governor, the Cherokees and some militia followed them.[155]

When Lyttelton changed his mind about the hostage taking is not known for certain; it was probably after he left Charleston, for his letter of 23 October to the Board of Trade makes no mention of it. But by the time the column met Round O's party at Amelia township the delegates were being treated as prisoners. The two parties of Indians were kept apart by encircling militia, and at the Congarees all pretence was abandoned: all the delegates were arrested and placed under armed guard. Four Cherokees – The 'May Aple' of Keowee, Arraskante of Stecoe, Jucah of 'Wattoger' and Skinakah of Nequassee – managed to escape and carried a tale of breathtaking arrogance and treachery into the Lower Towns.[156] Lyttelton's inability to conceive of treating with Indians on equal terms had made war inevitable.

Meanwhile Stuart had reached Fort Loudoun on 24 October to find that Attakullakulla had returned. Contrary to the rumours spread by Moitoi, the Carpenter's party had not gone to Fort Toulouse; instead they had ambushed a large French vessel on the Mississippi, inflicted several casualties, taken some scalps and brought back a French prisoner.[157] On 2 November a series of conferences with the Cherokees culminated in an important Talk by the Carpenter.[158] The latter was in an unenviable position. To Lyttelton's demands for satisfaction he could only respond with an offer to protect Fort Loudoun, whose garrison had come 'at my Desire' to 'defend us'. He asked to see Lyttelton again to discuss the reopening of trade, and for the removal of the black beads from the string the governor had given him in April. In return he and Willinawaw would once more go to war against the French.[159] But he said nothing at all about 'satisfaction'. Old Hop, who gave his Talk after Attakullakulla's, was even more evasive; he refused to say anything until Occonostota had returned from Charleston with his report. Neither Cherokee dared offer to hand over the men Lyttelton wanted.[160] Indeed, had Lyttelton the wit and humility to see it, they had proposed an attractive bargain: the safety of Fort Loudoun, which Lyttelton had already conceded could not be relieved from South Carolina, in return for releasing the hunting ammunition and dropping the question of retribution. But Lyttelton, as we have seen, could not conceive of negotiating except from strength, and had in any case reason to believe that the headmen would be unable to restrain the young men.

The Carpenter's offer was in any case nullified on the morning of 9 November by the arrival at Keowee of the four escapees from the Congarees, and by the appearance next day of John Elliot with one of the delegates, the Raven of 'Nachasee', and Lyttelton's dispatches from the Congarees. The Raven was carrying a secret Talk from Occonostota which left the Lower Towns in no doubt as to the full horror of the situation. About an hour later a 'War-hoop' and gunfire were heard on the northern path. Minutes later two warriors appeared with the news that the Mankiller of Sugar Town had just been killed and scalped in a scuffle with some Catawbas. The raid by South Carolina's Indian allies, and the news that a band of white men lay between the Catawba towns and Keowee, and that many Catawbas had been killed by small-pox, which might well spread to the Cherokee towns, 'alarm'd the Men & affrighted the Women'. All thoughts of peace collapsed, the Mankiller's brother set up his own 'War-hoop', and the young men vowed revenge. That evening in Keowee town house men from all the Lower Settlements heard the Raven tell how 'the Great Warrior, Round O and all their People' were now held 'like Slaves'. His mission, he said, was to warn the towns that Lyttelton meant to destroy them, and to see if sufficient warriors could be mustered to ambush him somewhere north of Ninety Six. At daybreak runners sped to call in the hunters and the women prepared to take their children into hiding in the hills.[161] A day or two later a messenger set off to the Creeks with 'a Painted Tomahawk' – an invitation to war.[162]

But the Lower Cherokees were still divided. The most attractive option – certainly the most emotionally satisfying – was to ambush Lyttelton at the difficult crossing of the Twelve Mile River. In the daily discussions which followed the Raven's arrival the young men overwhelmingly supported this course. The headmen, on the other hand, would not consent to an action which might mean the deaths of the Cherokee captives. Rather than risk that, they argued, some of the murderers should be given up to Lyttelton. By 14 November only this concern for the hostages prevented the young men from organizing an immediate attack, and Coytmore, getting wind of the situation, warned Lyttelton to watch his prisoners closely.[163] A week later on 21 November a ball play was held between Keowee and Sugar Town; these festive, if violent, sporting occasions involved whole towns either as players or spectators, and this particular one was a fairly transparent cover for a mass meeting of the Lower Townsmen. The meeting seems to have concerted tactics to try and organize the release, or escape, of the Cherokee prisoners. Two days later a warrior called Big Sawney led a four-man delegation from Keowee and Sugar Town to see Coytmore; their mission was to plead for peace, and, more concretely, to arrange for two warriors to visit the hostages.

> This Belt of Friendship we the People of Keohee and the Sugar Town send to my Brother the Governor who is coming along. He is long on his march and has many of our People with him – we long to hear from them. At each end of the Belt is the representation of a man. Let therefore the Governor take one End and the Other Warriors of our Nation the other and Let them come like hand in hand with Good thoughts – we Expect to hear soon from the Governor be it ever so little a talk that we may be sure our Warriors are safe – We send the Slave Catcher of Kittaway and a young fellow of Keohee with this talk to accompany the white man ...[164]

That evening Big Sawney returned to Fort Prince George to say that the Overhills had agreed to surrender the nine murderers in their towns, and would hand them over to Lyttelton when he appeared. The two Cherokee messengers were dispatched with one Thomas Leppard, who carried the beads and Coytmore's letter to Lyttelton. But from Estatoe came two of Beamer's frightened packhorse men with the news that all the towns were ready to attack Lyttelton if only they could discover a way to free his hostages. Coytmore surmised, not unreasonably, that the Lower Cherokees had resolved to make enough concessions to free their headmen, and then to strike with every warrior they could muster.[165] When the two messengers returned from Lyttelton's camp late on the evening of 28 November they brought a tale which roused the frustrated fury to fever pitch. Next morning they told it to a shocked and angry town house. They had only been allowed to see the captive headmen, ringed by white soldiers, at a distance. Lyttelton had not allowed them to speak to the hostages, nor even offered a meal, before ordering them out of camp. Immediately Seroweh, who was fast becoming the leader of the young militants, led a cry for action.[166] If Coytmore's analysis had been wrong on 24 November, it was undoubtedly correct now.

In the Overhill towns there was less turmoil but no less tension. The winter hunt had begun, and the settlements were almost empty when Stuart heard that Elliot had brought in Lyttelton's Talk to the Middle Towns. Stuart sent runners to bring the Carpenter back from his hunting; Elliot arrived on the 14th; and next day there was a conference at Fort Loudoun. But if Demeré thought that Attakullakulla would agree to organize the handing over of the murderers he was sadly mistaken. The Carpenter listened quietly to Demeré's reading of the Talk, and to Lyttelton's approbation of 'his Late behaviour', before asking if the governor had invited him to Charleston. Demeré answered evasively that Lyttelton would be bound to make him welcome if he chose to go. There was a little silence. Then Attakullakulla brought out a few home truths. It would be beyond the headmen's powers to stop any trouble, he said, as the news of Lyttelton's advancing army would spread dread among his people. Nor would he defuse the tension by appeasement, for 'Giving Satisfaction & Delivering up their people he did not approve of'. Instead he returned to his old offer of a peace based on a fighting alliance against the French 'as the properest way of making up matters'. Stuart and Demeré, seeing a way forward, invented a codicil to the Talk, to the effect that Lyttelton would meet Atakullakulla at Keowee.[167] In the Carpenter's mind a door opened slightly and at once his mood brightened: for there was now just a chance of an acceptable peace.

> Now I am quite satisfied and well pleased, and I am going to send a Runner to Willeleway, to tel[l] him to come immediately, and we shall consult together, and do everything for the best. There are but few Men in the Towns, they are already a hunting, but I am told, that Runners have been sent everywhere to order them to come to their Towns.[168]

Attakullakulla even tried to lure Gunninghame to his house so that Demeré's men could arrest him. Although this stratagem failed – 'some

Busy Body seeing some of our Men with the Little Carpenter, went and told him to hide himself for that we intended to take him'[169] – both sides were cautiously optimistic and friendly. Only the Small Pox Conjuror still actively tried to stir the young Overhills into an attack on the fort.[170] Stuart thought that the towns were now too frightened to do anything to upset the whites. 'The Indians are very cruel', he observed, 'but cannot hide their fears.' They were still supplying Fort Loudoun with corn, hogs and fowls and sent no more runners to the Creeks or French.[171] But that did not mean that the Overhills were prepared to give Lyttelton his satisfaction. Indeed apprehensions that Attakullakulla would promise just that erupted in an open quarrel with Connecorte in the Chota town house on 3 December. Old Hop accused the Carpenter of being an enemy to the nation, of servility towards the British, of constantly thwarting by his raids the Fire King's efforts to court the French, and of being a feeble warrior, 'no better than an old woman'.[172] 'This greatly incensed the Little man', who renounced his allegiance to Old Hop and threatened 'that he himself would supply his place' in future. Stuart concluded that Attakullakulla, having burnt his boats at Chota, would use his standing with Lyttelton to win a peace and establish his own authority. After two further days of conversations with his people he set out for Keowee.[173]

At the conference with Lyttelton the Carpenter was not in a strong position. With the mortally ill Old Hop against him and the Lower Towns seething for revenge, the pressures to defy South Carolina and put himself at the head of the war party were almost irresistible. Yet to do so would be politically devastating – he would be abdicating to those who wanted war – and diplomatically it would be a disaster. Attakullakulla's great distinction was his unwavering conviction that the nation could not survive without good relations with its powerful British neighbours and trading partners. No other Cherokee appreciated this truth so clearly and consistently. More immediately, Lyttelton's possession of the hostages gave him the whip hand, for an attack on the militia would probably mean their deaths. Even more galling for the Carpenter must have been the knowledge that this dilemma was not of his own making. In the circumstances it was to his credit that he managed to spin out the negotiations for several days.

Lyttelton's opening Talk was perfectly logical by its own terms, and as he proceeded his listeners could see that the governor really believed his action to be an unavoidable public duty. He repeated his argument that the 1730 treaty unequivocally bound the nation to hand over the killers of white men, without mentioning that it also bound the British to punish the murderers of Cherokees. Once again he pointed out that in November 1758 a six-man Cherokee delegation had promised to abide by that treaty, and had been given presents as compensation for the blood shed in Virginia, and again revealed his ignorance of – or contempt for – the Cherokee revenge law. Now, he said, he had come to take the satisfaction which the Cherokees should have freely offered in keeping with their obligations. In reply Attakullakulla managed, as Hewatt observes, to be conciliatory, yet 'cautiously avoided making any offer of satisfaction'. After expressing annoyance at the Cherokees' treatment in Virginia he promised to urge his countrymen to give up those who had taken their revenge upon the whites; but he added that he did not expect them to comply, and that he had neither the authority nor the inclination to compel them. But, he hinted, there might be progress should Lyttelton release some of his more influential captives first. The Cherokees, he concluded, had been treated worse than enemies, worse than the Choctaws who had killed some Carolinian settlers and not been pursued for satisfaction.[174]

No doubt Lyttelton would have liked to break the impasse by threatening fire and sword if his demands were not met at once. But that was out of the question. His little force, never more than 1300 strong and 'wretchedly' fed and clothed, was already depleted by desertions. When smallpox broke out in a nearby town and his men began to flee in droves,[175] Lyttelton knew he could stay no longer. Reluctantly he released Occonostota, Tistoe and the Warrior of Estatoe – three leading men, not two as Alden says – and next day these three with equal reluctance allowed the Carpenter to hand over two Cherokees. Gunninghame was also given up. The fact that Lyttelton made the first move is important, Alden, by putting it the other way round made the Carpenter's diplomacy look far more abject than it was.[176] But the treaty subsequently concluded on Boxing Day 1759 satisfied no one. Lyttelton was given no more captives but left 22 of his own against the future surrender of as many Cherokees. Confined in Fort Prince George, the hostages were to be released one by one as the alleged murderers arrived. Frenchmen entering the nation were to be either killed or handed over to South Carolina. The trade embargo would then be lifted and the Cherokees would allow the traders to return to their towns.[177] The Carpenter knew perfectly well that the nation would go to war rather than accept these terms, and he had already told Lyttelton as much. At least one of his five co-signatories, Occonostota, would never rest until he had avenged his humiliation; Henry Ellis, when he heard of it, saw at once that the treaty was 'too mortifying to be observed by the Cherokees',[178] an opinion echoed by almost every historian since. As Alden puts it, Lyttelton had 'neither appeased the Indians, nor impressed them with British power' and made war inevitable by breaking his word.[179] For two years wiser men would labour in vain to rebuild the trust which Lyttelton's folly had destroyed, before they could obtain a treaty which both sides could respect.

As Lyttelton withdrew down the country the infuriated Cherokees prepared their revenge. A few days before 13 January a trader called John Kelly was killed at Notally, apparently at the instigation of the Cockeyed Warrior, whose son was one of the hostages. Kelly's body was cut into pieces and displayed on bushes around the town. Meanwhile the Middle and Valley warriors were gathering to liberate the hostages from Fort Prince George.[180] This began a stampede of the remaining traders and packhorse men to the forts; at the Long Canes and other places above Fort Moore the settlers were packing their waggons to get as far away as possible.[181] On 19 January Seroweh tried to capture Fort Prince George by a ruse. Having sent a message that he would be coming to give up three or four killers for as many hostages, he appeared outside the fort asking to see Coytmore. But when the gates were opened his whole party attempted to push in and overwhelm the defenders. The gates were forced shut, but in the melee two hostages managed to escape. Frustrated, Seroweh departed to slay as many traders as he could catch. At John Elliot's house he and his warriors killed Elliot, who had so recently acted as Lyttelton's messenger, and 12 others.[182] Then came the first major raids on the South Carolina frontier.

By the end of January every building down to the Bush River had been destroyed, except for one small stockade where a handful of settlers held out. On the Broad River two men were killed on 22 January and John Downing and his four friends only escaped because 'the Mankiller' protected them. The ten Indians at Downing's boasted that they would take Fort Prince George and lay waste the settlements.[183] At Raybourn's Creek 27 settlers were killed, and on 1 February 100 Middle Cherokee horsemen caught and killed over 50 Long Canes fugitives as they fled towards Augusta.[184] Fort Moore was blockaded and Atkin thought that Lachlan Shaw, who came up to relieve Outerbridge, was lucky to get through unscathed.[185] The raiders were principally from the Middle and Lower settlements, but there were signs that the Overhills would join in too.[186] On 27 February Fort Dobbs in North Carolina was unsuccessfully attacked, and on

3 February and 3–4 March Ninety Six withstood assaults.[187] Refugees were fleeing far below the Congarees, the remaining settlers were penned up in a few log forts and the Cherokees were raiding down as far as Orangeburg.[188] The Indians had rolled back the frontier by a hundred miles and were pressing hard against the British posts. Meanwhile the Lower Cherokees had invested Fort Prince George. Although some weeks passed before there was any firing it was impossible for anyone to leave, and smallpox was killing soldier and hostage alike. By mid-February five of the latter had died and Attakullakulla and Occonostota, who had been to the Overhills, came to demand the release of the survivors. Coytmore refused and thereby signed his own death warrant. Two days later Occonostota returned at daybreak, having already concealed a party of gunmen under the banks of the Keowee river. Luring Coytmore, Bell and the interpreter to the water's edge he signalled his warriors to open fire. Both officers fell, and although both were carried into the fort Coytmore was clearly beyond help.[189]

What exactly happened next is unclear. If we are to believe Miln, Coytmore's successor in command, the enraged garrison wanted to kill the hostages. Miln then persuaded them to put the Indians in irons, but the Indians had concealed weapons and hatcheted the first soldiers to enter their crowded prison. The soldiers then shot and hacked the lot to death, despite Ensign Miln's valiant attempts to stop them. He added that afterwards a jar of poison, doubtless meant for the fort's well, was found buried under the floor.[190] This touch, to say nothing of the suddenly materializing hatchets and knives, is too theatrical to require comment. The truth is probably much nearer to the version provided by Adair: according to this the hostages were shot to death from outside their room, by soldiers firing through holes in the roof.[191]

When the would-be Cherokee rescuers realized that all their comrades had been killed they began firing into the fort from the hills dominating it. The shooting, to which the garrison could make no effective reply, was kept up for some days; thereafter the fort was closely blockaded.[192] The massacre destroyed what remained of Attakullakulla's peace party, and ensured that the frenzied raids on the settlements would continue.[193] For the nation would not now rest until it fully avenged those who died at Fort Prince George.

Thus Lyttelton had been lured into an impossible situation by actions which, given his perception of Indians as inferior, dependent and savage, were perfectly rational, indeed even inescapable. Yet his ruthlessness had shattered Cherokee faith in negotiation and driven almost all the headmen into hostility. Moreover he had done so without first securing sufficient strength to impose a solution by force. There was no sign of the promised help from his neighbours: the North Carolina militia refused to serve outside their own province, while the Virginian House of Burgesses would allow only defensive action. Amherst had offered him two regiments and Lyttelton was obliged to swallow the bitter pill of acceptance.[194] The coming of the regulars, as we shall see in the following three chapters, allowed a perceptive and strong-minded officer to step into the role of arbiter, and give the Cherokees a generous peace. In doing so he showed the home government the way in settling matters on this piece of frontier. But by the time the redcoats began to disembark in the spring of 1760 Lyttelton was past caring. He was packing his bags for Jamaica.

4

'The Sweet Bond of Human Things': Soldiers Seeking Peace, 1760

Sir Jeffrey Amherst was angry. Late the previous night on 23 February 1760 Lyttelton's appeal for help had arrived in his headquarters,[1] presenting him with an irritating distraction from the imminent drive on Montreal. For that operation he would need every unit at his disposal. But the treachery, as he saw it, of the Cherokees could not be ignored, and now he was framing the orders which would send Montgomery back to South Carolina with the best part of two regiments. The 'Royal' and Montgomery's own 77th, both Highland formations, were to produce a four-company battalion each, to be commanded by Majors Hamilton and James Grant respectively. To provide a coherent force of skirmishers, so necessary in Indian warfare, each regiment was to provide a company of light infantry, the pair to be brigaded under the elder of the two captains. A similar half-battalion of grenadiers provided a powerful reserve.[2]

He went on, spelling out the retribution he expected the expedition to inflict. 'With these four Corps', he told Montgomery, 'I am not in the least Doubt but you will Effectually Protect the colony and punish the Indians for their infamous breach of the peace, which they has so lately made ...'[3] Two weeks later, as the expedition and its transports were assembling at New York,[4] the commander-in-chief further unfolded his intentions. Montgomery was to wreak a swift and terrible vengeance upon the Cherokees 'by Destroying their Towns', the just 'punishment of those barbarian Savages for their Inhuman acts of Cruelty'.[5] The primary objective of the expedition was thus to be the pacification of the Cherokees by burning the settlements nearest to South Carolina. The direct relief of Fort Loudoun was not even mentioned.

For Amherst was preoccupied with the need for speed. He wanted Montgomery's 1373 seasoned regulars[6] back in the north in time for the summer campaign. For that reason the transports would wait in Charleston Harbour, ready to re-embark the men for the return voyage. On his march into the Cherokee country Montgomery must take live cattle to avoid the delays to be expected in assembling and moving a large waggon train.[7] Having crushed the Cherokees he was to march his whole force back to the waiting transports.

> ... [I]t is not my intention that You should remain with the
> Corps in South Carolina for any defensive Operations or
> that You are to Garrison any of the Forts on the Frontiers,
> unless some emergency occasions and that on such an
> Event, You Shall Judge it absolutely necessary for the good
> of His Majesty's Service.[8]

The resolution of the Cherokee war would thus depend upon the wider concerns of a distant commander-in-chief, and the decisions of a local commander restrained by his orders and already none too friendly to the citizens of South Carolina. The promotion of Grant to lieutenant-colonel by brevet on 8 March, and his simultaneous appointment as Montgomery's second-in-command,[9] ensured that no accident could put the expedition into the hands of a provincial officer. Both men had had a very unhappy experience of colonists and colonial politics during the quartering dispute. By contrast Grant had rather enjoyed meeting the Cherokees in Virginia in 1758. Moreover, by the time he and Montgomery were ordered to South Carolina both officers must have been aware of the growing anxiety in London to safeguard Indian lands. Finally, there was their old association with Bouquet, who had recently rejected the Ohio Company's bribes at Fort Pitt. There is no documentary evidence that he was in direct contact with either after 1758, or that they knew of the company's approach from other sources. But it is difficult to believe that the three did not share some common attitudes which were encouraged by the orders from London.

Grant turned out to be more opinionated than Montgomery, more devious, and even less sympathetic to colonial war aims. As early as 1758 Grant had been the linchpin of the then young and in-experienced Highlanders; after his capture Forbes had feared they would disintegrate, unless their major was speedily exchanged.[10] Because he was also much more robust of health, and because Montgomery liked to delegate authority to his able friend, Grant's mind gradually became the directing force behind operations in the

[marginalia: Bad Experiences During the Quartering Dispute with Colonial Officials. Knew of the general feeling in London of the need to protect Indian lands.]

south. While in South Carolina Grant quickly came to believe that the Cherokees were too frightened to make peace, and that the colonists did not want it. Historians have so far left it at that: Grant was a humane man who had to forsake his personal feelings for the sake of duty. Even Grant's recent biographer, while noting his sympathy for the Cherokees, makes no attempt to connect it to his behaviour.[11] Yet the very same sources, principally Grant's own papers at Ballindalloch Castle in Scotland and the Amherst Papers in the Public Record Office, show that this connection is inescapable. *(Connection b/t sympathy + behaviour.)*

The little convoy of five transports and one warship[12] dropped anchor in Charleston harbour on 1 April. Montgomery and Grant landed at once and went straight to Lyttelton. Here they found a situation which confirmed all of their prejudices against colonial authorities. For neither Lyttelton nor Bull would take the responsibility of organizing supplies of bread, cattle and waggons.[13] 'The Governor ready to embark', Grant told Amherst, 'had for some time declined Business & the Lieut-Governor would not act, while the other continued in the Province.'[14] Although Lyttelton had advertised for waggons, he had not set a price; on top of that there was smallpox in the town, so that the farmers and planters who could have supplied carriages dared have no contact with Charleston. Nor had Lyttelton arranged for the impressment of waggons, as he had done for his own expedition. Grant thrust a model warrant under the governor's nose, but Lyttelton objected that his powers to impress for the militia did not extend to regulars. Nor would he approach the Commons House of Assembly to authorize conscriptions and payments.[15] There were therefore no waggons and little prospect of getting any, even when Grant, by Montgomery's order, told the contractors to offer cash for both carts and cattle.[16] The truth was that Lyttelton would not assist an expedition which he did not control. He left for Jamaica on 5 April, having done nothing to resolve a problem largely of his own making.

Montgomery prudently landed his men seven miles from town and Grant marched them the additional thirty-odd miles to Monk's Corner, high up the Cooper River. Here was plentiful fresh water, a shady wood and a healthy camp; here too, schooners could bring cargoes of bread and flour from the transports. But the troops could not move without waggons and cattle, and even at Monk's Corner none of the country people would come near them. Montgomery therefore ordered Grant back to Charleston to help him extract the necessary supplies from the civil authorities.[17]

Grant hammered away at the unfortunate Bull, the councillors, and members of the Commons, pointing out that they would be responsible if the expedition had to be delayed or abandoned.[18] This threat to go back to New York was not taken seriously at first, for when the Commons finally met on 16 April the Bill which the lieutenant-governor laid before it was thrown out. Thereupon Grant persuaded Bull to repeat Montgomery's threat to abandon the province. That did the trick: the Bill was given a second reading and Grant, well pleased with himself, took a schooner back to the camp. On 18 April the Bill passed the Commons.[19] On 23 April the little army marched from Monk's Corner at last; after nine days of slogging through deep sand they reached the Congarees, where they waited a further 17 days for their waggons to bring up more provisions from 'the Corner'. On the morning of 23 May, almost exactly a month after setting out, they reached Ninety Six.[20]

Transport was not the only reason Montgomery had to curse 'the Shameful backwardness of this Province in every Particular; tho' I must do the Lt. Govr. the Justice to say that he seems desirous to promote the Service as Much as [is] in his Power'.[21] There was still the matter of provincial forces to reinforce the regulars. The provincials and Rangers so far raised were a rag-tag collection, including 'not a single man that is of any consequence in the Province'.[22] The Provincial Regiment, supposed to be 1000 strong, 'consisted of about eighty' men, half of them useless and under officers inclined to desert for lack of pay.[23] Three-quarters of the 400 Rangers would be essential as scouts and to drive the cattle, 'which in this Country are as Wild as Deer', but they were totally without discipline.[24] Yet Bull and the Commons were not prepared to let him have even these. The lieutenant-governor told the Board of Trade that he would allow Montgomery 200 provincials out of the notional 1000, but he asked Montgomery to detach a lieutenant and 30 rank and file to man one of the lesser frontier forts. Nor would he overrule James Francis' demand that the Ninety Six garrison should be left intact. As for the Rangers, Montgomery could have only 200.[25]

His reasoning was simple and familiar: South Carolina was a slave colony in which the blacks far outnumbered the whites, and their proportion of able-bodied males was far higher still. 'Thus our Strength is lessened by an interior Enemy.'[26] Beyond that peril lay the very real danger of a Creek war. The treaty signed by Atkin and the Albama Creeks on 10 October 1759 had been balanced by the famous attempt on the Superintendent's life, and the general pledges of neutrality given to him on 27 March 1760 only thinly veiled the deep divisions within that nation.[27] Two of the most important war leaders, the Gun Merchant and the Mortar, remained hostile and troublesome for some time.[28] Bull took good care to keep in touch with the Creeks on his own account,[29] notwithstanding which there were continual alarms.[30] There were only a few Savannah River Chickasaws and Catawbas, Georgia was weak, and North Carolina seemed unlikely to help at all.[31] Thus between slaves and Creeks, Montgomery was lucky to get the 37 Catawba scouts Bull sent up from Charleston.[32] '[S]uch a Set of People', exploded Montgomery, 'I never saw; tis my opinion that if there were no troops in the Country that a dozen of Indians might go to Charles Town; tho' in Conversation they are for putting all the Cherokees to Death, or Making Slaves of them.'[33]

In the circumstances it is not surprising that Montgomery and Grant wanted to make peace, not war. As early as 17 April Grant had expressed the opinion that the Indians, far from wishing to serve the interests of the French, were looking for an honourable way of making peace.

[T]he Indians have of late had some conversation with the Garrison [of Fort Prince George] ... and from what I can learn I fancy many of them are sory [sic] for what has happened and I make no Doubt but they will be glad to come into Terms when they find that there is a body of Troops upon their March, tho' whatever Dispositions they may have to peace, 'tis a Measure which would by no means be acceptable to the greatest part of this Province.[34]

Certainly there were signs that the war faction was weakening. Occonostota had gone hunting in mid-March, thus prudently disassociating himself from Ostenaca's attempt on Fort Loudoun. On the Tennessee River about 100 miles below the fort he had met a white man named McCormick, an escapee from northern Indians, and brought him safely in on 28 March. By 5 April the beleaguered garrison were admitting Cherokee emissaries in groups of three to parley.[35] At Fort Prince George, Tistoe of Keowee was acting as go-between for Seroweh and for Standing Turkey himself.[36] Tistoe, one of Lyttelton's victims of 1759, was displaying a remarkably tenacious commitment to peace.

Tistoe raised the matter of exchanging those of Lyttelton's hostages still held in Charleston. Miln very properly referred the question to Bull, but kept discussions open by promising to press the lieutenant-governor to agree. Meanwhile he gave the Cherokees the names of the nine survivors.[37] It was clear that the Indians were also in contact with the northern nations friendly to the French – messengers had set out on 5 April – and with the French at New Orleans,[38] so that Bull suspected 'that they only intend to amuse us till they can learn the Success of their several Embassies, and know what part the Creeks will take in this War'.[39] Nevertheless, he thought the genocide being demanded in Charleston both dangerous and abhorrent. Even if the Cherokees could be 'quite extirpated' or driven out of their lands, the whole South Carolina frontier would be open to raiders from further afield. Worse, their remote but fertile mountain valleys could become refuges for communities of runaway slaves, like the Maroons of Jamaica.[40] Force would certainly be necessary, but its end should be a peace based upon restored trust. Bull claimed he had opposed Lyttelton's treatment of the Cherokee delegation in 1759, and urged Grant to give the nation 'hopes that we do not intend to extirpate or exterminate them, but only chastise the most guilty, & then restore to them Peace and Trade as formerly'.[41] By mid-May the lieutenant-governor and the military commanders could at least hope for an early and moderate peace.

Trust and hope were alike exploded by Ensign Miln, in a single act of folly hardly less great than Lyttelton's. During the talks at Fort Prince George the Cherokees (so Miln said later) had promised to give up one of their white captives. On 7 May Tistoe and the Wolf of Keowee appeared on the Keowee side of the river with 200 other Cherokees, but no white man. Miln let the two leaders and six other headmen into the fort and berated them as liars. If the promised prisoner was not delivered next day, he said, the negotiations would be at an end. Miln seems to have taken their failure as a personal affront – 'trifling' with him, he called it – and when the Cherokees made some disparaging allusion to his youth he lost his dignity completely. The Cherokees solemnly promised to discuss his demand that night at Sugar Town, but Miln was sure he was being laughed at. Discomfited, he could think only of revenge. When the Cherokees accepted his invitation to dinner he secretly stood the whole garrison to arms. A marquee was pitched outside the fort and when the Indians were safely seated armed troops rushed in and seized them. Eight warriors and a little girl were bundled into the fort and tied up. The Wolf was released to carry a dreadful message to Standing Turkey: if the Cherokees did not give up their white hostages there would be another massacre at Fort Prince George.[42]

Miln's news reached Montgomery and Grant at the Congarees six days later. They were furious. Grant quickly drafted two letters. The first, which went to Bull, pointed out that 'publick Faith should not be broke even with Savages'; while Miln's action had been overzealous rather than malicious, it would have destroyed any confidence the Indians might have had in the British. The chances of getting them to accept and adhere to treaties were now much reduced. The second, which went out over Montgomery's signature, gave Miln a stinging rebuke and ordered him to neither mistreat nor exchange the prisoners until the army arrived.[43] Bull, confronted with the unpleasant prospect of having to dismiss Miln for locking up Indians, rushed to temporize. He agreed with Grant (and Grotius) that 'faith was the sweet Bond of Human things' and that the 'reputation of Faith is sacred between Enemies'; otherwise peace would be impossible except through outright victory. 'Faith is to be kept with Slaves and even with those that are perfidious', just as the Romans had kept their word to the treacherous Carthaginians. But surely the damage was not as great as Grant and Montgomery feared: they could still look to 'the moderate Men in the Cherokee nation, among whom we still have friends, besides the Little Carpenter, Cesar and the good old warrior of Estatoe'. Miln was young and inexperienced and should be excused.[44]

The soldiers were not impressed. In their view the Old Warrior had genuinely tried to secure a peace, and Miln had made that peace impossible.[45] Though prepared to accept that Bull was doing his best, Montgomery was more than ever convinced that the Cherokees had been both abused and misrepresented. Probably he had been lectured on the subject by Grant, for he expressed his feelings to Amherst in words very similar to those used by his deputy in April. '[T]hose Indians are Rogues as they all are', he wrote from Ninety-Six, 'but I fancy they have sometimes been hardly dealt by, and if they could tell their own story I doubt Much if they are so much to blame as has been Represented by the People of this Province.' The Cherokees were, he added, 'much divided Amongst themselves Many of them Sorry for What has happened'.[46]

That raised the question of the peace terms which would now have to be imposed rather than agreed, and who was to impose them. Bull insisted that South Carolina alone should decide, not the intercolonial commission proposed by Fauquier of Virginia.[47] He had little choice for otherwise he would have had to explain to the Commons why South Carolina's traditional primacy in Cherokee affairs had been abandoned. That was why he went out of his way to get Amherst's support on this point.[48] Amherst was perfectly prepared to recognize South Carolina's claims, largely to keep the army out of embarrassing political entanglements. Late in April James Glen, itching to meddle in Cherokee affairs again, had written from Philadelphia to offer his services as intermediary.[49] Although, or perhaps because, Glen pressed his claim as an expert and stressed the Cherokees' virtues, Amherst rejected the offer, 'as I do not think that an accommodation with the Indians is of my Department, but that it lays with the Legislature of the Province of South Carolina'.[50] Both he and Bull would have accepted Edmond Atkin as South Carolina's agent, but Atkin had not returned to Charleston until the end of March. There he stayed on various pretexts, perhaps preoccupied with his penchant for good dinners,[51] or perhaps by ill health.[52] He was still in Charleston on 12 May[53] even though he had promised to meet King Hagler of the Catawbas first at Fort Moore, then in the Catawba country, and again at the Congarees by 1 May.[54] When the warriors met Montgomery at the Congarees on 4 May and found Atkin had still not come, Hagler was not amused.[55] Nor were Montgomery and Grant. 'I don't understand Indian affairs', Grant told him; 'you must come to talk to them.' After that, he added acidly, Atkin could go back to Charleston to avoid a fatiguing and disagreeable campaign.[56] Suitably stung,[57] Atkin left for the Congarees on or just after 15 May,[58] but the lieutenant-governor had already decided to give Grant and Montgomery 'proper powers' to conclude a peace. This would also ensure that Bull's claim to primacy in these matters was recognized, and prevent the Superintendency from acquiring an independent authority. 'I do not see', he wrote, 'that Mr. Atkin has any such [treaty making powers] by his Commission or otherwise'.[59] Thus the two soldiers found themselves in possession of a diplomatic role which their own commander-in-chief would have denied them, but which circumstances made almost inevitable.

These powers could not be exercised, however, until South Carolina had determined its basic demands. But Bull was very slow in formulating them. His problem was the vengeance mania in Charleston, which he abhorred but found very difficult to resist. He must have known that the blood lust had even infected his power base[60] in the Council, and avoided consulting his advisers on the subject for as long as possible. Pressed by Montgomery, he would only offer a list of the 16 'Chief Malefactors and Incendiaries'.[61] When he finally went to the Council on 24 May, when Montgomery was already at Ninety Six and about to attack Keowee, it was only to obtain its ratification of the harsh proposals[62] which he had sent up to Montgomery (significantly not to Atkin) the previous day.[63] Fifteen of 'the principal Incendiaries', including Seroweh, must be executed by the Cherokees, or handed over for execution, five hostages to be named by Bull – all sons of leading headmen, 'not under 20 years of age' – must be given up to be kept at Charleston against future good behaviour. These young men would be exchanged for others after a year, and a committee of up to five headmen would be allowed to visit them every six months. Only when the executions had been carried out and the first batch of hostages handed over should Montgomery leave the Cherokee country. All prisoners in Cherokee hands, black or white, and all Frenchmen, were to be given up and all scalping parties called in. When all this had been done a Cherokee delegation 40 strong might visit Charleston to ratify the treaty. Only after ratification of this treaty would trade be resumed.[64]

Bull, who had opposed Lyttelton's hostage taking in 1759, could have had no illusions about the likely Cherokee response to this demand for more. The executions clause was even worse. Bull's eulogistic biographer is almost certainly right when he argues that he never expected the Cherokees to accept. As this writer points out, when it came to the means of imposing the terms, Bull drew the line at burning the Indians' crops to threaten them with starvation.[65] No doubt he expected the terms to be ameliorated during the negotiations. But the argument is less convincing when it asserts that Bull himself would have taken charge of the amelioration, as (the argument goes on) he was to do in fact after Grant's successful campaign the next year. In 1761, as we shall see in the next chapter, Bull allowed Grant to water down his proposals and then tried to abandon him when Commons proved awkward. There is no reason to suppose that he would have been braver in 1760. The very letter in which he proposed these terms was the one in which he tried to excuse Miln,[66] in order to avoid a row with the Councillors over hostage taking. He was also a little too anxious to invite Montgomery to put his name to the preliminaries, and to keep the whole business quiet. Montgomery was asked to convey the terms to Atkin, 'whose Secrecy is to be relied upon, and in whose Hands I shall place the Execution of the Treaty in my name on the behalf of His Majesty, which you will also I presume chuse to sign as the Commander of His Majesty's Forces.'[67] Significantly, Montgomery was also asked to send proposals for additional terms by express. Bull had weakened Atkin's position by explicitly involving Montgomery, asserted his own supreme authority over Indian affairs, and prepared to blame his agents for any weakening of the original terms.

Whatever Bull's intentions may have been, Montgomery now had very considerable powers. He had Amherst's original licence to leave

South Carolina as soon as possible with his entire force, the very authority he and Grant had used to bully the Commons in April, and which Montgomery was now yearning to use in earnest. From Ninety Six he promised Amherst that he would expedite the campaign, being 'not a little desirous to Return to the Northwards where all of us wish to be Most Heartily'.[68] That wish, and his open sympathy for the Cherokees certainly coloured Montgomery's notion of the degree of force he would have to use. He hoped to get up to Fort Prince George without resistance, after which he would burn one or two towns and so bring the Cherokees to terms. He expected that the treaty he had in mind, which would punish only the most guilty, would 'by no Means be Acceptable to the Majority of the Province'.[69] Nevertheless he would conclude it and leave the vicious and obstructive South Carolinians behind.[70] Bull's own terms were already on their way, but Montgomery was in no mood to observe them religiously. Rather he was likely to use Bull's explicit permission to conduct the preliminary talks to impose terms of his own.

There were also powerful military arguments against a protracted campaign. The Cherokee mountains were high and formidable, with passes 'like those of the Alps'.[71] Getting supplies up to Fort Prince George was proving difficult enough, with a desperate shortage of draught bullocks and healthy cattle,[72] but beyond there they would have to depend on packhorses and live cattle alone. Bull had suggested that 30 days' campaigning would require 300 horses, each carrying 150 lb of bread and flour.[73] Bull had also suggested a route from Keowee to Fort Loudoun[74] and supplied a list of guides,[75] but there were no reliable maps. This was all the more serious, because the traders who were to be the guides knew only the main paths.[76] Bull sent up a sketch map[77] but the dangers were obvious. A prudent commander – and Montgomery was certainly one – would think twice before risking his whole force in such a country.

In fact Bull himself had long assumed that the best – perhaps the only – hope for Fort Loudoun must lie with a thrust from Virginia. Early in May he considered abandoning the fort to secure peace, and rejected it because it would open a door to the French.[78] By 6 May he had written to Fauquier urging him to march swiftly on Fort Loudoun by the inland river valleys, a route offering no difficult passes, while the hostile Cherokees were busy watching Montgomery.[79] Fauquier was not encouraging. He was sure that the Virginian Assembly would vote the £32 000 needed to add 700 men to the 300 already serving on the Cherokee frontier, and he was prepared to use those men even if

North Carolina offered nothing at all. But he feared that Fort Loudoun would fall before he could raise and march the Virginian force down the Holston River. If the fort did fall he would disband his Virginian provincials unless Bull sent him a clear plan of action concerted with Montgomery.[80] At a time when Fort Loudoun garrison was reduced to a pint of corn per man per day and not expected to survive beyond 16 June,[81] this was depressing news. The best Bull could do was to send up two brave messengers with some paint and ribbons, which the Indian women connected with the garrison might be able to exchange for food.[82] Meanwhile there was nothing for it but to hope that Fauquier's expedition would be in time,[83] or that Montgomery, by burning a few of the Lower Towns, would divert the Cherokees[84] or even compel them to a peace.

On 28 May Montgomery marched from Ninety Six. Four days and over 80 miles later, at 11 o'clock in the morning, the column reached the Twelve Mile River a dozen miles below Keowee: a 'very Difficult Pass',[85] where the young men had wanted to ambush Lyttelton in November. To everyone's surprise there was no opposition at all as the troops struggled through the water and up the steep and slippery bank. Until 4 p.m. teams of soldiers toiled to push the waggons up the muddy slopes and still no Indians appeared.[86] The speed of the advance had taken the hostile warriors by surprise and Montgomery meant to keep his advantage. His most obvious course was to thrust straight for Keowee and Fort Prince George next day. Instead he and Grant gave their exhausted men only a brief rest before falling them in at 8 p.m. Leaving their tents standing, they marched into the gathering dark, not on Keowee but for 'the most considerable and Distant of the Cherokee Towns in the lower Nation': Estatoe.[87] (Map 6)

But in night marches the best laid plans often go astray. After miles of silent marching, with no sound but the crunching of boots on the path, and nothing to be seen but the black silhouettes of trees, scouts in front heard a dog bark. Then one of the guides found a few houses about a quarter of a mile from the path.[88] They had stumbled across Little Keowee. Montgomery detached a light infantry company of the Royal with orders to surround the houses and attack with bayonets only. All the men were to be killed, but women and children were not to be touched.[89]

But unknown to the soldiers a war party passing the night in the settlement was camped outside the houses. Some of these warriors were awake, saw the redcoats closing in, and opened fire. The light infantry fired back and charged. Almost all the men in and about the houses

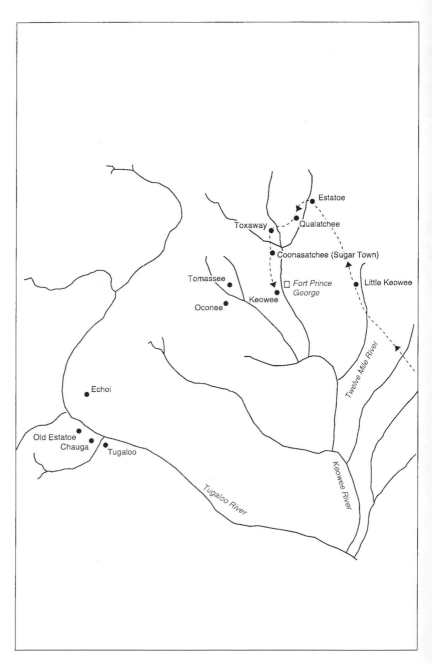

Map 6   Montgomery's route through the Lower Towns, 1760

were killed with bayonets, and some women and children died too before the officers could regain control.[90] Grant, shocked by the slaughter, 'could not help pitying them a little';[91] Montgomery was dismayed that 'Some [of the women and children] could Not be Saved'.[92] But there was no pause as the column pressed on to Estatoe and attacked in the early morning. Most of the Cherokees had fled, leaving their beds and breakfasts still warm; but ten or twelve stragglers were killed as they ran for the woods, and more were burnt as the houses went up in flames. The army marched on to burn Toxaway and Qualatchee.[93] So terrible was the destruction that they would have spared the last – Sugar Town – but for finding the mutilated and tortured corpse of a man killed that morning. So Wawatchee's Coonasatchee went up in flames.[94] In all the Cherokees had lost 60 to 80 dead and 40 men, women and children taken prisoner. Their dreadful work completed the troops stumbled on to Fort Prince George, having marched 60 miles without sleep.[95]

The carnage and havoc had been considerable by any standards, and Grant and Montgomery – both tough warriors well seasoned to the brutalities of North American warfare – were awed by what they had done. Montgomery described Estatoe and Sugar Town as 'Towns more considerable than could be imagined, their Houses Neat and Convenient and Well Provided with every necessary of life'.[96] Grant, to whom the ailing Montgomery had now delegated operational responsibilities as well as the task of communicating with Bull,[97] thought the Cherokees' punishment 'pretty severe'.[98] Though Montgomery was pleased with his men's performance, and especially with Grant's,[99] neither man could allow himself a single note of triumph. They would countenance no more destruction. Distant Tugaloo, Oconee and Tomassee remained untouched and – as Bull had wished, but to the chagrin of at least one Fort Prince George officer later on – all the Lower Towns' crops were left alone.[100]

Montgomery and Grant had firmly decided to go no further, and certainly not to attempt to reach Fort Loudoun. Grant thought that the Cherokees might easily ambush them if they tried, and that in any case the Indians had been so roughly handled already that they would quickly make peace.

> In my own opinion it is next to impossible for us to think of proceeding over the Mountains, and if they had not been surprised, the very Country we have just been in was unpracticable, if they had Spirit, which I much doubt of ...

The correction you'll allow has been pretty severe, I dare say the whole nation will readily come into terms, and will not be very fond of breaking them and I think peace with them is a very desirable event for this province.[101]

Montgomery agreed in every particular, and in almost the same words, including the desirability of peace for South Carolina.

From the very best Accounts I have been Able to Pick up I find, tis Almost impossible to proceed over the Mountains, and indeed it does not appear to be necessary in the Present situation of *Affairs*, there can be no great advantage in Continuing a War against those Savages. [T]he Lower Cherokees who were the Most Guilty have been sufficiently Corrected for their Insolence and if a peace can be made with the Whole I think, tis the best thing which can happen to this province.[102]

The two soldiers had moved with the logic of their orders, military reality and their own humane instincts, from the conduct of a campaign to the determination of Indian policy. Miln's 'improperly confined' hostages were released in stages and Tistoe and the Wolf were to convey a double-edged message to the nation: peace talks could be begun if Attakullakulla came down to conduct them, and if Fort Loudoun was given food. But if he did not come within a few days 'he may expect to see his Towns in Ashes – A threat by the Way we could hardly Put in Execution, but I dare say it will have the Desired Effect in their Present Consternation'.[103] Grant and Montgomery had decided to substitute bluff for force, which meant that the proposed peace terms might have to be weakened in the interests of a quick settlement and an early return to New York.

These implications disconcerted both Bull in Charleston, and Amherst in the middle of his march to Lake Champlain and Montreal. Bull, though quite prepared to support the negotiations, was certain that the colonists would fail to see the virtues of an early peace; he carefully deleted the decision not to cross the mountains before giving Grant's letter to the *South Carolina Gazette*.[104] Amherst had been sufficiently alarmed by Montgomery's despatch from Ninety Six to pen him a curt order to stay out of colonial politics. 'You must not think of Coming away till you have most Effectually punished these Scoundrel Indians', he had written. Once the Cherokees had been so crippled as to be no danger to South Carolina ever again a treaty might be made, but only by the colonial legislature, 'as my Intentions are not to Interfere in their Treaties, and so much I have said to the Lt. Governor'.[105] When he received the Fort Prince George letter he was careful to praise both Montgomery and Grant, and to approve of the approach to Attakullakulla. But Amherst once again insisted that peace was a matter for the South Carolina assembly alone, and that there could be no such peace until the Cherokees had been severely punished. 'This, indeed', he concluded, 'is the only method of treating Indians.'[106] He was too late. Before either of his letters could arrive in South Carolina Montgomery's negotiations had failed, the first 'battle' of Etchoe had been fought, and the expedition was on its way down to Charleston: without a treaty.

The negotiations began promisingly enough. When Bull's peace proposals arrived Montgomery made it clear that he would not adhere to them. Seroweh must be captured dead or alive, but Montgomery could see no advantage in demanding the others. The deaths of Lyttelton's captives had put the British into an untenable position when it came to demanding executions. As for demanding further hostages, that was the worst possible way to secure a peace; the Indians could not distinguish between hostages and slaves, and Lyttelton's hostage taking had caused the renewal of the war. Moreover the release of prisoners must be reciprocal, not confined to the Cherokee side. Finally, Miln must go. He knew himself that the Cherokees detested him and would kill him sooner or later, treaty or no treaty, and wanted to be relieved. To avoid future errors he should be replaced by Lachlan McIntosh, an ensign in the Carolina Independents whom the Cherokees knew and liked.[107] Bull, who was already contemplating sending McIntosh up from Fort Moore 'as soon as it is safe to travel through the Woods',[108] wanted to go further and withdraw Bell.

I believe it would be prudent to remove Mr. Bell from Fort Prince George on the settling of the peace, as his Behaviour was excepted against by the Indians last October, when Tistoe was in the Council Chamber, of which the Governor would take no notice.[109]

He also fell obligingly into line on the question of hostages, and made a considerable concession over the executions, as he had probably always intended. He certainly tried to give the impression that his views had been long thought out, and did not represent a sudden change of mind. Indeed, in this matter, as in the removal of Bell, he went out of his way to show his disapproval of Lyttelton's policies.

> I believe there will be great difficulty in obtaining, and little security in keeping the Hostages, for as they have no national Honor, or Governing Families from whence to take them, I fear that the confinement of Hostages will only irritate those, who are related to them, and prove no manner of Check to those who are not. I should therefore think upon the whole this article might be relaxed or omitted, and that immediate execution of some of the principal Delinquents by their own People, if they cannot deliver them up to our for our executioners, would be the most likely method of putting an End to the General fear of punishment ... [Even then it would be some time before the resentment of surviving Cherokee relations would subside]. This is not Cherokee nature only, it has been known in Italian quarrels to the third and fourth Generation. These public examples with the surrendering up of all prisoners of whatever complexion, and delivering up our Enemies the French, I think will be very sufficient preliminaries whereupon to establish a lasting peace ...[110]

While imposing their policy upon the willing lieutenant-governor, Montgomery and Grant had begun their approaches to the Cherokees. The hostages were released, Tistoe and the Wolf were sent into the nation, and the message to Attakullakulla via Demeré dispatched. At first there were some signs, despite the continued activity of scalping parties,[111] that their overtures might be accepted. From Grant's friend John Stuart at Fort Loudoun came confirmation of the dire effects of Miln's treachery. '[A]ll our Sham Friendship with the Indians has vanished', he wrote. 'Irritated to the highest degree at the seizure of Tistoe by Mr. Mills [sic], they determined to be avenged on us.'[112] There was therefore some reason for the soldiers to hope, with Bull,[113] that the release of those prisoners would relieve hostility and engender trust. A fortnight later Bull heard more of the conduct of Coytmore, Miln and Bell, though his news did not reach Keowee until the negotiations had failed. Two of Lyttelton's prisoners, still in irons in the Charleston barracks, told him that they had been provoked into war by officers in the garrison,[114] which gave greater urgency to the proposals to remove the two surviving culprits. Better still, Attakullakulla really was living at Fort Loudoun,[115] as had previously been reported.[116] Surely he would come down with his friend Stuart, whom Bull gave leave to be absent from the fort,[117] to negotiate a lasting peace.

Three weeks went by and no Cherokee deputies appeared, not even the Carpenter. Attakullakulla's return and his residence in Fort Loudoun were genuine marks of his commitment to the cause of peace with the British. But they were not, as Bull, Grant and Montgomery seem to have believed, proof of the reviving fortunes of the peace party. Grant had heard of the taunts he had to endure from the warriors besieging the fort on 3 April, when Lieutenant Maurice Anderson and a packhorseman called Thomas Smith had been killed.[118] But they had too easily assumed that the threat of the approaching army, the actual destruction of the Lower Towns, and the release of Miln's prisoners, would have produced a more flexible frame of mind. On the contrary, Miln's action had caused deep bitterness that required revenge almost as much as the deaths on 16 February. Tistoe and the Wolf, being Miln's principal victims, did not make enthusiastic peacemakers. Worse than their thirst for revenge was the fear of another delegation receiving similar treatment. Unknown to the soldiers the messengers' fears had been worked on by one of Montgomery's own guides, a trader named Welsh. When the pair had gone into the nation they had carried with them not only Montgomery's Talk, but Welsh's warning that it was a trap.[119] It may even be that renegade traders from Georgia were still playing upon Cherokee fears to keep the war going and Carolina traders out of the market. Finally, none of the three British leaders appreciated that Attakullakulla could not commit his people to a peace without a genuine consensus of the nation behind him. Used to a political culture in which the influence of great men was crucial, even Bull found this point difficult to grasp. Whatever the actual balance of causes no deputies came. By 23 June Montgomery and Grant were forced to admit that though some headmen wanted to treat 'the Whole are Afraid to trust us'.[120] They could no longer avoid further action and the army was busy making flour bags from 'Waggon Clothes and Soldiers' Tents' and 'Pack Saddles of Bear Skins'.[121] The march against the Middle Settlements was to begin the next day.[122]

Even now they had no intention of crossing the mountains to the Overhill country. The army, moving without tents or baggage and dependent upon their packhorses for food, could neither sustain a long campaign nor resupply Fort Loudoun. Relief would have to come from the Virginians or not at all. Yet with the Lower Cherokees fled, the Middle Settlements short of ammunition, and the Overhills short of food for the refugees amongst them, one more push might bring the war to an end. That could not come too soon for Montgomery. 'I long', he said, 'to get out of this Indian War and to return to the Army.'[123] It is difficult to avoid the conclusion that Montgomery intended no more than a swift raid into the mountains, and if that did not quickly produce peace, he would retire to the coast.

On 24 June the army marched on Etchoe (Map 1), the nearest of the Middle Settlements. Montgomery was awestruck by the ruggedness of the mountains and of the passes which, he thought, could have been defended by a mere 200 warriors.[124] The Cherokees did not disappoint him: they were gathering in a defile six miles from Etchoe[125] at a place Adair calls 'Crow's Creek'.[126] It was an ideal place for an ambush. On one side rose a high mountain, on the other low hills. The narrow valley between was bisected by a river with steep muddy banks and choked with dense bushes and trees. Here, where it was impossible to see more than ten feet ahead, the soldiers might be caught like Braddock's men: hemmed in and unable to use their superior firepower.[127] How large the Cherokee force was is unclear, but it must have been considerable. According to prisoners later questioned through interpreters, nearly all the men from the Lower and Middle Settlements (in which they may have included the Valley towns) were there, with some Overhills, and a few Choctaws and Creeks.[128] Anger and the confidence born of ignorance – none of them had fought large formations of British regulars before – had made them ambitious: for their plan was nothing less than to meet Montgomery head on in the narrow wooded pass and bring him to an annihilating halt. Shortly after eight o'clock on Friday 27 June the British vanguard ran straight into them.

All was quiet as the British column approached the defile and Montgomery sent a Ranger company forward to comb the thickets. The hidden Cherokee gun men opened fire, driving in the scouts and killing Captain Morrison their commander. Morrison's men had fled even before he fell. Montgomery sent his light infantry and grenadiers forward to support the fleeing Rangers, and a sharp struggle for the ravine ensued. In the first charge a light infantry captain was shot down, a surgeon attempting to help him was badly hit, and two soldiers died trying to recover his body. Here the undergrowth was thick and the Cherokees so well concealed that only their own firing betrayed their positions. The fighting became hand to hand. Unseen Indians hurled abuse in English at the troops, and everywhere Seroweh could be heard, urging his men to stand their ground. The Royal Scots reeled back into the open ground, still under heavy fire. A few of the warriors had rifles which greatly outranged the soldiers' muskets, and the grenadiers' habit of firing by platoons hampered their response. It was some minutes before they could reform and halt the Cherokee counter-attack.[129]

But Montgomery had now extended his line, pushing the rearward companies of Highlanders out to the left and the Royals to the right. Finding their right turned and their retreat threatened, the Cherokees fell back leftwards – straight into the arms of the Royals. After a sharp fight the Indians rapidly retreated to a rise just out of reach of the advancing British. Having thrust his opponents aside, Montgomery ordered his battalions to press on through the pass to Etchoe. Seeing this movement the Cherokees slipped away behind their hill and raced to warn the town.[130] But they had not given up. Montgomery's advance had brought his vulnerable supply train into the ravine. A sudden attack on the packhorse and cattle train in the rear threatened to cripple the army completely, and only after some anxious minutes was it driven off.[131]

Perhaps 50 Cherokees and 21 British soldiers had died in this engagement and nearly 60 of Montgomery's men were wounded.[132] The Cherokees had fought valiantly and had caused Montgomery twice the losses that Amherst sustained that season in his advance from Oswego to Montreal.[133] While far from scoring the brilliant tactical success depicted by Fortescue, Montgomery certainly had not suffered the 'disaster' painted by Hatley.[134] The road to Etchoe lay open and the British destroyed the town next day, though they had suffered dearly for it.

Montgomery now had to decide what to do next. Etchoe had been evacuated by the Cherokees just as the British arrived; they had removed their possessions (but not their food) already 'for fear of Accidents'.[135] It was painfully obvious that the destruction of this one town could not bring the Cherokees to their knees, and perhaps not even burning all the Middle Settlements would do so. 'The destroying of an Indian Town when the Savages have time to carry off their Effects is a Matter of no great consequence', he told Amherst. '[T]his one cost us rather too Dear ...'[136] Each town burned would cost him more heavy losses for no noticeable effect. Even now he was burdened with 55 wounded who could be neither sent back nor abandoned, and who must therefore be carried in litters supported by packhorses. That meant the destruction of a considerable quantity of flour,[137] which in turn meant a severely circumscribed radius of operations. If further proof were needed of the likely scale of Cherokee resistance, it was provided by the handful of Cherokee riflemen who began firing into the camp at extreme range; a sortie was needed to drive them away.[138] Montgomery really had no choice but to withdraw to Fort Prince George.

As we have seen already, the question of relieving Fort Loudoun was not at issue, and Alden is wide of the mark when he suggests that a more determined commander would have won through.[139] Similarly Hatley is wrong to suggest that Montgomery's twin objectives were the 'relieving of Fort Loudoun and the scouring of the Cherokee towns'.[140] Adair and Robinson correctly stress both the huge advantages given to the defenders by the mountains and Montgomery's logistical problems.[141] But Weir is considerably nearer to the truth when he traces Montgomery's attitudes back to the quartering dispute and suggests that the combat at Crow's Creek justified a 'decision for which he had been seeking an excuse since coming to South Carolina'.[142] He is also right to place rather less emphasis upon Montgomery's orders to return as quickly as possible to the north;[143] as we have seen, Montgomery needed no urging on this point. However, Montgomery's and Grant's preference for Cherokees over colonists was surely the most important factor. No mere negative prejudice generated by dislike of South Carolinians, this preference arose from the disturbing suspicion that their own cause was unjust. All their manoeuvres so far had been intended to bring the Cherokees to the conference table by using the least possible degree of force, and once there to present them with terms which they could genuinely accept. Etchoe had demonstrated their failure. On 30 June the retreat began.[144]

Montgomery started his march at night to get clear of the most dangerous passes before the Cherokees could react. But the warriors allowed him no respite. No less than three harassing attacks were beaten off by his flankers, who managed to surprise one party in camp.[145] Even the loss of a dozen men in these skirmishes did not deter the Indians,[146] who seem to have dogged the troops all the way to Fort Prince George. Here a saddened but unrepentant Montgomery spent two days resupplying the fort, before beginning his long-awaited march to the coast. The surviving settlements were still untouched, and everywhere in the Lower Towns the corn stood ripening in the fields.

The retreat of British troops in the face of hostile Indians caused a stir even in London. The South Carolina merchants there often heard news from the colony before Whitehall, due to merchant captains' habit of dropping into their masters' coffee house en route to the government offices.[147] For no very clear reason the merchants became very agitated, although there was never any prospect of the Cherokees laying waste the tidewater rice plantations or raiding Charleston, though perhaps those with creditors in the Cherokee trade had reason to wish for a speedy conclusion. Someone, probably Halifax at the Board of Trade, saw fit to mention the rumour to Pitt; he added that the papers to hand did not refer to the affair at all, 'which gives hopes that the Carolina news is not true'.[148] If Montgomery's retreat could make such an impact in the imperial capital, the consternation in Charleston may be imagined. Hatley points out that the good citizens saw the withdrawal as yet another subordination of South Carolina's needs to the demands of the northern colonies and of imperial strategy.[149] Bull, whose own procrastination in getting rid of Miln[150] had played its part in the failure, was horrified.

Bull received the bad news in a letter written by Grant from Keowee on 3 July.[151] He at once published the letter and laid it before the Council and Commons.[152] There was uproar. Both chambers clamoured for Bull to press Montgomery to stay, or at least to wait for specific orders from Amherst. Bull sent Montgomery the addresses and added some arguments of his own. Amherst's original orders, he reasoned, had been framed when the colony had been expected to raise 1000 infantry and 520 'light horse' for itself; nothing like that number of foot had been found, and mounted Rangers were undisciplined and unreliable in action, 'as you were witness to at Etchoe'.[153] Bull was also genuinely frightened of a Creek war; already he had ordered the Independents to abandon Fort Moore, had reinforced Fort Augusta, and was prepared to lead 700 militia to the latter's relief in case of an attack.[154] He was engaged in precarious negotiations with a Creek leader, the Wolf King,[155] and had been bombarding Montgomery with ingenious schemes for intimidating hostile Indians. At one moment he had hoped that the Creeks would join the Cherokees against Montgomery, and so expose themselves to a discrediting drubbing.[156] At the next he had wanted to persuade the Cherokees to slaughter the Creeks among them, thus 'sowing inextinguishable Jealousy hereafter between the two Nations, whereby the Balance of power would naturally rest in our Hands'.[157] But the news of the retreat ruined all these prospects, and threatened to encourage the Mortar with 'the imaginary triumphs of the Cherokees'.[158] Finally, the French were likely to seize the opportunity to execute 'their long concerted plan against this Province', which would allow them to supply their West Indian islands and make them masters of 'all the Indians lying West of the Six Nations ..., an Advantageous Exchange for the frozen clime and inconvenient situation of Quebec.'[159] The possibility of a

Franco-Cherokee-Creek coalition supported by the Choctaws ('always at their disposal'),[160] though it existed chiefly inside Bull's own head, terrified him. Perhaps even more worrying was the probability of being blamed for any unpleasant consequences; he told Montgomery that his request was intended to avoid just that situation.[161] Two days later, just for good measure, he repeated his fears for the colony's 'very precarious State' to Grant.[162]

This combination of panic and political trimming did not impress the two commanders. They believed that South Carolina's military effort had been so feeble only because the colonists preferred to let the regulars fight their disreputable little war for them, a view which they knew to be shared by Amherst.[163] Nor could men anxious to be in at the storming of Montreal have taken the imaginary French threat very seriously. As for the Cherokees, they had too little food to think of forming war parties to harass the Carolina frontier.[164] Grant and Montgomery did not halt at the Congarees as Bull had hoped, and they asked the naval officer commanding the vessels waiting in Charleston harbour to be ready to receive their exhausted men.[165] By the end of the month Grant was in Charleston to liaise with Bull and to prepare for the embarkation.

Bull, having failed to persuade them to stay, was still trying to persuade them to leave a small detachment to guard the frontier. The soldiers were not unsympathetic, for Bull, whatever his faults, had been a sturdy ally and as anxious for a just peace as they. Grant particularly did not wish to leave him politically embarrassed before the obnoxious Commons. Then they acquired an embarrassment of their own. On 30 July Grant, staying at Bull's house, opened Amherst's response to Montgomery's pre-Etchoe letters of 24 May and 4 June. The order it contained, that the Cherokees must be rendered incapable of hurting South Carolina again, seemed to require far more vigorous action against the Middle Towns.[166] Though quite capable of exploiting loopholes, Grant had no wish to be accused of direct disobedience; if Amherst had made his wishes clear to begin with, 'I most certainly for my own part should have been of Opinion to Destroy every Town in the Middle Settlements tho' [it] had been certain that our loss would have been considerable'.[167] It was too late to go back now – the troops had marched too far down the country and the waggons had been discharged. Bull seized his chance and a bargain was struck. The lieutenant-governor promised to justify the soldiers' actions to the commander-in-chief. In return, Grant told Montgomery, they 'must' agree to the lieutenant-governor's 'reasonable' request for some regulars to guard his frontiers.[168] Adopting a tone which implied that the roles of commander and subordinate had now been completely reversed, Grant instructed Montgomery to order Hamilton back to the Congarees with four companies of Royal Scots.[169] The whole transaction must be kept secret until Bull could pen his formal request for the troops; in that way the notion would seem to come from him, and Montgomery could justify this direct breach of Amherst's orders.

This is the most delicate point you ever had to transact. Consider the Contents of this Letter with the utmost attention. Do not show it to any Mortal, & do not tell any body that You have received it or that any Application has been made to you by the Governor. Give your orders to Major Hamilton without telling him how or why it happens any further than that it is in Obedience to the Commands which you have Received.[170]

One wonders whose 'Commands' Grant had in mind! Montgomery did send the four companies back to the Congarees, although Hamilton objected, knowing he was being punished for malingering after Etchoe.[171] Bull did ask for them to be left in South Carolina,[172] and Montgomery, still bowing to Grant's insistence, and with feigned reluctance, agreed.[173] Thus Bull could feel pleased that he had at least kept some regulars in the colony, and Amherst, who was on the whole satisfied with Montgomery's efforts, appears to have been mollified.[174] The army embarked in the second half of August, and by early September they were at Albany. Ironically, Montreal had already fallen and they were ordered to find winter quarters on Long Island.[175]

As for Grant, he had done more than to demonstrate arrogance and a capacity for prevarication. He had emerged as the strongest personality in the power vacuum of southern Indian affairs, where there was little cooperation between colonies and where the Superintendent had little influence. Atkin had gone with the army at least as far as Keowee, but he appears to have taken no part in the peace initiatives and nothing is heard of him after 5 July.[176] Bull, of course, had admirable sentiments, but was much too wary of conflict with the legislature. Under such conditions a strong man with an army at his back could decide both the course of the war and the terms of peace.

This would have been of but passing importance had South Carolina resolved the conflict after his departure. Bull certainly did his best. To him the Montgomery expedition had confirmed the folly of trying to invade the Cherokee country. Although the Indians had been 'defeated as far as Indians Generally can be defeated by Regulars', they were 'not subdued'.[177] On 18 August he received a letter from Demeré, telling him that Fort Loudoun had surrendered. To Bull that made peace essential. The Cherokees could make terrible use of the captured ammunition and cannon, and even their promise to escort the garrison to safety had its perils. For if the Cherokees found Montgomery's 33 prisoners no longer at Fort Prince George, they would think them dead. The Indians were elated at Montgomery's repulse and, although their messenger McLemore – a renegade white trader – brought overtures of peace, Bull knew that this was not an admission of weakness. Rather, it arose from 'their Apprehension of their Wants', through lack of trade. If the Cherokees were attacked again the long-feared Creek–Cherokee alliance might come to pass. That would not only lead to further rapine amongst the back settlements; it would threaten the very existence of Georgia. Arthur Dobbs of North Carolina shared this view, and had already appealed to Amherst for some of the troops freed by the conquest of Canada.[178]

Bull therefore went wholly upon the defensive. Although the Commons voted a regiment with which to continue the war, Bull declined to raise it. As he pointed out, 1000 provincials and seven troops of Rangers would be quite insufficient to obtain a clear-cut victory. That would require substantial aid from Virginia and Amherst, and could only be thought of in the winter, when the bare trees could offer no cover for ambush.[179] Instead he relied wholly upon the militia and the settlers' own frontier stockades for defence, and tried to find ways to open negotiations. He conducted discussions with the Creeks carefully, with a view to separating them from the Cherokees. On 22 August he sent a Talk to the Cherokees themselves.[180] He did not know that 29 people from Fort Loudoun had already been massacred and the survivors were all prisoners.

Even after Montgomery's retreat the Cherokees had wanted to avenge Lyttelton's hostages and had still distrusted South Carolina. The net tightened around Fort Loudoun where the food was almost exhausted. The ribbons and paint sent up by Bull had bought only two weeks' food. By June the garrison was subsisting upon whatever food their Indian wives and mistresses could bring them. These women were exceptionally brave, meeting threats of violence from Wawatchee or Seroweh with promises of clan vengeance if they were killed.[181] But they could bring little; the Overhills themselves had little food, and some of it may have been hidden from the women. On 4 June the last communication from Carolina reached the fort, and at the end of the month the Cherokees began to boast that they had destroyed Montgomery. Weak and ill from lack of food, the men despaired of rescue. In ones and twos they began to slip over the stockade at night, hoping either to walk through the woods to safety, or simply to join the Indians. The crisis came at the beginning of August. On 4 and 5 of that month large numbers of soldiers left, and the remainder threatened to go unless the officers surrendered. Next day, 6 August, Demeré and his officers decided to capitulate.[182]

Stuart and Adamson went into Chota to settle the terms. The Cherokees agreed to let the whole garrison, women and children included, march out of Fort Loudoun. Each man was to be allowed to carry his arms, ammunition and baggage. The whites were to be given horses and escorted on their way to either Virginia or Fort Prince George by Cherokees who would hunt for them. The Cherokees would care for the sick and disabled until fit to be taken to Fort Prince George. For their part the soldiers had to give up the fort with its cannon, spare ammunition and forge, without fraud. On 7 August Demeré signed the surrender document. Next day the English colours were lowered and the troops marched out.[183]

What went wrong can only be surmised. It may be, as the whites alleged afterwards, that the Indians had always intended to break the agreement. Or, perhaps, the more vengeful warriors were beyond the control of the moderate headmen, and insisted upon retribution for the murders at Fort Prince George. It may even be that the garrison were found to have broken the pact themselves, by hiding ammunition before surrendering the fort. Whatever the reason, the Cherokee escort which began to march with the expelled garrison on 9 August gradually melted away. It is said that Occonostota turned back claiming to have dropped a prized match coat. When the refugees camped for the night near Cane Creek, perhaps ten miles from the fort, they had no escort at all.[184]

At first light on 10 August the party was fired on by hundreds of Indians hidden in the long grass. In the brief combat which followed Demeré himself, three other officers, 23 rank and file and three women were slaughtered. Stuart was seized by a warrior and dragged across the stream to safety, while one of the headmen cried out and stopped the killing. Altogether 120 whites were made prisoners. The massacre seemed to satisfy the Cherokees. The prisoners were certainly humiliated. They were slapped in the face with freshly taken scalps, and upon arriving in their captors' towns they were beaten and made to dance. One man was gradually tortured to death. After that the violence stopped. The captives still had to dance in the evenings, and on one occasion they were all brought to Chota to perform for the Mortar's party of Creeks. There were even suggestions, possibly serious, of forcing the whites to fight for the Cherokees. Some ex-sailors with knowledge of artillery were to help take the captured guns across the mountains and plant them before Fort Prince George; Stuart was to command them. But the plan was dropped when Stuart was allowed to escape.[185]

The more sober of the hostile headmen, notably Occonostota, knew that the British would inevitably seek revenge. The Great Warrior was anxious to send Carolina a signal that the war was over for the Cherokees. His instrument was Stuart. 'Bushyhead', as the Cherokees called him, had survived because the Indians knew and liked him. His particular friend, Attakullakulla, used all his worldly possessions to buy Stuart from his captor and kept him for a time inside the fort. Occonostota and the others must have expected the Carpenter to help Stuart to flee. But when the Second Man announced that he was going hunting with his family and his new slave, no one tried to stop him. The little party comprised Attakullakulla, his brother, two young warriors 'and three Wenches', with Stuart, his servant and an old doctor. Once in the woods this group made full speed for the Great Island. On 8 September 1760 they reached the Virginian camp. Attakullakulla, having thus preserved his credentials as the friend of the British, was able to open negotiations with Byrd. Meanwhile, now that the blood of the Fort Prince George hostages had been avenged, Occonostota and Ostenaca began to sway the Overhill and Middle Settlements in favour of peace. By October tentative arrangements were made for a mutual exchange of prisoners at Ninety Six.[186]

But all the initiatives came to nothing. Attakullakulla was offered terms even more draconian than those demanded by Lyttelton. Occonostota and Ostenaca were still angry and suspicious; while Seroweh was claiming a military victory and demanding renewal of the war. As for Bull, the news of the massacre had already destroyed his peace plans. No longer could he withstand public demands for vengeance. He wrote to Byrd, urging him to advance and burn the nine Overhill towns. Meanwhile he would form an army in South Carolina, hopefully including Hamilton's men, for the relief of Fort

Prince George. For the offensive operations which he could delay no longer, he called for another large force of regulars.[187] The British side, unable to overlook the massacre, could not offer the Cherokees the terms their strength and dignity appeared to deserve. The Cherokees, especially Occonostota, feared a repetition of Lyttelton's treachery. Faith between enemies was indeed the sweet bond of human things, and without it there was no end in sight.

The massacre at Fort Loundon prevented Governor Bull & the British military commanders from settling for peace, since the actions taken by the Cherokees demanded retribution.

5

The Carpenter and the Colonel

On 29 August 1761 a Cherokee and a Scot sat down to smoke a pipe of peace. The scene was the British camp outside Fort Prince George and the Cherokee was Attakullakulla, come to save what he could from the wreckage of defeat. The Scot was James Grant, now the British commander in South Carolina, whose little army had just burned the houses and crops of 15 of the Middle Settlements. Grant's raid had forced the Cherokees to negotiate or starve. But he had deliberately left the Middle Settlements alone, and he never intended to attack the Overhills at all. In fact Grant had applied what he thought to be just enough force to discredit the war faction. Now having 'chastised' the Cherokees as his orders required, and having won *de facto* control of the peace-making, he was prepared to settle for terms far less harsh than those demanded by South Carolina.

The colonel had sound military reasons for his policy. After a month in the mountains his men were crippled by exhaustion and sickness. Plagued by desertion, short of food and shoes, and with a worn out waggon train, Grant knew that he could not remain in the Cherokee country much longer. Historians have usually taken this explanation,[1] spelled out by Grant in his letters to Sir Jeffrey Amherst,[2] at face value. But as in 1760 Grant was driven by a motive less professional and perhaps more powerful: his conviction that the Cherokees had the greater justice on their side. This argument was well in tune, as Grant must have known, with the imperial government's continuing concern for the protection of Indian lands. On 12 August 1760, just before Montgomery and Grant had returned from South Carolina to New York, Monckton had repeated Bouquet's assurance that the British did not intend to take the Ohio Indians' lands.[3] Even before Monckton's pronouncement the Board of Trade had warned Fauquier not to let the

Ohio Company take up lands promised to Virginian volunteers in 1754.[4] At the same time New York had been told it could open its northern frontier to soldier-settlers only if Indian rights were protected.[5] Finally, the Board had forbidden further settlement west of the Appalachians until further notice.[6] Grant cannot have failed to know of these developments; nor could he have failed to notice that soldiers' promises about the limits of settlement were being given sanction from home.

Thus, in peppery alliance with William Bull, he had set out to reach a settlement which the Cherokees could accept and which would consequently prove lasting. Indeed, had he been allowed, he would have done so without fighting. So it was that the Carpenter and the Colonel met at Fort Prince George less as adversaries than as collaborators. Grant's presence in the Lower Towns ensured that the nation would let Attakullakulla negotiate; the Colonel's sympathy and logistical situation allowed the Carpenter to obtain honourable terms.

Grant had been brought back to South Carolina by the fall of Fort Loudoun. On 15 December Amherst had sent him his written orders to undertake the new expedition against 'these perfidious Savages'. He was to have four companies of light infantry, two battalions made up from independent companies newly arrived from Britain, and the four companies of Royals still in South Carolina, as well as some Mohawks and Stockbridges. These would be augmented with Carolinian provincials and rangers, and by local Indians. Amherst envisaged a late winter to early spring campaign 'as the Season of the Year when you may most probably arrive there, is the best in that hot climate to pursue operations, and you will have before you a sufficient period of mild Weather, entirely to Effect the Service you are going upon'. Grant's objective was 'to reduce [the Cherokees] to the absolute necessity of Sueing for Pardon and Effectively to put it out of their power of Interrupting the Peace, which it may be thought Expedient to Grant them'. Grant was to decide for himself when this had been achieved and then to 'come away',[7] a sensible discretion which he was later to put to vigorous use.

Grant at once began to raise difficulties. An early campaign was out of the question for 'the Want of Grass in the Woods & the weakness of the Cattle should make it very difficult to march up the Country ...'; and what if the Cherokees could not be made to surrender? 'After cutting up the Indian Settlements and following the Cherokees as far as Troops can, with any degree of Safety, supposing they retire only, and don't ask for Peace, what is to be done?'[8] Grant, who had seen both the Carolinian settlers and the Cherokees' mountains at first hand, was still thinking of a limited campaign and a compromise peace. He then made his first attempt to get full control of the peace-making process, using as a lever the fragmentation and incoherence of British policy towards the Cherokees.

> If the Cherokees offer Terms, I know Your Excellency does not chuse that the Commanding Officer should settle the Articles of Peace, but who is to conclude it? as they are at War with four Provinces can any one Governor settle the differences of the Whole?[9]

It was a pretty point, born of experience out of a humane and ambitious mind. While it ignored Atkin's existence altogether (not surprisingly in view of his performance in 1760) it recognized the reality that no one except the military commander on the spot would be in a position to negotiate a coherent peace. But Amherst would allow no leeway. Grant was not to return 'until You have compelled them into a Peace, or that you receive orders for so doing ...', and the terms of that peace were to be settled by South Carolina.[10] So Grant swallowed his orders for the time being and sailed for Charleston on 23 December. His little convoy was scattered by a storm, but by 10 January all the transports were safely inside Charleston bar.[11]

Within a week Grant tried once again to obtain a modification of his orders. He had probably already received the unsigned letter written by someone at Amherst's headquarters (perhaps the great man's secretary, John Appy) describing a visit from Henry Ellis en route to England. The writer, an old school friend of the former Georgia governor, had been able to obtain and pass on a minute account of Ellis's conversations with Amherst. Ellis's purpose was to persuade Amherst that the southern colonies were dangerously exposed to attack by a French-sponsored 'secret Combination of all the different Nations of Savages' frightened by Britain's military power and 'Ambitious Views'. These peoples, made fearful by the British war upon the Cherokees believed, thought Ellis, that 'We intend to extirpate the whole Race Tribe by Tribe'. This peril, he had long thought, made a speedy 'accommodation' with the Cherokees vital, or, if that was not possible, Amherst must provide 'some Assistance for this Province before it is too late ...'[12] The worst possible action, from his point of view, was to forfeit any hope of a compromise by attacking the Cherokees with a force inadequate to subdue them. Arriving in New York only days after Grant's departure, he had lost no time in presenting his demands to the commander-in-chief.

Ellis, with 'a certain bluntness of conversation', had badgered the commander-in-chief about 'the inadequate force' given to Grant, the lack of forage in the woods, the lack of growing corn to destroy at that season, the 'inaccessible' position of the Overhill towns, the difficulty of getting carriages and colonial troops. If none of these things caused disaster, Ellis predicted, the expedition would still fail, for the Indians would never accept action unless certain of victory. According to this correspondent, Amherst had been able to think of no more adequate answer than to offer tea. The writer, 'too near the throne' to speak too favourably of the Indians himself, invited Grant to make what use he could of his report, but begged him to 'throw this Letter into the fire for reasons which are obvious'.[13] Grant could thus hope that Ellis had shaken Amherst's former resolve, and that the time might be ripe to try again for himself.

At all events the difficulties raised by Grant in his letter of 17 January were very similar to those pointed out by Ellis. As both men had predicted, there was no grass in the woods, and there would probably not be enough for the cattle and horses until April at the earliest. Both Bull and Major Thompson of the Rangers agreed that this alone would make a campaign impossible for some time. The waggons were not ready and the provincial forces had not yet assembled. As Grant put it, 'The Regt. is at the Congarees and the Rangers are scattered up & down the face of the Earth.'[14] He then made it just a little too plain that his delay was at least partly motivated by hopes of a fresh overture from the Cherokees, or even of initiating one himself. He pointed out the near-quiescence of the Indians since the fall of Fort Loudoun, and recommended concessions.

> Notwithstanding the great Apprehension of the People here of the Reports we had to the Northwards of the Cruelty & Barbaritys of the Indians, I find the Province exactly in the same state as when I left it. Since that time three or four People have been killed & indeed their Differences still subsist, but there are Faults on both sides & if both Parties were heard, I fancy the Indians have been the worst used, and yet I believe that the greatest part of them are sory for what has been done, & would be glad to make Peace, if they knew how to bring it about.[15]

Indeed John Stuart had told him that peace talks had been very close in 1760. Only now did he learn that the fear of treachery fanned by Welsh had prevented them. As Grant said:

the Treatment their Hostages had met with induced them to believe this Report the more readily, so an End was made to our making Peace, which I never could account for til now, tho' indeed before we left this Province, there was a sort of Surmise that such a Report had been spread in the Indian Nation.[16]

The Charleston people, by contrast, wanted to continue the war for their own ends, including a liking for the profits to be made from the presence of a regular force. Almost everyone, especially anybody with frontier 'plantations', was caught up in the hysteria emanating from Miln, Bell and a third officer at Fort Prince George. These men, whose removal he had recommended in 1760, he would unseat when 'a Convoy of Provisions is to be thrown into the Fort, and at the same time put Lachlan McIntosh into Miln's place.[17]

There was much merit and even wisdom in these remarks. If most of the Cherokee were not actually 'sorry' they would almost certainly have grasped at a reasonably dignified peace, and if the Fort Prince George alarms were understandable[18] (and Ellis too was very frightened) they were out of proportion to the real danger. Moreover, it had been Miln's and Coytmore's misbehaviour in 1759 and 1760 which had materially contributed to the mischief. More recently, from 5 November until 12 January, Miln had censored letters leaving the garrison, clearly to ensure that only his version of events got out.[19] But neither Ellis's arguments nor Grant's impressed the commander-in-chief. Ellis was brushed off with a mendacious promise of troops for both Georgia and Grant.[20] Even a visit from Byrd, who agreed with Ellis that the expedition was fatally flawed,[21] did not shake him. Once again Amherst, while prepared to yield to Grant's judgement on technical matters (such as the grass) and warmly approving the decision to get rid of Miln, was quite inflexible as to the main objective.

That the greatest part of the Indians are sorry for what has been done I can scarcely prevail upon myself to Credit, unless it is owing thro' the apprehension they are under at the Chastisement that attends them; to avoid which they now feign a Repentance, the Insincerity of which we have too often Experienced to be again allured with: punished therefore they must be, and that severely too, before Peace is granted them; for until they have Undergone a due Correction & are thoroughly Convinced of the weight of His Majesty's Displeasure, there can be no Safety for the Inhabitants of his Southern American Colonies.[22]

That silenced Grant's direct importunities but it did not stop him from searching for ways of evading his orders. Already he had incited Bull to make a fresh approach to the Cherokees. Officially Bull was anxious to recover white prisoners in the nation before Grant's advance should put their lives in peril; he planned to ransom them with trade goods, ironically a notion which derived from Miln. On 22 January Bull had asked the Council to consider the scheme; by 29 January the necessary funds had been voted by the Commons House of Assembly, and the goods bought. That day they were sent up country with McIntosh and a large food convoy. McIntosh had also been ordered to promise the release of all the Cherokee prisoners taken by Montgomery in 1760 in return for all the whites in the nation, 'As any difficulty on that Subject might render this humane scheme abortive, and prove fatal to all the English captives'.[23] Bull knew that he had some time in hand, for Grant and he had agreed that lack of feed would make an advance beyond Monk's Corner impossible until April at the earliest. It may or may not be coincidence that they each wrote letters on this subject from Charleston on the same day.[24]

The convoy reached Fort Prince George without incident, Miln and another officer were relieved, and McIntosh delivered his Talk. The returning Ranger escort were so sure of safety that they camped without sentries at Six Mile Creek, allowing Seroweh to relieve them, undetected, of 129 horses. Yet even in this phase there was hope, for to Grant's amazement at least, the warriors did not take a single scalp.[25] The more sober Cherokee leaders took Bull's gesture to signal the chance of an honourable peace. While in Virginia to return 16 British captives, Attakullakulla may have received a private Talk from Bull and sent a messenger ahead before hurrying back to Carolina himself.[26] On 10[27] or 15 March,[28] no doubt briefed by the Chota Council to probe for concessions, he appeared before Fort Prince George with a Talk from 'several of their principal men'.[29] Attakullakulla admitted that Seroweh was out with a war party and would not have peace at any price, and that another band had gone out from Sugar Town. To convince the waverers he wanted one of Montgomery's captives as a pledge of faith.[30] For his part McIntosh received the Carpenter warmly and gave presents to him and his followers. Monypenny, whose source was McIntosh's report to Grant, thought this was going too far. Peace was certainly desirable, but the Fort Loudoun massacre and subsequent raids had been too 'flagrant' to be overlooked. The presents, he felt, should have been confined to the Carpenter himself.[31] But McIntosh had, of course, been executing a policy devised by Bull and Grant.

Monypenny's reaction shows that to secure peace Grant was prepared to go beyond what his colleagues thought prudent. But there were signs that he was justified. On 24 March the hitherto hostile Ostenaca sent a conciliatory Talk from Tomotly,[32] and on 1 April Seroweh himself came to plead that his depredations had been provoked by ill-treatment by Miln. By way of good faith he brought McIntosh a string of white wampum and 13 bullocks earlier stolen from white settlers. McIntosh packed talk and beads off to Grant, who was eager to believe Seroweh's story.[33]

Bull was inclined to give the Cherokees encouraging replies, but he had to be very careful not to offend the war-hysteria still strong in Charleston. Lyttelton's shambles of an expedition had made the Commons unwilling to trust even a governor who promised strong action, and Bull's passive policy in 1760 had made him doubly suspect. Even the Council would not hear of negotiations until all Cherokee hostilities ceased.[34] Thus Bull, in any case inclined to shy away from conflict, could offer little to the Cherokees. His Talk to Attakullakulla praised the Carpenter for his loyalty, but insisted that the release of all the remaining white prisoners must precede any talk of peace. Cherokees who continued to resist would suffer at the hands of Grant's men, but those who surrendered would be well treated. As proof he had allowed Tistoe to resettle with his people near Fort Prince George.[35] This was hardly the concession Attakullakulla had hoped for; not one Indian prisoner was released and the Cherokees were required to surrender without conditions. Not surprisingly the next weeks passed without a reply from the nation, but at the time Grant – at least in his letters to Amherst – chose to remain optimistic. '[A]s [Tistoe] puts himself entirely in our Power, he deserves Protection, I shall give him no Trouble when we march up.'[36]

Optimism was essential to his purpose. While blandly assuring Amherst that he did not intend to 'interfere about the Peace', Grant was preparing his superior's mind for the compromise which he intended to conclude himself, far from the clamouring politicians of Charleston. He had clearly already discussed such a peace with Bull, a peace which would require the lieutenant-governor to moderate the harsh terms of 1760. Provided, he wrote, that 'we are lucky enough to give them a Blow, the Lieut. Governor should not insist upon hard Terms, & from what he has told me, that is not his Intention'. The subsequent treaty would prove more durable if signed in a Cherokee town house than if concluded in Charleston. Moreover, the need to consult Bull at every turn would paralyse the army, possibly for weeks at a time. If the troops were kept idly waiting on peace negotiations which might well fail, they might have to withdraw before forcing the Cherokees to surrender. After all, it would be difficult enough to supply nearly 3000 men at Fort Prince George, which could be reached by waggons, 'but it is next to impossible to do so for any length of time after we pass that Fort, & are reduced to Pack horses only'. He had therefore asked Bull for a copy of his peace proposals in advance, so that he could ensure that the Cherokees were committed to accept them before operations ceased.[37] On 12 April he followed up this argument by sending Seroweh's Talk and beads on to Amherst, in another attempt to sway his chief.[38] All this time Grant was still at Monk's Corner, having been continually delayed by torrential rain.[39] The Cherokees had been given plenty of time in which to negotiate.

As far as Amherst was concerned, the stratagem worked; unable to resist the military logic of Grant's proposition, he gave his assent by return.[40] But he was quick to remind Grant that this was not a licence to change Bull's terms or to presume to settle a treaty on his own.

> I need not say anything about the *Talk* sent to the Lieut-Governor, or Your not interfering about the Peace, as my Instructions on this point have been very full; I am certain that you will Exert Yourself in Effecting the Service You are on which I wish to see Compleatly done, as other Services will call for the Troops ...[41]

His response to Scrowch's approach and the release of the prisoners was openly cynical: 'I rejoice to get people out of the hands of those Barbarians; they never give them up but when they are afraid of Us.'[42] Nevertheless, when he reached Fort Prince George at the end of May, Grant had in his hands Amherst's permission to obtain the terms from Bull and to conduct the preliminary peace talks.[43]

Grant's aim was to pin Bull down to the concessions which he had already made in private. Bull certainly cannot have been anxious to abdicate control of the peace-making in this way, for whatever terms he proposed, Grant – knowing that without his army there would be no peace at all – could chop and change them at will. Nor can he have relished the thought of the consequent onslaught in the Commons. At all events he hesitated. But Grant kept at him; as late as 10 and 11 April he wrote from Monk's Corner asking for the peace terms.[44] When Bull did reply, three days later,[45] Grant was already starting for the Congarees; he arrived on 22 April,[46] by which time the courier must have overtaken him. Here Grant learned that Bull, while disposed to moderate the very severe terms of 1760, was prepared to do nothing which the Commons might reject.

The first clause, for example, no longer required the executions of 15 named Cherokees, but deaths there must be. The lieutenant-governor required 'one or two Cherokee (Offenders) from each of their Four Settlements to be delivered up to be put to Death in your Camp', or the Indians might themselves execute 'in their own way, those whom they shall pitch on as having been instrumental in bringing these Disturbances in our Settlements and those Distresses on themselves. In the latter case the Scalps of the Executed to be brought Fresh to your head quarters.' All white prisoners were to be handed over at once, but no Cherokees would be released until the Indians had carried out the remaining terms of the treaty,[47] a clear abrogation of the ransom and mutual exchange proposals of January. The cannon taken from Fort Loudoun were to be returned, and South Carolina was to have in future the right to build whatever forts it thought necessary. The animals, fields and pastures of such forts were to be forbidden to the Cherokees, and all Frenchmen in the nation were to be expelled or given up. Moreover the nation – or rather the Lower Towns – were to surrender all their lands below the Twenty-Six Mile River, that is more than 26 miles from Keowee[48] (Map 8). This new demand for territory, with its echoes of Glen's schemes, was clearly no more than a sop to the expansionist demands of the settlers. The treaty was to include South Carolina's allies, the Chickasaws and Catawbas, and Attakullakulla was 'to be declared by us and Acknowledged by them as their Emperor', his reward for 'inviolable Attachment to the English'.[49] This blatant attempt to set up a puppet ruler drew its inspiration from Sir Alexander Cuming's 'treaty' of 1730, and if meant seriously displayed an astonishing ignorance of the realities of Cherokee polity. The rest of the terms were hardly better. Future Cherokee murderers of whites were to be executed by the nation, while the colonial authorities would deal with white offenders. Finally, trade would be resumed only when the preliminaries settled by Grant had been ratified in Charleston.[50] It was a high price to ask for peace and it doomed Grant to fighting the Cherokees before negotiation. It was certainly not a proposal which, given his already trenchantly expressed opinions, he could accept without protest.

Bull, apparently expecting objections, went out of his way to stress the necessity of the executions. 'I consider', he wrote, 'the first as the Grand Article that must be insisted on to Satisfy our Honor, but will meet with the greatest difficulty in their submitting to it'; this would be especially

the case as, while the 'Old Men' wanted peace, 'their Young men entertain no very respectable Opinion or Dread of the English manner of
Fighting'. Thus only a 'Spirited and Successful action' would get them to
comply.[51] Bull's message was plain: Grant was not at liberty to drop the
executions clause, and if Bull himself was obliged to do so he would
blame Grant. However, he was not nearly so insistent about the boundary clause. The Cherokees might think 'the New Limits set to their
Hunting ground an encroachment on their Ancient possession and
claim on those Lands', and, although Bull added that 'the woods are
wide enough to compensate for loss of territory', he did not make the
cession an absolute condition of peace. He took much the same position
about the emperorship, which he expected to be resisted by 'the Rivals in
Power, the Standing Turkey and Judd's Friend [Ostenaca]'.[52] It is there
fore conceivable that Bull intended these two clauses only as bargaining
points, the dropping of which might make the executions a little more
palatable. But the executions he regarded as politically essential. He may
even have expected them to establish a lasting peace, by establishing
Cherokee respect for British power and justice. At least, that is what he
told Amherst.[53]

Sure enough, Grant did not waste his time over the executions.
Instead he at once attacked the boundary clause as 'unreasonable and
improper', the colonists having 'already too great an Extent of Country
which is not settled & which they have not the people to inhabit', an
objection in which Bull 'readily acquiesced'.[54] Bull, who did not want
to drive the Cherokees 'to despair', and who now thought that Grant's
advance alone would render the nation 'sincerely disposed to make a
Peace on Terms which we may think reasonably Satisfactory',[55] was
happy to let that important demand drop. Having distanced himself as
far as possible from the amendment he took the further precaution of
concealing the whole transaction from the Commons until September,
when peace talks had already begun. Even then he did not mention
the dropping of the boundary clause.[56] For his part Grant 'forgot'[57] to
tell Amherst until writing from Fort Prince George on 2 June, when it
was already too late for the commander-in-chief to object. To his credit
Amherst accepted the *fait accompli*, again approving Grant's possession
of the peace proposals and his intention to conduct the preliminaries,
but ignoring his meddling with the terms.[58] Grant's earlier arguments –
he had objected to unnecessary executions in 1760 – and later actions
show that the commander in South Carolina had still more changes in
mind. But for the time being he held his peace. For he had gained two
fundamental points: authority to act as Bull's agent in the preliminary

peace talks; and, the land issue having set a precedent, the right to insist upon further concessions as diplomacy demanded. The Cherokees would certainly have been driven 'to despair' by Bull's proposals, had they known of them. Even their response to his comparatively mild Talk of 30 March was ambivalent to say the least. As we have seen, the Chota council apparently decided not to send Attakullakulla back to McIntosh with a reply. Instead they awaited the outcome of negotiations they had begun with the Senecas, with the French at Fort Toulouse, where Occonostota had gone; and with Virginia, where Willinawaw was trying for a separate peace. Only a few of Tistoe's people, and few of those young men, had chosen to settle with him under the guns of Fort Prince George. Those who came were so poor that Tistoe himself had to go back to the Middle Towns to beg for corn; in his Keowee house he left only a woman and a boy. Given time, perhaps more Cherokees might have plucked up the courage to abandon war and trust the English. But that chance was promptly ruined by Grant's Chickasaws. At the very end of April, about a month after Tistoe's first arrival, a scouting party raided Keowee, killing the woman and wounding the boy. The triumphant Chickasaws rejoined the army at '12 mile run' below Saluda on the road to Ninety Six. Monypenny was horrified. 'This', he wrote acidly, 'is exactly true Indian Assistance.'[59] Grant did not mention the incident to Amherst.

But even this little tragedy did not dash all hopes of a settlement. The prospect of peace, food and clothes was too much for some of the towns, and ransomed white prisoners still trickled into Fort Prince George. By 25 April another 13 or so had appeared, making 113 in all, including at least 16 Independents and 21 provincials 'that belonged to Fort Loudoun'; and about 13 bullocks had been returned as presents.[60] At about the same time Ostenaca sent in another Talk to McIntosh.[61] Up to this point Chota and the war faction were clearly playing a waiting game, just as Corkran suggests;[62] taking good care to hold out the prospect of peace provided South Carolina would offer real concessions. The more warlike headmen, certainly Seroweh and now perhaps Tistoe, were convinced that they could repulse Grant as they had done Montgomery. These warriors would not give way until they had suffered a serious military reverse.[63] But by the beginning of May Chota had been forced to change its tune, for Grant was at last approaching Keowee with a formidable force.

At the Congarees he had been joined by Thomas Middleton's South Carolina regiment and Hamilton's four companies of Royals.[64]

Henceforth his progress had been retarded less by the need to complete his forward magazines than by ferocious weather[65] (a cyclone had struck Charleston on 4 May[66]). Between deep mud, floods and damaged waggons he did not reach Ninety Six and Thompson's 401 Rangers until 18 May. By 20 May it had been raining for three weeks and Grant was to lose 14 days on the last leg of his journey up to Fort Prince George.[67] But he was bringing up over 2800 fighting men including Indians – Mohawks, Stockbridges, Chickasaws and Catawbas – supported by 250 waggoners.[68] If this army were to get in among the Middle Settlements it would be too late for Chota to negotiate at all.

The situation was all the more serious because elsewhere Chota's diplomacy had failed. Occonostota was back with no more than a French commission and eight pack-horse loads of ammunition and other presents.[69] Nothing had been heard of the Senecas;[70] not surprisingly, for the Iroquois were themselves short of ammunition and consequently anxious to please the British by making ostentatious preparations *against* the Cherokees.[71] It is true that the Senecas proposed a wide-flung conspiracy against the British, which would have involved a hundred-strong embassy to the Cherokees.[72] But, although Wilbur R. Jacobs erects this into a full blown plot thwarted only by alert British agents,[73] the idea was never adopted. Virginia would not make a separate peace.[74] Occonostota himself, irritated and alarmed by his cool reception at Mobile,[75] opposed the wilder spirits who wished to fight.[76] No doubt the threat of Grant's advance had helped to keep the prisoners coming into Fort Prince George; now, in the Chota town house, Attakullakulla was at last able to sway the majority in favour of peace. But a majority was not a consensus, and the council would still not make peace without Carolinian concessions. Attakullakulla was given 12 days in which to reach an agreement with Grant and report back to the nation.[77] He went on to Tomotly where he 'found things very pleasant'.[78] But the war faction had not given up. That night a runner came to warn him that some of the young warriors were planning to attack Grant before he could reach Keowee. Attakullakulla met the plotters and warned them that if they did fight 'they would Spoil all', and the raid was stopped.[79] But the Little Carpenter knew that he could not hold them for long.

Knowing that failure would mean disaster, he once more hurried over the mountains to Fort Prince George, arriving on 22 May. To his astonishment a war party from Settico[80] had already arrived to try to wreck the negotiations.[81] He at once presented McIntosh with a Talk which frankly acknowledged the limits of his credentials – 'I am but a Messenger sent by Occonostota' – but suggesting that the Great Warrior was ready to treat.[82] Grant, who was then still struggling through flooded creeks, received this Talk by McIntosh's courier next day. The colonel found himself obliged 'to have some Intercourse with him sooner then I intended'.[83]

Monypenny used exactly the same phrase, 'sooner than intended', in his journal, as though he were repeating words he had just heard from Grant. The last word, however, was for Amherst's benefit; 'expected' might have been more accurate. Grant at once composed a careful reply, superficially sticking to his orders to reject all overtures until the Cherokees had been punished, but containing enough encouragement to keep Attakullakulla at Fort Prince George until the army arrived. '[H]e had always had a good opinion of the Carpenter, would be glad to see him, when convenient, but would not now detain him.' The Fort Loudoun prisoners must be released, and the Cherokees' breach of faith on that occasion was contrasted with Montgomery's release and arming of Miln's hostages in 1760. Grant would march into the Middle Settlements, but provided the Cherokees remained quietly in their towns he would do no harm there. Peace talks could be held if Occonostota would come in person, and Grant specified how the Great Warrior should approach the camp.[84] Grant and Monypenny must have calculated that Amherst could not reasonably object to peace on this basis; as Grant pointed out to Attakullakulla, it was a carbon copy of the commander-in-chief's own treatment of the Canadian Indians a year before.[85] But a meeting at Fort Prince George would be much harder to justify, and the fact remains that Grant was very anxious to have one. The horseman who carried this message had to run the gauntlet of Seroweh's marksmen to reach McIntosh on 24 May – only to find that he had missed Attakullakulla by a matter of hours,[86] and Grant's advance guard did not sight Fort Prince George for a further three days.[87] Had Grant really wished to avoid meeting the Carpenter he had opportunity and excuse enough.

He explained this serious breach of his orders in almost exactly the terms used by Bull in his letter to Grant in 1760, and more recently to the Board of Trade:

[I]t was not proper to refuse absolutely coming to terms and so deprive him of all hopes for an accommodation, tho' I was determined not to hearken to any Proposals until I got into their Country. I did not chuse to tell him what I intended & yet was resolved not to deceive him, as I think Faith is to be kept with Indians, as well as with other men.[88]

The ambivalence of this last sentence – and its jibe at the likes of Lyttelton, Coytmore and Miln – was significant. Grant might have little room for manoeuvre but he was determined to make the most of what he had. He hurriedly added that he had to tread carefully, as Bull had not sent him a copy of the Talk of 30 March, the document which, Grant supposed, had brought Attakullakulla to the fort.[89] This was disingenuous for, as we have seen, Grant probably knew the *contents* of that Talk already, even if he did not possess a copy. Besides he certainly had a copy of the lieutenant-governor's peace proposals, a fact which he admitted in the postscript to his letter, as an afterthought.[90] Thus his claim that he did not know how Bull wanted him to proceed, or what had already been said to the Cherokees, was really a smokescreen for his own determination to open negotiations at once.

Meanwhile Attakullakulla had lost patience. The days were slipping away and his allotted time might well expire without any tangible result. It might perhaps be better to be in Chota, where he might yet dissuade the headmen from pursuing the war. On 24 July, only hours before the arrival of Grant's express, he decided to go.[91] Gathering his escort about him, the Carpenter began the long weary journey back to the Overhill country. Hardly had he started than he was overtaken by a breathless galloper from McIntosh: Grant's message had arrived, and the army itself was barely a day's march from the fort. At once Attakullakulla wheeled his party about and hastened back to Keowee.[92]

On 27 May the first of Grant's Indian Corps – including 60 to 70 volunteers from the white regiments – appeared on the traders' path below Fort Prince George, whereupon most of the 30 or so Indians hovering around the fort fled. As the army coiled itself into a camp on a hill overlooking the rain swollen river, here fifty to sixty yards wide, only Attakullakulla and five companions remained to greet Colonel Grant.[93] Christopher French, a captain in Monypenny's regiment, was pleased as Punch to meet the famous Little Carpenter. '[H]e is', wrote French, 'a well looking Man, has always a smile on his Countenance, & has the Character of a King.'[94] It was probably on this occasion that Attakullakulla let it be known that the attempt on the messenger's life had 'vex'd him prodigiously'.[95] He was, as French observed, 'a man of great Sense'.[96]

To read Grant's account of what happened next one would suppose that the pair at once fell to bargaining.[97] But that, as Dorothy Jones reminds us, would have been quite contrary to the protocol of Indian diplomacy, where every public Talk expressed an agreement already reached behind the scenes. French's and Monypenny's journals, and that of the *South Carolina Gazette*'s anonymous correspondent, show that formal exchanges took place the next day,[98] leaving plenty of time for discreet conversations. Did such conversations take place? French tells us that a Talk was indeed held that evening at the fort, and his silence as to the details implies that it was private. (French, who went to the fort himself, was confined to the noisy Indian ceremonies which included firing volleys into the air.) He goes on, by speaking of *another* Talk between them the following day, to imply that Grant and Attakullakulla were the principals.[99] For some reason Corkran, who made extensive use of French, ignored this evidence and accepted Grant's version of events.[100] Perhaps, not realizing that Grant wished to mislead Amherst, and not having seen Monypenny's journal, he missed the significance of this first Talk.

We can reconstruct the outlines of what passed that evening through the discrepancies between the Carpenter's public Talk and the accounts of Monypenny and Henry Laurens. Monypenny was, of course, Grant's prospective successor and would have had to be privy to any private deal. Lieutenant-Colonel Laurens was Middleton's second in command and may already have become, as he certainly was later, one of Grant's favoured circle. Where either of these two mentions details referred to neither in Attakullakulla's official words, nor in Grant's letter to Amherst, we may cautiously infer that they are describing a different meeting altogether: that of the evening of Wednesday, 27 May. For example, only Monypenny mentions Settico, the attack on the messenger and Occonostota's efforts to procure peace; only Laurens mentions the Carpenter asking for a specific period of grace.[101]

Grant could not violate his orders further by beginning open negotiations unless the Cherokees met his demands of 23 May. Attakullakulla did not have the authority to commit Occonostota and the nation, and the smallness of his retinue betrayed the weakness of his following. The Carpenter did his best, offering to have the leading troublemakers – and specifically the Settico party – put to death. But in the end he was reduced to begging for a further ten days in which to consult the nation and return with a reply; he would even take one of Grant's officers to meet the Great Warrior in the Overhill country. Occonostota, he stressed, was so anxious for peace that he had already prevented an attack on Grant's army. Moreover, a Creek delegation which had come to Hiwassee with a bloody tomahawk, offering yet another fighting alliance against the British, had been sent packing on pain of death.[102] Grant replied that he had given his Talk and would not alter it. As for the proffered executions, such satisfaction 'should flow from themselves & not be extorted & those who had disturbed the peace should be punished by their own Country Men in the presence of our Army'.[103] In other words, he would not necessarily insist upon any executions at all, and he would certainly not order them to be carried out by British soldiers. But the circumstantial evidence strongly suggests that he went a stage further: Attakullakulla could have his ten days.

Grant could not delay his march without a reasonable excuse. Fortunately one was at hand. Next morning, 28 May, the troops were put to work making ready for the invasion of the Middle Settlements.

> The Carpenter's [*sic*] at work making frames of pack-saddles. The Taylors in making baggs to carry Flour, & Sodds to put under the Pack Saddles. Sadlers, Harness makers, & collar makers at work cutting Hydes into thongs for cruppers and Breast Pieces. They are cut & put green into Salt & water.[104]

As each horse was to carry no more than 150 lbs into the mountains, the men were making equipment for no less than 600 animals. The 150 waggons which Grant decided to keep at Fort Prince George had to be protected with fortifications, but sandy soil and lack of suitable timber for stockades or fascines made construction difficult. Captain Dudgeon, the engineer, solved the problem by starting two wattle fences two feet apart, the gap to be filled with sand. This would form a redan breastwork backing onto the fort and enclosing a number of storehouses.[105] The Cherokees could see that the British would be engaged at Fort Prince George for some time.

Later Grant, his officers, Grant's Indians and the Cherokees held their public negotiations at the fort. Attakullakulla put his case again, asking for 'a limited Time' in which to persuade the nation to meet Grant's conditions. Grant, of course, politely refused to wait for even half an hour. He would march, he said, as soon as his waggon camp adjoining Fort Prince George had been entrenched, and when the pack saddles and flour bags had been made.[106] This was as good as saying that he would not move for at least a week, and as we have seen, Grant had probably already said so in private. The conference ended with Grant giving Attakullakulla some rum, and other presents to his companions. As Monypenny put it, 'Coll Grant was very civil to him',[107] and everyone on the British side thought that peace was in the air. Monypenny wrote on 28 May:

> This day the Indians, of whom 40 more had join'd viz, 20 Chikesaws, & 20 Catawbas observ'd the civilitys paid to the little Carpenter, were not much pleas'd with them, & said the War was over; but, the Head Man of the Chikesaws. is said, to have taken his young man [*sic*] aside, & told them, words are nothing, look at the Pack Saddles.[108]

Next day, Friday 29 July, Monypenny carried on his ostentatious labours.[109] French went to the fort to see a new arrival, the Tail of Estatoe, 'who has been remarkable for his activity against us'.[110] The Tail, reputedly Seroweh's right-hand man, and his companion Moitoi of Keowee, asked to be allowed to settle peacefully and plant corn under Grant's protection.[111] Later that day Attakullakulla set out to see Occonostota, as French believed, about a peace. Many more Lower Cherokees began to come in, including 'the White Owl & some others of Note', and were allowed to settle near the fort.[112] By 2 June 'a good many' – 60 or 70 of them – had arrived and been taken under Grant's protection.[113] These people were 'almost starved', being reduced to a diet of wild strawberries and acorns in lieu of corn; though they were said to have had some meat, there could not have been much.[114] They were not allowed to hunt in the woods, and had had no time to plant crops. In any case they had no seed – they had to be given seed corn and peas to plant. As Grant pointed out, it would be some time before these Cherokees could recover sufficiently to threaten the frontier again.[115]

The Tail's hint that even Seroweh might be prepared to negotiate, the sight of scores of hungry Cherokees coming in to surrender, the absence of enemy action and the Carpenter's insistence that he would return created a widespread impression that the war faction was about to collapse. By 2 June it was rumoured that the army would march to Estatoe in time to meet the Carpenter on his return journey. There the Cherokees, squeezed between Byrd and Grant, would cheerfully accept South Carolina's terms. On 5 June a white escapee from Chota arrived to confirm Occonostota's disappointment with the French.[116] Monypenny, ever the conscientious brigade major, worried that the prospect of peace was making the men careless.

> The nation must be much inclined to Peace, as a Scalp has not been taken as yet, tho our waggoners, & even Soldrs. (contrary to orders)

cross the River, & ramble all round the opposite hills, picking straw-
berrys unarm'd. Till one is kill'd, they will never believe there is any
danger.[117]

Thus beneath the bustle of warlike preparation – the checking and
mending of weapons, the completion of the breastwork, the building
of storehouses inside it, the making of cartridges[118] – dwelt a conviction that peace was practically assured.

Grant, who knew from the Carpenter that Cherokee opinion was
balanced on a knife edge, was more cautious. 'Tho' these Indians seem
at present very desirous to come to terms', he wrote to Amherst on
2 June, 'want of Confidence in us or some other reason, may make
them alter their Opinion, the Carpenter is honest, the others are not to
be trusted.'[119] He would therefore be on the look out for an ambush on
his march into the Middle Settlements, which he planned to begin in
three days' time. He had already explained his plan to trade clemency
for non-resistance, but he did not mention that as much had been
offered to Attakullakulla.

If they submit when we get into their Country and remain quietly
in their Towns treating them with Severity could answer no good
End, seeing that they are in our Power will be sufficient, Examples
no doubt must be made, some of the guilty must be put to Death by
themselves, in our Camp, as a Proof of their Sincerity, and as a
Security for their good Behaviour.[120]

He made no mention of such executions not being extorted; nor did
he enclose a copy of his Talk of 28 May. There is another curious dis-
crepancy. Grant left this letter open and put off sending it. Next day he
wrote to Bull giving his expected starting date as 7 June.[121] He had
decided to give Attakullakulla two more days, but he could not offer
this explanation to Amherst. On the day he wrote to Bull, 3 June, the
rains began again and did not cease for two days. All work had to stop.
Only then did Grant add a postscript to his letter to Amherst, explain-
ing that the rain had delayed his march by 48 hours.[122] When at
6 a.m. on 7 June the army snaked away from the fort to ford the waist-
deep Keowee River,[123] the Little Carpenter had been given most of the
time he had desired.

In his letter Grant made no mention of the Valley towns, and he certainly never intended to attack the Overhills. Having supplies for only
a month he argued that an offensive against Chota was Byrd's respons-

ibility, a responsibility Byrd had clearly already abandoned.[124] Bull also assumed that the Cherokees would be able to retire to the Overhill country, out of Grant's reach, 'especially as they have nothing to fear from the Virginia troops on the other side'.[125] That being so Grant almost certainly intended a swift punishing raid, enough to force the war party to sue for peace, but no more.

Having crossed the Keowee and half expecting an attack, the army pressed on towards the towering Oconees. The Carpenter had still not come and already there were signs that Tistoe and Seroweh at least intended to fight. Three days earlier The Tail, perhaps acting for Tistoe, had been caught trying to excite fear of mountains and Cherokees amongst Grant's Indians.[126] Next day Grant began to hurry his men through the dangerous Oconee defiles, and still the Carpenter did not come. The path along War Woman's Creek (which ran very fast knee deep and had to be crossed twice) was commanded on all sides by steep mountains.[127] By 9 June Henry Laurens was convinced that Attakullakulla's talk of peace had been but a delaying tactic, designed to give the Cherokees time to get their crops safely in.[128] Yet Grant did not give up hope of meeting Cherokee 'deputies' until the morning of 10 June,[129] exactly 12 days after the Carpenter's departure from Fort Prince George.[130] By then there was clearly a large force of Cherokees across his path, ready to do battle.

What happened in the Cherokee country during those 12 days can be discerned in outline. Attakullakulla had been unable to persuade Occonostota that it was safe to go to Grant's camp. Nor could he persuade the nation to disgorge more of its captives while Cherokees remained imprisoned in South Carolina.[131] Seroweh seems to have remained implacably hostile – he may have already gone to the Middle Settlements to prepare the resistance – and Tistoe understandably was against all compromise with the treacherous foe. Eight packhorse loads of ammunition – four or five hundredweight of powder and perhaps twice that of ball – had just arrived from Fort Toulouse on the Albama;[132] little enough to be sure, but perhaps enough for another Etchoe. At all events, the Carpenter's pleas were rejected and hundreds of young warriors flocked to resist the invasion. How many came is not known. A Fort Loudoun deserter living among the Cherokees thought that there were 2500.[133] This is improbable, but the more modest estimates are impressive enough. Grant guessed 'at least 600'. But a prisoner taken on 10 June claimed all the Valley and Middle Settlements men were there, which by Laurens's estimate would have made the

Cherokee force over 1200 strong.[134] There were also warriors from the Lower Towns, some women, and about ten Creeks.[135] Still, this was little more than half of Grant's strike force[136] and with proportionately less firepower. Moreover, the speed of Grant's advance through the Oconee ravines forced them to fight in the last defile before Etchoe (Map 7). There could be no question of repeating the mistake of the first Etchoe, by coming to grips with the enemy head on. Instead the Cherokees would attack from the flanks of the defile, where Grant's superior numbers and armament could not be brought to bear. Fighting at long range to minimize losses, they would force Grant to hurry on towards open ground. Then, when his pack train had been drawn into the ravine, they would charge in to kill as many packhorses as possible. The British would be brought to a halt in the pass while Grant tried to defend his vital supplies, and in the ensuing melee he would suffer crippling losses in men and animals. Like Montgomery, Grant would be forced to retire and the Cherokees would have won another great victory. That this was the Cherokee plan can be deduced from the events of the battle. But what happened was rather different.

Long before the invaders reached the ravine the Indians had begun a psychological attack. On the afternoon of 9 June Cherokee scouts began to show themselves to Grant's advance patrols. On an isolated tree they left a threatening carving: of a soldier being dragged away by two Indians.[137] When the British halted for the night at Estatoe Old Town, 17 miles south of Etchoe, a scouting party saw many tracks and fires.[138] That night the Cherokees closed in again. The troops were roused at 3 a.m. and were ready to march at six. For the first time Grant, certain at last that he would have to fight, ordered his men to load. The Indian Corps scouts led the way, followed by the brigaded light infantry which now included a company of provincials. They were followed by the Independents, now formed into a regiment (Burton's), and Middleton's provincials. As the rearguard of cattle-herders and Rangers rode out of the camp-ground, a spattering of musketry followed them. Grant, with the experience of 1760 behind him, at once reinforced his rear. Two hours later, at about 8 a.m. and six miles into the march, Captain Quentin Kennedy's scouts approached the defile.[139]

Here the path ran between a steep mountain on the right and the wood-fringed Cowee River on the left. The Cherokees were deployed behind the river and on the slopes of the mountain, where a small outpost was quickly detected by Kennedy's Indians. Firing broke out at

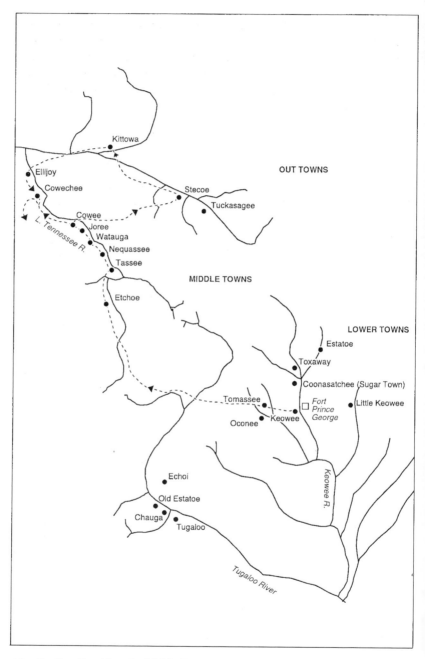

Map 7 Grant's raid on the Middle Towns, 1761

once.[140] The Cherokee 'Yelp' went up on both flanks, from front to rear. With an impassable river on his left and an invisible enemy on both sides, Grant ordered his men to press on, hoping to find open ground where he could fight on his own terms. As the main column entered the ravine the firing became heavier. Grant deployed light infantry and Rangers to clear the mountain slopes and the Indians prudently fell back before them. But the warriors safe behind the river poured shot and arrow in upon the opposite flank.[141] French's men, slowed by horses floundering on the path ahead, soon had to cross a patch of savannah which gave the Cherokee marksmen an excellent field of fire. At Grant's order, he 'sent a platoon to amuse the Indians that were on the far side of the River', while the rest of the company pressed on.[142] At 8.30 the tip of the column reached a ford, and Grant glimpsed open grassland. But even as his light infantry were forcing a crossing the vulnerable pack train entered the ravine.

At once the Cherokees stormed it, killing six Rangers and drivers, wounding many more, and slaughtering between 40 and 60 horses. For a moment the escort commander panicked. But Grant was not caught. Sending back 175 provincials to rescue the pack train, he drove his main force on through the cordon of Cherokees defending the ford. French's company stormed across and took possession of a hill which covered the passage of the main army. The attack on the pack train was beaten off and by mid-morning the whole force was safely across and drawn up in line of battle. The Cherokees kept up a distant firing for some time but would not be drawn into a frontal attack. At about 11.30 they ran out of ammunition and withdrew.[143]

The Cherokees had not been defeated. Their skirmishing tactics had kept their losses to only 30 or so dead and one man taken prisoner.[144] This was astonishingly better than at the first Etchoe. But Grant's casualties had been even lighter – 12 killed (including one Catawba) and 52 wounded[145] – and he still had adequate pack animals and supplies. His army was still perfectly capable of pressing on, while the Cherokees, with no powder, had no way of stopping him. The Middle Settlements were doomed and the Indians hurriedly abandoned them. Their best chance now was to stay out of reach until Grant's supplies ran out.

Grant knew that time was against him. If he could catch the fleeing warriors he might still just obtain a decisive victory. If not – and this was the very dilemma he had put to Amherst in December – he might have to withdraw with nothing resolved. The only escape lay in the complete destruction of the Middle Towns and their crops; then hunger and distress might break the prestige of the hostile headmen and force them to a conference. Grant did not hesitate. He gave his men two hours in which to rest, sink the dead in the river, see to the wounded and build litters.[146]

Then they were off, marching at a killing pace for Etchoe which they entered at 9 p.m. Grant's order to 'put every Soul to Death', as Christopher French misleadingly expressed it,[147] was probably meant for warriors only, but it was ruthless enough. Fortunately it was not put to the test, for all the people had gone. The houses, rebuilt since Montgomery's visit, were all pulled down and the debris fired. The men cooked their suppers in the open; then, leaving Middleton's regiment to guard the wounded and the supply train, they fell in and marched two miles to surprise Tassee. That town, like Etchoe, was deserted. At midnight Tassee went up in flames and the column pressed on, hoping to take the next town unawares. At dawn the exhausted soldiers stumbled into empty Nequassee. Here they posted strong piquets and slept on their arms.[148] The warriors had escaped.

That day the work of serious destruction was begun. Middleton and the wounded arrived, and the town house – 'a large Dome, surrounded with resting places made of Kane & pretty enough'[149] – was converted into a hospital. It was too late for Ensign Munro of 22 Regiment, shot through the body during the battle: he had died on the march. He was buried under a house, which was then pulled down and fired to conceal his grave.[150] All the other houses were demolished and 'wigwams' were made out of the remains.[151] Over the next three days the soldiers tore up the town's rows of peas and beans, let their horses into the fields of ripening corn and cut down the peach trees.[152]

Meanwhile the hunt for Cherokee war bands went on, with spectacularly little success. Grant's Indians raided and burned Neowi and Canuga, towns built by refugees from the Lower Settlements, and on 12 June a strong detachment missed a large Cherokee band at Joree. Only 12 Cherokees were found there, and of these 10 escaped. The raiders returned with one scalp and one old woman prisoner. She displayed astonishing courage, smiling blandly at her captors and refusing to say anything. Eventually French and his fellows helped her to escape, hoping to save her from the Catawbas, but to no avail. She went straight home to Joree where the Catawbas found and scalped her. Their only other capture was another old woman whom they scalped and threw into the river.[153] Indeed the Savannah River Chickasaws and Catawbas had had enough; on 14 June they made off for Carolina to collect the bounties on their scalps.[154] Grant's army had begun to wreak its havoc, but already the process of disintegration had commenced.

On 14 June the army moved on to complete its grim task. By 2 July they had, in Henry Laurens's words,

> burnt upwards of 800 (houses) in 15 Towns in a circuit of 150 miles, & plucked up at least 1500 acres of Corn, Beans, Mellons &. This work tho necessary often makes my heart bleed. The Cherokees has totally abandoned these Towns & fled with their wretched Women & Children across the Mountains into the Valley settlements. They have already suffer'd greatly & will be reduced to extreme misery as the Winter advances. We took in their Towns or rather by outscouts five prisoners and four more were killed.[155]

Another participant added that almost five thousand Cherokees had been driven into the mountains 'to starve'.[156] At Joree a decision had to be made. Despite the appalling sack of the Middle Towns Grant had neither brought the warriors to a second battle, nor forced them to send peace deputies. From Joree he could have turned into the Valley and spread destruction there. But there were two sound arguments against it. First, the column was hardly fit to go further. About 1000 men had worn out their shoes, the other supplies were nearly gone, and everyone was tattered and exhausted. Over 300 were already wounded, sick or lame[157] and every day more men fell ill.[158] Exhaustion brought lapses of vigilance. Up till now the little bands of warriors stalking the army had not taken a single scalp. But on 3 July a party 'supposed to be five in number' killed a packhorseman and escaped, 'notwithstanding they came within our advanced Guards'.[159] Still, an autocratic and determined officer like Grant could have driven them on for a few more days, long enough to raze a couple of the Valley towns and strike terror into the rest. But as we have seen, wholesale destruction was never part of Grant's purpose. Even now he feared that he might have gone too far. As he later told Amherst, the Cherokees 'must certainly starve or come to Terms, & even in that Case, I think 'tis hardly in the power of the Province to save them'.[160] Already, judging by the number of carcasses on the paths, the Cherokees were killing and eating their own horses.[161] Humane feeling and military prudence pointed in the same direction. At 6 a.m. on Saturday 4 July the army marched for Fort Prince George.[162]

The decision ignited a long smouldering quarrel with Thomas Middleton, who from the start had resented having to serve under a mere lieutenant-colonel. Being a relative and an important political supporter of the lieutenant-governor, Middleton had been in a position to do something about it. By 2 April he had wrung from Bull two extraordinary letters. The first had instructed Middleton to obey Grant's orders only until Bull directed otherwise. This had provoked a volcanic protest from Grant; he alone, as the commander-in-chief's appointee, was in military command in South Carolina.[163] Bull had kept the second letter, permitting Middleton to leave the expedition, whenever it should become 'irksome and disagreeable' to him, a secret. He did this partly to avoid conflict, but partly, as he told John Rattray later, out of pique with Grant over the commissioning of Ranger officers.[164] By the time the army reached Keowee Grant had won his point over the Ranger commissions but the two incidents had not improved his opinion of the lieutenant-governor. On 2 June he had informed Amherst that Bull had taken far too much upon himself in the past six months. 'I imagine', he went on, 'his being appointed to sign the Peace led him to think that his Powers was much extended.'[165] What he might have said had he known of the second letter can be left to the imagination.

Though Grant had already given the provincials the same status as the regulars – which Monypenny thought unparalleled in North America[166] – the invasion of the Middle Settlements had brought on a series of petty disputes. It may be that Grant's habit of taking all the decisions himself – nothing extraordinary in a military commander – irked the amateur provincial colonel. It may even be that the quarrel reflected much deeper provincial resentment of being marginalized by British regular officers, and by the northern focus of British strategy in general. Even more alarming, at least to provincial patricians like Middleton, was the realization that Grant – an unelected imperial agent – was taking over the direction of local Indian policy. In mid-June at Cowee,[167] seventh of the 15 towns to burn, there had been words about an express sent back to Fort Prince George. Middleton complained that it had gone without his knowledge, thus depriving him of an opportunity to send letters home.[168] Probably Middleton had been urging stronger measures for some time, and the real argument was about whether to invade the Valley. Perhaps Grant, suspecting that Middleton wanted to rouse public opinion in his favour, let him miss the express on purpose. Now, furious at his advice and seniority being set at naught, the provincial colonel produced Bull's letter, announcing that he would use it when the army reached Keowee. He was as good as his word. On the evening of 10 July the troops sighted Fort Prince George and at once he withdrew from his 'voluntary' subordination to Grant. In the morning Middleton set out for Charleston.[169] In effect, he had deserted his regiment. This was hardly surprising behaviour from a man who had spent the winter in Charleston, while his men at the Congarees had frozen, sickened and died.[170] Once back in Charleston he found the parochial-minded and belligerent citizens only too willing to listen to his accusations. By 18 July it was common talk that Grant, by sparing the Valley Towns, killing so few Cherokees and destroying so much food had only encouraged the Indians to raid South Carolina again.[171] By the end of the month Peter Timothy was publishing Middleton's diatribes in his *South Carolina Gazette*. Here Grant was additionally accused of failing to reinforce his cattle train on 10 June (that had allegedly been Middleton's initiative) and of failing to swing round behind the Cherokees to give them a crushing blow.[172]

Had it not been for this public attack, Grant would have let Middleton go quietly; he declined to question the authority of Bull's letter, and did not even mention the matter to Amherst until the press campaign was well under way.[173] But once he was openly assailed Grant raged from Keowee against Middleton and Bull. The latter, unwilling as ever to take a firm position, left the public to judge whether Middleton had acted correctly. Eventually he tried to appease Grant by the token gesture of suspending Middleton from his now rapidly disintegrating command. But there was no sign of Middleton's resignation, nor of a court-martial. Henry Laurens, now in command of the disappearing provincials, thought the lieutenant-governor's behaviour incomprehensible.[174] Grant's friend on the Council, John Rattray, had laboured to pour oil upon troubled waters, but even he was disgusted with Bull's prevarication. 'The Govr.', he declared, 'has been Halting & still Halts between Duty and Convenience.'[175] Meanwhile, as Rattray observed, this 'Halting' had encouraged the bloodthirsty majority into ludicrous but chilling extremes:

> If the Army could kill 9/10th of the Cherokee Nation & give ample proof of it – yet many would not believe it & many would still remain unsatisfied without a Certificate from Hell that their souls were Damned to all Eternity.[176]

Thus long before the deputies came down to treat at Fort Prince George most colonists had come to believe that Grant had saved the Cherokees and humiliated South Carolina. In this atmosphere the sacking of 15 little towns seemed like the tenderness of a collaborator. Through Middleton public opinion had sensed Grant's true motives and been prepared for greater betrayals to come.

For seven anxious weeks, while the rage against him in Charleston grew, Grant waited for the Cherokee delegates. The problem was no longer the obduracy of the war faction, which had been totally discredited by Grant's raid. Already, on about 1 July, the Little Carpenter had persuaded the Chota council to seek peace. But Occonostota still wielded sufficient support to insist upon their making the first approach to Virginia, not to Grant. In this way the nation's enemies might be divided and honourable terms might yet be obtained. The council saw the sense of making overtures to the weaker, less aggrieved and less active enemy, and commissioned Attakullakulla as its envoy. Grant's raid had now restored the Carpenter to something like his old position of chief diplomat. However, the council was still very far from empowering him to sue for peace. Not surprisingly, when he reached Byrd's camp on the Holston on 18 July the whole manoeuvre collapsed. Far from exploiting Virginian jealousy of South Carolina's primacy in Cherokee affairs, Attakullakulla discovered that Amherst had ordered Byrd to leave the peace preliminaries to Grant. He could only blame the war upon his absent rivals – Occonostota, Ostenaca and Standing Turkey – and carry Byrd's Talk to these warriors back to Chota.[177]

With Attakullakulla temporarily out of the way Occonostota had begun his own contacts with Grant. Perhaps afraid that the Scot would once again take the offensive, and almost certainly bent on outmanoeuvring the Carpenter, he sent Old Caesar of Chatuga to Grant on or about 14 July.[178] Thus even before Attakullakulla had reached Byrd, the Great Warrior was trying to take over the peace negotiations himself. Caesar, long known as an advocate of peace, was the ideal messenger. At the same time Grant sent out two messengers of his own, the Mankiller of Nequassee and the White Owl of Toxaway, with an ultimatum: if an embassy did not come by 29 July he would march on Chota. Grant's pair met Caesar en route and brought him back to the British camp. There on 21 July he asked for peace, promising that even Seroweh – who had gone to raid Georgia – would be held to it on pain of execution.[179] But he offered no specific terms[180] and Grant knew that to make the peace secure he must deal with a properly accredited delegation. He sent Caesar back with a demand for Occonostota himself.

To the Great Warrior, this was unwelcome news. He was deeply afraid of a repetition of Lyttelton's and Miln's treachery and dared not go.[181] Attakullakulla was back with the news that Virginia would not make a separate peace, and if Occonostota did not go to Grant the Carpenter would recover the initiative. There was one chance: Grant might be persuaded to deal with Occonostota and the rest by proxy, through hitherto hostile Cherokees of the second rank. He and Standing Turkey assembled a number of headmen and insisted that the hatchet be buried. They then sent Tistoe of Keowee and the Slave Catcher of Tomotly to Grant with two strings of beads, a pipe adorned with a white feather, and some tobacco.[182]

This pair reached Keowee on Sunday 9 August and saw Grant at a public conference next day. The Great Warrior and Standing Turkey, they declared, had 'gone hunting': Cherokee code for refusal to come. Grant replied that he wanted 'to mend & Brighten the Chain' of friendship, but insisted that he must have 'the first voices' – Occonostota, Ostenaca, Attakullakulla (and Standing Turkey). The Slave Catcher and Tistoe were given 'Twelve Sleeps' to return with a satisfactory reply – or he would renew the war.[183] They left with John Watts, now a captain of Rangers and Grant's interpreter.[184] Occonostota had to choose between risking a personal appearance, and allowing the war to resume.

He almost chose to take the risk. He gathered a party of headmen and took them down as far as Little Hiwassee. There, to his dismay he found Seroweh with stolen horses and one of two kidnapped Georgia Rangers. The headmen confronted the Young Warrior who, in Watts's hearing, said that he did not know that peace was being discussed. No one believed this story, and Occonostota was terrified that the British would seize him in revenge. He obtained the release of the Ranger, and sent him to Grant with a message that he was looking for the other man and the horses. With this excuse he handed over all his negotiations to the Carpenter.[185] For the Chota council had decided that it could no longer wait.

The most intractable problem was hunger. Almost the whole Cherokee population was now dependent upon the resources of the Overhill and Valley towns, adequate for perhaps a third of their number.[186] Grant's tattered force was visibly less of a threat to the Overhills than an obstacle to the reoccupation of the destroyed settlements, while Byrd had not moved for months. But without food or trade the distressed nation would be helpless against the winter raids of Chickasaws from further down the Tennessee River,[187] the Shawnees (who were now at peace with the British)[188] and the Iroquois. Even hitherto friendly Creeks were already making overtures to Bull.[189] Those who survived the cold, hunger and scalping might well face a renewed British offensive in the spring. In short the Cherokees might suffer at the hands of the British the fate dealt out to the Natchez by the French: annihilation.[190] Peace must be made, even if the three great headmen would not risk their persons to conclude it. On or about 21 August Attakullakulla was given command of an eight-man delegation to negotiate a reasonable peace.[191]

The others were Old Caesar, the Raven of Tomotly and the Mankiller of Nequassee, Connecorte's son Cappy, Moitoi of Hiwassee, Half-Breed Will of Nequassee and Willinawaw. The party set out with a white flag before it and accompanied by a number of other Cherokees.[192] One of these was Occonostota, who had decided to come close enough to Fort Prince George to intervene in the talks by messenger if need be.[193] His presence caused a little confusion. On Tuesday, 25 August a Cherokee runner came into Keowee with a white man – a former deserter from Fort Loudoun – and a message: Occonostota was coming down to treat. The British were jubilant.[194] But on 28 August it was Attakullakulla who appeared at the fort with his fellow delegates, 'a few Attendants' and Watts.[195] He admitted leaving some important headmen, including Occonostota, some distance away. The jubilation in the camp turned to frustration. '[W]e were much disappointed', wrote Christopher French, 'at not seeing the great Warrior as we judged his absence must prolong our Treaty.'[196] Nevertheless a properly authorized embassy had come and the serious work of treaty-making could begin.

Thus it was that on Saturday, 29 August the Carpenter and the Colonel sat down to smoke their pipe of peace. Just as Grant had predicted, the Cherokees had been able to retreat deep into their mountain fastnesses, well beyond the reach of destruction. The peace would now have to be the honourable compromise he and the Carpenter had always wanted and worked for. It cannot be said that Attakullakulla was glad to meet the destroyer of the Middle Towns. But he may have already recognized a fellow spirit.

* Grant applied means which he believed were enough to make the Cherokees ask for peace.

* Grant believed, as did many imperial gov't officials, that the Cherokees deserved a lenient peace, since the colonials had provoked them into war.

* The imperial gov't had forbidden the violation of Natt. rights in Ohio & the New York frontier, so they allowed Grant to see a general feeling

* Rivalries among the Cherokee about who to negotiate & the need for food.

6

The Carpenter, the Corn Puller and the 'Town of Lyes'

Grant's threat of renewed hostilities was pure bluff. His men had endured 33 days of long marches over wild and rugged mountains which some thought more formidable than the Alps. They had cheerfully endured open bivouacs, rough and precipitous tracks, 'and what the men thought worse than all, no Rum'.[1] Grant was proud of them, even of the once suspect Independents and unruly Rangers, and would ask no more of them at present.[2] The only Cherokee towns within reach were the pathetic remains of the Lower Settlements, and as early as 10 July he had determined to leave them alone. 'I shall', he had told Amherst, 'in a few days send to the Great Warrior & the Little Carpenter ... Till I receive their Answer I shall endeavour to save the small Remains of the Lower Towns.'[3] Indeed, as we have seen, he spared them for seven whole weeks under conditions which might have driven a less scrupulous man to action.

A second thrust into the mountains had become even less conceivable than at Joree. Middleton's desertion had encouraged large numbers of the provincials to follow suit. Their pay was in arrears, their terms of enlistment had expired on 20 July, and by the time Attakullakulla reached Keowee they were walking off in bodies. 'The Regt.', Grant warned Amherst, will soon disband itself.'[4] The Rangers' term would be up on 10 October, unless Bull could persuade the Commons to sustain them for longer.[5] Many of the Catawbas and Chickasaws, who had proved so invaluable as scouts, were gone. The Mohawks were few and scalp hungry; even before the Middle Settlements raid their leader, Silver Heels, had committed a savage attack upon friendly Indians.[6] Grant could rely only upon the few staunch Upper Chickasaws – 'quite a different Species from any other Indians I have ever met' – whose outstanding loyalty and good behaviour he wanted to reward.[7] In any case the waggon train which kept him supplied at Fort Prince George was worn out. On his return Grant had reharnessed the pack horses to 140 of the 150 encamped waggons and sent them down to Ninety Six for stores. Only 63 had been able to make the return journey. The horses were so tired that animals from the broken down waggons had to be used to help the remaining teams, and Bull said he had no power to break into private premises to conscript replacements.[8] Even if Attakullakulla's embassy had not come, Grant would soon have had to march down the country.

The Virginians were, of course, a lost cause. Byrd, let down by the contractors appointed to supply him, had reached Stalnaker's on the Holston only on 19 July. On 1 August he was still there, 200 miles from the nearest Cherokee town, with no more than 670 men fit for duty. Even if he reached the Overhill settlements, behind him would lie 330 miles of road which would have to be protected 'in case of Accidents'. The Cherokee retreat in the face of Grant's raid had, he argued, made his task still more difficult, for many Indians were now concentrated in the Overhill towns 'where they seem to have nothing to fear from him'.[9]

> If Colonel Grant with his formidable Power could only burn fifteen towns & over-run the Country below the Mountains, not more than seventy miles from his advance Post, I do not imagine it can be expected that I can with my pittyful number proceed thro a Wilderness two hundred miles from my advance Post, which is one hundred and thirty Miles above the Inhabitants, to attack thirty two Towns in the Remotest Part of the Nation, defended by their united Force, with the most distant probability of success.[10]

The final humiliation had been Attakullakulla's approach, which Byrd's orders had obliged him to reject. Neither strong enough to frighten the Cherokees, nor authorized to make peace, Byrd was in an impossible situation. Never an enthusiastic leader, and possibly as sympathetic to the Cherokees as Grant, he resigned his command.[11]

The new commander, Adam Stephen, made a show of energy. He pushed the Virginians up to the Great Island in the Holston, about 100 miles from Chota, where he began to build a fort. But in the end he could do no more than Byrd. By the end of August he was still on the island, the fort half built.[12] Fauquier, who could not even get last year's Acts and legislative journals copied, could do nothing to help:

'Inactivity, Indolence & an aversion to Business prevailing universally thro' this Colony,'[13] he complained. He did not need to add that the House of Burgesses was not interested in augmenting an expedition beyond its own frontiers, and on what was for Virginia a secondary front. Grant knew from Byrd's letters of 19 and 22 July that the Virginians would remain passive, and the Carpenter must have guessed that as well.

Grant thus had a watertight military case to put to Amherst, who had instructed him to remain at Fort Prince George in case 'before a Peace is firmly Established, the Cherokees out of Despair should attempt a Revenge upon the Settlements'.[14] It followed that if the army had to go down the country, the preliminary peace terms should not be such as to drive them to desperation. Grant's reasoning would be less well received in Charleston, where the Middleton-inspired agitation was reaching a crescendo. But to Grant this was of small significance as long as he had Amherst's support. The commander-in-chief had agreed that had the Cherokees used the terrain 'or any Spirit to Oppose your passage, they must undoubtedly have done You great Mischief', but, he added characteristically, Indians were 'a Dastardly sett'. Now that the Cherokees had been so roundly defeated, South Carolina should have no trouble in looking after its own defence; consequently, the colony should not expect automatic support in future. Indeed, the punishment already meted out would surely force the Cherokees to accept whatever terms were offered; Grant, having done everything possible, could be 'very indifferent' to public opinion, and was given discretion to send some troops down as circumstances should dictate.[15] True, the peace would still have to be ratified in Charleston, but once Grant began to send detachments down the country the colony would have to accept his terms. Thus instead of the usual picture of a humane man driven to concessions by military necessity, we have a clever and powerful personality imposing peace terms he had always wanted.

Attakullakulla, on the other hand, knew he was in a far stronger position than in May. On 29 August he began proceedings by shaking hands with Grant and presenting a pipe, which Willinawaw handed 'round to each of us to smoak out of, which being ended the Talk began'.[16] The Carpenter announced that the pipe had been sent by 'the Prince of Chotee' – Standing Turkey – thus drawing attention to the absence of the 'first voices' insisted upon by Grant. He then presented beads from Chota, Settico, Chatuga and Great Tellico 'that all things may be Straight'. By thus demonstrating that a significant number of the hostile towns wanted peace, he managed to imply that other settlements were unconvinced. He was warning Grant not to press too hard. On the other hand, he accepted that the Middle Towns had brought their destruction on themselves, and asked Grant to pity the 'Dying, Naked & Starving' refugees. He promised that young men who, like Seroweh, went on raiding 'shall all be Quiet', and asked for peace on the basis of a mutual exchange of prisoners and restored trade. His speech ended with a pointed reminder of his past services to the British, including the rescue of John Stuart.[17] It was an impressive and dignified performance, and Grant was quick to take up his conciliatory tone. The Scot reminded the Cherokee that he had personally arranged the release of the Indians taken by Miln in May 1760, though the final peace would have to be based on the lieutenant-governor's terms and be ratified at Charleston. These terms he would present next day. The offer was plain enough: Grant would support any reasonable Cherokee demands, if the Indians in turn were prepared to be sensible. The overnight pause before presenting the formal terms was probably intended, in the usual way of Indian diplomacy, to allow time for a deal to be negotiated behind the scenes.

Just as in May, the existence of such a privy conference may be inferred from the outcome. Most likely Attakullakulla was given Bull's terms and at once pointed out that the nation would never accept the executions clause. Certainly Grant argued in these terms afterwards, although he had not done so before. The executions, he told Bull, would be 'hard' on the Cherokees as there had been 'a General War' in which the Cherokees had been 'Severely Corrected'.[18] Besides, the only means of compulsion in his power were both inadequate and distasteful.

> ... if a peace is ever to be made with the Cherokees too much has already been done on this Side, if they could have been brought to terms with a less Severe Correction for they must either Starve or be a Load to the Province for some time ... I could easily destroy the remains of the Lower Towns in a few hours, and I could send to Toogaloo, but these things are of so little Consequence that they are not worth mentioning and are better let alone for the late Chastisement will make them honest or nothing will.[19]

He had no power to delete a clause, especially the one which Bull had insisted was the key to peace. But to avoid a fatal breach he agreed to refer the matter to the lieutenant-governor. The Cherokees were 'much pleased', as they had thought South Carolina would make harder terms than they had hoped to get from Virginia.

The only other difficulty was over the proposal to make Attakullakulla emperor of the Cherokees. As Corkran points out,[20] probably it was the Carpenter himself who persuaded Grant that this measure

> would ruin his interest in the Nation, in the present Satuation [sic] of affairs. The Headmen of whom Several have as much Power as he has, would never come into it, and he neither has [n]or pretends to have influence enough to agree to a Peace or to bring it about without the Approbation and Concurrence of the Headman [sic] who have employed him to treat for the Nation ...[21]

Such confident intimacy with the Carpenter's mind must surely have come from another source than the formal exchanges of 29 and 30 August; moreover, it is a confidence not hitherto evident in Grant's writings. No doubt, as he listened to the Carpenter's arguments, Grant saw that his fruitless demands for the 'first voices', the advice of old traders like Watts, and even Bull's own apprehensions on this point, all pointed in the same direction. The clause was struck out.

The public negotiations of 30 August would thus appear to be a rehearsed confirmation of matters already decided. When Grant read out the peace terms the first clause, that demanding executions, was still there, but the emperor clause had gone. Attakullakulla promptly replied that he would have to consult the whole nation if the executions were to be insisted upon.[22] Grant as promptly gave him until the following day to answer. He had, he added, 'but one Tongue' and if the terms were not agreed to 'there could be no Peace'. After all, he was only asking for what he would have granted the Cherokees, had the English been guilty.[23] It is unlikely that Attakullakulla was genuinely taken aback by the first clause; in May he had offered to secure such executions himself. Moreover, the quickness of his and Grant's responses certainly suggests that each already knew what the other would say. Neither man could afford to give way too easily, and the further day's delay allowed each to appear to be haggling. It also gave the Carpenter time to consult Occonostota. Not surprisingly, the speeches exchanged on 31 August have even more of the smell of the lamp about them.

That morning Attakullakulla gave a long Talk – a 'very artful' one, thought Christopher French[24] – which may rank as a masterpiece of Indian rhetoric. He explained that he had been shocked by the harshness of the terms offered the day before, made much of his personal attempts to end the war and restrain the Overhills, and cleverly pointed out that time was running out. 'When he set out they gave him Ten Nights, Of which Six are gone, And that he will now have but three left to go [home] with it.' He recalled that he had brought warning of a Creek party at Hiwassee bent on attacking Grant's Chickasaws as they travelled homeward with their presents. Eventually he addressed the critical question. He would accept the general principle that Cherokees and whites who offended in future should die: 'it was so before.' But as for the immediate deaths of four Cherokees, 'he ... has looked all around him, but cant [sic] see them, for they are all grown better, but if any of them grow bad again they shall be killed.'[25] But more he could not do until he had consulted the nation in the short time remaining: 'he will soon let the people at home know what was told him Yesterday.'[26] He then softened the blow by agreeing to expel all French agents from the nation, as urged upon him by Byrd: 'for they were as nothing, And would soon be driven out of America by the English, And that the White and Red people must live in peace & friendship together.'[27] He concluded on a humble note, pointing out that the Cherokees needed peace so that the traders could return: he 'should be very glad to see them bringing Goods as formerly, which would Shew that they took Pity on their People.'[28] Nevertheless, his rejection of the first clause was clear and unambiguous.

Grant, with a show of impatience, replied that he had waited long enough, and that the Carpenter had already claimed to have the power to treat for the whole nation. Then he slipped in the means of escape.

> He observes that he answers but two Articles, and that [he] declines agreeing to the Performance of the first. He now desires him to Answer to every Article particularly except the first which they will talk of afterwards.[29]

The articles were then re-read and the Cherokee agreed to all of them individually. Grant followed this by declaring that he had 'Considered' both the Cherokees' objections to the executions and the terrible privations suffered 'by the People of the Middle Settlements'.[30] This was virtually a public admission of previous collusion, as Grant was never one to make important decisions in haste. There was, moreover, a feeling among his officers that Attakullakulla's refusal had made the first clause a dead letter; 'nor do I suppose', observed French, 'that we should have let them carry it out to the last extremity if they had agreed'.[31] Grant went on to point out that he could not delete Bull's first article on his own authority, and that the delegates would have to meet the lieutenant-governor face to face in Charleston. But should Bull agree 'to lay aside the First Article he [Grant] shall have no objection'.[32] This was as clear a declaration of sympathy and support as the Carpenter could have desired. He accepted with alacrity, electing to take Willinawaw, Cappy, Half-Breed Will, the Mankiller of Nequassee and the Raven as his companions. The others would return to the nation to discover 'whether they will agree to the first article if insisted upon by the Governor'.[33] This last mission was but a formality; everyone at Keowee knew what the reply must be. Far more significant was the speed with which the Cherokees made their – presumably prearranged – decision.

No wonder that the Cherokees were pleased. They had won a preliminary peace almost upon their own terms. Unless Bull made objections or alterations there would be no puppet emperor, no loss of land and no executions. Grant's promised support and the state of his army might prevent any modifications at all. Grant, who was fond of good living, hosted a celebratory dinner party. By the end of the meal, after the wine had flowed freely, it came out that Occonostota had promised to show his friendship by going to fight the French or any Indians hostile to the British. 'I believe the sincerity of this Offer the more', wrote Grant, 'as it did not come out till our business was Over here, ... from the Mankiller of Nequassee [who] got up from the Table, in great good humour and in the fullness of his heart to make Captain Watts tell me, as he thought it had been forgot.'[34]

But such boozy goodwill overlay a much more profound fear of what might happen in Charleston. It had taken a great deal of courage on the Indians' part to agree to enter the town where Occonostota had been betrayed in 1759, nor had they forgotten Miln's deception of 1760. The trust so painstakingly engendered by Grant was very thin, and that evening the renegade trader Gunninghame came close to pricking the bubble. Arriving late in the camp, and hearing of the projected embassy to Bull, he went straight to the Cherokees with dark tales of treachery. Charleston, he said, was racked with smallpox and the whites hoped that the Cherokee deputies would all die. Gunninghame, of course, wanted to delay the reappearance of rival traders in the nation, and he may even have believed that the Cherokees were walking into a trap. Whatever his motives he came near to wrecking the peace. All the deputies and their attendants – bar six or seven who clung to Attakullakulla – fled at once. From a safe distance they sent back a runner with two stray horses and a white turkey, 'to shew me that their hearts are straight tho' they are afraid'. Grant clapped Gunninghame into irons and would have hanged him if he had more than 'Indian Proof', a sentiment which that lover of simple direct justice, Amherst, would later heartily endorse.[35] Grant had won respect and a measure of confidence, but Lyttelton and Miln still cast long shadows.

On 3 September, having regained their courage, the Cherokees set out for Charleston. With them went Henry Laurens and four other officers. Well ahead of them went Grant's letter to Bull, putting their case in the strongest terms and making it perfectly clear that further military action was out of the question: in other words, that the peace terms were unalterable. Within a week the lieutenant-governor knew that the Indians were on their way.[36] He was now in the uncomfortable position of having to justify to the Commons a treaty which demanded neither land nor executions. True to form, he tried to evade the issue.

On 10 September he met the Council and laid before it Grant's letter, one from Laurens, and a copy of his own letter of the 14 April containing the original peace terms. Pointing out that the Cherokees seemed to genuinely desire peace, he asked the board for advice. Should he meet Attakullakulla en route with only the Council, or should they consult the Commons? The Council agreed that it would be prudent to consult the Commons, and that the meeting should take place at Shem Town near the Ashley River ferry, as there were rumours of yellow fever in Charleston.[37] This move would have the double effect of reassuring the Cherokee deputies frightened by Gunninghame, and of removing the discussions from the excited atmosphere of the colonial capital. There was no discussion of the letter of 14 April. But by tabling it Bull had drawn attention to the boundary clause, while Grant, supposing the matter to be dead and buried, had not mentioned the boundary at all. Knowing full well that he would have to face the Commons, Bull had made it appear that Grant had unilaterally dropped the land cession. This cannot possibly be regarded, as Bull's biographer would have it, as a negotiating ploy, for at no time in the subsequent negotiations did he use the boundary as a lever. Nor did he suggest such a course to the Council. Having thus done his best to divert the assembly's predictable anger, he took the further precaution of catching a diplomatic illness. When at last he had to face Grant's fury he was, as we shall see, able to plead a lapse of memory.

On the morning of Tuesday, 15 September at Shem Town Bull and three councillors – Othniel Beale, Austin and Egerton Leigh – welcomed Attakullakulla and his party. A peace pipe, lit by Attakullakulla, was passed round and the Carpenter presented strings of wampum from the whole nation as well as from Chota and the other towns. The formalities having been cordially dealt with, the meeting adjourned: officially to allow Bull to consider his reply.[38] In fact the delay permitted him to consult the Commons – due to meet that afternoon – and perhaps also to meet the Carpenter in private. Before the Commons Bull continued the deception he had begun with the Council. He tabled three letters: his own of 14 April, Grant's of 2 September, and one from Byrd pointing out that the Virginians would not attack the Overhills. The record of the Council's conference with the Cherokees that morning was then read and ordered copied into the journals.[39] The Commons were thus left in no doubt that they must accept a peace without executions, but with the boundary clause intact (Map 8).

The house was not pleased. Bull's message and the supporting papers were referred to a committee of nine members, of whom Middleton was one.[40] There could be little doubt as to what their verdict would be, and at 10 a.m. on 16 September they duly delivered it. Peace without executions, ran their first resolution, 'would be useless and dishonourable, and that no peace ought to be made with the Cherokees upon any other terms'. The committee also thought that the remaining terms ought to be subject to confirmation of the 1730 treaty;[41] by this means they hoped to obtain Cherokee recognition of British sovereignty, and to reinstate the emperor clause. As a gesture towards providing the necessary force they wanted to keep the Rangers enlisted and paid until 1 January. The house then passed a motion calling for a copy of Grant's journal of the negotiations at Keowee.[42] Having thus made it clear where it believed blame lay, the Commons deferred discussion of the committee's report till the following day.[43]

By then most of the members, though angry with Grant, had absorbed the unpalatable truth. Executions could not be had unless Grant enforced them, and Grant would do no such thing. The reading of Grant's journal only confirmed this verdict. With an ill grace the Commons voted to delete the executions clause, and the following day they agreed not to insist upon Attakullakulla becoming emperor. The rest of the 14 April terms were agreed to without important amendments, though the Cherokees were to be compelled to return black as well as white captives, and South Carolina would not again undertake the garrisoning or supply of Fort Loudoun. There was one significant exception. Bull was asked to prescribe the exact conditions under which Cherokees could cross the Twenty-Six Mile River, and to insist upon the surrender of renegade whites.[44] As Bull had anticipated, the house regarded the boundary clause as some kind of compensation for the lack of executions. Thus far his political instincts had been correct. Before noon on 18 September the business was done.[45]

Having accepted the *fait accompli*, however, the house appointed a second committee to record its feelings in the form of a reply to Bull's original message. The chairman of that committee was Grant's friend and fellow Scot John Rattray, whose contempt for the prevailing blood-lust was prodigious. But not even he could stem the members' anger. Of the six one was Middleton's most ferocious partisan, Christopher Gadsden, and another was Byrne, chairman of the previous commit-tee.[46] When the assembly resumed after lunch poor Rattray had to read out a report which roundly condemned his friend.

The committee echoed accusations already being made by Middleton in print. Grant, should have stuck to his original plan to conclude the preliminary peace in an Indian town house. This could have been done by invading the Valley, as many colonists had expected. The result of not attacking those towns had been too little salutary destruction. 'We dread the unhappy consequences that may attend Colonel Grant[']s depending too much on the importance of destroying the Middle Towns; a thing he made light of last year ...' Instead he should have pressed on, forced the Cherokees to accept battle again, and slaugh-tered as many as possible. 'The only way to fight a Cherokee War is to destroy as many of these People as we can & when an Opportunity Offers to miss it by no means.' Grant, on the contrary, had wilfully given up many such opportunities; as a result the Cherokees would still have insufficient respect for British arms. Middleton, however, whom Grant had ignored, was an officer 'of great Influence, merit and abili-ties, and well acquainted with the Interest of the Province & the proper method of Treating with the Cherokees'. But as Middleton would clearly never be consulted by a regular commander, and as South Carolina would not pay for a renewed war itself, the omission of the execution clause had to be accepted. The Rangers would also have to be continued, thanks to Grant's ineffectualness, but that did not mean that the colony should be saddled with the garrisoning of Fort Loudoun.[47] Bull had obtained what he considered to be the least severe terms which the province would accept, and left Grant with the subse-quent opprobrium. When he wrote to the Board of Trade he made much of the removal of the executions clause, and to Amherst he stressed the 'Reluctance' with which the peace had been achieved. He made no mention of the boundary.[48]

Thus on 22 September the Cherokee delegation attended a meeting of the Council to formally hear Bull's terms. The panic about fever having subsided, the whole conference had moved back to Charleston in the interim, and the reading took place in the council chamber.[49] Although he appears to have objected to the boundary clause in private, Attakullakulla was too glad to get rid of the executions to make difficulties in public. He must have known Grant's sentiments on the boundary, and Bull may have hinted that there was still room for negotiation on that point. That being so the two months until ratification could take place might be put to good use. Bull produced a pipe decorated with feathers left behind by another Cherokee embassy 'in time of peace'. All smoked from the pipe in honour of the new peace, after which the terms were read out. At the end Bull made a point of the omission of the executions clause, saying that he expected good faith in return; in particular he expected some headmen to come down to ratify the treaty which the Carpenter had agreed on their behalf. 'I am', replied Attakullakulla, 'extremely well satisfied with everything your Honour has proposed and said.'[50]

Next day the eight delegates came to see the solemn sealing of the treaty and to receive their own copy for the nation. As the copy was handed over, Bull urged the Carpenter to have it read to the Chota council by an honest interpreter, a plain allusion to the notorious Gunningham and his ilk. Attakullakulla then asked for and was promised presents for the headmen as a token of friendship, 'proper stuff for warm cloathing'. Although two war parties had gone against the Chickasaws before he left the nation, he undertook on his return to prevent further raids and to return with an embassy for the ratification. Bull, pointing out that what 'Mr. Cunningham told you of sickness ... you see to be a lie', urged him to hurry. Otherwise the headmen might not be thought sincere.[51] As tokens of his own goodwill he invited Attakullakulla to dinner, and promised to consider the case of a Fort Loudoun soldier who wanted to stay with the Cherokees. At the price, which might still be evaded, of giving up a swathe of the Lower Towns' land, the Overhill statesman had won for his people an honourable peace. On 24 September he set out for the nation.

In fact Bull was not at all sure that Occonostota and the others would come; that was his reason for harping on the machinations of the 'wicked whites' as he called them.[52] Like Grant he knew that the confidence restored in the Cherokees' minds was wafer thin, and the least accident could puncture it beyond repair. Over dinner that evening he had pinned Attakullakulla down to a timetable; he would reach Grant within 12 days and summon the Chota Council on 13 October. Allowing four days for discussion, the nation's reply should be at Fort Prince George by 21 October, and be in Bull's hands in six or seven days after that.[53]

Bull wrote at once to Grant to inform him of the outcome, presumably gritting his teeth in the knowledge that his deception would now be revealed. Perhaps he hoped that Grant would accept the treaty with no more than a growl of protest. If so, he gravely misjudged his man. Grant was furious when he found that the boundary clause had been reinserted behind his back. Quite apart from the insult to himself, he could not believe that such a land-grabbing peace could last.

> This Province is desirous to continue the War in order to keep the Troops in the Country, their Conduct shews it, for a Peace cannot be lasting if the intended Encroachment of seventy Miles, upon the Indian Country takes Place, and you'l please to observe that the Lieut. Governor has inserted that Article at the *Desire* of the Assembly, tho' he impowered me under his *hand* to leave it out.
>
> I expect the Indian Deputies every moment. I shall recommend to the Carpenter to be expeditious in returning with some of the Head men, according to the Lieut Governors Desire but Im afraid they'l not trust themselves so soon, the Alterations made in the Treaty at Charles Town will be no Encouragement.[54]

In Grant's mind the recovery of the Cherokees' trust was the central issue, and he was far from sure that Bull's timidity might not forfeit it at the last moment. But he was not short of a reply. He would, he told Amherst, very soon have to retire to Ninety Six where he could more easily obtain supplies, and where, as he said, 'the Frontier will be equally well protected'.[55] The colonel intended to withdraw from the Cherokee towns and stand on the defensive, even before ratification, so forcing the colony no choice but to accept the terms of 1 September.

Attakullakulla's progress up the country was unexpectedly slow. Not until 12 October did he reach Fort Prince George, grumbling about the threats he had received from settlers en route, but on the whole greatly pleased to have avoided the executions. He hoped, he told Grant next day, by appearing to save the nation from destruction, 'to become the leading Man in it'.[56] A day later Grant carried out an ostentatious display of his trust in the Carpenter and the nation in general.

The 14th I carryed some Officers with me to visit the small remains of the Lower Towns & I was so much convinced of the Sincerity of the Indians, that we went twelve Miles from Camp, through their Country without Arms or an Escort, with which the Cherokees were much pleased, indeed a little Encouragement is all that is necessary to make the Peace lasting, I made the Party with that View, it has already had the desired Effect. Lieut. McIntosh writes me that two hundred men, Women & Children are arrived to settle the Towns near the Fort.[57]

Next day he saw Attakullakulla safely on his way to Chota. Grant told him that as a demonstration of faith in his integrity he would move his men down to Ninety Six where he would await the Carpenter's return. For his part Attakullakulla promised to meet him there with a delegation of headmen within 'twenty five Sleeps'.[58]

Grant began his move down to Ninety Six the day after the Carpenter's departure, on 16 October. He had not started a moment too soon. His supplies at Fort Prince George had run so low 'that I could not bring a Bullock or a Barrell of Flour from thence ...'[59] The horses were so weak that the army had to halt for rest every second day, and supplies had to be sent up to them from Ninety Six. The troops took ten long days to get there. However, once at Ninety Six and comfortably supplied, he sent McIntosh a drove of hogs and 50 barrels of flour, as the latter 'cannot avoid giving Provisions now & then to Indian visitors'.[60] Even at this distance Grant wished to ensure that the Lower Towns would feel safe from immediate hunger. He also divested himself of the remnants of the provincials, sending them straight down to the Congarees to await Bull's decision to disband them. On 29 October the halt and lame from the regular regiments were sent after them, together with a number of waggons due to be discharged from service.[61]

About an hour before they started a Lieutenant Parker arrived with two letters from Amherst, dated 2 and 9 October.[62] The first was his reply to Grant's letter of 3 September, which had described the preliminary peace and the impossibility of keeping the army at Keowee. Amherst agreed to the withdrawal to Ninety Six, adding that, since the colony was unwilling to defend itself, Grant had better go no further until the peace was ratified, but Grant was to keep this order to himself.[63] Amherst, of course, was concerned to recover his troops for service elsewhere, and did not want to encourage the colony to neglect its own forces. In reality, however, he had authorized Grant to blackmail the colony into accepting his terms. The second letter, prompted by orders from London, modified these instructions significantly. Grant was to detach four companies of the 17 and 22 regiments under Monypenny, and send them down to Charleston where four transports would be waiting.[64] Nothing could have suited Grant better. Next morning, after an emotional leave taking, Monypenny began his march. (Though he did not yet know it, he was to be appointed Adjutant-General to Monckton, who was to lead an expedition against Dominica.)[65] Whatever lingering hopes the colonists may have harboured, the fact that the final peace must rest upon conciliation, not compulsion, was now inescapable.

> Our Business here [wrote Grant] I think is in a great measure over the Articles of Peace are signed & wil not soon be broke on the Part of the Cherokees, unless they are ill used and forced into a War by the Province. When the Carpenter returns here with the other head men, I shall consider the Treaty as finally concluded ...[66]

His optimism was more than justified. Among the 200 Cherokees resettling the Lower Towns were Tistoe and the Wolf. These people had come out of the mountains into Keowee on 31 October,[67] and that night the settlement had reverberated with celebration. 'We have danced all night', Tistoe told McIntosh next morning, 'for joy of coming home again.'[68] By 6 November 'Mrs. Carpenter, her Children and Attendants' were at the fort waiting for Attakullakulla and (most significantly) Ostenaca. A persistent rumour had it that Occonostota had gone with a war party against the French on 11 October.[69] But, as Grant feared, the boundary issue was still alive. For Tistoe and the other Lower Cherokees this was not merely a matter of dropping the Twenty-Six Mile River line, but of setting definite limits to white expansion.

> I send this earth to the Governor [Tistoe told McIntosh] to remind him of the Saluda agreement by which we were to hunt this side of the Long Canes to Tugaloo. It's what the White People will come and Settle it. It will be good for the White People to Settle at Turkey Creek and the Head of Broad River, and Leave the Middle Ground for both to hunt, The middle Settlements People have no right to Hunt to this Ground let them Hunt between them and Virginia and the over Hills to Hunt down the Rivers.[70]

Not only did he expect Bull to honour the Long Canes boundary; he wanted Grant's support for his demand. He gave McIntosh a pipe which he was to send 'to the Dreadful Warrior and the Governor. I desire that the dreadful Warrior may Smoak out of it, and then send it to the Governor to Smoak out of it, that we may Smoak out of the Same Pipe.'[71] Clearly, if the peace did not secure the Lower Towns' already rapidly shrinking hunting grounds it would be of short duration. Fortunately Grant's siege of poor Bull was about to bear fruit. A last letter from Grant – which Monypenny saw and thought far too gentle[72] – so upset the lieutenant-governor that on 13 November he asked the Council to strike the boundary clause out of the draft treaty. He pleaded that having fallen ill on 10 September while preparing the peace terms, he 'did not recollect what had passed and been agreed to by Colonel Grant and himself' concerning that article. The board, consisting at that meeting of Beale, Guerard and Leigh, agreed and the offending clause was removed.[73] There is no doubt that Bull's well-meant deception had caused him, as he put it, 'great uneasiness and concern'.[74] The episode had already earned him the scorn of John Stuart, who despised 'the impotent Malice of our Legislature' against Grant, and accused Bull of double-dealing. '[H]e knows well how to play with both hands', wrote Stuart to Grant. 'I wish to God he may meet with the just Reward of Disingenuity & Rotten Heartedness.'[75] The conciliatory John Rattray had died in October,[76] and Bull had no friend to intercede for him. He called in Henry Laurens to discuss Grant's 'last letter', but succeeded only in appearing embarrassed and shifty. Reluctant to reveal its details, and worried lest Laurens had already seen it, he seemed to be 'under much anxiety & discovered such an unwillingness to disoblige or differ with the General or yourself, that I cannot help pitying him most heartily'.[77] Even then Bull was not to be spared one last humiliation. Monypenny's entry into Charleston turned into a dramatic pro-Grant demonstration.

As the weary and travel-stained redcoats approached the outskirts of the city they were met by two provincial officers, Moultrie and Roberts, on horseback. Closer to town they were joined by Laurens, Stuart, Howarth and others who accompanied Monypenny as he led the march. As they drew level with Bull's window the lieutenant-governor raised his sash and looked out: to Monypenny's delight every officer ignored him.[78] Conversation with Laurens and the others softened his attitude, but only a little. 'Were he not so unfair a Wretch', he wrote that evening, 'by what I hear he is now to be pity'd He now blames himself, & is frightened about the result.'[79] Such was the depth of feeling in the town that Monypenny and his companions refused Laurens's offer of hospitality because it would make him a marked man, 'as we were resolv'd to take no Notice of the Governor'.[80] Grant's own response to Bull's explanation was no less scathing. '[I]t will appear I dare say extraordinary to Your Excellency', he wrote to Amherst, 'that he should forget the only Point of any Consequence which he ever had to settle during the course of the Indian War.'

Bull had given way in the nick of time. While Monypenny was marching into Charleston the Cherokee delegation was approaching Fort Prince George. This was a conspicuously more distinguished embassy than that of September. Attakullakulla was now accompanied by Occonostota's brother, the headman of the Cherokee mother town; like Standing Turkey, he was referred to as 'the Prince of Chota'. Also with him were Ostenaca's brother, six other headmen 'and a large Gang of Men and Women' who wished to hear the negotiations.[81] But it had taken the Carpenter longer than he had promised to persuade the nation to send them; the warriors, to adopt his euphemism, were away from home. Neither Occonostota, nor Standing Turkey nor Ostenaca had dared to come, while others had appeared at the last moment and were extremely nervous. Welsh, who had already slipped back into the nation,[82] and the Georgia packhorsemen already bringing goods and ammunition up from Augusta,[83] had no doubt been massaging the Cherokees' suspicions of the South Carolina authorities. Laurens was convinced that 'Villains of our own Country and Colour' – Proctor, Gunninghame and McLemore among them – were largely responsible for the trouble which followed; and Bull had been worried about their influence since September at least.[84] The Carpenter was particularly agitated by the lateness of those delegates bearing the vital 'Eagle's Wing', the symbol of his authority to conclude a treaty for the nation. Next day a sudden quarrel with McIntosh threatened to wreck the peace at the eleventh hour.

Two Cherokee women coming up from Ninety Six, where they had seen Grant's men repairing the fort and constructing store houses, reported that he was building a prison. There were, they claimed, two separate rooms so that men and women could be kept apart. At this most of the Cherokees fled and even Attakullakulla's nerve was shaken.[85] The Carolina people, he told McIntosh, were always telling lies. Now even Grant had betrayed him. '[T]he Dreadful Warrior as they call him, for my part I call him the Corn Puller', was going to lock up the Cherokees before driving them to Charleston 'like a parcel of Sheep'.[86] Angrily he demanded assurances in the form of presents for his followers and ransoms for the prisoners still in Cherokee hands. The price would be high – at least 15 lb of leather per prisoner – and until there were presents for his warriors as well he would not even send a Talk to Bull.[87]

McIntosh kept his temper in the face of what he considered 'a very impertinent Talk' and of the Carpenter's 'ever craving appetite'.[88] But overnight the panic died down. A long and anxious conference at Keowee concluded that Grant was to be trusted after all. But there was still a difficulty about the exchange of prisoners. Attakullakulla was all for dropping the question of ransom, which was contrary to the letter and spirit of the terms already agreed, and which had upset McIntosh and might alienate Grant. But the others pointed out that the warriors who had prisoners – meaning Seroweh and his followers would not give them up without compensation.[89] After all a Cherokee warrior's captive was his personal property, his slave, his legitimate booty. If the British had been prepared to buy back their people at the beginning of the year, when the war was still in progress, it would be unjust to refuse to pay now that peace was about to be concluded.[90] Moreover, the Chota council neither would nor could oblige Seroweh's people to comply. When Attakullakulla apologized to McIntosh next day he had to explain this unpalatable fact.[91]

When Grant heard about this episode he brushed aside the question of ransoms and presents. This kind of attempted blackmail (as he saw it) was annoying but it was hardly surprising or unusual. 'I have wrote Mr. Bull that they should not be humoured, and I shall threaten them for having mentioned it, but they have been so long accustomed to receive every thing they ask, that 'tis impossible to prevent them begging.' But as evidence of the Cherokees' deep-rooted fear, he took the incident very seriously indeed. 'Nothing but time', he wrote, 'will restore the Confidence which they formerly placed in the English, at present they are timorous beyond Conception.' So fragile were their nerves that, in Grant's view, even Welsh could scarcely do more damage, 'for in speaking of Charles Town they have for many years been accustomed to call it the Town of Lyes'.[92]

Reassured by McIntosh, albeit with some difficulty, the Cherokee delegates set out apprehensively for Ninety Six. On arrival they were welcomed by Grant, who sent them straight on to Charleston. Soon after their departure the colonel, already under orders to join the expedition against Dominica, began his own march to the sea. As the Cherokees approached the 'Town of Lyes' Bull reconvened the Commons for the ratification. There was no constitutional necessity for him to do so, and members were still angry at the Council's unilateral removal of the boundary clause. Presumably he wanted to placate the House by keeping it informed, but in sending it a message describing the incident at Keowee he was courting trouble. The members ignored the question of Cherokee trust and fastened at once upon the Carpenter's demand for presents. Noting that Bull had tabled only a copy of the Talk of 16 November, they demanded the more inflammatory one of the previous day. Bull hedged valiantly, saying a copy had not yet come, and that he had sent to Grant for it.[93] But it was clear that without a boundary clause in the treaty, and with talk of ransoms in the air, the lieutenant-governor was in for an uncomfortable time. By the time the Cherokees entered the capital, on Thursday, 11 December, Bull had once again contracted a diplomatic illness. Already he had handed over the negotiations to the President of the Council, his own father-in-law Othniel Beale. On the following Monday Beale formally received the Cherokees in the Council Chamber and announced the lieutenant-governor's indisposition.[94]

Bull was not to be let off so lightly. The Cherokees were inconveniently sympathetic and announced that they were willing to wait until the lieutenant-governor was better.[95] This forced Bull to insist that he was far too ill to see them for some time and to instruct the Council to prepare a draft of the final treaty.[96] Bull was now certain that he could weather the storm only if some kind of territorial concession was included. Accordingly the Council reinserted the boundary article, fixing the border at the Forty Mile River, considerably further from Keowee than the original 26 miles (Map 8). On Wednesday 16 December Beale presented the revised articles to the Indians.[97]

For the Lower Towns this would still mean a considerable loss of hunting grounds, but it was so much better than the September proposals that the Cherokees were glad to accept. Next day Attakullakulla told Beale that he was glad that the lieutenant-governor had taken his advice on this point.[98] The question of the exchange of prisoners was, however, a thorny issue. Had not McIntosh informed Bull that he, the Carpenter, had delivered up eight whites and one negro since his return, and that the rest had gone hunting with their captors and would be given up as soon as they returned? Beale was quick to blame Grant for not passing on McIntosh's message, but refused to allow the Cherokees anything in return until all the prisoners had been given up. There would be no trade until then, and, by implication, no presents. Nevertheless, Attakullakulla was too pleased with the new boundary to

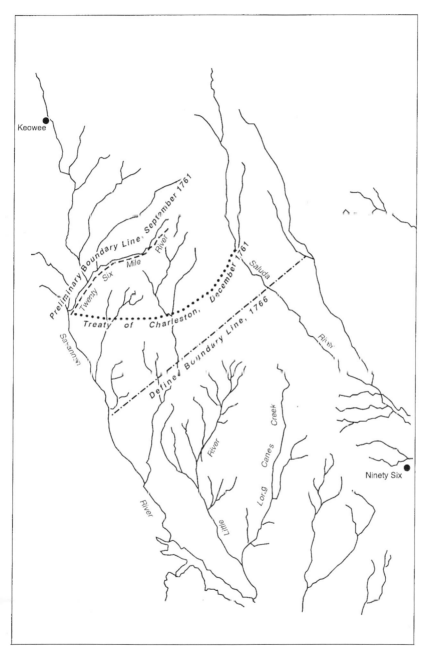

Map 8 The Cherokee–South Carolina boundary, 1761 and 1766

press the point. He only asked that, as it was now late, for the ratification ceremony to be postponed until the following day.[99] The Treaty of Charleston was solemnly ratified in council on 18 December 1761. The pipe left by Attakullakulla on his last visit was lit and passed around. Next the Prince of Chota lit and offered a pipe which, with two strings of wampum, he had brought from Standing Turkey and Occonostota. Attakullakulla presented more strings and an eagle's tail, 'the greatest present' the nation could send, reminding the council that Standing Turkey was Old Hop's successor. The Prince of Chota followed by giving an eagle's wing, a rattlebox and a pipe.[100] Thus the Cherokee delegation gave the nation's highest pledges of good faith. Even now, however, the question of the prisoners refused to die.

Attakullakulla once again promised to return all the remaining prisoners, if the doubters in the nation were now convinced. As tangible proof of the colony's good faith, he asked for two or three of the Cherokees in British hands. In view of the nine prisoners whose release the Carpenter had already obtained, this was a reasonable request. But to others it was capable of another interpretation. Watts, who was present, interjected that the Carpenter was really demanding ransoms again. Beale promptly reminded the Cherokees that there could be no question of presents; the redemption with trade goods at the beginning of the year had been 'an Act of Generosity and Compassion to the unhappy Prisoners'. Attakullakulla protested that he had neither asked for nor expected presents: only for two or three Cherokees. The little squall over, the Cherokees put their marks to the treaty. Beale, Attakullakulla and the Prince of Chota then carried the paper to Bull's town house where he signed and sealed it, and allowed the Cherokees to take home any two of the captives taken by Montgomery. A flag was raised over Grenville's Bastion and the battery fired a nine-gun salute.[101] The Anglo-Cherokee War was over.

Next day a much relieved Bull raised with the Commons the question of the customary presents for departing Indian delegations. No doubt such presents could not be as generous as in the normal days of peace. 'Yet when I Consider the length of their Journey, and the Inclemencies of the Season, which they must encounter before they return home, I recommend them as objects of Humanity that they may be furnished with th[o]se Necessaries only as will defend them against the Severity of the Weather.'[102] But a House which had only two days before voted to continue the Rangers until the end of March, because the final peace was not settled,[103] was not about to agree without protest. Angry at having been left out of the final negotiations, members insisted on having the ratified treaty and all the associated papers laid before it. In particular they returned to the quarrel over ransoms at Fort Prince George, again insisting on having Attakullakulla's intemperate speech of the previous day. Without it the Commons would not even consider giving clothing to the departing delegates.[104] The lieutenant-governor answered that Grant had sent him the Carpenter's only message, and had there been another Talk for him Grant would have sent it.[105] Bull, as usual, was being economical with the truth: strictly speaking there had indeed been no other Talk for him, since the speech of 15 November had been addressed to McIntosh. He produced this message all the same, together with all the other documents for which the Commons had asked.[106] But the House, having obtained the original papers, did not at once grant the presents Bull had asked for. Instead it postponed the whole issue for further debate. It was not until 24 January that it finally voted £500,[107] by which time the Cherokees had long gone.

Public and representative anger at the way the treaty had been concluded rumbled on into and beyond 1763. As 'Philopatrios' Gadsden or Middleton (or both) published a pamphlet extending Grant's crimes back to 1760, when he had been in virtual command of the Montgomery expedition, and pointing out that his Indian policy marginalized Americans, John Stuart's consistent campaigns for imperial control of the frontier, especially his opposition to traders taking payments in land, kept the underlying question alive; indeed, in the south it was a potent cause of resistance to the Stamp Act, and so perhaps a more fundamental cause of the Revolution.[108] The Commons in the winter of 1761–2 was not thinking of independence, but its members reflected a widespread sense that the treaty arose from improper imperial interference.

Thus when Grant and his men arrived in town they walked into a hornets' nest. Grant himself was hissed and booed whenever he appeared in the streets and in the end had to fight a duel with Middleton. Early one cold December morning they met to exchange pistol shots. Apparently Middleton fired first and missed, giving Grant a chance to kill his tormentor at leisure. Instead he raised his weapon and fired, as Henry Laurens put it, 'over his Calabash'. Grant rather optimistically told Amherst that his generosity had defused colonial hostility to him, but he could hardly have believed so himself. He and his men marched to their ships to the tune of jeers. But he never wavered in his conviction that he had achieved a just and lasting peace, and in this respect he never forfeited the respect of Laurens (who used Grant's own papers to defend his reputation for the next two years), Monypenny, Stuart, Moultrie and others.

The returning Cherokees, too, were victims of popular anger. On their way back to the nation with Lieutenant John Lloyd, who had helped Laurens to escort them down in September, they were robbed of 14 horses by hostile back settlers. Lloyd, profoundly embarrassed, apologized profusely. The culprits were, he said, 'some of the lower sort of people', and promised restitution. Attakullakulla accepted Lloyd's apology graciously, but could not resist a dry observation upon Carolinian self-righteousness: 'we believe it to be so, & you see that there is some bad amongst the White people too.'[109]

The Council provided fresh mounts and a proper escort, and the incident did not upset the new peace. Not only were the Cherokees for the time being unable to go to war again; the new definitive boundary, once surveyed, marked and enforced might give them better long-term security against settler encroachments. Fresh Cherokee raids, which might ruin this prospect of safety, were now highly unlikely. This was well understood by the back settlers themselves, who had begun to resettle old frontier areas at the Long Canes, around Saluda and Ninety Six, and along the Broad River by the beginning of December. New settlers, no doubt attracted by the combination of new lands and a defined frontier, were among them.[110] The Carpenter and the Corn Puller had brought about a peace which had at least a real chance of survival.

Epilogue: Toward Augusta

Meanwhile the Carpenter's rivals were still trying to outflank him. In November 1761, while Occonostota took himself off to Louisiana, Standing Turkey returned to the Virginian camp. There he invited Byrd's successor, Adam Stephen, to send an officer to put the peace terms before the whole Chota council. Stephen sent Ensign Henry Timberlake, who luckily for us published a memoir of his subsequent adventures in 1765.[1] With his servant, interpreter and a sergeant called Thomas Sumter, he was a witness to the still disturbed and anxious state of mind among the Overhill Cherokees. He went on to chronicle a Cherokee mission to Virginia, which became a colourful embassy to London in the summer of 1762.[2] These events, while essentially footnotes to the peace concluded at Charleston, were part of a complex process of reconciliation which led on to the great Congress of Augusta in the following year.

At Tomotly Timberlake was taken up by Ostenaca. The Mankiller probably saw in the young Virginian his own passport to restored influence among the whites, and consequent prestige at home. In the Chota council he rose to demand that the peace be accepted and strictly observed, and to point out that Timberlake was under his personal protection.[3] This was a necessary warning. The Overhills were still very suspicious of South Carolina and Virginia, and as several frankly admitted to Timberlake, they had sought peace principally to get the vital trade goods which the French could not supply.[4] The Cherokees had no reason to believe that the new governor of South Carolina, Thomas Boone, would be more flexible on this point than Glen or Lyttelton; and indeed he was not, believing that 'their wants are the best pledges for the faithful Performance of the Articles'.[5] In mid-January there were rumours of invasion and of Virginian encouragement of a Creek attack at the Great Island. Ostenaca spoke up for moderation, but he became very terse with Timberlake, and the young Virginian, having a rudimentary knowledge of the law of vengeance, began to worry about his scalp.[6]

Anxious to be gone, Timberlake asked Ostenaca to assemble all the British prisoners for repatriation.[7] Timberlake did not appreciate that their masters would resist handing over their property without payment, nor did he realize how reluctant the nation would be to give

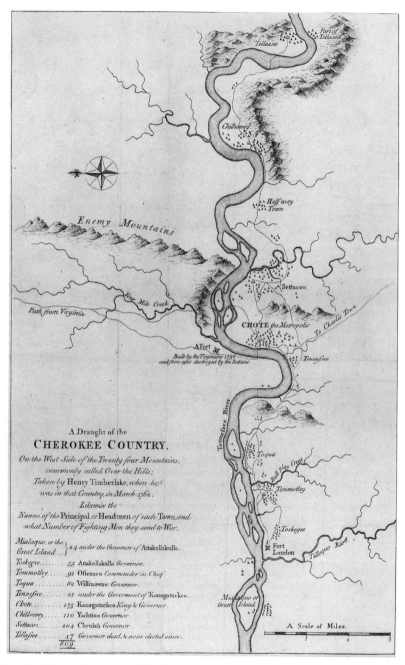

Map 9   Timberlake's map of the Overhill Towns, 1762

up their last guarantees against British treachery. Moreover, they could see no reason to return those whites who were unwilling to go. Ostenaca found himself facing exactly the same difficulty as Attakullakulla a few months before. Unwilling to upset his protégé by pointing out the facts of Cherokee life he procrastinated: the prisoners would be collected, he said, as soon as their owners brought them in from hunting. But even then Ostenaca refused to take Timberlake to Virginia.[8]

Attakullakulla's prolonged absence at the 'Town of Lyes' had made his countrymen very nervous. The deadline for his return had come and gone on 15 February, at the height of the rumours from the Great Island, and still the Carpenter had not come. Ostenaca was unwilling to trust himself to the white men until he knew what had become of his rival's party. Then one of the embassy, pushing on ahead, arrived with the news that South Carolina had already resumed the war. Ostenaca very sensibly declined to move until the Carpenter should come to confirm or deny the story. Not until 23 February did Attakullakulla appear, and then he could not categorically refute the rumour, which he said he had heard from someone anxious to make mischief.[9] Consequently the Overhills were in no hurry to comply with the treaty he brought. Trade was still important, but access to Virginia tempted the Overhills to make a show of reluctance. Not until May did the first captives reach Fort Prince George.[10]

Meanwhile it was sensible for Chota to seize the opportunity to restore relations with Virginia. Ostenaca was the obvious ambassador and it is probable that the council asked him to escort Timberlake home. Ambition overcoming his lingering doubts, the Mankiller agreed, and at the beginning of May he reached Williamsburg safely with Timberlake's party and a horde of Overhill warriors.[11] Fauquier saw that an understanding with Ostenaca would weaken Attakullakulla, and so undermine South Carolina's primacy in Indian affairs. He seems to have made much of the recently arrived Order-in-Council of December 1761, requiring the governors of royal colonies to suspend all grants of land in areas claimed by Indians.[12] Delighted with his welcome, Ostenaca asked to go to England to see the king. Fauquier at once saw the possibility of further deflating the Carpenter's prestige and impressing the Mankiller, and on 15 May the Ostenaca, two companions, Timberlake, Sumter and an interpreter sailed in *L'Epreuve*, a sloop of 16 guns escorting a convoy to Plymouth.[13] Unfortunately tuberculosis killed the interpreter early in the voyage, leaving Ostenaca and his friends with no effective means of communication with their hosts.[14]

But Lord Egremont, Pitt's portly and pleasure loving successor as Secretary of State for the Southern Department, could not ignore them. He knew that the security of the frontier, and common justice, required a coherent policy of Indian protection. Advised and assisted by Henry Ellis, Egremont was already working out the principle of a continuous fixed frontier. On 12 December 1761, the day the preliminary peace proposals of September landed on his desk,[15] the Privy Council had approved the ban on land grants which Fauquier had later explained to Ostenaca. On that same day Egremont had sent a letter to Amherst, ordering him to treat the conquered French Canadians and Indians with equal sensitivity and consideration.[16]

Unfortunately Egremont had misjudged his man. Amherst, of course, loathed Indians, and his embargo on presents to the hungry Algonquian peoples of the northwest led in little more than a year to a spectacular Indian war – Pontiac's. Though quite prepared to promise to protect Indian lands, and to support officers like Grant and Bouquet who actually did so, he saw no inconsistency in encouraging New York to open Mohawk land to military settlers.[17] But although Sir Jeffrey was the worst possible agent of conciliation and justice, Egremont's own commitment to that policy cannot be in doubt. The language of the letter of 12 December is not that of a man concerned only to keep the Indians quiet: it dilates upon 'the shameful Manner in which Business is transacted between Them and our Traders, the latter using every low Trick and Artifice to over reach and cheat those unguarded ignorant People in their Dealings with Them, while the French, by a different conduct, and worthy of Our Imitation, deservedly gain their Confidence...'[18] Thereafter, with impressive speed and energy, he displaced the Board of Trade from the influence it had enjoyed under Halifax (now at the Admiralty), and proceeded to impose his own solutions.

Thus by the summer of 1762 the Secretary of State knew that the future of the fragile Cherokee peace might well depend upon what Ostenaca would have to say about his treatment in Britain. When the Cherokees reached Plymouth on 16 June they were at once subjected to both the curiosity of the crowd and the solicitous attentions of their official hosts.[19] On Saturday, 18 June, the morning after they reached London, Egremont received the Cherokees at his Piccadilly home. A house was found near the Haymarket, and Egremont procured an audience with the king. On this regal occasion he saw to it that they met Montgomery, now an MP and brother of Lord Eglintoun, Lord of the Bedchamber, and he prudently equipped George III with a written address of conciliation and friendship, for the Cherokees to have translated on their return. He also seems to have arranged a series of uplifting sightseeing tours for the Cherokees designed both to educate and to impress: the Tower, St Paul's, Parliament, Westminster Abbey, the Mansion House, the Temple, Greenwich, naval dockyards, military displays.[20] So successful was this official programme that the Cherokees were not unduly alarmed when they discovered that their return passage in *L'Epreuve* was not to Virginia but to South Carolina. At 10 a.m. on Tuesday 24 August they sailed with Sumter from Portsmouth.[21]

In early November they reached Charleston, where the Mankiller assured Boone that he had been mightily impressed with the vast numbers of warriors he had seen, and had been very kindly treated. He would now use all his influence to overcome any lingering resentment in the nation. Indeed, as Boone quickly observed, Ostenaca still viewed his own enhanced influence as the main object of his embassy. He specifically asked that Sumter should accompany him to the Cherokee country, 'as it was a signal mark of the King's favour'.[22]

He, his companions and Sumter reached the Overhill country in the New Year, living proof that the British could, after all, be trusted. The headmen crowded into the town houses of Tomotly and Chota to hear his wondrous tales of England, to murmur their approval of the fuss that had been made of him, and to listen to his counsel. Only Occonostota, still nursing his hurt dignity, took himself off on yet another futile mission to Mobile.[23] Attakullakulla remained the principal Cherokee spokesman. But the still increasing pressures on the frontier gave great influence to anyone who – like the great Mankiller of Tomotly – could claim special knowledge of the British.

The nation to which Ostenaca returned was much reduced in numbers. According to one contemporary estimate, as early as the end of 1760 there were no more than two thousand warriors left, which would suggest a population of eight to ten thousand people. By these calculations disease, accompanied by war and hunger, had killed a third of the nation. If a still earlier estimate of five thousand warriors in 1757 is correct the catastrophe was even worse, and these figures take no account of the effects of Grant's campaign in 1761.[24] This may be too gloomy a picture, for Stuart, the new Superintendent of Indian Affairs, thought that there were 2750 fighting men in 1764, which would give a total population in excess of eleven thousand. But whichever of these somewhat dubious estimates we accept, the Cherokees were now clearly outnumbered by the Creeks, their nearest and most likely enemies.[25]

The fall in population, the devastation of the Lower and Middle Towns, and the interruption of the winter hunts, meant a sharp fall in the Cherokees' purchasing power. The Cherokees' efforts had to go into rebuilding the towns, replanting the orchards and gardens, and hunting for food rather than for trade leather. There may even have been a period of isolationist reaction, where European goods were shunned as much as possible, and where the prices of guns fell below those for objects needed for native rituals.[26] The new South Carolina trade law confined the new public monopoly to one post at Keowee, thus making buying and selling very difficult for all but the Lower Towns. But this in itself was a recognition that the bottom was falling out of the Indian deerskin trade, and that it was primarily a diplomatic, not an economic, activity.[27] Cherokees, with insufficient offerings from Virginia and Georgia, found themselves once again dependent upon South Carolina and therefore as vulnerable as ever to economic blackmail. A partial boycott may have seemed the only way to assert their independence.

But, as before, European goods could not be ignored altogether. Guns could not be abandoned in favour of bows and arrows; nor, for that matter, could stone arrowheads replace metal. The nation had to find alternative sources of supply and so free its hands for the boundary negotiations to come. Occonostota seems to have continued to favour the French. Canada had been lost, but Louisiana was still in French hands in 1762. But when the Peace of Paris gave everything east of the Mississippi (except New Orleans) to Britain, and awarded the rest of Louisiana to Spain, the convenient points of contact at Forts Toulouse and Massac were lost. Although France did not hand over her Mississippi settlements to the Spaniards until 1767, until when they remained a constant source of worry for British officials, their usefulness to the Cherokees was negligible. Occonostota remained aloof from the British, but probably did not believe that France could adequately supply the Cherokees. In May 1763 he even tried to interest Governor Wright of Georgia in opening a substantial trade.[28] The deep wound to his pride inflicted in 1759, and the fact that his rivals had taken control of Anglo-Cherokee affairs, were the main factors pushing him towards France.

But there were other good reasons for keeping in touch with the Bourbons. The treaty of 1761 had forbidden the Cherokees to hunt below the Forty Mile River, but did that constitute a boundary? Just because the Cherokees had agreed to stay well clear of the white settlements, did that allow the Long Canes settlers to push forward into the gap? Or, as the Cherokees had always argued, was the legal boundary still at Long Canes Creek? The settlers who flooded back into the Long Canes area in 1762 and 1763 were very clear about their own answers to these questions, and almost at once there was a wave of horse stealing by whites from Cherokees.[29] By the spring of 1763 over a thousand families had settled in the area and four hundred more were expected.[30]

To the north the Virginians were creeping back into the transmontane lands along the Kanawha and upper Holston rivers, abandoned at the start of the French and Indian War.[31] Samuel Stalnaker's settlement, the 'Stalnaker's' where Byrd had camped in 1761, had been destroyed by the Shawnees and their allies. A number of settlements even further down the Holston had likewise been abandoned. Large-scale speculators also had claims in the area, although the only legally valid prewar claim arose from the patent given to John Patton. But as late as 1760 a grant of a thousand acres on both sides of the Kanawha had been made to one John Chiswell, who opened a lead mine opposite a tributary called Cripple Creek. 'Chiswell's Mines' became a feature on maps of the time, and a convenient point of reference for both sides in postwar boundary negotiations. Once the French and Indian threat was removed from the Ohio in 1759 that river and all its tributaries were once again laid open to the inexorable tide of inland immigration.[32]

The British government, as we have seen already, moved to prevent the encroachments upon Indian lands from causing a new war. In 1760 the Board of Trade had ordered Fauquier to refrain from making land grants anywhere in the Ohio drainage system. Fauquier consistently maintained that land issues had nothing to do with the Cherokee War, or indeed with any of Virginia's frontier conflicts. He argued that it was the violence of the settlers, not their (already abandoned) Kanawha and Holston settlements, which had provoked the Cherokees. Lawless men, encouraged by a scalp bounty law which he took great pride in having had repealed, had been the root cause of the Cherokee raids. Although the Board steadfastly stood by its ban on new settlements, Fauquier was allowed to let genuine prewar settlers return.[33] The Cherokees, watching the renewed expansion close to the fringes of their hunting grounds were nervous. Did Virginia mean to steadily nibble away at the nation's lands? Or would Fauquier be prepared to draw a firm boundary in the neighbourhood of the Kanawha?

From the Cherokee point of view the British had not honoured their treaty obligations, and allowing French emissaries or traders into their nation – itself a breach of the Treaty of Charleston – was a concrete way of expressing their dissatisfaction and continuing lack of trust. By the spring of 1763 Boone was complaining that they were harbouring a Frenchman, trying to prevent his arrest, and responding to French intrigues.[34]

Thus when in May 1763 the Cherokees were invited to send delegates to a general congress of southern nations and British governors at Augusta, they already had a programme of objectives. The first was to establish trust between themselves and the British, without which particular agreements on trade or boundaries would have no meaning. To adopt the terms of family relationships used by Indians, the British must act as brothers towards the Cherokees, and the King must be their father. Some Cherokees, though they knew that harmonious relations with Britain were essential, remembered Lyttelton and Miln all too clearly. The Valley people feared to the last that the invitation was a trap, and not even Attakullakulla could induce them to do more than to send beads and a request for friendship.

Occonostota, proud and outmanoeuvred by Ostenaca and the Carpenter, refused to go, but he was not even then the militant nationalist depicted by Dorothy Jones.[35] He collaborated with the Carpenter, also jealous of Ostenaca's new prestige, to concoct a public message and a private one. The public Talk was a general expression of friendship and good will; the private one was a proposal that they should both embark for Britain in the spring of 1764. This suggestion was made partly to put Ostenaca in his place, but it was also meant as a way of offering and inviting a ritual expression of trust and brotherhood. Other Cherokees understood this very well. At Augusta Ostenaca spoke first, inviting the governors to examine the Talk given to him by the King; Seroweh, silent until the second day, observed that those who had been to England had the right to be heard first.[36]

However, the Congress of Augusta, and the Proclamation which preceded it, would not have occurred had not Cherokee unrest been part of a mosaic of discontents and hostility affecting Indian nations from the Great Lakes to Alabama. The virtual defeat of France in North America by 1761 had made all the eastern woodland nations extremely nervous about British intentions. Under the preliminary articles of the Peace of Paris, signed on 8 November 1762, Britain acquired Canada, Acadia, Cape Breton and eastern Louisiana from France, and Florida from Spain. Even before the ink was dry on the final treaty of

10 February 1763, the British were moving to take possession of their new territories. In the south the British occupied Pensacola and Mobile; Fort Toulouse was obviously next on the list. But from the Creek point of view Spain and France had been permitted to build and occupy those forts; they did not own them, nor had they been ceded the land. But now the British were taking them over, apparently laying claim to the freehold by virtue of an agreement with mere tenants. The Upper Creeks, led by the Mortar and the Gun Merchant, stirred ominously, and even the Lower Creeks were angry. When the northern nations erupted in May 1763, messengers from the Ohio–Great Lakes area urged the Creeks to take up the hatchet. Creek bands began to strike the frontier settlements, dangerously close to the Cherokees. In August raiders killed a man and two children on the south fork of the Catawba River, '& miserably cut a Woman lower down the country'. For the first time since the Cherokee war the settlers were building stockades and cramming inside for safety. On 25 August northern Indians ambushed and killed King Hagler of the Catawbas 'almost in the middle of our Settlements'.[37] There was a terrible danger of a general Indian war along the whole of the North American frontier.

However, the Proclamation was not a panic stricken response to the emergency; the policies embodied in it went right back to the War of the Austrian Succession. The Easton treaties of 1758 began a series of pragmatic, even enlightened, imperial interventions in Indian affairs.[38] Egremont, inheriting this trend, saw a unified boundary primarily as a means of restraining settlement, not, as is sometimes said, as a precondition for orderly imperial expansion. A great deal of the advice given to Egremont and his successor Halifax was concerned with mercantilist economic aims, which required restricting settlement to the seaboard; their achievement was to show that these arguments were in perfect harmony with the need to protect Indian lands.[39] This argument is worth unfolding a little further if we are to understand not only the Proclamation, but the Congress of Augusta which followed it in November 1763.

We have seen that as early as December 1761 the Privy Council had used the means of an Order-in-Council to restrain western settlement while a more permanent policy was being worked out. It has been suggested that the end of the Cherokee War may have, as Stagg himself puts it, 'focused and sustained British concern for Indian affairs'.[40] While the news of Grant's preliminary peace may have reached London too late to influence the 1761 Order, it almost certainly helped to form Egremont's thinking on Indian affairs in 1762. The copy of the journal of the Keowee conference which he had made for his own use is to be found in his papers in the Public Record Office: between a deposition and a letter about southern Indian affairs in the 1730s, and a representation written on the question of an Indian boundary by William Bull's father in 1738.[41] Clearly Egremont was doing his homework, and not only on the boundary. In January 1762 the Privy Council resolved to carry out the long awaited attack on Louisiana, and papers about Oglethorpe's attempt on St. Augustine can be found in the same file.[42]

No doubt the visit of Ostenaca and his friends in the summer of 1762 helped Egremont to keep the Indian question in mind even while preoccupied with the peace negotiations which would make a permanent general policy essential. On 15 December Henry Ellis argued that the expected alarm of the southern Indians at the coming British occupation of Florida and Louisiana could only be averted by three key measures. These were the prevention of settlements, at least for the time being; the provision of trade; and the demolition of Forts Loudoun, Tombigbee and Toulouse. For while taking possession of these places would generate a new war and make the garrisons, as in 1759–69, 'Hostages in their hands and a security for our submission to their Enormities', levelling them would 'remove the jealousies of the Indians'. To ensure that the southern nations understood Britain's benign intentions Egremont should organize a general conference.[43] None of these ideas was very new or very radical, and when in February he asked the Board of Trade for advice, he made it plain that he wanted a report embodying Ellis's proposals.[44] On 16 March 1763 Egremont made them official policy. On that day he sent out a circular letter to John Stuart, Atkin's successor as Superintendent, and the four southern governors, ordering them to convene a general meeting between themselves and the leaders of the Cherokees, Creeks, Choctaws, Chickasaws and Catawbas. In a separate letter he informed Amherst of the intended conference, and asked him to suggest additions 'to what is directed to be said to the Indians'.[45]

However, merely ordering the congress did not settle the direction of future British policy. As Egremont collected opinions and information, he found two distinct strands of British interests dovetailing neatly together. A defined general Indian boundary would guarantee the Indians' lands against encroachment and thus help to ensure the security of the colonies. But it would also have the desirable effect of preventing American settlement inland, beyond the reach of British goods and economic control. By the autumn, when Halifax had taken over the Secretaryship, it had been decided to adopt the heads of the eastward flowing rivers – in other words the Appalachian watershed – as the line of a general Indian–white boundary, but this was subject to recognition of established Indian rights (such as those of the Cherokees) further to the east. The choice of a Royal Proclamation to announce it was made less for the sake of speed than because of it had greater legal force than Additional Instructions to governors. Furthermore, the decision was probably made before the full scope of the Indian war in the north was known. The Proclamation of October 1763 was thus the embodiment of a long maturing policy, not a desperate attempt to stave off disaster in the American backwoods.[46]

Meanwhile in America the preparations for the Augusta conference were well advanced. Stuart had not received Egremont's 16 March circular until 1 June. He had at once written to the governors, and on 3 July to the Indian nations, convening the meeting at Augusta on 15 October. Boone, who had received his copy of the circular a little earlier than Stuart, had already suggested 25 September as the earliest possible date. As both he and Stuart realized, the Chickasaws and Choctaws would have to cover enormous distances – 'seven Hundred Miles' in the case of the Choctaws – and all except the Creeks would have to pass through hostile or potentially hostile territory. The Choctaws, after grave consideration, sent only two delegates on the long and perilous trek through the Creek towns – and they had to pretend to be Chickasaws. Even the Cherokees were nervous about going to Augusta, as two of their people had just been killed by Creeks. In the end Stuart's date was the one agreed to.[47]

By late October the governors were assembling at Charleston. Here Dobbs, who was unwell, persuaded Fauquier and Boone, who may have been jealous of Georgia as the host colony, to move the venue to Dorchester, about twenty miles from the South Carolina capital. Stuart, however, would have none of it, conceiving it his duty to be at Augusta to greet the delegates at the agreed time. On 6 October he went on, alone. Five days later he was at Augusta, and on 15 October – punctual as clockwork – the Chickasaw, Choctaw, Catawba and Upper Creek delegates arrived. When Stuart put to them the proposed change of venue – perhaps implying his own disapproval – the Indians refused to go a step further. Stuart accordingly summoned the errant governors. While he and the Indians waited the Lower Creeks and Cherokees came. The Cherokees had sent 15 high-ranking delegates, including Attakullakulla, Ostenaca, the 'Prince of Chota', Willinawaw,

Tistoe of Keowee, the Wolf, the 'Good Warrior' of Estatoe and even Seroweh. When Boone, Fauquier and Dobbs arrived on 1 November there were over 840 Indians 'of all Ages and Sexes' to greet them.[48]

After a pause of four days, which doubtless left time for the usual consultations behind the scenes, the Congress formally opened. Wright, as the host governor, welcomed his Indian guests and looked forward to settling all the differences which lay between them. One by one, nation by nation, the Indian delegates rose to reply. The Cherokees spoke last.[49] Ostenaca, flaunting his new status, reminded the governors of his personal relationship with the King. The Prince of Chota then offered a string of beads with knots at either end and in the middle. The ends he announced, were Chota and Charleston, the middle knot Fort Prince George.[50] Fort Prince George, then, was to be the link between the two peoples; but the absence of a knot to represent Fort Loudoun was, perhaps, significant. Although the Treaty of Charleston required the Cherokees to return the Overhill fort, they would rather it remained empty. So far Ellis's instincts about the wilderness posts were justified. Nothing more was said on the subject, but it is not quite true to say, as the British representatives did later, that the question had not been aired at all.

Then Attakullakulla rose to deliver the main Cherokee message. He gave Stuart the string of beads from Occonostota, and a belt of wampum to support Chota's pledge of peaceful intentions, and to ask for a more abundant trade. He gave another belt to represent the headmen's pledge to restrain their young men in future. But, he pointed out that although the Overhills were ready for an accommodation, the Valley was afraid.[51] Thus he and the others placed the fundamental objective of the restoration of mutual trust at the very top of the Cherokee agenda.

The Carpenter then turned to trade. Again his theme was less economics than a stress upon the fulfilment of obligations. He wanted traders to come back to live in the Cherokee towns, where their safety would be guaranteed from all but outside attack. The store at Keowee was clearly useless to the Overhills and the Virginians struck hard bargains. He asked for trade to be carried 'over the Mountains and a Price set on the Goods. Some people did come from Virginia but had exorbitant prices, & got their Skins for almost nothing...' Had the governors taken steps to control prices? He wanted the matter cleared up.[52] Next day, when the delegations were asked if they had anything more to add, he repeated his request for traders at Chota, provided they were 'Staid Men, not Young Riotting Fellows...' Asked which governors he was addressing he said that traders from all four colonies would be welcome. Seroweh, interpreted by Beamer, added that not even all the Lower Towns found the Keowee store convenient. Georgia had sent traders immediately after the war, and now perhaps South Carolina would do the same.[53] Thus, as Jones points out, the Cherokees were very anxious for the benefits of a competitive market which would drive up the price of leather, and for an official ceiling to hold down the prices of Virginian goods.[54] But to the Indians the trade was more than an economic activity. The return of traders to the towns would be a symbol of trust; by providing adequate goods at assured prices the British would be behaving like brothers, and the King as a father. Nor is it true to say that the Cherokees' public Talks dwelt almost exclusively upon trade.[55]

On that second day of open discussions the Carpenter raised the matter of the Long Canes and Kanawha boundaries. He complained that whites had settled beyond Long Canes; and although they might remain, there must be no trouble between white and Cherokee hunters.[56] He was insisting that although the Cherokees had promised to recognize the Forty Mile River as the limit of their hunting, Long Canes remained the frontier of white settlement. In the same way he insisted that the Virginians should remain on the far side of the Kanawha, for otherwise the Cherokees' hunting grounds – and with them their livelihood – would be eroded. Seroweh supported him. While promising to respect the boundary, he implied that any settlers above Long Canes Creek were trespassing. 'The Lines run out between the English & them, he is satisfied with, tho' they are small for his people.' The trespassers might remain, he added magnanimously, as long as no more settlements were made.[57] The Cherokees, as they admitted later, were using the time-honoured ploy of demanding far more than they were prepared to settle for, and even more than they could seriously claim. They were prepared to be beaten down. But at the same time they were drawing attention to the obligations which Virginia and South Carolina must fulfil if mutual trust and coexistence were to be preserved. Just boundaries must be agreed, defined, marked and actively maintained.

The British reply, delivered by Stuart, on Wednesday, 10 November, only partially satisfied these aspirations. Its remarks on trade were positively distressing. The Cherokees, the governors claimed, already had goods coming 'from almost all the colonies over which we preside', but would not pay prices sufficiently high to encourage more than a handful of traders to come to their towns. The Cherokees, the Talk went on, could attract more traders themselves, by offering reasonable prices for their goods. South Carolina, still the Cherokees' most considerable trading partner, had provided ample goods at Keowee, at least as cheaply as could be offered by any private trader. In any case, there was no chance of altering the law and allowing the traders to go back into the towns, the excuse being that the matter had now gone before the King. Virginia did not have the power to compel traders to settle in the Cherokee towns, nor could the colony regulate their prices.[58] The Cherokees were 'Mortified at the Refusal of Traders from South Carolina'.[59] They were poor and short of goods, and they had been promised trade as before the war once they gave up their prisoners. It was therefore their brothers' duty to supply them amply, conveniently and cheaply. Until both colonies sent traders to the towns and regulated prices for their goods, they would not have created the atmosphere of trust necessary for a stable and happy relationship.

But on the more vital boundary questions there was significant progress. Stuart explained that Virginia had made substantial grants on the Kanawha and Holston rivers before the French and Indian War, and that the resulting settlements had drawn no breath of complaint from the Cherokees. However, no new settlements would be allowed and Fauquier promised strictly to examine and enforce all past agreements. That would not stop unofficial settlements, but the colony was prepared to take action against them.[60]

> It is probable some Idle persons may set down on Lands without any authority whatever, but this you ought not to consider as an Act of the Government which does not nor ever will countenance and protect People settling in that manner, but heartily concur with you in removing them on complaint made by you to the governor for that Purpose.[61]

As for the settlements beyond the Long Canes, they were 'allowed and agreed to' in the peace treaty with South Carolina.[62] At this the Cherokees cheerfully admitted that they 'had claimed more than were their Hunting Grounds and what they desired was, that they might not be molested in hunting as far as the Spring Head of the Holstein River'.[63] They were willing to strike a mutually agreeable bargain.

It is true that there was no hint of such a bargain in the Treaty of Augusta signed on 10 November 1763. The Creeks had negotiated a new boundary with Georgia, and the Catawbas had been promised a survey of their pathetically small 15 miles-square reservation. However, of a new Cherokee line there was no sign.[64] Yet there may already have been progress towards a compromise in informal discussions which, as Jones observes, were referred to on later occasions by Attakullakulla, Occonostota and, most sweepingly, by Dobbs who thought that the Cherokees had settled their boundaries with both Carolinas and Virginia.[65] Stuart mentioned at the time that the distribution of the King's presents allowed him to see each delegation privately at the end of the conference, and of course there had already been the opportunity of the four-day gap before the talks began. At the very least the Cherokees believed that they had secured the lands behind the Forty Mile River, while leaving the Long Canes issue open. It can be no coincidence that the following year Boone demonstrated his willingness to enforce the existing boundary by removing a settlement of trespassers and burning their huts. But the critical question of the lands between Long Canes and the Forty Mile River was not finally settled until October 1765. Then a line was agreed which protected the existing white settlements, but which at the same time was markedly more favourable to the Cherokees than the Forty Mile River limits. In 1766 this new line became the first formally surveyed and marked border between South Carolina and the Cherokee nation, and part of the definitive general boundary delineated in principle in the Proclamation of 1763 (Map 8). William Bull, by then once more in charge of the South Carolina government, was less helpful in dealing with intrusions by white poachers. But South Carolina and Georgia were now garrisoned with regulars from the Royal American Regiment under Captain Gavin Cochrane, and Cochrane and his subordinate commander at Fort Prince George, Ensign George Price, were prepared to act on their own.[66] This was a far cry from the deliberate vagueness of the Long Canes boundary, and from South Carolina's demands of 1761. The policy of generosity and consensus begun by James Grant in the teeth of South Carolina's resistance was bearing promising if imperfect fruit.

The question of sovereignty did not become a major issue at Augusta, perhaps because both sides knew that it was intractable. Egremont's intention to explain the dislodgement of Spain and France before the Indians heard of it from another source had been foiled by the long distances and delays. To the relief of the British participants at Augusta, Egremont's offer to demolish Loudoun and the two other forts deflected even Creek anger, though there was no suggestion that the British might also give up Pensacola and Mobile.[67] However, something important had changed. The new drive to define and coordinate policy from London was based on the assumption that the ceded areas were British possessions. But at Augusta both sides carefully avoided giving offence to the other on this matter; in the Cherokee case, this was remarkable evidence of the renewed mutual trust which had been building since 1761.

Between 1756 and 1763 British policy had been moving slowly and imperfectly towards a more centralized and coordinated system, and one based on the assumption that the tranquillity of the American frontiers depended upon recognition of the just claims of the Indians. In the sphere of Anglo-Cherokee affairs the main issues had been the boundary question, the related matter of trade, and lurking in the background the matter of sovereignty. However, at least until 1763, there was little effective direction from London and little cooperation between colonies.

This situation, the inevitable result of vast distances and wartime preoccupations, had led to a chaotic environment where strong-willed individuals on the ground could exercise disproportionate influence. Too often this influence was malign, whether from lowly villains like Elliot, arrogant young men like Coytmore and Miln, or from high-minded officials with a deep contempt for Indians such as Lyttelton and Amherst. But on occasion such independence could operate in the opposite direction. James Grant was probably not the only middle ranking officer to feel a deep respect for, if not a thorough understanding of, his Indian allies and opponents. But it was Grant's distinction to be placed in a situation, far from effective control by the commander-in-chief, where he could insist upon a moderate end to a violent and tragic situation.

Grant, Montgomery, McIntosh, Bull and others reached out to the Cherokees, to rebuild their trust in British intentions. But it was the Cherokees' readiness to reach out from their side that made a peace possible. Here individuals were even more important than among the British. Attakullakulla deserves his reputation for statesmanship, but Connecorte, Standing Turkey, Ostenaca and Occonostota had always preferred peace with the British to war. Where they differed was in their perceptions of how far the British could go before their arrogance and treachery became insupportable. Even Seroweh, the younger arch-advocate of violence, had always been careful to leave open the door to an honourable peace, and at Augusta he took a public part in building it. These men, all in their different ways leaders of immense moral and physical courage, struggled to find their way out of a war they had not wanted, and which seemed likely to destroy their nation. They were not to know that at Augusta they had won a settlement which would endure, with periodic revisions, until the very eve of the American Revolution. But as they journeyed homewards, they shared in general a sense – on both sides – that Anglo-Indian relations in the south had entered a new and more prosperous era.

Competition among rivals in the Cherokee leadership to gain stature by obtaining the best terms of peace from the colonials.

The British needed to secure the friendship of the Cherokee in order to secure peace + stability on the frontier

Between 1756-63 British policy towards the Cherokee became more centralized in order to promote stability on the frontier, but the lack of cooperation between London + the colonies + the pursuit of individuals on the ground both helped + hindered that process

Boundaries, trade + sovereignty were the main questions affecting Anglo-Cherokee relations in this period.

Appendix: Prominent Cherokees

Attakullakulla (the Little Carpenter). Leading Cherokee diplomat and right-hand man to Connecorte. Remarkable for his consistent support for an accommodation with the British. Rival of Occonostota, who competed with him for supremacy at Tomotly.

Connecorte (Old Hop). The lame Fire King (Uku) of Chota, nominal leader of the Cherokees. He died in early 1760.

Kanagatucko (Standing Turkey). Connecorte's successor. Associated with, and apparently influenced by, Occonostota and Ostenaca.

Occonostota (the Great Warrior). The Great Warrior, or titular war leader of the Cherokee nation. He was also the Warrior of Chota. In favour of peace until his humiliating arrest by Lyttelton in 1759. Thereafter he was the most important of the war faction, and tried to build an alliance with the French. In 1760 he organized Coytmore's death. He gave way to the Carpenter in the peace talks of 1761, but was probably consulted during the negotiations.

Ostenaca (Outacité, or Mankiller, of Tomotly). Also known as Judd's Friend or Judge's Friend. Attakullakulla's rival. Specialized in building relations with Virginia until the Cherokee war, and took the lead in rebuilding them afterwards. Frightened into hostility by Lyttelton's treatment of the peace delegations in 1759, but on the whole favoured peace. Visited London with two companions in 1762.

Round O. Warrior of Stecoe and most important leader in the Out Towns. In favour of peace. Led a peace delegation which, with Occonostota's, was arrested by Lyttelton in 1759.

Seroweh (the Young Warrior of Estatoe). The most implacable of the war leaders, and the junior war leader of Estatoe. Seroweh was the last important Cherokee leader to accept the peace of 1761.

Tistoe. Headman of Keowee. Worked hard for peace until driven into hostility by the actions of Coytmore, Miln and Lyttelton. Returned to rebuild Keowee in 1761.

Willinawaw. Attakullakulla's brother and closest supporter.

Wawatchee (Ohatchie). Lower Towns headman, frightened by the advance of the South Carolina settlers. Appealed to Ellis to persuade Lyttelton to enforce the Long Canes boundary. In 1761 argued that Long Canes must remain the limit of settlement, though not of white hunting.

Notes

The following abbreviations are used in the notes:

BL Add. MS   British Library Additional Manuscript
CO   Colonial Office documents in the Public Record Office, Kew, London
DRIA   McDowell, William L. (ed.), *Colonial Records of South Carolina. Series 2. Documents Relating to Indian Affairs 1754–1765.* University of South Carolina Press for the South Carolina Department of Archives and History, Columbia, 1970.
GD   Gifts and Deposits: document class at the NRA(S)
NRA(S)   National Register of Archives (Scotland)
PRO   A document class at the Public Record Office, Kew
WO   War Office documents in the Public Record Office

Chapter 1 Long Canes Creek: Anglo-Cherokee Relations to 1756

1. The numbers and locations of these towns were subject to fluctuation. See Betty Anderson Smith, 'The Distribution of Eighteenth Century Cherokee Settlements', in Duane H. King (ed.), *The Cherokee Indian Nation: A Troubled History* (University of Tennessee Press, Knoxville, 1979) 46–60.
2. Timothy Silver, *A New Face on the Countryside: Indians, Colonists and Slaves in the South Atlantic Forests 1500–1800* (Cambridge University Press, New York and Cambridge, 1990) 82; James Adair, *The History of the American Indians, Particularly Those Nations adjoining to the Mississippi, East and West Florida, Georgia, South and North Carolina, and Virginia* ... (Edward and Charles Dilly, London, 1775) 227; Fred Gearing, *Priests and Warriors: Social Structures for Cherokee Politics in the Eighteenth Century* (American Anthropological Association, vol. 64, no. 5, pt 2, October 1962, Memoir 93) 113n. The most recent work of Cherokee demography suggests that 20 000 may be too high a figure. Russell Thornton, *The Cherokees: A Population History* (University of Nebraska Press, Lincoln and London, 1991) 17–23.
3. R. C. Simmons, *The American Colonies From Settlement to Independence* (Longman, London, 1976) 177.
4. James Glen, governor of South Carolina, to the Duke of Newcastle, Secretary of State for the Southern Department, 3 February 1747, CO 5/389, f. 42; David H. Corkran, *The Cherokee Frontier: Conflict and Survival 1740–1762* (University of Oklahoma Press, Norman, 1962); J. R. Alden, *John Stuart and the Southern Colonial Frontier* (University of Michigan Press, Ann Arbor, 1944)

8–9; Chapman J. Milling, *Red Carolinians* (University of North Carolina Press, Chapel Hill, 1940), 280; T. R. Reese. *Colonial Georgia: A Study of British Imperial Policy in the Eighteenth Century* (University of Georgia Press, 1963) 106; Thornton, *The Cherokees*, 28–30.

5. Alden, *John Stuart*, 8–12; Silver, *A New Face on the Countryside*, 82–3; Wilbur R. Jacobs, *Dispossessing the American Indian: Indians and Whites on the Colonial Frontier* (University of Oklahoma Press, Norman, 1985) 80n; Reese, *Colonial Georgia*, 106–7. James H. Merrell, *The Indians' New World: Catawbas and Their Neighbours from European Contact Through the Era of Removal* (University of North Carolina Press, Chapel Hill and London, for the Institute of Early American History and Culture, Williamsburg, Virginia, 1989) 193–5.

6. Simmons, *American Colonies*, 177.

7. Ibid.

8. Ibid.

9. Dorothy V. Jones, *License for Empire: Colonialism by Treaty in Early America* (University of Chicago Press, 1982) 39; Thornton, *The Cherokees*, 10, 23ff.

10. M. Eugene Sirmans, *Colonial South Carolina: A Political History 1663–1763* (University of North Carolina Press, Chapel Hill, for the Institute of Early American History and Culture, 1966) 57; Alden, *John Stuart*, 8–9; John Phillip Reid, *A Better Kind of Hatchet: Law, Trade and Diplomacy in the Early Years of European Contact* (State University Press of Pennsylvania, Pennsylvania and London, 1979) 2–3.

11. P. M. Hamer, 'Anglo-French Rivalry in the Cherokee Country 1754–1757', *North Carolina Historical Review*, vol. II, no. 3 (July 1925) 303–22.

12. Cherokee belonged to the Macro-Siouan language group, of which Iroquoian was a subdivision. The Creeks, Chickasaws and Choctaws spoke Muskogean languages, while the Shawnees and the vanished nations of the Powhatan confederation used Algonquian tongues, both of which belonged to the Macro-Algonquian group. W. Stitt Robinson, *The Southern Colonial Frontier 1607–1763* (Greenwood Press, Westport, Connecticut, 1979), 2–3. Of the Cherokees' neighbours only the Catawbas spoke Macro-Siouan languages, and these were Siouan rather than Iroquoian. Merrell, *Indians' New World*, 9–10.

13. Despite the linguistic relationship to the Iroquois, many modern scholars prefer a local emergence explanation of Cherokee origins over the migration theory. Thornton, *The Cherokees*, 17–23.

14. Gearing, *Priests and Warriors*, 5.

15. Gearing, *Priests and Warriors*, 1–3; Reid, *A Better Kind of Hatchet*, 4; Henry Timberlake, *The Memoirs of Lieutenant Henry Timberlake* (London, 1765) 32 [59]. Page numbers in [brackets] refer to the 1927 Watuga Press reprint edition, edited by Samuel Cole Williams. Corkran, *Cherokee Frontier*, 4–5, has a vivid description of Cherokee buildings.

16. Gearing, *Priests and Warriors*, 18. It has been suggested that 'Slave Catcher' became an increasingly common title after 1730, as the Cherokees fulfilled their obligation to capture and return runaway black slaves. R. Halliburton, *Red Over Black: Black Slavery Amongst the Cherokee Indians* (Greenward Press, Westport, Connecticut, and London, 1977) 8.

17. Gearing, *Priests and Warriors*, 47; Tom Hatley, *The Dividing Paths; The Cherokees and South Carolina Through the Era of Revolution* (Oxford University Press, New York, 1993) 102.

18. John Phillip Reid, 'A Perilous Rule: The Law of International Homicide', in King (ed.), *The Cherokee Indian Nation*, 33–41.

19. Ibid., Gearing, *Priests and Warriors*, 87–8.

20. CO 5/4, ff. 211–14. Alexander Hewatt, *An Historical Account of the Rise and Progress of the Colonies of South Carolina and Georgia*, vol. II (London, 1779). 3–11; Sirmans, *South Carolina*; Verner W. Crane, *The Southern Frontier* 276–80, 295–9.

21. South Carolina itself did not formally recognize the treaty until 1738. Corkran, *Cherokee Frontier*, 15–16.

22. Gearing, *Priests and Warriors*, 86-88 Corkran, *Cherokee Frontier*, 17–21; David H. Corkran, 'The unpleasantness at Stecoe', *North Carolina Historical Review*, vol. 32 (1955) 358–75.

23. Gearing, *Priests and Warriors*, 88–94; Corkran, *Cherokee Frontier* 18–19; Alden, *John Stuart*, 32.

24. Gearing, *Priests and Warriors*, 96–7.

25. Robinson, *Southern Colonial Frontier*, 194–5.

26. Lieutenant-Governor William Bull to the Duke of Newcastle, 11 February 1740, CO 5/388, ff. 103–4.

27. J. R. Jones, *Britain and the World 1649–1815* (Fontana, London, 1980) 201–2.

28. Howard H. Peckham, *The Colonial Wars 1689–1762* (University of Chicago Press, Chicago and London, 1964) 89–95.

29. Glen to Newcastle, Saturday 2 May 1746 (duplicate), CO 5?388, ff. 158–9.

30. Ibid.

31. Glen to Newcastle, 24 July 1746, CO 5/288.

32. Alden, *John Stuart*, 34–5.

33. Copy of a letter from Glen to Vaudreuille, enclosed in Glen to Bedford, 23 December 1749, ibid., 146–7.

34. Glen to Bedford, 2 October 1750, CO 5/389, 208–9.

35. Grant, when governor of East Florida from 1763, built up an indigo plantation with over 40 slaves whom he had sold in Charleston for cash when that colony was regained by Spain. Paul David Nelson, *General James Grant: Scottish Soldier and Royal Governor of East Florida* (University Press of Florida, Gainesville, 1993) 66, 147.

36. Alden, *John Stuart*, 36.

37. Ibid., 37

38. William De Brahm to William Henry Lyttelton, Keowee, 25 August 1756, Lyttelton Papers, microfilm Reel 1, Clements Library.

39. Alden, *John Stuart*, 45; Sirmans, *South Carolina*, 296–300.

40. Ibid., 299–300.

41. Alden, *John Stuart*, 45.

42. Ibid., 45–6; Corkran, *Cherokee Frontier*, 59; *South Carolina Gazette*, 24–31 July 1755.

43. Corkran, *Cherokee Frontier*, 60; Sirmans, *South Carolina*, 299; W. Stitt Robinson, *James Glen: From Scottish Provost to Royal Governor of South Carolina* (Greenwood Press, Westport, Connecticut, and London, 1996), 101; the treaty is at CO 5/375, f. 113.

44. J. M[urray] to Mr Oswald, Charleston, 31 January 1756, Murray of Murraythwaite Muniments, National Register of Archives (Scotland), GD 219/290, f. 3.
45. Alden, *John Stuart*, 46; Hewatt, *Historical Account*, II, 202–4; Sirmans, *South Carolina*, 299.
46. J. R. Alden, *John Stuart*, 32; Sirmans, *South Carolina*, 296, 299; Hatley, *Dividing Paths*, 75–8.
47. Sirmans, *South Carolina*, 300.
48. Alden, *John Stuart*, 25.
49. Ibid.; George Croghan to William Johnson, 10 September 1755, *William Johnson Papers*, cited in Wilbur R. Jacobs, *Wilderness Politics and Indian Gifts*, 160.
50. See Chapter 2 below.
51. Hewatt, *Historical Account*, II, 297–8.
52. W. S. Willis, 'Colonial conflict and the Cherokee Indians 1710–1760', unpublished PhD thesis, Columbia University, 1985. David Duncan Wallace, *The Life of Henry Laurens: With a Sketch of the Life of Lieutenant-Colonel John Laurens* (G. M. Putnam and Sons, the Knickerbocker Press, New York and London, 1915) 96–7.
53. Hewatt, *Historical Account*, II, 10–11.
54. Robinson, *Southern Colonial Frontier*, 171–2; Simmons, *American Colonies*, 174 8, 184; Louis De Vorsey, *The Indian Boundary in the Southern Colonies 1763–1775* (University of North Carolina Press, Chapel Hill, 1966) 112; Alden, *John Stuart*, 22; Robert L. Meriwether, *The Expansion of South Carolina 1729–1768* (Southern Publishing, Kingsport, Tennessee, 1940) 123–5.
55. De Vorsey, *Indian Boundary*, 116–7; Murray to Oswald, Charleston, 31 January 1756, Murray of Murraythwaite Muniments, NRA(S), GD 219/290, f. 3; Robinson, *Southern Colonial Frontier*, 171–2, includes a fine map of the Long Canes surveys.
56 . De Vorsey, *Indian Boundary*, 50–2.
57. Ibid.
58. S. C. Williams, 'An Account of the Presbyterian Mission to the Cherokees 1757–1759', *Tennessee Historical Magazine*, 2nd ser., vol. I (1931) 137. This article quotes verbatim most of Richardson's journal of his stay with the Cherokees between November 1758 and February 1759. He thought there was 'too much Truth' in these complaints.
59. Timberlake, *Memoirs*, 74–5 [96–8].
60. R.M. Weir, *Colonial South Carolina: A History* (KTO, Millward, New York, 1983) 269.
61. Ibid.
62. Silver, *A New Face on the Countryside*, 90–1.
63. Ibid., 90–7.
64. Glen to Bedford, 27 July 1748, CO 5/389, 66–8; Corkran, *Cherokee Frontier*, 20–1.
65. Gearing, *Priests and Warriors*, 87.
66. Glen to Bedford (duplicate), 15 July 1750, CO 5/389, 205–11; Corkran, *Cherokee Frontier*, 23–4; Alden, *John Stuart*, 32; Sirmans, *South Carolina*, 288.

67. Gary C. Goodwin, *Cherokees in Transition: A Study of Changing Culture and Environment Prior to 1775* (University of Chicago Department of Geography Research Paper no. 181, 1977).
68. Gearing, *Priests and Warriors*, 87; David H. Corkran, *The Creek Frontier 1540–1783* (University of Oklahoma Press, Norman, 1967) 146ff.
69. Mary U. Rothrock, 'Carolina Traders Among the Overhill Cherokees 1690–1760', *East Tennessee Historical Society's Publications*, no. 1 (1929) 21–22, 27–29.
70. Francis Jennings, *The Ambiguous Iroquois Empire: The Covenant Chain Confederation of Indian Tribes with English Colonies from its beginnings to the Lancaster Treaty of 1744* (Norton, New York, 1984) 370–372; Jones, *License for Empire*, 38.
71. Wilbur R. Jacobs, *Wilderness Politics and Indian Gifts* Lincoln, Nebraska, 1966) 124.
72. De Vorsey, *Indian Boundary*, 50.
73. This treaty, with its obvious threat to the South Carolina supremacy, may have spurred Glen on to Saluda. Hatley, *Dividing Paths*, 75.
74. Jacobs, *Wilderness Politics*, 139–141.
75. Otis K. Rice, 'The Sandy Creek Expedition of 1756', *West Virginia History*, vol. 13 (1952) 5–19.
76. Corkran, *Cherokee Frontier*, 67–71; Alden, *John Stuart*, 47–8. Christopher Gist, who was both a Virginian agent and Edmond Atkin's deputy, organized the distribution of presents. Jacobs, *Wilderness*, 160–4.
77. Corkran, *Cherokee Frontier*, 70.
78. Lewis to Captain Raymond Demeré [commanding officer at Fort Prince George, and commandant designate of Fort Loudoun], Chota, 7 July 1756, Lyttelton Papers, Reel 1.
79. Corkran, *Cherokee Frontier*, 72; Francis Fauquier to the Board of Trade, Williamsburg, 1 May 1762, CO 5/1330, f. 125; Carolyn Thomas Foreman, *Indians Abroad 1493–1938* (University of Oklahoma Press, Norman, 1943); Timberlake, *Memoirs* (Williams ed., 1927,repr. 1971) 74n.
80. Hardy to Lyttelton, New York, 21 September 1756, Lyttelton Papers, Reel 1; Halifax to Lyttelton, Horton, 13 August 1756, ibid.
81. Captain John McNeill to Ostenaca, Augusta Courthouse, 28 October 1756, Loudoun Papers, Box 86, LO 3670; Lewis to Ostenaca, Augusta, 30 October, 22 November, 1756, ibid; Dinwiddie to 'the Sachems, Warriors, and Headmen of the lower and upper Towns of the Cherokee Nation of Indians', ibid; Dinwiddie to Ostenaca, nd., ibid; McNeill to Ostenaca, Roanoke, 27 November 1756, ibid; Lieutenant John Allen to John Watts, Fort Loudoun,24 December 1756, Ibid; 'Answer to the Governor of Virginia's Letter by Conneeaughtehe, the Little Carpenter, Willinawaw, Judge's Friend & his Brother, the Old Bark, & two more Old Men. At the House of Otacitte Ouestenaco'. 21 December 1756 (copy), ibid., Box 55, LO 2378; Raymond Demeré to Loudoun,. Fort Loudoun, 23 December 1756, ibid., LO 2392.
82. Dinwiddie to Lyttelton, Williamsburg, 7 August, 2, 18 September, 20 November 1756, 24 January 1757, Lyttelton Papers, Reel 1; Dinwiddie to Halifax, Williamsburg, 9 November 1756, 4 January 1757, CO5/1329,

ff. 21, 24;, and Whitehall, 19 November 1756, Lyttelton Papers, Reel 1; Dinwiddie to Loudoun, Williamsburg, 1 December 1757, Loudoun Papers, Box 109, LO 4930; and 23 December Ibid., Box 55, 2392; 'At a council held [in Virginia]', 28 January 1757, Ibid.' Box 61, LO 2723; Loudoun to Lyttelton, New York, 24 April 1757, Ibid., Box 75, LO 3448.

83. Corkran, *Cherokee Frontier*, 66–72.
84. Jennings *Iroquois Empire*, 354. Shawnees killed a settler at Monk's Corner, only thirty miles from Charleston, as late as 1753. Alden, *John Stuart*, 24–5.
85. Sirmans *South Carolina*, 215–16.
86. James H. Merrell, '"Their Very Bones Shall Fight": The Catawba-Iroquois Wars', in Daniel K. Richter and James H. Merrell (eds), *Beyond the Covenant Chain: The Iroquois and Their Neighbours in Indian North America 1600–1800* (Syracuse University Press, Syracuse, New York, 1987) 115–33.
87. Theda Perdue, 'Cherokee Relations with the Iroquois in the Eighteenth Century', in ibid.,135–48.
88. Ibid., 216; Alden, *John Stuart*, 24.
89. 'Mr. Charles's Proposal Relating to the Indians in America', Newcastle Papers, BL Add. MSS 33029, ff.147–8.
90. J. E. Stagg, 'Protection and Survival: Anglo-Indian Relations 1748–60 – Britain and the northern colonies'. Unpublished Ph.D. thesis, Cambridge, 1984, 163–4.
91. Ibid., 163–180.
92. Ibid., Chapter IV, 'Imperial and Colonial Ideas for the Management of Indian Affairs on the Eve of the French and Indian War', 148ff., *passim*.
93. Peckham, *Colonial Wars*, 120–9, contains a useful survey of these French expeditions.
94. Stagg, 'Protection and Survival', 180–8.
95. Ibid., 100–9.
96. The admonitory tone of the Board's letter is remarked upon by Simmons, *American Colonies*, 277.
97. Stagg, 'Protection and Survival', 220–4.
98. Loudoun to Hardy, Albany, 21 November 1756 (copy), Bouquet Papers, BL Add MS 21631, ff. 3–6.
99. Jack P. Greene, 'The South Carolina Quartering Dispute 1757–58', *South Carolina Historical Magazine*, vol. 60, 1959, 193–203.
100. Part of a letter from John Forbes [1758], Correspondence and Miscellaneous Papers, NRA(S) 0017 4.
101. Wilbur R. Jacobs (ed.), *The Appalachian Indian Frontier: The Edmond Atkin Report and Plan of 1755* (University of Nebraska Press, 1967) reproduces Atkin's scheme in its entirety.
102. Loudoun to Lyttelton (private) 13 February 1758 (extract); 13 February 1758 (extract), Forbes Papers, University of Virginia Library, microfilm M2374 P, reel 1, Item 44.
103. Byrd to Forbes, South Carolina, 21 March 1758, Ibid., 85. For the context of this remark, see Chapter 2 below.
104. Jack P. Sosin, *Whitehall and the Wilderness*, 32, 42–3; Richard White, *The Middle Ground: Indians, Empires and Republics in the Great Lakes Region 1650–1815* (Cambridge University Press, Cambridge and New York, 1991)

254–5; James H. Merrell, *Into the American Woods: Negotiators on the Pennsylvanian Frontier* (W.W. Norton, New York and London, 1999) 209ff., 242–9.

105. Ibid., 43, 46–8.
106. White, *Middle Ground*, 50.
107. Dowd, '"Insidious Friends"', 114–150, *passim*.

Chapter 2: 'Two Brothers Falling Out': the Slide to War, 1756–59

1. Alden, *John Stuart*, 52–53
2. Ibid. The British usually called it 'Fort L'Assumption' or 'Assomption'.
3. Ibid., 61–62.
4. Loudoun to Johnson, Halifax, 1 July 1757, in J. Sullivan (ed.), *The Papers of Sir William Johnson*, vol. 2 (University of the State of New York, Albany, 1922) 729; copy of the peace preliminaries, dated New Orleans, 25 November 1756, ibid., 9 (1939), 574–81; Lyttelton to the South Carolina Assembly, 5 April 1757, enclosing Kelérec to Ministre de la Marine, 13 December 1756, and the articles of peace, 25 November 1756, Lyttelton Papers, Reel 1.
5. Demeré to Lyttelton, Fort Loudoun, 29 October, 7 November, 8 December 1756, *DRIA*, II, 265–6, 268–71, 295–7; Alden, *John Stuart*, 62.
6. Ellis to Lyttelton, Savannah, 24 May 1757, Lyttelton Papers, Reel 1.
7. 'Captain Raymond Demeré's account of the evidence given to him by the Old Warrior of Tomotly', 25 November 1756, CO 5/386, ff. 85–7; Ostenaca's talk to Raymond Demeré, 25 November 1756, ibid., ff. 95–6; Indian Information [of Cornelius Doherty as reported to Raymond Demeré], English Camp, 2 December 1756, Loudoun Papers, Box 55, LO 2309; 'Information given to Capt. Demeré by an Indian wench called Nancy Butler', Fort Loudoun, 20 December 1756, ibid., LO 2392; The information of 'Capt.Caesar of the Town of Chatuga...', Fort Loudoun, 21 December 1756 (copy), ibid., LO 2325; Demeré to Loudoun, Fort Koudoun, 23 December 1756, ibid., LO 2392; Talk of the Blind Slave Catcher of Chatuga, Fort Loudoun, 2 January 1757, *DRIA*, 305–6.
8. Corkran, *Cherokee Frontier*, 12–14; Gearing, *Priests and Warriors*, 64; Goodwin, *Cherokees in Transition*, 100.
9. Raymond Demeré to Lyttelton, Fort Loudoun, 4, 6, 12, 13, 15 January 1757, *DRIA*, 306–10, 311–16; Demeré to Lieutenant Robert Wall, Fort Loudoun, 10 January 1757, ibid., 311; Talk of Lieutenant Wall to the Tellico Indians, Great Tellico, 11 January 1757, ibid., 317–19; Talk of the Mankiller of Tellico to Raymond Demeré, Fort Loudoun, 15 January 1757, ibid., 319–20; Wall to Raymond Demeré, Fort Loudoun, 13 January 1757, ibid., 321–4; Alden, *John Stuart*, 63.
10. Milling, *Red Carolinians*, 289–91; Alden, *John Stuart*, 63–64.
11. Stuart to Lyttelton, Fort Loudoun, 12 June 1757, Lyttelton Papers, Reel 2. Incidents of this kind may have given Coytmore the taste for arrogant behaviour which eventually killed him and helped to spark off the Anglo-Cherokee War. See Chapter 3 below.

12. Milling, *Red Carolinians*, 288–99.
13. Stuart to Lyttelton, Fort Loudoun, 12 June 1757, Lyttelton Papers, Reel 2.
14. Demeré to Lyttelton, Fort Loudoun, 26 June 1757, ibid.
15. Demeré to Lyttelton, Fort Loudoun, 11 July 1757, enclosing Daniel Pepper to Demeré, New Windsor, South Carolina, 27 June 1757, ibid; John Bogges to Lyttelton, Fort Prince George, 16 July 1757, enclosing Bogges to Lyttelton, 10 July 1757, ibid.
16. Alden, *John Stuart*, 64.
17. Raymond Demeré to Lyttelton, Fort Loudoun, 9 July 1757, Lyttelton Papers, Reel 1; Stuart to Lyttelton, Fort Loudoun, 11 July 1757, Ibid., Reel 2.
18. Demeré to Lyttelton, Fort Loudoun, 4 July 1757, ibid.
19. Stuart to Lyttelton, Fort Loudoun, 29 May 1757, Lyttelton Papers, Reel 2.
20. Silver, *A New Face on the Countryside*, 93.
21. Stuart to Lyttelton, Fort Loudoun, 11 July 1757, Lyttelton Papers, Reel 2.
22. Raymond Demeré to Lyttelton, Fort Loudoun, 20 July 1757, ibid.
23. John Bogges to Lyttelton, Fort Prince George, 16 July 1757, ibid.
24. Raymond Demeré to Lyttelton, Fort Loudoun, 20 July 1757, ibid.
25. Ibid.
26. Ibid.; Stuart to Lyttelton, Fort Loudoun, 23 July 1757, ibid.
27. Paul Demeré to Lyttelton, 31 August 1757, ibid.
28. Ibid.
29. Ibid.
30. Ibid.
31. Ibid.
32. 'Copies of Original Papers shewn the 27 June 1757 by Outossity Oustenoika, The Chief Warrior of Tomotly in the Upper Cherokee Country to His Majesty's Agent and Superintendent of Indian Affairs', Loudoun Papers, Box 80, LO 3670.
33. Dinwiddie to Lyttelton, Williamsburg, 22 July 1757, Lyttelton Papers, Reel 2.
34. Dinwiddie to Lyttelton, Williamsburg, 27 August 1757, ibid.
35. 'Old Hop, Little Carpenter, Great Warrior, William A. Waugh, Standing Turkey to the Governor of Virginia', Fort Loudoun, 23 August 1757 (copy), Fort Loudoun, 23 August 1757; Loudoun Papers, Box 95, LO 4294; 'Old Hop, Great Warrior, Standing Turkey' to Ostenaca and John Watts, Chota, 23 August 1757, ibid.
36. Paul Demeré to Lyttelton, Fort Loudoun, 11 October 1757, Lyttelton Papers, Reel 2; Atkin's Talk 'To Cunnicahtarkty Governor of the whole Nation of Cherokee Indians', Winchester, 4 August 1757 (copy), Loudoun Papers, Box 91, LO 4049.
37. J.E. Stagg, 'Protection and Survival', 327 ff.; Theda Perdue, 'Cherokee Relations with the Iroquois in the Eighteenth Century', in Daniel K. Richter and James H. Merrell (eds), *Beyond the Covenant Chain: The Iroquois and their Neighbours in Indian North America, 1600–1800* (Syracuse University Press, Syracuse, New York, 1987) 140; Loudoun to Forbes, New York, 26 April 1758, Dalhousie Muniments, NRA(S) GD 45/2/65/19; Forbes to Abercromby, Philadelphia, 4 May 1758, *Writings of Forbes*, 85; William Johnson feared that a Cherokee expedition to the Ohio would drive the

Iroquois into the hands of the French, Johnson to Atkin, Fort Johnson, 21 June 1757, *Johnson Papers*, 9, 785.
38. Jones, *License for Empire*, 43. The best account of the meaning of gifts, which Jones also relies on, is Jacobs, *Indian Gifts*, 11–28.
39. Corkran, *Cherokee Frontier*, 115.
40. Ibid.
41. Ibid.
42. Clement Read to Dinwiddie, Luneburg, 5 April 1757 (copy), Loudoun Papers, Box 86, LO 3670; Dinwiddie to Lyttelton, Williamsburg, 28 May 1757, Lyttelton Papers, Reel 1.
43. Corkran, *Cherokee Frontier*, 116–17.
44. Not to be confused with Fort Loudoun in the Cherokee country, nor with a third Fort Loudoun in Pennsylvania, which will assume some importance later in this chapter.
45. Atkin to Lyttelton, Williamsburg, 25 May 1757, Lyttelton Papers, Reel 1; Dinwiddie to Lyttelton, Williamsburg, 28 May 1757, ibid.
46. Dinwiddie to Lyttelton, Williamsburg, 22 July 1757, ibid., Reel 2.
47. Washington to Brigadier-General John Stanwix, Fort Loudoun [Virginia], 15 June 1757 (copy), Loudoun Papers, Box 85, LO 3838.
48. Atkin to Lyttelton, Winchester, 13 August 1757, ibid.
49. 'Copies of Original Papers shewn the 27 June 1757 by Outossity Oustenaika, the Chief Warrior of Tomotly in the Upper Cherokee Country to his Majesty's Agent and Superintendent of Indian Affairs', ibid., Box 86, 3670; Atkin's Talk to Connecorte, Winchester, 4 August 1757 (copy), ibid., Box 91; 'Instructions to Christopher Gist, Esqr...', Smithfield, Virginia, 16 November 1757, ibid, Box 106, 4847.
50. Dinwiddie to Lyttelton, Williamsburg, 22 July 1767, Lyttelton Papers, Reel 1.
51. Silver, *A New Face on the Countryside*, 96.
52. Glen to Edward Fenwick, Saxegotha Township, 1 June 1756, Lyttelton Papers, Reel 1.
53. Dobbs to Lyttelton, New Bern, 2 August 1756, ibid.
54. John Fairchild to Lyttelton, 'In the Fork between Broad and Saludy Rivers', 1 January 1757, *DRIA*, 324–5.
55. 'The Intelligence brought by Rosq, or Silver Heels, a Seneca. Also Peter an Oneida Indians Intelligence', *Johnson Papers*, 9, 612–14.
56. Joseph Chatwin to Lyttelton, New Hope, Savannah River, 4 December 1757, *DRIA*, 421; John Fairchild to Lyttelton, 10 December 1757, ibid; Captain William West to Lyttelton, Little Saluda, n.d., ibid., 424–5; James Francis to Lyttelton, [Ninety Six], 23 December 1757, ibid., 425–6; James Beamer to Lyttelton, Estatoe, 25 February 1758, ibid., 441–2.
57. The Headmen of the Lower Towns and the Warriors of Keowee to Lyttelton, Fort Prince George, 2 March 1758, ibid., 444.
58. Ibid.
59. 'Talk from his Excellency to the Headmen and Warriours of the Lower towns of the Cherokee Nation', [March 1758], ibid., 479–80.
60. Ibid., 480.
61. Ibid., 479.
62. Ibid.
63. Alden, *John Stuart*, 78–9 n.; Milling, *Red Carolinians*, 291.

64. Warriors of Estatoe to Lyttelton, Fort Prince George, 20 March 1758, *DRIA*, 451.
65. George Turner to Lyttelton, Fort Prince George, 20 May 1758, enclosed with Turner to Lyttelton, Fort Prince George, 19 May 1759, ibid.
66. Milling, *Red Carolinians*, 292–4; Alden, *John Stuart*, 78 n.
67. 'Examination of Jerome Courtonne', South Carolina Council Journals, CO 5/476, f. 3.
68. Cashin, *Henry Ellis*, 82–5.
69. Ibid.
70. Ellis to Lyttelton, Savannah, 25 August 1757, Lyttelton Papers, Reel 2.
71. Cashin, *Henry Ellis*, 85.
72. Bouquet to Paul Demeré, Charleston, 28 July 1757, Letterbook 1757, Bouquet Papers, BL Add. MS, 21,631, f. 47.
73. Bouquet to Loudoun, Charleston, 25 August 1757, ibid., f. 81.
74. Bouquet to Paul Demeré, Charleston, 10 September 1757, Letterbook 1757–58, ibid., ff. 2–3.
75. Bouquet to Shaw, Charleston, 17 September 1757, ibid., ff. 6–7
76. Bouquet to Croghan, 10 August 1759, quoted in White, *Middle Ground*, 257.
77. Bouquet to Loudoun, Charleston, 10 December 1757, Loudoun Papers, Box 110, LO 4993.
78. Sosin, *Whitehall and the Wilderness*, 42–3.
79. See Chapters 4–5 below.
80. Cashin, *Henry Ellis*, 85; Ray Allen Billington (with James Blaine Hedges), *Westward Expansion: A History of the American Frontier* 4th edn (Macmillan, New York, 1974) 138.
81. White, *Middle Ground*, 288, citing a letter from Bouquet to Amherst, 15 July 1763.
82. Ibid.
83. Pitt to Lyttelton, Whitehall, 30 December 1757, Lyttelton Papers, Reel 2; Pitt to Lyttelton, Whitehall, 27 January 1758, ibid., Pitt to Lyttelton, Secret, Whitehall, 7 March 1758, ibid.
84. Abercromby to Lyttelton, New York, 16, 22 March 1758, ibid.
85. Atkin to Loudoun, Williamsburg, 8 October 1757, Loudoun Papers, Box 101, LO 4006; '...Goods proposed by Mr. Atkin to be provided by the Government of Virginia for the Indian Parties coming to its Assistance', October 1757, ibid., LO 4723; Atkin to Nathaniel Walthoe, 'Clerk of the Council at Williamsburg, Virginia', New Bern, 26 January 1758 (copy), ibid., Box 118, LO 5473; 'Copy of Mr. Atkin's Representation against an Act passed in Virginia, for establishing a Trade with the Indians in Alliance with His Majesty', 26 January 1758, ibid., oversize, LO 5987; Atkin to Lyttelton, Williamsburg, 28 October 1757, Lyttelton Papers, Reel 2; Dinwiddie to Lyttelton, Williamsburg, 23 November 1757, ibid. Dobbs to Lyttelton, New Bern, 24 October 1757, ibid.
86. Atkin to Lyttelton, New Bern, North Carolina, 23, 29 November 1757, 6 January 1758, ibid., Dobbs to Lyttelton, New Bern, 8 January 1758, ibid., Atkin to Lyttelton, Georgetown, 19 March 1758, ibid. On the boundary question and the Catawba fort see Dobbs to Lyttelton, New Bern, 24 October 1757, enclosing affidavit of the Catawba headmen, 29 September 1757, and Catawba Headmen to Dobbs, 5 October 1757, ibid.

87. William Byrd to Loudoun, 'Keawee', 30 April 1758, Marion Tinling (ed.), *The Correspondence of the Three William Byrds of Westover, Virginia*, vol. 2 (University Press of Virginia, Charlottesville, for the Virginia Historical Society, 1977) 649–50; Atkin to Forbes, Charleston, 20 May 1758, Forbes Papers, Reel 2, Item 235.

88. South Carolina Council Journals, 4, 9 April 1759, CO 5/476, f. 30.

89. Lyttelton to the Board of Trade, 8 August 1758, CO 5/376, ff. 45, 46, 47.

90. Ibid., ff. 47–8.

91. Ibid.

92. Ibid., f. 45.

93. Lyttelton to the Board of Trade, Charleston, 7 August 1758, CO 5/376, f. 45.

94. Lyttelton to the Board of Trade, Charleston, 30 November 1757, ibid., f. 20.

95. Lyttelton to the Board of Trade, Charleston, 7 August 1758, CO 5/376, ff. 45–6.

96. Ibid.

97. Fox to Loudoun, Whitehall, 12 May 1756, Loudoun Papers, Box 23, LO 1142.

98. Atkin to Loudoun, Craven Street [London], 14 May 1756, ibid., LO 1148; Atkin to Loudoun, New York, 6 October 1756, ibid., Box 45, LO 1979; Atkin to Loudoun, Albany, 20 October 1756, ibid., LO 2045; Atkin to Loudoun, Albany, 26 November 1756, ibid., Box 53, LO 2282; Atkin to Loudoun, Philadelphia, 20 March 1757, ibid., Box 70, LO 3178.

99. Loudoun to Lyttelton (private), New York, 13 February 1758, Lyttelton Papers, Reel 2.

100. Ibid., Loudoun to Bosomworth, New York, 15 February 1758 (copy), Forbes Papers, Reel 1, Item 47; Bosomworth to Loudoun, York Town [Virginia], 23 February 1758, Loudoun Papers, Box 121, LO 5651.

101. Loudoun to Atkin New York, 14 February 1758 (copy), ibid., Box 120, 5586.

102. Byrd to Forbes, Charleston, 21 March 1758, Forbes Papers, Reel 1, Item 85.

103. Byrd to Loudoun, Charleston, 21 March 1758, WO 34/47, ff. 192–3. Published in *Byrd Correspondence*, 2, 640–1.

104. Ibid., Lyttelton to Loudoun, Charleston, 21 March 1758 (extract), Forbes Papers, Reel 1, Item 84; Byrd to Forbes, Charleston, 21 March 1758, ibid; 'Governor Lyttelton to Old hop and the Cherokee Headmen and Warriours', *DRIA*, II, 478–9; 'Governor Lyttelton to O Tacite', and 'Governor Lyttelton to the Raven of Highwassie', ibid., 480; Lyttelton to the Board of Trade, 7 August 1758, CO 5/376, ff. 41–2.

105. Atkin to Byrd, Charleston, 24 March 1758, CO 34/47, f. 194, enclosing Atkin 'to the Cherokee governour Cunnicahtarkly', CO 34/47, f. 194 ff; copies of both documents in Forbes Papers, Reel 1, Item 88. The letter is printed in *Byrd Correspondence*, 2, 642–3, with a long extract from the Talk, 643–4 n.

106. Paul Demeré to Lyttelton, Fort Loudoun, 20 February, 2 March 1758, Lyttelton Papers, Reel 2.

107. Byrd to Lyttelton, Keowee, 10 April 1758, Lyttelton Papers, Reel 2; Paul Demeré to Lyttelton, Fort Loudoun, 10 April 1758, ibid., Byrd to [Forbes?], Keowee, 30 April 1758, Forbes Papers, Reel 1, Item 158; Byrd to Loudoun, 'Keawee', 30 April 1758, *Byrd Correspondence*, 2, 649; Lyttelton to Forbes, Charleston, 21 May 1758, Dalhousie Muniments, NRA(S), GD 45/2/49/3.

108. Paul Demeré to Lyttelton, Fort Loudoun, 20 February 1758, Lyttelton Papers, Reel 2.

109. Ibid.
110. Ibid.
111. Ibid.
112. Byrd to Lyttelton, 'West's on Little Saluda', 31 March 1758, Lyttelton Papers, Reel 2; printed in *Byrd Correspondence*, 2, 644–5.
113. Ibid., Byrd to Loudoun, Keowee, 30 April 1758; printed in *Byrd Correspondence*, 2, 649.
114. Ibid.
115. Byrd to Lyttelton, Keowee, 1 May 1758, Lyttelton Papers, Reel 2; printed in *Byrd Correspondence*, 2, 651.
116. Ibid.
117. Ibid.
118. Ibid.
119. 'Little Carpenter and the Great Warrior of Chota to Governor Lyttelton', [Keowee], 2, May 1758, *DRIA*, 478.
120. Byrd to Glen, Winchester, 23 June 1758, Dalhousie Muniments, NRA(S), GD 45/2/44/3b.
121. Byrd to [Forbes], Keowee, 30 April 1758, Forbes Papers, Reel 1, Item 158.
122. Ibid., Byrd to Lyttelton, Keowee, 1 May 1758, Lyttelton Papers, Reel 2; printed in *Byrd Correspondence*, 2, 650–1.
123. Ibid.
124. McIntosh to Lyttelton, Fort Prince George, 19, 26/27 May 1758, Lyttelton Papers, Reel 2; George Turner to Lyttelton, Fort Prince George, 19 May 1758, ibid; Paul Demeré to Lyttelton, Fort Loudoun, 20 May 1758, ibid., Lyttelton to Forbes, Charleston, 21 May 1758, NRA(S) GD 45/2/49/3.
125. McIntosh to Lyttelton, Fort Prince George, 26 May 1758, Lyttelton Papers, Reel 2.
126. Byrd to Loudoun, 'Keowee', 30 April 1758, ibid.
127. Milling, *Red Carolinians*, 292–4.
128. Hewatt, *Historical Account*, II, 218. Milligan practised medicine in South Carolina for many years, but his valuable description of the colony was published under the name of Milligan Johnston. George Milligan Johnston, *A Short Description of the Province of South Carolina with an Account of the Air, Weather, and Diseases, at Charles-Town Written in the Year 1763* (London, 1770), reprinted in Chapman J. Milling (ed.), *Colonial South Carolina: Two Contemporary Descriptions by Governor James Glen and Doctor George Milligan-Johnston* (University of South Carolina Press, Columbia, 1951) 187–8.
129. Turner to Lyttelton, Fort Prince George, 20 May 1758, enclosed with Turner to Lyttelton, Fort Prince George, 19 May 1758, ibid. What may have been a separate incident occurred at about the same time, but in this case the Indians were attacked because they had stolen horses. Milling, *Red Carolinians*, 293–4.
130. Byrd to McIntosh, 'N. Yadkin', 12 May 1758, *Byrd Correspondence*, 2, 633.
131. Virginia President and Council, Minute, 27 May 1758, ibid., 655.
132. Milling, *Red Carolinians*, 292–3.
133. Bouquet to Forbes, Carlisle, 25 May 1758 (copy), Bouquet Papers BL Add. MS, 21,640, f. 39; Amherst to Bouquet, Philadelphia, 29 May 1758, ibid., Virginia President and Council. Minute, 6 June 1758. *Byrd Correspondence*, 2, 659.

134. Forbes to Johnson, Philadelphia, 4 May 1758, *Johnson Papers*, 9, 897–8. This was indeed a wish born of despair. Forbes himself had earlier reminded Abercromby that the Cherokees were outside Johnson's jurisdiction. Forbes to Abercromby, Philadelphia, 22 April 1758, *Writings of Forbes*, 69.
135. Forbes to Abercromby [Philadelphia], 20, 22 April 1758, Abercromby Papers, Box 4, AB 175, 185, printed in *Writings of Forbes*, 65, 68–9; Forbes to Loudoun, 27 April 1758, *Writings of Forbes*, 69. Some leading Pennsylvanians seem to have feared that arming the Cherokees would renew the war with the Delawares, and so lead to raids on their plantations. Forbes, who thought the Cherokees vital to his expedition, was unimpressed by a nation which 'would not make a breakfast for the Cherokees' and was therefore determined 'of giving the last the preference in everything'. Forbes to Abercromby, Philadelphia, 24 April 1758, ibid., 72. On the shortages in Virginia being made worse by Pennsylvanian parsimony see Christopher Gist to Forbes, Winchester, 12 April 1758, NRA(S) GD 45/2/43/3; John Blair to Forbes, Williamsburg, 9 April 1758, ibid.
136. Forbes to Johnson, Philadelphia, 4 May 1758, *Johnson Papers*, 9, 898; Forbes to Abercromby, Philadelphia, 4, 7 May 1758, Abercromby Papers, Box 5, AB 230, 237; Ferrell Wade to Forbes, Philadelphia, 4 May 1758 (copy), ibid., AB 232; Forbes to Pitt, Philadelphia, 'May latter end 1758', Dalhousie Muniments, NRA(S) GD 45/2/52/2.
137. John Blair, President of the Virginia Council, to Bosomworth, [Williamsburg], 8 April 1758, Abercromby Papers, Box 3, AB 132.
138. Bosomworth to Abercromby, Williamsburg, 8 April 1758, ibid., 133.
139. 'Speech of Captain Bosomworth to the Headmen, Chiefs and Warriors of His Majesty's faithful Friends and Allies the Cherokees and Catawbas...', Fort Loudoun [Virginia], 21 April 1758, ibid., Reel 1, Item 132; Forbes to Abercromby, Philadelphia, 1 May 1758, Abercromby Papers, Box 5, AB 221.
140. Ibid.
141. Bosomworth to Forbes, 'For the Better regulation and Management of a Body of Indians going to Warr...', Philadelphia, 2 May 1758, Forbes Papers, Reel 2, Item 166; Atkin to Forbes, Charleston, 20 May 1758, ibid., Item 236.
142. Bosomworth to Forbes, Carlisle, 1 June 1758, ibid., Item 285; Bouquet to [Amherst?], Carlisle, 2 June 1758, docketed 'Copy to Genl. Forbes', Bouquet Papers, BL Add. MS. 21,640, f. 56.
143. Amherst to Bouquet, Philadelphia, 6 June 1758, ibid., ff. 58–69.
144. Forbes to Stanwix, Philadelphia, 29 May 1758, Abercromby Papers, Box 7, AB 294; Forbes to Pitt, 'Carlisle, west of Susquehannah', 10 July 1758 (copy), Dalhousie Muniments, NRA(S) GD 45/2/524a; Forbes to Abercromby, Shippensburg, 4 September 1758, Abercromby Papers, Box 12, AB 610; Forbes to Abercromby, [Raestown, September] 1758, ibid., Box 13, AB 709.
145. Johnson to Abercromby, Fort Johnson, Fort Johnson, 18 June 1758, ibid., Box 8, AB 380; Abercromby to Forbes, Fort Edward, 24 June 1758, ibid., AB 364; Forbes to Abercromby, Carlisle, 9 July 1758, ibid., Box 9, AB 428.
146. Glen to Forbes, South Carolina, 29 March 1758, Dalhousie Muniments, NRA(S) GD 45/2/44/1; Forbes to St. Clair, Philadelphia, 8 June 1758 (draft), ibid., 45/2/22/9.

147. Forbes to Abercromby, Philadelphia, 15 June 1758, Abercromby Papers, Box 8, AB 175; Forbes to Bouquet, Philadelphia, 22 May, 16, 27 June 1758, Bouquet Papers, BL Add. MS. 21,640, ff. 36, 66, 71.

148. Forbes to Abercromby, Philadelphia, 15 June 1758, *Writings of Forbes*, 113; Glen to Forbes, Fort Cumberland, 13 July 1758, Dalhousie Muniments, NRA(S) GD 45/2/44/3a.

149. Bosomworth to Forbes, Carlisle, 25 May 1758, Forbes Papers, Reel 2, Item 260; Forbes to Bosomworth, Carlisle, 1 June 1758 (copy), ibid., Item 284.

150. For example, Forbes to Pitt, Philadelphia, 19 May 1758 (copy), *Writings of Forbes*, 91; Forbes to Stanwix, 29 May 1758, CO 34/35, f. 7; Forbes to Abercromby, Philadelphia, 7 June 1758, Abercromby Papers, Box 7, AB 334.

151. 'Plan of Operations on the Mississippi, Ohio &', New York, 1 February 1758, *Writings of Forbes*, 35; Forbes to Abercromby, New York [sic – should be Philadelphia], 20 April 1758, Abercromby Papers, Box 4, AB 175; Forbes to Pitt (corrected copy), Philadelphia, 1 May 1758, Dalhousie Muniments, NRA(S) GD 45/2/52/1.

152. Forbes to Loudoun, Philadelphia, 23 April 1758, Loudoun Papers, Box 124, LO 5813.

153. Halkett to Washington, Philadelphia, 4 May 1758, *Writings of Forbes*, 83.

154. Nelson, *James Grant*, 18–19.

155. Forbes to Abercromby, Philadelphia, 4 May 1758, Abercromby Papers, Box 5, AB 230.

156. Paul Demeré to Lyttelton, Fort Loudoun, 24 June 1758, Lyttelton Papers, Reel 2.

157. Thompson to Bosomworth, Fort Loudoun, 23 May 1758, Forbes Papers, Reel 2, Item 247; Bosomworth to Forbes, Carlisle, 1 June 1758, ibid., Item 285; Bouquet to [Amherst], 3 June 1758, Bouquet Papers, BL Add. MS 21,640, f. 57; Forbes to Bouquet, Philadelphia, 10 June 1758, ibid., f. 59, printed in *Writings of Forbes*, 112.

158. William Trent to [Forbes?], Fort Loudoun, 5 June 1758, Forbes Papers, Reel 2, Item 294; Forbes to Bouquet, Philadelphia, 10 June 1758, Bouquet Papers, BL Add. MS, f. 59, printed in *Writings of Forbes*, 112.

159. Byrd to Glen, Winchester, 23 June 1758, Dalhousie Muniments, NRA(S) GD 45/2/44/3b. He expresses a fear that Turner may have been killed in 'the Quarrels in Bedford'.

160. Glen to Forbes, Fort Cumberland, 13 July 1758, NRA(S), G.D. 45/2/44/3; Bouquet to Forbes, Camp near Raestown, 21 July 1758 (copy), Bouquet Papers, BL Add. MS, 21,640, f. 102.

161. Forbes to Pitt, 'Carlisle, west of Susquehannah', 10 July 1758 (copy), Dalhousie Muniments, NRA(S) GD 45/2/52/4; Bouquet to Forbes, 8 August 1758, Bouquet Papers, BL Add. MS, 21,640, f. 126, printed in *Writings of Forbes*, 172; Major Halkett to Bouquet, Carlisle, 10 August 1758, ibid., f. 135; Lieutenant Orry to Forbes, Fort Loudoun [Virginia], 9 August 1758, Forbes Papers, Reel 3, Item 458; Nelson, *James Grant*, 19.

162. Halkett to Bouquet, Carlisle, 10 August 1758, Bouquet Papers, BL Add. MS, 21,640, f. 35; Bouquet to Forbes, 8 August 1758, ibid., f.126; Nelson, *James Grant*, 18–19.

163. Grant to Forbes, Fort Loudoun, 16 August 1758, Forbes Papers, Reel 3, Item 476. Grant's biographer makes very little of this episode, which he sees as an example of Grant's intimacy with Forbes. Nelson, *James Grant*, 19.
164. Grant to Forbes, Fort Loudoun, 16 August 1758, Forbes Papers, Reel 3, Item 476.
165. Ibid.
166. Forbes to Pitt, Philadelphia, 17 June 1758, Fort Loudoun, Dalhousie Muniments, NRA(S) GD 45/2/52/3, 56.
167. Forbes to Lyttelton, Shippensburg, 16 August 1758, Lyttelton Papers, Reel 2; draft in Forbes Papers, Reel 3, Item 477.
168. Ibid.
169. Ibid.
170. Forbes to Atkin, Shippensburg, 16 August 1758, ibid.
171. 'At a Meeting held in Augusta by the Honbl. Edmond Atkin Esq....', 2 November 1758 (copy of advertisement), Lyttelton Papers, Reel 3.
172. [John] Appy, 'Secretary [to the Commander-in-Chief]' to the Governors of Pennsylvania, Maryland, Virginia, South and North Carolina, Albany, 24 June 1758, Lyttelton Papers, Reel 2. Although Lyttelton's copy of this circular is docketed as received on 28 September, Forbes may have received his much earlier.
173. McIntosh to Lyttelton, Fort Prince George 26/27 May 1758, enclosing Byrd to McIntosh, 12 May 1758, ibid.
174. Attakullakulla's Talk to Byrd, [Keowee], 27 May 1758 (John Watts interpreter), *Byrd Correspondence*, 2, 656. From an MS once kept in fragments at Berkeley, James River, Virginia, and published in *Southern Literary Magazine*, vol. 6 (January 1840) 40 (p. 657n.).
175. Turner to Forbes, Fort Loudoun, 'Upper Cherokees', 23 June 1758, Forbes Papers, Reel 3; Turner to Byrd, Winchester, 4 August 1758, Virginia Papers, Draper Collection, 4ZZ53, printed in, *Byrd Correspondence*, 2, 664–5; Lyttelton to the Board of Trade, 7 August 1758, enclosing Attakullakulla to Lyttelton, Fort Prince George, 3 June 1758, CO 5/376, ff. 42, 51–2; Turner to Lyttelton, Fort Prince George, 2 July 1758 (extract), CO 5/376 f. 53.
176. Ibid; 'Affadavit' of Little Carpenter, Occonostota, Old Hop, the Conjurer, Willinawaw, Standing Turkey and Moitoi before Paul Demeré and other officers, Fort Loudoun, 22 June 1758, Virginia papers, Draper Collection, 4ZZ52.
177. Ibid; Demeré to Lyttelton, Fort Loudoun, 24 June 1758, Lyttelton Papers, Reel 2.
178. Ibid. Lyttelton too, not surprisingly, thought Attakullakulla had been stringing Byrd and Turner along for the sake of presents. 'I am truly sorry that after all this he should have play'd false in the manner he has done...' Lyttelton to the Board of Trade, Charleston, 7 August 1758, CO 5/376, f.42.
179. Turner to Lyttelton, Fort Prince George, 2 July 1758 (extract), ibid., f. 55.
180. McIntosh to Lyttelton, Fort Prince George, 21 July 1758, Lyttelton Papers, Reel 2.
181. 'The Talk of Tistoe and the Wolf' to Lyttelton, Fort Prince George, 12 July 1758, ibid.
182. Ibid.

183. 'Talk of Tistoe and the Wolf and the rest of the Headmen of the Lower Towns' to Lyttelton, Fort Prince George, 7 August 1758, CO 5/376, f. 60.
184. McIntosh to Lyttelton, Fort Prince George, 21 July 1758, enclosing Tistoe and the Wolf to McIntosh, Fort Prince George, 29 July 1758; Ohatchie [Wawatchee] to Lyttelton, Fort Prince George, 1 August 1758; and Ohatchie, Tistoe and the Wolf, Fort Prince George, 1 August 1758, ibid., Demeré to Lyttelton, Fort Loudoun, 30 July 1758, ibid., McIntosh to Lyttelton, 21 August 1758, ibid.
185. James Beamer to Lyttelton, Estatoe, 16, 19 September 1758, ibid., McIntosh to Lyttelton, Fort Prince George, 18 September 1758, enclosing 'The Talk of Ohatchie and the Young Warrior of Estatoe', ibid., Thomas Beamer to Atkin, Estatoe, [18? September] 1758, ibid., Atkin to Thomas Beamer, Charleston, 17 September 1758, ibid. McIntosh had raised the problem of the quality of his men and of the need for a magazine inside the fort over a month before. Less than half were capable of going beyond a twelve mile radius of the fort; if not superannuated or worn out they had 'some other Empediment about them'. McIntosh to Lyttelton, Fort Prince George, 5, 8 August 1758, Ibid. Gearing, *Priests and Warriors*, 92, merely observes that some towns had already sent parties against Virginia.
186. Demeré to Lyttelton, Fort Loudoun, 30 September, Lyttelton Papers, Reel 2,
187. 'Articles of Friendship and Commerce proposed by the Lords Commissioners for Trade and Plantations to the Deputies of the Cherokee Nation in south Carolina...', 7 September 1730 (copy), Lyttelton Papers, Reel 1.
188. Fauquier to Lyttelton, Williamsburg, 8, 16 June, 13 October 1758, Lyttelton Papers, Reel 2; Lyttelton to the Board of Trade (duplicate), Charleston, 2 October 1758, CO 5/376, ff. 55–56.
189. Minute of discussion of Fauquier's letter of 16 June, 4 July 1758, South Carolina Council Journals, 4 July 1758
190. 'Governor Lyttelton to the Lower and Middle Cherokee Headmen and Warriours' (copy), CO 5/376, ff. 61–2; printed in *DRIA*, II, 481.
191. Dowd, '"Insidious Friends"', 144.
192. Atkin to Lyttelton, Purysburgh, 15 October 1758, enclosing Thomas Beamer to Atkin, [September] 1758, and Atkin to Beamer, 27 September 1758, Lyttelton Papers, Reel 2.
193. McIntosh to Lyttelton, Fort Prince George, 13, 21 October 1758, ibid., 'The Talk of the fourteen towns of the Lower and Middle Cherokees in Answer to his Excellency the Governor's Talk of 26th of September 1758, spoken by Ohatchie [Wawatchee]', Fort Prince George, 16 October 1758, ibid., 'The Young Warrior of Estatoe's Talk', ibid., James Beamer to Lyttelton, Estatoe, 20 October 1758, ibid., Talks of the Estatoe headmen to Lyttelton, Estatoe, 20 October 1758, ibid., Atkin to Lyttelton, Augusta, 4 November 1758, ibid., Ellis to Lyttelton, Savannah, 5 November 1758, enclosing Alexander McGillivray to Ellis (extract), 24 October 1758, ibid., South Carolina Council Journal, 7 November 1758, CO 5/476, ff. 12–13.
194. Ibid., 8 November 1758, ff. 14–16, copy enclosed with Lyttelton to the Board of Trade, Charleston, 1 December 1758, CO 5/376, ff. 65, 67–70; McIntosh to Lyttelton, Fort Prince George, 21 December 1758, Lyttelton Papers, Reel 2.

195. South Carolina Council Journals, 10 January 1759, CO 5/476, f. 21.
196. Glen to Old Hop, Fort Cumberland, 11 December 1758, Lyttelton Papers, Reel 2; Demeré to Lyttelton, 1 January 1759, ibid., Robinson, *James Glen*, 122.
197. Demeré to Lyttelton, Fort Loudoun, 26 March 1759, ibid.
198. Demeré to Lyttelton, Fort Loudoun, 1 January, 26 February 1759, ibid., McIntosh to Lyttelton, Fort Prince George, 31 January 1759, ibid., Richardson to Lyttelton, 14 March 1759, ibid., Williams, 'Presbyterian Mission', 130–8.
199. Demeré to Lyttelton, Fort Loudoun, 26 January, 26 March, 6 April 1759, ibid., Lyttelton to the Board of Trade, Charleston, 14 April 1759, CO 5/376, f. 83.
200. Alden, *John Stuart*, 79.
201. Ibid., Attakullakulla to Lyttelton, Fort Prince George, 20 March 1759, Lyttelton Papers, Reel 2; Robinson, *James Glen*, 122.
202. Forbes to Abercromby, [Raestown, September] 1758, Abercromby Papers, Box 13, AB 709, Forbes to Abercromby, 'Rays Camp', 8 October 1758, ibid., Box 14, AB 736; Forbes to Abercromby, Raestown Camp, 16 October 1758, ibid., Box 15, AB 767.
203. Ibid., Forbes to Abercromby, Raestown, 24 October 1758, ibid., Box 15, 788; Forbes to Burd, 'New Camp, 20 miles west of Loyal Hannan', 19 November 1758, printed in *Writings of Forbes*, 256–8; McIntosh to Lyttelton, 14 January 1759, Lyttelton Papers, Reel 2; J. Oglethorpe to Lyttelton, 27 January 1759, ibid., Attakullakulla to Lyttelton, 20 March 1759, ibid., Bosomworth to Forbes, Raestown, 7 December 1758, Dalhousie Muniments, NRA(S) GD 45/2/89/2; Peckham, *Colonial Wars*, 177–8; Hatley, *Dividing Paths*, 102–3. Alden, *John Stuart*, 78–9; Robinson, *James Glen*, 122.
204. Alden, *John Stuart*, 79–80; Fauquier to Byrd, Williamsburg, 23 January 1759, Virginia Papers, Draper Collection, 4ZZ46, printed in *Byrd Correspondence*, 2, 670; Fauquier to Lyttelton, Williamsburg, 14 December 1758, Lyttelton Papers, Reel 2; McIntosh to Lyttelton, Fort Prince George, 4 March 1759, ibid., Attakullakulla to Lyttelton, Fort Prince George, 20 March 1759, ibid.; *South Carolina Gazette*, 14–21 April 1759.
205. Philip Morison to James Fergusson of Craigdarroch, Charleston, 10 April 1759, Fergusson of Craigdarroch Muniments, NRA(S), G.D. 77/200, Document 6.
206. South Carolina Council Journal, 17 April 1759, CO 5/475, f. 30.
207. Ibid., 17, 18, 21 April 1759, CO 5/476, ff. 31–3, 34–5; Lyttelton to Old Hop and the Little Carpenter, CO 5/386, f. 115; *South Carolina Gazette*, 14–21 April 1789; Alden, *John Stuart*, 80.

Chapter 3 Lyttelton's Folly: How the Anglo-Cherokee War Began

1. Alan Calmes, 'The Lyttelton Expedition of 1759: military failures and financial successes', *South Carolina Historical Magazine*, Vol. 77 (1976), 10–33.
2. Sirmans, *South Carolina*, 331–2.

3. Ibid.; Weir, *South Carolina*, 268–9; Robinson, *Southern Colonial Frontier*, 219–20.
4. 'Instructions to William Henry Lyttelton', 4 November 1755, CO 5/403, 141; Jack P. Greene, *The Quest For Power: The Lower Houses of Assembly in the Southern Royal Colonies 1689–1776* (Norton, New York, 1963) 310–21; Sirmans, *South Carolina*, 318–9.
5. Ibid.
6. Forbes to Bouquet, 25 October 1758, Bouquet Papers, BL Add. MS, 21,640, f. 191; printed in *Writings of Forbes*, 248.
7. Robert Wood to Lyttelton, Whitehall, 11 August 1759, Lyttelton Papers, Reel 3. Halifax, however, did not offer his congratulations until November. Halifax to Lyttelton, Downing Street, 15 November 1759, ibid.
8. Sirmans, *South Carolina*, 318–9; Greene, *Quest For Power*, 321–3.
9. Robert Wood to Lyttelton, Whitehall, 6 June 1759, Lyttelton Papers, Reel 3.
10. Greene, 'Quartering Dispute', *passim*.
11. Nathan Alexander to Lyttelton, 4 May 1759, *DRIA*, 485; Coytmore to Lyttelton, Fort Prince George, 8 May 1759, ibid., 487–8; 'Information Taken on Oath by Samuel Wyly Esq', Pinetree Hill, 5 May 1759, enclosed with Wylie to Lyttelton, Mount Pleasant, 5 May 1759, ibid., 485–6; Lieutenant James Anderson to Lyttelton, Wateree, 5 May 1759, ibid., 486–7; *South Carolina Gazette*, 12 May 1759; Coytmore to Lyttelton, Fort Prince George, 11 June 1759, Lyttelton to the Board of Trade, Charleston, 1 September 1759, CO 5/386, ff. 110–3; Alden, *John Stuart*, 80.
12. Paul Demeré to Lyttelton, Fort Loudoun, 12 May 1759, *DRIA*, 488.
13. Milligan, *Description*, 88.
14. Paul Demeré to Lyttelton, Fort Loudoun, 12 May 1759, *DRIA*, 488.
15. Paul Demeré to Lyttelton, Fort Loudoun, 2 May 1759, ibid., 484.
16. Paul Demeré to Lyttelton, 12 May 1759, ibid., 488.
17. Ibid.
18. Ibid.
19. Coytmore to Lyttelton, Fort Prince George, 8 May 1759, ibid., 487.
20. 'The Lower Towns to the Goveror [sic] spoke by Wawatchee', Keowee, 11 May 1759, ibid., 491–2.
21. 'The Town of Keowee to the Governor Spoke by Tistoe', 13 May 1759, Lyttelton Papers, Reel 3. The wording of the Indian Book copy printed in *DRIA*, 492, differs slightly.
22. Ibid.
23. The previous day Demeré had received Coytmore's account of the Carpenter's arrival. Paul Demeré to Lyttelton, Fort Loudoun, Lyttelton Papers, Reel 3. Indian Book copy printed in *DRIA*, 493.
24. Ibid. The Carpenter left behind two young men, on pretence of their being lame, to hear Lyttelton's reply to the Lower Towns. Coytmore to Lyttelton, Fort Prince George, 11 June 1759, Lyttelton Papers, Reel 3.
25. Coytmore to Lyttelton, Fort Prince George, 23 May 1759, ibid.; Indian Book copy printed in *DRIA*, 495.
26. 'Letter from some of the Headmen of the Cherokee Nation to His Excellency Wm. Hnry. Lyttelton, dated 16 May 1759', Lyttelton Papers, Reel 3. Indian Book copy printed in *DRIA*, 494–5.
27. Ibid.

28. Ibid.
29. Demeré to Lyttelton, Fort Loudoun. 1 June 1759, Lyttelton Papers, Reel 3; Talk by Old Hop and the Little Carpenter, Fort Loudoun, 2 [*sic*] June 1759, CO 5/386, f. 118; Lyttelton to the Board of Trade, 1 September 1759, ibid., f. 110.
30. Demeré to Lyttelton, Fort Prince George, Lyttelton Papers, Reel 3.
31. South Carolina Council Journals, 21 May 1759, CO 5/476, f. 88.
32. Lyttelton to Old Hop and the Little Carpenter, 22 May 1759 (copy), ibid., ff. 115–16; Lyttelton to the Board of Trade, 1 September 1759 (extract), ibid., ff. 110–11.
33. Ibid.
34. Demeré to Lyttelton, Fort Loudoun, 10 July 1759 (copy), CO 5/386, ff. 121–3; Lyttelton to the Board of Trade, 1 September 1759 (extract), ibid., 110.
35. South Carolina Council Journals, 19 March 1759, ibid., f. 26.
36. Demeré to Lyttelton, Fort Loudoun, 2 May 1759, *DRIA*, 483–4.
37. Ibid.; Milling, *Red Carolinians*, 294.
38. Ibid., 294–5; Coytmore to Lyttelton, Fort Prince George, 11 June 1759, Lyttelton Papers, Reel 3.
39. William Shorey to Demeré, 8 May 1759 (Indian Book copy printed in *DRIA*, 491) enclosed with Demeré to Lyttelton, Fort Loudoun, 15 May 1759, ibid.
40. Demeré to Lyttelton, Fort Loudoun, 2 June 1759, ibid.; Coytmore to Lyttelton, Fort Prince George, 11 and 23 July 1759, ibid.
41. Coytmore to Lyttelton, Fort Prince George, 23 July 1759, Lyttelton Papers, Reel 3.
42. Coytmore to Lyttelton, Fort Prince George, 11 June 1759, ibid.; Account of 'the Buffalo Skin', 1 August 1759, ibid.
43. Cashin, *Henry Ellis*, 79.
44. Outerbridge to Lyttelton (two letters), Fort Augusta, 2 July 1759, ibid.
45. Ibid.
46. Evidence of Stephen Bull, Northcote Webber and 'Prince', South Carolina Council Journals, 9 July 1759, CO 5/474, ff. 5–6; J. Kinloch Bull, *The Oligarchs in Colonial and Revolutionary Charleston: Lieutenant-Governor William Bull II and His Family* (University of South Carolina Press, Columbia, 1991) 53.
47. Merrell, *Indians' New World*, 162–7.
48. South Carolina Council Journals, 24 April 1759, CO 5/476, ff. 35–6.
49. Ibid., f. 35. Merrell, *Indians' New World*, 162, mentions the intercolonial rivalry over the fort as part of a pattern of Catawba exploitation of such situations. He thus fails to notice that in this case the Indians had no choice: if South Carolina did not build the fort no one would. Similarly, though he mentions the two murdered women on page 158, as an example of a deeply entrenched cycle of blood vengeance, he does not explain its connection to the fort issue.
50. South Carolina Council Journals, 24 April 1759, f. 36.
51. Wylie to Lyttelton, Mount Pleasant, 5 May 1759, *DRIA*, 485.
52. 'Information Taken on Oath Before Samuel Wyly Esq', Pinetree Hill, 5 May 1759, ibid., 486; Adamson to Lyttelton, Wateree, 5 May 1759, ibid.
53. Captain Johnny's Talk to Lyttelton, South Carolina Council Journals, 30 May 1759, CO 5/476, f. 39.

54. Ibid., 38–9.
55. Ibid., f. 38.
56. Lyttelton's Talk to Captain Johnny, ibid., f.39.
57. King Hagler and the rest of the Catawba Warriors to Lyttelton, 11 June 1759, Lyttelton Papers, Reel 3.
58. Ibid.
59. John Evans to Lyttelton, English Santee, 20 June 1759, ibid.
60. Ibid.; Hagler's Talk to Lyttelton, 11 June 1759, ibid.
61. Evans to Lyttelton, English Santee, 7 September 1759, Lyttelton Papers, ibid.
62. Adair, *American Indians*, 246.
63. Milling, *Red Carolinians*, 295.
64. See, for example, Alden, *John Stuart*, 82.
65. Merrell, *Indians' New World*, 100.
66. Demeré to Lyttelton, Fort Loudoun, 27 June 1759, Lyttelton Papers, Reel 3; Coytmore to Lyttelton, Fort Prince George, 23 July 1759, ibid.
67. Coytmore to Lyttelton, Fort Prince George, 23 July 1759, ibid.
68. Ibid.
69. Ibid.
70. Tistoe's Talk to Lyttelton, South Carolina Council Journals, 19 October 1759, CO 5/474, f. 21.
71. See Chapters 4 and 5 below.
72. *South Carolina Gazette*, 21 February, 7 March 1761, Margaret Carrere McCue, 'Lieutenant-Colonel James Grant's Expedition Against the Cherokee Indians, 1761' (unpublished MA thesis, University of South Carolina, 1967) 47.
73. 'Proceedings of a Court of Inquiry held at the Camp at Fort Prince George the 5th Day of September 1761', Ballindalloch Muniments, Bundle 3/8.
74. Charles Woodmason, 'Injunctions to the Rangers, [delivered] At Swift Creek, Wateree River', [December 1767 or January 1768], in R.J. Hooker (ed.), *The Carolina Backcountry on the Eve of the Revolution* (University of North Carolina Press, Chapel Hill, for the Institute of Early American History and Culture, Williamsburg, 1953), 283.
75. Demeré to Lyttelton, Fort Loudoun, 22 July 1769 (extract), CO 5/386, f. 125.
76. Ibid.; Demeré to Lyttelton, Fort Loudoun, 28 August 1759, Lyttelton Papers, Reel 3.
77. Coytmore to Lyttelton, Fort Prince George, 3 August 1759, ibid; the Board of Trade's copy is at CO 5/386, ff. 127–31.
78. Ibid.
79. Ibid.
80. Ibid.
81. Ellis to Lyttelton, Savannah, 14 September 1759, ibid.
82. Coytmore to Lyttelton, Fort Prince George, 23 August 1759, ibid.
83. South Carolina Council Journals, 6 June, 4, 31 July, 19 September, 7 November, 5 December 1758, 2 January, 6 February, 6, 23 March, 4 June 1759, CO 5/476, ff.1, 4, 7–8, 10, 13, 17, 21–3, 25, 29.
84. Lyttelton to the Board of Trade, 1 September 1759 (extract), CO 5/386, ff. 110–13.
85. Ellis to Lyttelton, Georgia, 27 August 1759, Lyttelton Papers, Reel 3.
86. Ibid.
87. Ibid.

88. South Carolina Council Journals, 13, 14 August 1759, CO 5/474, ff. 8–10.
89. Ibid.
90. Ibid.
91. Fauquier to Lyttelton, Williamsburg, 19 June, 6 September 1759, Lyttelton Papers, Reel 3; Coytmore to Lyttelton, Fort Prince George, 23 July 1759, ibid.
92. South Carolina Council Journals, 14 August 1759, CO 5/474, f. 10.
93. Fauquier to Lyttelton, Williamsburg, 5/13 September 1759, Lyttelton Papers, Reel 3.
94. Ibid.
95. South Carolina Council Journals, 28 August 1759, CO 5/474, f. 10.
96. Ibid.
97. Ibid.
98. Ibid., ff. 10–11.
99. Lyttelton to the Board of Trade, 1 September 1759 (extract), CO 5/386, ff. 110–13.
100. Ellis to Lyttelton, Savannah, 8, 25 September 1759, Lyttelton Papers, Reel 3.
101. Coytmore to Lyttelton, Fort Prince George, 23/24 August 1759, ibid.
102. Paul Demeré to Lyttelton, Fort Loudoun, 28 August 1759, ibid.
103. Ibid.
104. Ibid.
105. Ibid.
106. Ibid.
107. Nathan Alexander to Lyttelton, 27 June 1759, ibid.
108. Demeré to Lyttelton, Fort Loudoun, 28 August 1759, enc. the account of the Buffalo Robe, 1 August [1759], ibid.
109. Stuart to Lyttelton, Congarees, 2 September 1759, Lyttelton Papers, Reel 3.
110. Shaw to Lyttelton, Charles Town, August [1759], ibid.; James Francis, Ninety Six, 21 August 1759, ibid.; Captain John Fairchild to Lyttelton, 'Dated between Long Canes and 96', 24 August 1759, ibid.; Coytmore to Lyttelton, Fort Prince George, 30 August 1759, ibid.; Patrick Calhoun to Lyttelton, Long Canes, 21 September 1759, ibid.
111. Coytmore to Lyttelton, Fort Prince George, 8 September 1759, ibid.
112. Ibid.; Demeré to Lyttelton, Fort Loudoun, 13 September 1759 (copy), CO 5/386, f. 147; James Beamer to Lyttelton, Estatoe, 10 September 1759, Lyttelton Papers, Reel 3.
113. Ibid.
114. Stuart to Lyttelton, Fort Prince George, 6 October 1759, ibid.; Occonostota's Talk to Lyttelton, 19 October 1759, CO 5/474, f. 21.
115. Paul Demeré to Lyttelton, Fort Loudoun, 13 September 1759, Lyttelton Papers, Reel 3 (copy at CO 5/386), f. 147; Maurice Anderson to Coytmore, Fort Loudoun, 12 September 1759 (copy), ibid.
116. Paul Demeré to Lyttelton, Fort Loudoun, 13 September 1759, Lyttelton Papers, Reel 3.
117. Ibid.
118. Ibid.; *South Carolina Gazette*, 29 September – 6 October 1759.
119. Stuart to Lyttelton, Fort Prince George, 26 September 1759, CO 5/386, f. 150.
120. Anderson to Coytmore, Fort Loudoun, 12 September 1759 (copy), Lyttelton Papers, Reel 3; Paul Demeré to Lyttelton, Fort Loudoun, 1 October 1759, ibid.
121. Ibid.

122. Ibid.
123. Coytmore to Lyttelton, Fort Prince George, 8 September 1759, ibid.
124. Ibid.
125. Ibid.
126. Stuart to Lyttelton, Fort Prince George, 26 September 1759, CO 5/386, f. 150.
127. Stuart to Lyttelton, Fort Prince George, 6 October 1759, Lyttelton Papers, Reel 3.
128. Ibid.
129. Ibid.
130. Alden, *John Stuart*, 83.
131. Coytmore to Lyttelton, Fort Prince George, 26 September 1759, CO5/386, f. 145.
132. Outerbridge to Lyttelton, Fort Augusta, 23 September 1759, Lyttelton Papers, Reel 3.
133. Coytmore to Lyttelton, Fort Prince George, 8 September 1759, ibid; South Carolina Council Journals, 17 September 1759, CO 5/474, f. 12.
134. Calmes, 'Lyttelton Expedition', 12.
135. Ibid.; South Carolina Council Journal, 1 October 1759, CO 5/474, ff. 13–14; Lyttelton to the Board of Trade, 16 October 1759, CO 5/386, f. 141.
136. Stanwix to Lyttelton, 'Pittsburg Camp', 5 December 1759, enc. with Fauquier to Lyttelton, Williamsburg, 4 February 1760, Lyttelton Papers, Reel 3.
137. South Carolina Council Journals, 4 October 1759, CO 5/474, f. 15; Calmes, 'Lyttelton Expedition', 12. He did alert the remaining militia companies on 12 October, but for internal security and defensive duties only. Lyttelton to the Board of Trade, Charleston, 16 October 1759, CO 5/386, ff. 142–13.
138. Lyttelton to the Commons, 5 October 1759, CO 5/206, ff. 152–3; Lyttelton to the Board of Trade, 16 October 1759, ibid., f. 142; Calmes, 'Lyttelton Expedition', 12.
139. Lyttelton to the Board of Trade, Charleston, 16 October 1759, CO 5/386, ff. 142; Commons to Lyttelton, 6, 11, 12 October 1759, ibid., ff. 154–5, 158, 160-1; Lyttelton's messages and speech to the Commons to the Commons, 6, 12, 13 October ibid., 156, 160- 161; South Carolina Council Journal, 11 October 1759, CO 5/474, f. 17; for copies of the messages and the speech see Lyttelton Papers, Reel 3.
140. *South Carolina Gazette*, 29 September – 6 October 1759.
141. Lyttelton to the Board of Trade, 16 October 1759, CO 5/386, f. 142.
142. South Carolina Council Journals, 14, 15 October 1759, CO 5/474, f. 19.
143. Lyttelton to Amherst, Charleston, 16 October 1759, WO 34/35, ff. 128.
144. South Carolina Council Journal, 15 October 1759, CO 5/474, ff. 19–20.
145. Ibid., 7, 14 October October 1759, ff. 16–17, 19.
146. Lyttelton to the Board of Trade, Charleston, 23 October 1759, CO 5/386, ff. 164–5.
147. South Carolina Council Journals, CO 5/474, f. 20.
148. Ibid.
149. Ibid., 19 October 1759, f. 21.
150. Ibid.
151. Milligan, *Description*, 188–9; Bull to Grant, 15 May 1760, Ballindaloch Muniments, Bundle 394; Bull, *Oligarchs*, 54.
152. South Carolina Council Journals, 19 October 1759, f. 21.

153. South Carolina Council Journal, 22 October 1759, CO 5/474, ff. 23–4; Lyttelton to the Board of Trade, Charleston, 23 October 1759, CO 5/386, f. 164–8; Lyttelton to Amherst, Charleston, 23 October 1759, WO 34/35, ff. 134–5; Milligan, *Description*, 189–90.

154. South Carolina Council Journal, 19, 22 October 1759, CO 5/474 ff. 22, 23–4; Lyttelton to the Board of Trade, Charleston, 23 October 1759, CO 5/386, f. 164.

155. Sirmans, *South Carolina*, 333; *South Carolina Gazette*, 20–27 October, 27 October – 3 November 1759; Bull, *Oligarchs*, 56.

156. Coytmore to Lyttelton, Fort Prince George, 11, 14, 21 November 1759, Lyttelton Papers, Reel 3; 'Names of the Indian Deserters from the Congarees', ibid.; Milling, *Red Carolinians*, 296; Sirmans, *South Carolina*, 333; Hatley, *Dividing Paths*, 123.

157. Paul Demeré to Lyttelton, Fort Loudoun, 3 November 1759, Lyttelton Papers, Reel 3.

158. Attakullakulla to Lyttelton, Fort Loudoun, 2 November 1759, ibid.

159. Ibid.

160. Paul Demeré to Lyttelton, Fort Loudoun, 3 November 1759, ibid.

161. Coytmore to Lyttelton, Fort Prince George, 7 November 1759, ibid.

162. Coytmore to Lyttelton, Fort Prince George, 14 November 1759, ibid.

163. Ibid.

164. Coytmore to Lyttelton, Fort Prince George, 24 November 1759 (first letter), ibid.

165. Coytmore to Lyttelton, Fort Prince George, 24 November 1759 (three letters), ibid.

166. Coytmore to Lyttelton, Fort Prince George, 3 December 1759, ibid.

167. Stuart to Lyttelton, Fort Loudoun, 15 November 1759, ibid.

168. Ibid.

169. Paul Demeré to Lyttelton, Fort Loudoun, 21 November 1759, ibid.

170. Demeré to Lyttelton, Fort Loudoun, 23 November 1759, ibid.

171. Stuart to Lyttelton, Fort Loudoun, 3 December 1759, ibid.

172. Ibid.; Hewatt, *Historical Account*, II, 218–19.

173. Stuart to Lyttelton, Fort Loudoun, 3 December 1759, Lyttelton Papers, Reel 3.

174. Hewatt, *Historical Account*, 2, 218–19; *South Carolina Gazette*, 8–12 Janaury 1760.

175. Ibid.; Hewatt, *Historical Account*, II, 226.

176. Ibid.; *South Carolina Gazette*, 12–19 January 1760; Alden, *John Stuart*, 86–7; Milling, *Red Carolinians*, 296–7.

177. 'Treaty of Peace and Friendship concluded by His Excellency William Henry Lyttelton Eqr,...with Attakullakulla (or the Little Carpenter) Deputy of the whole Cherokee Nation and other Headmen and Warriors thereof at Fort Prince George the 26 Day of December 1759', CO 5/386, ff. 180–3; *South Carolina Gazette*, 29 December – 5 January 1760.

178. Ellis to the Board of Trade, 15 February 1760, cited in Sirmans, *South Carolina*, 334; Ellis to Pitt, Georgia, 15 February 1760, *Pitt Correspondence*, 254–6.

179. Alden, *John Stuart*, 101.

180. Affidavit of Isaac Atwood, 31 January 1760, enclosed with Outerbridge to Lyttelton, 2 February 1760, Lyttelton Papers, Reel 3. The Hiwassee people

appear to have also been involved. Affadavit of John Downing, James Butler, Barnet Hues, Andrew Kerns and John McPeerson before John Vann, Broad River, 29 January 1760, enclosed with Atkin to Lyttelton, Fort Moore, 31 January 1760, ibid. Coytmore was told that the murder happened at Hiwassee. Coytmore, Miln and Bell, 'A Copy of a journal kept at Fort Prince George', 13 January 1760, enc. with Coytmore to Lyttelton, Fort Prince George, 7 February 1760, ibid.

181. Affidavit of Isaac Atwood, ibid.; Atkin to Lyttelton, Fort Moore, 1 February 1760, ibid.
182. 'Copy of a journal...', 19, 23 January 1760, ibid.
183. Affidavit of John Downing, ibid.; John Pearson to Lyttelton, 8 February 1760, ibid.; Milling, *Red Carolinians*, 298.
184. Ibid., 298–9; Outerbridge to Lyttelton, Fort Augusta, 2 February 1760, Lyttelton Papers, Reel 3; Ellis to Lyttelton, Savannah, 4 February 1760, ibid; Atkin to Lyttelton, Fort Moore, 5 February 1760, ibid.; Pearson to Lyttelton, 8 February 1760, ibid; *South Carolina Gazette*, 2–9, 16–23 February, 8–15 March 1760; Milling, *Red Carolinians*, 298–9; Hatley, *Dividing Paths*, 127.
185. Ellis to Lyttelton, Georgia, 5 February 1760, Lyttelton Papers, Reel 3. Atkin to Lyttelton, Fort Moore, 5, 21 February 1760, ibid.; Outerbridge to Lyttelton, 12, 15 February 1760, ibid.; Shaw to Lyttelton, 21 February 1760, ibid.
186. 'Copy of a journal...', 19 January 1760, ibid.; Affadavit of Isaac Atwood, ibid.
187. *South Carolina Gazette*, 9–16 February, 8–15, 15–23 March 1760; James Francis to Lyttelton, 'Fort 96', 6 March 1760, Lyttelton Papers, Reel 3 (Indian Book copy printed in *DRIA*, 504–5); Alden, *John Stuart*, 104; Milling, *Red Carolinians*, 301–2.
188. Pearson to Lyttelton, 8 February 1760, Lyttelton Papers, Reel 3; Henry Gallman to Lyttelton, Saxegotha, 12 February 1760, ibid; Benjamin Waring to Lyttelton, 15 February 1760, ibid; Atkin to Lyttelton, Fort Moore, 16 February 1760, ibid.; George Pawley to Lyttelton, 27 February 1760, ibid.; Captain John Grinnan to Lyttelton, 'Turners Fort', 6 March 1760.
189. Journal signed by Miln and Bell, enc. with Miln to Lyttelton, Fort Prince George, 24 February 1760, ibid.
190. Ibid.
191. Adair, *American Indians*, 250. The two versions are weighed by Milling, *Red Carolinians*, 299–300; Alden, *John Stuart*, 103–4, is sceptical of Miln's over-coloured account.
192. Miln's journal, 16–24 February, 1760, Lyttelton Papers, Reel 3; Miln to Lyttelton, Fort Prince George, 28 February 1760, ibid.; *South Carolina Gazette*, 9–16 February 1760.
193. Milling, *Red Carolinians*, 301.
194. Amherst to Lyttelton, New York, 26 February 1760, Lyttelton Papers, Reel 3.

Chapter 4 'The Sweet Bond of Human Things': Soldiers Seeking Peace, 1760

1. Amherst to Montgomery, New York, 24 February 1760, WO 34/48, f.1.
2. Ibid.
3. Ibid.

4. Amherst to Grant, New York, 3 March 1760, ibid., f. 3.
5. Amherst to Montgomery, New York, 6 March 1760, ibid., f. 5.
6. The order of embarkation, ibid., f. 12.
7. Amherst to Montgomery, New York, 6 March 1760, ibid., ff. 4, 5.
8. Ibid.
9. Grant's commission, Ballindalloch Muniments, Bundle 478; Amherst to Grant, New York, 8 March 1760, WO 34/48, f. 10. Grant's rank became permanent on 26 July, according to the Army List, WO 65/9, ff.13, 100 (microfilm).
10. Forbes to Abercromby, Rays Town Camp, 16 October 1758, Abercromby Papers, Box 15, AB 767
11. Nelson, *James Grant*, chapters 2 and 3 *passim*. Unfortunately the letter to Amherst of 28 April 1760 (n. 18), alluded to on pages 26–7, was written by James *Glen*. See Glen to Amherst, Philadelphia, 28 April 1760, WO 34/47, ff. 11–12.
12. Order of embarkation WO 34/48, f. 12.
13. *South Carolina Gazette*, 29 March–7 April 1760; Montgomery to Amherst, Charleston, 12 April 1760, WO 34/47, ff. 4–5; Grant to Amherst, Charleston, 17 April, ibid., f. 6.
14. Ibid.
15. Ibid.; Montgomery to Amherst, Charleston, 12 April 1760, ibid., ff. 4–5.
16. Ibid., f. 5.
17. Ibid., ff. 4–5; Grant to Amherst, Charleston, 17 April 1760, ibid., f. 6.
18. Ibid., f. 7; Montgomery to Amherst, Charleston, 12 April 1760, ibid.
19 . Grant to Amherst, Charleston, 17 April 1760, ibid., ff. 6–7; Montgomery to Amherst, Camp at Monk's Corner, 22 April 1760, ibid.; South Carolina Commons Journal, 16, 17, 18 April 1760, CO 5/473, ff. 97–9. Bull gives the date of the Commons' first meeting and the passage of the Bill as 15 April, and that of his assent as the 19th. He mentions neither the Commons' initial rejection, nor Montgomery's threat. Bull to the Board of Trade, Charleston, 6 May 1760, CO 5/377, f. 8.
20. Montgomery to Amherst, Camp at Ninety Six, 24 May 1760, WO 34/47, f. 12.
21. Ibid.
22. Ibid.
23. Ibid.
24. Ibid.
25. Bull to Grant, 29 April 1760, Ballindalloch Muniments, Bundle 394; Bull to Montgomery, Charleston, 30 April 1760, ibid., Bundle 561; James Francis to Lyttelton, Fort 96, 6 March 1760, *DRIA*, 504–5; Bull to the Board of Trade, Charleston, 6 May 1760, CO 5/377, f.8;
26. Bull to the Board of Trade, Charleston, 29 May 1760, CO 5/377, f. 18.
27. Atkin to Pitt, Charles Town, 27 March 1760, in G.S. Kimball (ed.), *Correspondence of William Pitt when Secretary of State with Colonial Governors and Military and Naval Commissioners in America*, vol II (Macmillan, New York and London, 1906) 268–72; Corkran, *Creek Frontier*, chapter 12, 193–210, *passim*.
28. Jacobs (ed.), *Appalachian Indian Frontier*, introduction, xxvii. Adair, whose feud with Atkin went back to the time of the so-called Choctaw Revolt,

met him briefly at Augusta on his way to the Creeks. Adair, who believed that a Cherokee–Creek alliance already existed, put the subsequent troubles down to Atkin's slowness, pomposity and general incompetence. Adair, *American Indians*, 253–5.

29. Bull to Grant, Charleston, 24 April 1760, Ballindalloch Muniments, Bundle 394.
30. Bull to the Board of Trade, 14, 29 May 1760, CO 5/377, ff. 13–14, 17–19.
31. Bull to the Board of Trade, Charleston, 29 May 1760, CO 5/377, f.18.
32. Bull to Montgomery, Charleston 5 May 1760, Ballindalloch Muniments, Bundle 561.
33. Montgomery to Bull, Camp at Ninety Six, 24 May 1760, WO 34/47, ff. 12–13.
34. Grant to Amherst, Charleston, 17 April 1760, WO 34/47, f. 7.
35. *South Carolina Gazette*, 26 April–3 May 1760; Bull to Montgomery, Charleston, 29 April 1760, Ballindalloch Muniments, Bundle 561.
36. Bull to Montgomery, Charleston, 5 May 1760, ibid; *South Carolina Gazette*, 12–19 April 1760.
37. Miln's Talk to Standing Turkey, Fort Prince George, 22 April 1760, Ballindalloch Muniments, Bundle 561.
38. Bull to Montgomery, Charleston, 29 April 1760, ibid.; Bull to the Board of Trade, Charleston, 3 May 1760, CO 5/377, f. 11.
39. Ibid.
40. Ibid.
41. Bull to Grant, 15 May 1760, Ballindalloch Muniments, Bundle 394.
42. Miln [to Montgomery or Grant], Fort Prince George, 9 May 1760, Ballindalloch Muniments, Bundle 561, Miln to Montgomery, Fort Prince George, 21 May 1760, ibid, Corkran, *Cherokee Frontier*, 206, wrongly gives 9 May, the date of Miln's first letter, as the date of the incident.
43. [Grant] to Bull, Camp at Congarees, 13 May 1760 (draft), Ballindalloch Muniments, Bundle 561; [Montgomery] to Miln, ibid. The evidence for the actual signatures is in the replies: Miln to Montgomery, Fort Prince George, 21 May 1760, ibid., and Bull to Montgomery, Charleston, 23 May 1760, ibid., Bundle 394, in which he accepts Grant's views about keeping faith.
44. Bull to Montgomery, Charleston, 23 May 1760, Ibid.
45. Montgomery [to Bull, Camp near Fort Prince George, 31 May 1760], ibid.
46. Montgomery to Amherst, Camp at Ninety Six, 24 May 1760, WO 34/47, ff. 12–13.
47. Bull, *Oligarchs*, 70.
48. Bull to Amherst, Charleston, 29/31 May and 6 June 1760 (misdated 1759), WO 34/35, 200–1; Bull, *Oligarchs*, 70.
49. Glen to Amherst, Philadelphia, 28 April 1760, WO 34/47, ff. 11–12.
50. Amherst to Glen, Albany, 31 May 1760 (copy), WO 34/48, f. 25.
51. See Alden, *John Stuart*, 155 n.
52. Jacobs, *Appalachian Frontier*, xxviii n.
53. Atkin to Grant, Charleston, 12 May 1760, Ballindalloch Muniments, Bundle 511.
54. Grant to Atkin, Congarees, 5 May 1760 (draft), ibid.
55. Ibid.
56. Ibid.

57. Atkin to Grant, Charleston, 12 May 1760, ibid.
58. Bull to Grant, 15 May 1760, ibid., Bundle 394.
59. Ibid.
60. For an excellent account of the Bull family's domination of the Council, and of the alliances which allowed it, see Bull, *Oligarchs*, chapter 2, *passim*.
61. Bull to Montgomery, Charleston, 5 May 1760, Ballindalloch Muniments, Bundle 561,
62. South Carolina Council Journals, 24 May 1760, CO 5/474, ff. 64–5.
63. Bull to Montgomery, Charleston, 23 May 1760, Ballindalloch Muniments, Bundle 394. Bull, *Oligarchs*,70, wrongly implies that he did this after the Council proved 'unhelpful'. The fact that only three councillors turned up next day – and Bull's comment that he was sorry that the other members had chosen not to come – suggests that his manoeuvre had been seen through. South Carolina Council Journal, CO 5/474, f. 64. It is, of course, perfectly possible that Bull had previously consulted the members in private, but there is no evidence that he did so.
64. Ibid., ff. 64–5.
65. Bull, *Oligarchs*, 70; Bull to Montgomery, Charleston, 23 May 1760, Ballindalloch Muniments, Bundle 394.
66. Ibid. See pages 160–1 above.
67. Bull to Montgomery, ibid.
68. Montgomery to Amherst, Camp at Ninety Six, 24 May 1760, WO 34/47, f. 12.
69. Ibid.
70. Ibid.
71. Bull to Montgomery, Charleston, 5 May 1760, Ballindalloch Muniments, Bundle 561.
72. Montgomery to Amherst, Camp at Ninety Six, 24 May 1760, WO 34/47, ff. 12–13.
73. Ibid.
74. Ibid.
75. Ibid.; Bull to Montgomery, Charleston, 1 May 1760, ibid.
76. Bull to Grant, Charleston, 24 April 1760, ibid., Bundle 394.
77. Ibid.; Bull to Montgomery, Charleston, 29 April 1760, ibid.
78. Bull to the Board of Trade, Charleston, 3 May 1760, CO 5/377, f. 11.
79. Bull to the Board of Trade, Charleston, 6 May 1760, ibid., f. 8.
80. Fauquier to Bull, Williamsburg, 24 May 1760 (copy), Ballindalloch Muniments, Bundle 561.
81. Bull to the Board of Trade, Charleston, 6 May 1760, CO 5/377, f. 8.
82. Ibid.
83. Ibid.
84. Bull to the Board of Trade, Charleston, 29 May 1760, CO 5/377, ff.18–19.
85. Montgomery to Amherst, Camp near Fort Prince George, 4 June 1760, WO 34/47, f. 14.
86. Ibid.
87. Ibid. Hatley, *Dividing Paths*, 131, wrongly identifies Keowee as the first town reached, a consequence of using neither WO 34/47 nor the Ballindalloch Muniments.
88. Montgomery to Amherst, Camp near Fort Prince George, WO 34/47, ff. 14–15.

89. Thomas Mante, *The History of the Late War in North America and the Islands of the West Indies including the Campaigns of MDCCLXIII and MDCCLXIV against His Majesty's Indian Enemies* (London, 1772) 287; Hewatt, *Historical Account*, republished in B.R. Carroll (ed.), *Historical Collections of South Carolina*, vol. I (Harper & Bros, New York, 1836), 455.

90. Montgomery to Amherst, Camp at Fort Prince George, 4 June 1760, WO 34/47, ff. 14–15.

91. Grant to Bull, Camp near Fort Prince George, 4 June 1760, enclosed with Bull to the Board of Trade, CO 5/377, f. 21 *et seq.*

92. Montgomery to Amherst, Camp at Fort Prince George, 4 June 1760, ibid., ff. 14–15.

93. Ibid.; *South Carolina Gazette*, 10–14 June 1760.

94. Grant to Bull, Camp near Fort Prince George, 4 June 1760, CO 5/377.

95. Montgomery to Amherst, Camp near Fort Prince George, 4 June 1760, WO 34/47, ff. 14–15.

96. Ibid., f. 15. Montgomery's impressions were supported by the correspondent of the *South Carolina Gazette*: 'The neatness of these towns and their knowledge of agriculture would surprise you; they abounded in every comfort of life, and may curse the day we came among them.' Another correspondent added that Estatoe had consisted of 'about 200 houses'. *South Carolina Gazette*, 12–19 July 1760; the article is also quoted in Hatley, *Dividing Paths*, 130.

97. Ibid.; Grant to Bull, Camp near Fort Prince George, 4 June 1760, CO 5/377.

98. Ibid.

99. Montgomery to Amherst, Camp at Fort Prince George, 4 June 1760, WO 34/47, f. 15.

100. *South Carolina Gazette*, 20–27 September 1760.

101. Grant to Bull, Camp near Fort Prince George, 4 June 1760, CO 5/377.

102. Montgomery to Amherst, Camp at Fort Prince George, 4 June 1760, WO 34/47, f. 15.

103. Ibid.

104. Bull to the Board of Trade, Charleston, 17 June 1760, and enclosures: *South Carolina Gazette*, 7–10 June 1760, and a full copy of Grant's letter, CO 5/377, f. 21 *et seq.*; Bull to Grant, Charleston, 11 June 1760, Ballindalloch Muniments, Bundle 394.

105. Amherst to Montgomery, Albany, 18 June 1760, Ibid., Bundle 468.

106. Amherst to Montgomery, Fort Herchkeimer, 29 June 1760, WO 34/18, ff. 28–9.

107. Montgomery to Bull, Camp at Fort Prince George, 7 June 1760 (draft), Ballindalloch Muniments, Bundle 561.

108. Bull to Grant, Charleston, 11 June 1760, ibid., Bundle 394.

109. Bull to Montgomery, Charleston, 20 June 1760, ibid., Bundle 561. In the version of his speech recorded in the Council Journals Tistoe complains of Fort Prince George officers in general, and does not mention individuals. South Carolina Council Journals, 19 October 1759, CO 5/474, f. 21. But Bull, who was present, apparently heard Bell mentioned by name.

110. Bull to Montgomery, Charleston, 20 June 1760, Ballindalloch Muniments, Bundle 561.

111. Montgomery to Bull, Camp at Fort Prince George, 7 June 1760, Ballindalloch Muniments, Bundle 561.

112. Stuart to Grant, Fort Loudoun, 6 June 1760, Ballindalloch Muniments, Bundle 517.
113. Bull to the Board of Trade, Charleston,17 June 1760, CO 5/377, f. 21.
114. Bull to Montgomery, 20 June 1760, Ballindalloch Muniments, Bundle 561.
115. Stuart to Grant, Fort Loudoun, 6 June 1760, ibid., Bundle 517.
116. Montgomery to Amherst, Camp at Ninety Six, 24 May 1760, WO 34/47, ff. 12–13; Bull to the Board of Trade, Charleston, 29 May 1760 (postscript), CO 5/377, f. 19; Montgomery to Amherst, Camp at Fort Prince George, 4 June 1760, WO 34/47, f. 15.
117. Bull to Grant, Charleston, 11 June 1760, Ballindalloch Muniments, Bundle 394.
118. Stuart to Grant, Fort Loudoun, 6 June 1760, 1760, ibid., Bundle 517.
119. Grant to Amherst, Charleston, 17 January 1761, WO 34/47, f.37.
120. Montgomery to Amherst, 'Camp at Keowee Town', 23 June 1760, WO 34/47, f. 16; Montgomery [to Bull], n.d. [23 June 1760], Ballindalloch Muniments, Bundle 561.
121. Montgomery to Amherst, 'Camp at Keowee Town', 23 June 1760, W034/47, f. 16.
122. Ibid.
123. Ibid.
124. Montgomery to Amherst, Camp at Fort Prince George, 2 July 1760, WO 34/47, f. 17.
125. Ibid.
126. Adair, *American Indians*, 253. Corkran identified the site as 'Tessuntee old town'. Corkran, *Cherokee Frontier*, 212.
127. Ibid.; Hewatt, *Historical Account*, II, 232.
128. Montgomery to Amherst, Camp at Fort Prince George, 2 July 1760, WO 34/47, f. 17. Some of the Rangers from the advance guard thought they had been ambushed by 500 Cherokees, but they had run away so quickly that this could only be guesswork at best. *South Carolina Gazette*, 5–12 July 1760.
129. Hewatt, *Historical Account*, II, 232–3; Corkran, *Cherokee Frontier*, 212–13; J.W. Fortescue, *A History of the British Army*, vol. II (Macmillan, London 1910) 407. *South Carolina Gazette*, 12–19, 19–26 July, 18–26 October 1760 *Maryland Gazette*, 7 August 1760; Hatley, *Dividing Paths*, 131.
130. Fortescue, *British Army*, 2, 407; Hewatt, *Historical Account*, 2, 232–3.
131. Corkran, *Cherokee Frontier*, 213.
132. Ibid.; 'Return of the Killed and Wounded...', Ibid., f. 19.
133. Fortescue, *British Army*, 2, 407.
134. Ibid. Hatley makes his case by emphasizing the difficult fighting in the ravine and the British losses, and by omitting Montgomery's subsequen dislodgement of the Cherokees. *Dividing Paths*, 132. Hewatt, anxious to write up a Cherokee success, paints a very vivid picture of the combat in the defile, but does not mention that the warriors were driven out *Historical Account*, II, 232–3
135. Montgomery to Amherst, Camp at Fort Prince George, 2 July 1760 WO 34/47, f. 18.
136. Ibid., ff. 18–19.
137. Ibid.
138. Ibid.; Mante, *History of the Late War*, 492.

139. Alden, *John Stuart*, 112.
140. Hatley, *Dividing Paths*, 132.
141. Adair, *American Indians*, 253; Robinson, *Southern Colonial Frontier*, 221.
142. Weir, *South Carolina*, 270.
143. Ibid. For a contrasting view see Sirmans, *South Carolina*, 33, who places stress on the orders.
144. Montgomery to Amherst, Camp at Fort Prince George, 2 July 1760, WO 24/47, f. 19.
145. Ibid.
146. Ibid.
147. Alison Olsen, 'Coffee House Lobbying', *History Today*, vol. 41 (January 1991) 35–41.
148. Memo, undated and unsigned, Chatham Papers, PRO 30/8, Volume 96 (America and West Indies), f. 237. Unfortunately the contextual papers in this volume bear no relation, chronologically or in content, to the events of 1760, and so cannot be 'the enclosed' referred to in the memo.
149. Hatley, *Dividing Paths*, 132.
150. Only in early July did he order McIntosh to Fort Prince George, and even then he procured a further delay by allowing him to settle his affairs in Charleston first. Bull to Montgomery, Charleston, 7 July 1760, Ballindalloch Muniments, Bundle 561. In the event Miln was left in command until the early spring of 1761.
151. There is no copy of this letter in the Ballindalloch Muniments and Bull's personal papers seem to have been destroyed by bombing in London during the Second World War. Bull, *Oligarchs*, 'Notes on Primary Sources', 325–8.
152. Bull to Montgomery, Charleston, 12 July 1760 (copy), CO 5/377, f. 189.
153. Ibid., f.190.
154. Ibid.; Bull to the Board of Trade, 29 May 1760, CO 5/377, ff. 17–19; Bull to Grant, 2 June 1760, Ballindalloch Muniments, Bundle 394; Bull to the Board of Trade, 17 June 1760, CO 5/377, f. 21; Bull to Montgomery, 20 June 1760, Ballindalloch Muniments, Bundle 561.
155. Bull to Montgomery, Charleston, 7 July 1760, ibid., Bundle 561.
156. Ibid.
157. Bull to Grant, Charleston, 8 July 1760, ibid., Bundle 394.
158. Bull to Montgomery, Charleston, 13 July 1760, CO 5/377, f. 190.
159. Ibid.
160. Ibid.
161. Ibid.
162. Bull to Grant, 14 July 1760, Ballindalloch Muniments, Bundle 394.
163. Montgomery to Amherst, Camp at Ninety Six, 24 May 1760, WO 34/47, ff. 12–13; Amherst to Montgomery, Albany, 18 June 1760, Ballindalloch Muniments, Bundle 468.
164. Montgomery to Bull, n.d. (draft), ibid., Bundle 561.
165. Montgomery to officer commanding HM ships at Charleston n.d. (draft), ibid.
166. Amherst to Montgomery, Albany, 18 June 1760, ibid., Bundle 468. In mid-June Amherst had not yet heard of the destruction of the Lower Towns, and when he did he assumed that peace would follow 'from the measures you have so wisely taken...' Amherst to Montgomery, Fort Herchkeimer,

29 June 1760 (copy), WO 34/48, f. 28. Amherst, of course, did not yet know that the Cherokees had not made peace, nor that Montgomery had failed to do much against the Middle Settlements.

167. J[ames] G[rant] to Montgomery, dated '30th, 8' at night', Ballindalloch Muniments, Bundle 561.

168. Ibid.

169. Ibid.

170. Ibid.

171. Montgomery to Amherst, 4 September 1760 (draft), ibid., Bundle 468; Montgomery to Amherst, Albany, 11 September 1760, WO 34/47, f. 21.

172. Bull to the Board of Trade, Charleston, 15 August 1760, CO 5/377, ff. 29–30.

173. Montgomery to Amherst, Albany, 4 September 1760 (draft), Ballindalloch Muniments, Bundle 468; Montgomery to Amherst, Albany, 11 September 1760 (copy), WO 34/47, f. 20.

174. Amherst to Montgomery, Camp of Montreal, 10 September 1760, WO 34/48, f. 32.

175. Ibid.

176. Jacobs, *Appalachian Frontier*, introduction, xxvii; Alden, *John Stuart*, 133. Hewatt, *Historical Account*, II, 456, says that it was Atkin who sent Tistoe and the Wolf into the nation with the abortive overtures of June, which would suggest he reached Fort Prince George. The initiative, however, was clearly Montgomery's and Grant's.

177. Bull to the Board of Trade, Charleston, 15 August 1760. CO 5/377, f. 29; Sirmans, *South Carolina*, 337.

178. Dobbs to Amherst, Brunswick, 3 August 1760, WO 34/35, f. 12.

179. South Carolina Commons Journals, 5, 14 August 1760; Sirmans, *South Carolina*, 337; Bull to the Board of Trade, Charleston, 31 August 1760, CO 5/377, f. 27.

180. Ibid.; Bull to the Board of Trade, Charleston, 31 August 1760, CO 5/377, f. 27.

181. Timberlake, *Memoirs*, 65–6 [89–90]; *South Carolina Gazette*, 31 May–7 June 1760.

182. Ibid., 16–23 August 1760.

183. Ibid.

184. Ibid., 20–27 September 1760.

185. Ibid., 6–13, 13–20, 20–27 September, 11–18 October 1760.

186. Bull to the Board of Trade, Charleston, 21 October 1760, enc. Major Andrew Lewis to Byrd, n.d. (copy), CO 5/377, ff. 1–3 (copies in the Hardwicke Papers, BL Add. MS, 35,910, 108–10); *South Carolina Gazette*, 18–25 October 1760.

187. Bull to the Board of Trade, 21/24 October 1760, and duplicate with additional postscript, CO 5/377, Pt. 1; ff. 31–8.

Chapter 5 The Carpenter and the Colonel

1. Corkran, *Cherokee Frontier*, 254; Alden, *John Stuart*, 128–9; Sirmans, *South Carolina*, 338–9; D. E. Leach, *Arms For Empire* (Macmillan, New York and London, 1973) 491.

2. Amherst Papers, WO 34/47.
3. Sosin, *Whitehall and the Wilderness*, 32.
4. Ibid., 44–5, citing Board of Trade to Fauquier, 12 June 1760, CO 5/1367, 409–12.
5. Ibid., 46–7.
6. Ibid., 43.
7. Amherst to Grant, New York, 15 December 1760, WO 34/48, ff. 38–44.
8. Grant to Amherst, New York, 20 December 1760, WO 34/47, ff. 30–1.
9. Ibid.
10. Amherst to Grant, New York, 21 and 22 December 1760, WO 34/48, ff. 50–2, 58.
11. Grant to Amherst, 17 January 1761, WO 34/47, f. 36; Alexander Monypenny, Order Book, 24 December 1760 – 13 January 1761, typed transcript, Gilcrease Museum, Tulsa, Oklahoma.
12. Ellis to the Board of Trade, Georgia, 5 September, 25 October 1760, CO 5/640, ff. 15, 20. He was not alone in his belief that a conspiracy had already been hatched. A report reaching New York at the beginning of December had brought rumours of a Creek–Chickasaw–Cherokee alliance, potentially 7000–8000 warriors strong, and had convinced a London observer that the Cherokee war was 'likely to break out again with redoubled vigour...' Editorial comment and letter dated New York, 4 December [1760], *Royal Magazine*, January 1761 (vol. 4, January–June 1761).
13. [John Appy?] to Grant, 1 January 1761, Ballindalloch Muniments, Bundle 378. Fortunately for historians Grant did not burn the letter, but carefully preserved it. On 19 January this correspondent sent a second letter, illegibly initialled, describing an equally pessimistic visit from William Byrd. Ibid.
14. Grant to Amherst, Charleston, 17 January 1761, WO 34/47, ff. 36–7
15. Ibid., f. 37.
16. Ibid.
17. Ibid.
18. For example, the scalping of two privates cutting wood outside the fort on 21 January, and another of other minor, but menacing, incidents. *South Carolina Gazette*, 31 January – 2 February, 28 February – 7 March 1761.
19. Much to the chagrin of the *South Carolina Gazette*, whose anonymous Fort Prince George correspondent was unable to file his reports. *South Carolina Gazette*, 17–24 January 1761.
20. James Wright, Lieutenant-Governor of Georgia, to Grant, Savannah, 4 March and 20 May 1761, Ballindalloch Muniments, Bundle 378.
21. [Appy?] to Grant, 19 January 1761, ibid.
22. Amherst to Grant, 13 February 1761, WO 34/48, f. 61.
23. South Carolina Council Journal, 22 January 1761, CO 5/477, ff. 68–9; Bull to the Board of Trade, 29 January 1761, CO 5/377, ff. 51–2.
24. Bull to the Board of Trade, ibid.; Grant to Amherst, 29 January 1761, WO 34/47, f. 42.
25. *South Carolina Gazette*, 21–28 February, 28 February – 7 March 1761; Grant to Amherst, 13 March 1761, WO 34/47, f. 54.
26. Alexander Monypenny, Journal, 23 March 1761, 1–2, typed transcript, Gilcrease Museum, Tulsa, Oklahoma.
27. Ibid.

28. South Carolina Council Journal, 25 March 1761, CO 5/477, f. 52.
29. Monypenny, Journal, 1–2.
30. South Carolina Council Journal, 25 March 1761, CO 5/477, ff. 52, 53.
31. Monypenny, Journal, 4, 5.
32. South Carolina Council Journal, 13 April 1761, CO 5/477, f. 55.
33. 'A Talk from the Young Warrior of Estatoe to Mr. McIntosh', Fort Prince George, 21 April 1761 (copy), enclosed with Grant to Amherst, 12 April 1761, WO 34/47, ff. 59–60.
34. South Carolina Council Journals, 25 March 1761, CO 5/477, f. 53.
35. Bull to Attakullakulla, 30 March 1761 (copy), Ballindalloch Muniments, Bundle 560. Amherst's copy is at WO 34/47, ff. 90–2. See also Corkran, *Cherokee Frontier*, 242–3. The deal with Tistoe was already over a week old, for Monypenny, then with the army at Monk's Corner, had heard of it on 23 March; see Monypenny, Journal, 23 March 1760, 2.
36. Grant to Amherst, 30 March 1761, WO 34/47, f. 58.
37. Ibid.
38. Ibid.; Grant to Amherst, Monk's Corner, 12 April 1761, WO 34/47, f. 59.
39. Ibid., ff. 59–60.
40. Amherst to Grant, New York, 7 May 1761, WO 34/48, f. 76.
41. Ibid.
42. Amherst to Grant, New York, 12 May 1761, WO 34/47, f. 77.
43. Grant to Amherst, Camp near Fort Prince George, 2/5 June 1761, WO 34/47, f. 81.
44. South Carolina Commons Journals, Thursday 5 September 1761, CO 5/477, ff. 113–14.
45. Bull to Grant, 14 April 1761, ibid., ff. 113–14. He was obviously testing the political water first: the day before the Council had discussed Seroweh's Talk of 1 April. South Carolina Council Journal, 13 April 1761, CO 5/377, f. 55.
46. Grant to Amherst, Camp at Congarees, 25 April 1761, WO 34/47, f. 64.
47. Bull to Grant, 14 April 1761, South Carolina Commons Journals, CO 5/477, ff. 113–14.
48. Ibid.
49. Ibid.
50. Ibid.
51. Ibid., f. 114.
52. Ibid.
53. Bull to Amherst, Charleston, 15 April 1761, WO 34/35, f. 145.
54. Grant to Amherst, Camp at Fort Prince George, 2/5 June 1761, WO 34/47, f. 82.
55. Bull to the Board of Trade, Charleston, 30 April 1761, CO 5/377, ff. 73–4.
56. South Carolina Commons Journals, 5 September 1761, CO 5/477, ff. 113–14.
57. Grant to Amherst, Camp at Fort Prince George, 2/5 June 1761, WO 34/47, f. 82.
58. Amherst to Grant, Albany, 13 July 1761, WO 34/48, f. 60.
59. Monypenny, Journal, 8.
60. Bull to Amherst, Charleston, 15 April 1761, WO 34/35, f.194; Grant to Amherst, Camp at 22 Mile Creek, 5 May 1761, WO 34/47, ff. 66–7.
61. South Carolina Council Journal, 6 May 1761, CO 5/477, f. 57.
62. Corkran, *Cherokee Frontier*, 243.

63. Ibid.
64. Ibid.
65. Grant to Amherst, Camp at Twenty-Two Mile Creek, 5 May 1761, WO 34/47, f. 66.
66. Bull to the Board of Trade, 16 and 20 May 1761, and the enclosed copy of the *South Carolina Gazette* of Wednesday, 6 May 1761, CO 5/377, ff. 75–8.
67. Corkran, *Cherokee Frontier*, 246; Monypenny, Journal, 3–5 May, 7–8 May, 10–14 May 1761, 8–12; Grant to Amherst, Camp at Fort Prince George, 2/5 June 1761, WO 34/47, f. 81. Monypenny was quite impressed by the rank-and-file Rangers, many of whom had 'good Riffled pieces', but despaired of the corruption of their captains. He goes on to describe in moving detail the miserable labours of the troops to build bridges across flooded streams.
68. Corkran, *Cherokee Frontier*, 246, citing *South Carolina Gazette*, 23 and 30 May, 20 June 1761.
69. Ibid.
70. Ibid.
71. Sir William Johnson to Lieutenant Daniel Claus, Castle Cumberland, 10 March 1761 (postscript), *Johnson Papers*, 3, 356.
72. Nicholas B. Wainwright (ed.), 'George Croghan's journal, 1759–1763', *Pennsylvania Magazine of History and Biography* (1947), 411; Croghan to Johnson, Fort Pitt, 10 February 1761, *Johnson Papers*, vol. 3, 329–37.
73. Wilbur R. Jacobs, *Dispossessing the American Indian: Indians and Whites on the Colonial Frontier* (University of Oklahoma Press, Norman, 1985) 85.
74. Corkran, ibid.
75. The Little Carpenter's Talk to Colonel Grant, WO 34/47, f. 89.
76. Monypenny, Journal, 28 May 1761, 19.
77. Ibid.; The Little Carpenter's Talk to Colonel Grant, Fort Prince George, 27 May 1761, WO 34/47, f. 89, Corkran, *Cherokee Frontier*, 246.
78. The Little Carpenter's Talk to Colonel Grant, WO 34/47, f. 89.
79. Ibid.
80. Monypenny, Journal, 28 May 1761, 19.
81. The Little Carpenter's Talk to Colonel Grant, WO 34/47, f. 89.
82. 'A Talk from Occonostota & the Little Carpenter to Lt. Mackintosh', Fort Prince George, 22 May 1761, Ballindalloch Muniments, Bundle 511. The dating of this Talk, delivered by Attakullakulla on arrival, suggests that the council meeting at Keowee took place rather later than Corkran's suggested date of 1 May; 14 May may be nearer the mark.
83. Grant to Amherst, Camp at Fort Prince George, 2/5 June 1761, WO 34/47, f. 61.
84. Monypenny, Journal, 23 May 1761, 16–17.
85. Ibid., 17.
86. Four Indians fired at the express as a party sallied out of the fort to meet him. Ibid., 28 May 1761, 19. The *Gazette's* correspondent, who thought that the galloper had left Grant's camp on 21 May – i.e. the day *before* Attakullakulla's Talk was written down – was clearly mistaken. *South Carolina Gazette*, 13–20 June 1761; Corkran, *Cherokee Frontier*, 244.
87. Ibid., 27 May 1761, 18.
88. Grant to Amherst, Camp at Fort Prince George, 2/5 June 1761, WO 34/47, f. 84.

89. Ibid.
90. Ibid.
91. *South Carolina Gazette*, 20 June 1761.
92. Corkran, *Cherokee Frontier*, 246; Attakullakulla's Talk to Colonel Grant, Fort Prince George, 27 May 1761, WO 34/47, f. 81.
93. French, Journal, Wednesday, 27 May 1761, 93; *South Carolina Gazette*, 13–30 June 1761.
94. French, Journal, Wednesday, 27 May 1761, 93.
95. Monypenny, Journal, 28 May 1761, 19.
96. French, Journal, Wednesday, 27 May 1761, 93.
97. Grant to Amherst, Camp at Fort Prince George, 2/5 June 1763, WO 34/47, f. 81.
98. French, Journal, Thursday, 28 May 1761, 94; Monypenny, Journal, 28 May 1761, 19–20; *South Carolina Gazette*, 13–20 June 1761.
99. French, Journals, 27–28 May 1761, 94.
100. Corkran, *Cherokee Frontier*, 246.
101. Monypenny, Journal, 28 May 1761, 19; Laurens to John Etwein, Camp of Keowee, 11 July 1761, Philip M. Hamer and George C. Rogers (eds), *The Papers of Henry Laurens Vol. Three: Jan. 1 1759–Aug. 31 1763* (University of South Carolina Press, Columbia, 1972) 74–5. The *Gazette*'s man at Fort Prince George, it seems, was not a direct witness of even the public Talk; he admitted himself that his account relied on second-hand description and rumour. *South Carolina Gazette*, 20 June 1761.
102. Grant to Amherst, Camp near Fort Prince George, 2/5 June 1761, WO 34/47, f. 81; The Little Carpenter's Talk to Colonel Grant, ibid., f. 89; French, Journal, 28 May 1761, 94; Monypenny, Journal, 28 May 1761, 19; Henry Laurens to John Etwein, Camp of Keowee, 11 July 1761, *Laurens Papers*, 3, 74.
103. Grant to Amherst, Camp near Fort Prince George, 2–5 June 1761.
104. Monypenny, Journal, 28 May 1761; *South Carolina Gazette*, 20 June 1761.
105. Monypenny, Journal, Thursday, 28 May 1761, 20.
106. Ibid.
107. Ibid.
108. Ibid.
109. Monypenny, Journal, 29 May 1761, 20.
110. French, Journal, Friday, 29 July 1761, 94.
111. *South Carolina Gazette*, 13–20 June 1761.
112. French, Journal, Friday, 29 May 1761, 94.
113. Grant to Amherst, Camp near Fort Prince George, 2/5 June 1761, WO 34/47, f. 81; Bull to the Board of Trade, Charleston, 19 June 1761, CO 5/377, f. 81.
114. *South Carolina Gazette*, 13–20 June 1761.
115. Ibid.
116. *South Carolina Gazette*, 20 June 1761.
117. Monypenny, Journal, 30 May 1761, 21.
118. Ibid., 29, 30 May 1761, 19–20; Bull to the Board of Trade, Charleston, 19 June 1761, CO 5/377, f. 82.
119. Grant to Amherst, Camp near Fort Prince George, 2/5 June 1761, WO 34/47, f. 82.

120. Ibid., f. 81.
121. Bull to the Board of Trade, Charleston, 19 June 1761, CO 5/377, f. 82.
122. Grant to Amherst, Camp near Fort Prince George, 2/5 June 1761, WO 34/47, f. 82.
123. French, Journal, Sunday, 7 June 1761, 96–7.
124. Grant to Amherst, Camp near Fort Prince George, 2/5 June 1761; Byrd to Grant, Williamsburg, (22?) April 1761 (extract), WO 34/47, f. 92; Monypenny, Journal, 21 May 1761, 14.
125. Bull to Amherst, Charleston, 30 April 1761, WO 34/35, f. 199.
126. South Carolina Gazette, 13–20 June 1761; Corkran, Cherokee Frontier, 247.
127. French, Journal, Monday, 8 June 1761, 98–9.
128. Laurens to Etwein, Laurens Papers, 3, 74.
129. 'Journal of the March and Operations of the Troops under the Command of lieut. Colonel Grant of the 40th Regiment, upon an Expedition from Fort Prince George against the Cherokees', 10 June 1761, WO 34/40, f. 95.
130. Grant, Journal, 10 June 1761, WO 34/40, f. 95.
131. Corkran, Cherokee Frontier, 246.
132. Bull to Amherst, Charleston, 6 June 1761, WO 34/35, f.201.
133. French, Journal, Tuesday, 25 August 1761, 158.
134. Laurens to Etwein, Laurens Papers, 3, 74. Grant, Journal, 10 June 1761, f. 96.
135. Ibid.
136. 1433 regulars and 537 provincial effectives, not counting the Rangers and Indians. 'Return of His Majesty's Forces in South Carolina commanded by Lt. Coll. Grant, with all Casualties since last Return of 4th May 1761', WO 34/47, f. 85; 'Return of Colonel Middleton's Provincial Regiment', 1 June 1761, ibid.
137. French, Journal, Tuesday, 9 June 1761, 101. The soldiers thought it might also mean that the Cherokees had captured a missing soldier of 17 Regiment, hitherto supposed drowned.
138. Ibid.
139. Ibid., Wednesday, 10 June 1761, 102; Grant, Journal, 10 June 1761. The creation and brigading of the provincial light infantry had taken place on 31 May. Monypenny, Journal, 31 May 1761, 21. Unfortunately this is Monypenny's last surviving entry.
140. French, Journal, Wednesday 10 June 1761, 102.
141. Grant, Journal, 10 June 1761; Maryland Gazette, 13 August 1761; Corkran, Cherokee Frontier, 248.
142. French, Journal, Wednesday, 10 June 1761, 103.
143. Ibid., 249; Corkan, Cherokee Frontier, 249; Grant, Journal, 10 June 1761, f. 96; Proceedings of the court martial of Captain John Dargan of the Rangers, Camp at Fort Prince George, 4 August 1761, Ballindalloch Muniments, Bundle 378; Adair, American Indians, 253.
144. '[T]he Carpenter declared before Some Gentlemen of veracity here that the Indians lost Twenty Two men & Some women on the 10th of June & that in Col Montgomery's action they lost more than Double the Number, which they agreed among themselves should be kept a secret from the white people.' John Stuart to Grant, Charleston, 17 October 1761, Ballindalloch Muniments, Bundle 378. The prisoner is mentioned in Laurens to Etwein, 11 July 1761, Laurens Papers, 3, 75, and may be the man

brought in and later butchered by a Catawba who had lost a relative in the engagement. French, Journal, Wednesday, 10 June 1761. Laurens later claimed that the Carpenter had admitted to 32 Cherokee dead, which tallies with the estimate given to Stuart. Laurens also claimed that John Bench, a Fort Loudoun survivor released after the battle, thought 38 had died, while Old Caesar would only admit to ten men and one woman. Laurens' own estimate was 35.'A Letter Signed Philolethes', *Laurens Papers*, 3, 288. Three of the prisoners taken after 10 June said that every town [presumably meaning the Middle settlements] had lost men. *South Carolina Gazette*, 25 July – 1 August 1761.

145. 'Return of the Killed and Wounded...',10 June 1761, WO 34/47, f. 97; French, Journal, Wednesday, 10 June 1761, 103–4. These sources and other witnesses confirm that the Cherokees made their main effort against the centre and rear of the column; the leading light infantry escaped lightly. See the letter dated 'Col. Grant's head-quarters, near Fort Prince George', 10 July 1761, *Royal Magazine*, vol. 5 (September 1761), 153–4.

146. Ibid.; Grant, Journal, 10 June 1761. The bodies were put into the river to protect them from the Cherokees. But over a week later French's men found the corpse of one of Burton's sergeants floating down the stream. French, Journal, Thursday, 18 June 1761, 132–3.

147. French, Journal, Wednesday, 10 June 1761, 105. Hatley fastened on this isolated and unproven order to argue that the level of violence had risen sharply since the attack on Little Keowee in 1760. Hatley, *Dividing Paths*, 139. However such an interpretation is quite inconsistent with Grant's earlier and later actions.

148. French, Journal, Wednesday, 10 June 1761, 105.

149. Ibid.

150. Ibid., Wednesday, 10, Thursday, 11 June 1761, 103–104, 106–107.

151. Ibid.

152. Ibid., Friday, 12, Saturday, 13 June 1761; Grant, Journal, 12–14 June, WO 34/40, ff. 95–6; Corkran, *Cherokee Frontier*, 250.

153. French, Journal, Friday, 10, Sunday, 14, Tuesday, 16 June 1761, 126–7, 129, 130.

154. Corkran, *Cherokee Frontier*, 251; Grant, Journal, f. 96; *South Carolina Gazette*, 4–11 July 1761. The Catawbas had a particularly well established reputation for indiscipline, savagery and leaving when they felt like it. Merrell, *Indians' New World*, 161–2. There is rich irony here, in view of the Catawbas' derision of the Cherokees for leaving Forbes in 1758.

155. Laurens to Etwein, 11 July 1761, *Laurens Papers*, 3, 75.

156. Letter dated 'Col. Grant's head-quarters...', 10 July 1761, *Royal Magazine*, September 1761, vol. 5 (1761) 154–5.

157. 'Extract of a letter from an Officer in Col. Middleton's regiment', 10 July 1760, ibid.

158. Grant, Journal, f. 96.

159. French, Journal, Friday, 3 July 1761, 148.

160. Grant to Amherst, Camp at Fort Prince George, 10 July 1761, WO 34/47, f. 94.

161. Grant, Journal, f. 98. Next day French saw about twenty skeletons as well as some freshly killed. French, Journal, Saturday, 4 July 1761, 148.

162. Ibid.

163. Grant to Bull, 23 April 1761, Letterbook 1761, Ballindalloch Muniments, Bundle 772, cited in Nelson, *James Grant*, 33, n.5. This Bundle is now missing. 'Copy of Colonel Middleton's Letter to Colonel Grant, Camp Near Fort P. George, 10 July 1761', *Laurens Papers*, 3, 291–2; Bull, *Oligarchs*, 86–7.

164. John Rattray to Grant, Charleston, 16 August 1761, Ballindalloch Muniments, Bundle 378. This letter, and Grant's April letter cited by Nelson, explode the assertion of Bull's biographer that Grant knew of and approved the discretion given to Middleton. Bull, *Oligarchs*, 99; Grant to Amherst, Camp at Fort Prince George, 3 September 1761, WO 34/47, ff. 98–9.

165. Grant to Amherst, Camp near Fort Prince George, 2/5 June 1761, ibid., f. 82.

166. Monypenny, Journal, 29 April 1761, 7.

167. French, Journal, Tuesday, 16 June 1761, 129.

168. Grant to Amherst, Camp at Fort Prince George, 3 September 1761, WO 34/47, ff. 98–9.

169. Ibid.; 'Copy of Colonel Middleton's Letter to Colonel Grant[,] Camp near Fort P. George', 10 July 1761, *Laurens Papers*, 3, 291 2.

170. Weir, *South Carolina*, 271.

171. John Rattray to Grant, 18 July 1761, Ballindalloch Muniments, Bundle 378.

172. Timothy admitted that Middleton had been the author of the letter 'inserted in my last [the issue of 18–25 July] ... I think little Good can result there-from; but I am so circumstanced that refuse or publish, I am equally exposed to Censure...I shall only add, that my Press is as free and open to your Correspondent as to mine...' Timothy to Lieutenant John Grey, Charleston, 29 July 1761, Ballindalloch Muniments, Bundle 378. Two more anonymous letters, the first dated Charleston, 28 July 1761, appeared immediately afterwards; these appear to have been replies to pro-Grant pieces in Charleston's other *Gazette*, copies of which have not survived. But the extent of Timothy's embarrassment is evident. the first part of the second letter was obliterated by another report. *South Carolina Gazette*, 25 July – 1 August, 1–8 August 1761.

173. Grant to Amherst, Camp at Fort Prince George, 3 September 1761, WO 34/47, ff 98–9.

174. Bull, *Oligarchs*, 99. Laurens was now firmly within Grant's circle of friends. 'My best wishes are always with you & with Maj. Monypenny & those other Gentlemen who used to incircle your Evening Table at Keowih!' Laurens to Grant, Charleston, 11 February 1762, Ballindalloch Muniments, Bundle 378. It seems that these 'Gentlemen' included other provincial officers such as Moultrie. A[lexander] M[onypenny] to Grant, Forbes's House [Charleston], 14 November [1761], ibid.

175. Rattray to Grant, Charleston, 16 August 1761, ibid.

176. Ibid.

177. Byrd to Grant, Camp at Stalnaker's, 19 and 22 July 1761; with the latter was enclosed Byrd's Talk to 'Occonostota, Jud's Friend, Tistoe, Scalyousca and all the Warriors of the Cherokees', Camp at Stalnaker's, 19 July 1761. Ballindalloch Muniments, Bundle 378. See also Byrd to Bull, 26 July 1761, and South Carolina Commons Journal, 15 September 1761, CO 5/379, f. 115.

178. *Maryland Gazette*, 10 September 1761, cited in Corkran, *Cherokee Frontier*, 256–7.

179. Ibid.; French, Journal, 21 July 1761, 153.

180. Ibid.
181. *South Carolina Gazette*, 24 August 1761, cited in Corkran, *Cherokee Frontier*, 257.
182. Ibid.; French, Journal, Monday, 10 August 1761, 156.
183. Ibid.
184. Grant to Amherst, Camp at Fort Prince George, 3 September 1761, WO 34/47, f. 99.
185. Grant to Bull, Camp at Fort Prince George, 2 September 1761, South Carolina Commons Journals, CO 5/479, f. 115.
186. Attakullakulla's Talk to the Council, S.C. Council Journal, 18 December 1761, CO 5/477, ff. 97–100; Corkran, *Cherokee Frontier*, 255. Even while the raid had been in progress the offal left behind had shown that the Cherokees were slaughtering precious horses for food. 'A Letter Signed Philolethes', 2 March 1763, *Laurens Papers*, 3, 286–7.
187. Corkran, *Cherokee Frontier*, 255.
188. Ibid., citing the *South Carolina Gazette*, 20 June 1761.
189. Bull to Amherst, Charleston, 17 June 1761, WO 34/35, ff. 202–3.
190. Corkran, *Cherokee Frontier*, 255.
191. French, Journal, Friday, 28 August 1761, 159.
192. Ibid., 159–60.
193. Corkran, *Cherokee Frontier*, 257–8, citing *Laurens Papers*, no. 49, 108–9.
194. French, Journal, Tuesday 25 August 1761, 158–9.
195. Ibid., Friday, 28 August 1761, 159.
196. Ibid.

Chapter 6 The Carpenter, the Corn Puller and the 'Town of Lyes'

1. Grant to Amherst, Camp at Fort Prince George, 10 July 1761, WO 34/47, f. 94.
2. Ibid.
3. Ibid.
4. Grant to Amherst, Camp at Fort Prince George, 3 September 1761, ibid., ff. 98.
5. Ibid., f. 99.
6. Amherst, Monypenny and other officers had thought he should have been shot out of hand. But when Grant heard of it he 'did not chuse to have it done' in cold blood. Grant to Amherst, Camp at Congarees, 25 April 1761, WO 34/47, f. 64; Amherst to Grant, New York, 12 May 1761, WO 34/48, f. 77; Monypenny, Journal, 15 April 1761, 5–6.
7. Grant to Amherst, Camp at Fort Prince George, 10 July 1761, WO 34/47, f. 94.
8. Grant to Amherst, Fort Prince George, 3 September 1761, ibid., f. 99.
9. Byrd to Amherst, Camp at Stalnaker's, 1 August 1761, ibid., f. 136.
10. Ibid.
11. Ibid., ff. 136–7.
12. Timberlake, *Memoirs*, 0–10 [36–38].
13. Fauquier to Amherst, Williamsburg, 29 August 1761, CO 5/1330, f. 73.

14. Amherst to Grant, Albany, 1 August 1761, WO 34/48, ff. 83–4.
15. Ibid.
16. French, Journal, Saturday, 29 August 1761, 160.
17. 'Attakullakulla's Talk to Col. Grant', Camp at Fort Prince George, 29 August 1761, WO 34/47, f. 163.
18. Grant to Bull, Camp at Fort Prince George, 2 September 1761, South Carolina Commons Journals, CO 5/479, f. 114.
19. Ibid.
20. Corkran, *Cherokee Frontier*, 260.
21. Grant to Bull, Camp at Fort Prince George, 2 September 1761, South Carolina Commons Journals, CO 5/479, ff. 114–15.
22. Ibid., f. 119.
23. Ibid.
24. French, Journal, Monday, 31 August 1761, 160–1.
25. South Carolina Commons Journal, CO 5/479, ff. 119–20
26. Ibid., f. 120.
27. Ibid.
28. Ibid.
29. Ibid.
30. Ibid.
31. French, Journal, Monday, 31 August 1761, 160–1.
32. Ibid.
33. Ibid., ff. 81–2.
34. Grant to Bull, Camp at Fort Prince George, 2 September 1761, South Carolina Commons Journals, CO 5/479, f. 115.
35. Ibid.; Amherst thought Gunninghame 'should have no Mercy shewn to him', having interfered in crucial public business for 'private advantage'. Amherst to Grant, Staten Island, 2 October, 1761, WO 34/10, f. 07.
36. South Carolina Council Journals, 10 September 1761, CO 5/477, f. 79.
37. South Carolina Council Journals, 10 September 1761, CO 5/477, f. 79.
38. Ibid., 15 September 1761, CO 5/477, ff. 81–2.
39. South Carolina Commons Journals, 'At the House of Mr. Legge in Shem Town', Tuesday 15 September 1761, CO 5/479, ff. 112–6.
40. Ibid., f. 116. The other members were Colonel Byrne of the provincial militia, Thomas Smith, John Savage, Logan, Goddsdon, Sommers, Manigault and Pinkney.
41. Ibid., f. 117.
42. Ibid.
43. Ibid.
44. Ibid., 17, 18 September 1761, CO 5/479, ff. 117–21.
45. Ibid., f.121.
46. Ibid.
47. Ibid., ff. 121–2.
48. Bull to the Board of Trade, Charleston, 23 September 1761 (duplicate) CO 5/377, f. 85; Bull to Amherst, Charleston, 24 September 1761 (copy), CO 5/61, ff. 526–7.
49. South Carolina Council Journals, Council Chamber, 22 September 1761, CO 5/477, f. 83.
50. Ibid., ff. 83–5.

51. Ibid., f. 85.
52. Bull to the Board of Trade, Charleston, 23 September 1761, CO 5/377, f. 85. An abstract of this letter was sent to Egremont, then Secretary of State, on 11 December. CO 5/386, ff. 15–18.
53. Bull to Amherst, Charleston, 24 September 1761, CO 5/61, ff. 526–7.
54. Grant to Amherst, Camp at Fort Prince George, 6 October 1761, WO 34/47, ff. 108–9.
55. Ibid., f. 214.
56. Grant to Amherst, Camp at Ninety Six, 5 November 1761, WO 34/47, f. 111.
57. Ibid., Christopher French, who went with him, records that they went via Sugar Town, Toxaway, 'Qualasatchee', Estatoe and 'Cholunna' – nine miles in all. French, Journal, Wednesday, 14 October 1761, 165.
58. Grant to Amherst, Camp at Ninety Six, 5 November 1761, WO 34/47, f. 111.
59. Ibid.; French, Journal, Friday 16 October 1761, 166.
60. Grant to Amherst, Camp at Ninety Six, 5 November 1761, WO 34/47, f. 111.
61. Ibid.
62. Ibid., f. 112.
63. Amherst to Grant, Staten Island, 2 October 1761, Ballindalloch Muniments, Bundle 468. It also deplored Grant's 'little paper War' with Middleton and Bull, and ordered him to stop his part in it.
64. Amherst to Grant, Staten Island, 9 October 1761, Ibid.; Amherst to Captain Campbell, officer commanding His Majesty's Ships of War at Charles Town, Staten Island, 9, 10 October 1761, ibid.
65. Ibid.; A[lexander] M[onypenny] to Grant, Forbes's House, [Charleston], 14 November 1761, Ballindalloch Muniments, Bundle 378.
66. Grant to Amherst, Camp at Ninety Six, 5 November 1761, WO 34/47, f. 112.
67. McIntosh [to Grant], Fort Prince George, 6 November 1761, Ballindalloch Muniments, Bundle 378.
68. A Talk from Tistoe and the Wolf to Capt. [*sic*] Mackintosh, Fort Prince George, 1 November 1761, ibid.
69. McIntosh [to Grant], Fort Prince George, 6 November 1761, ibid.
70. 'A Talk from Tistoe and the Wolf...', Fort Prince George, 1 November 1761, ibid.
71. Ibid.
72. A[lexander] M[onypenny] to Grant, Forbes's House, [Charleston], 14 November [1761], ibid. He wished that Grant 'had rubb'd up his Candour in the rough Rice and Wood Cattle' and concluded 'showing what you had a Right to expect from a Lt. Governor so candid & well inform'd'.
73. South Carolina Council Journals, 13 November 1761, CO 5/477, f. 89.
74. Ibid.
75. Stuart to Grant, Charleston, 17 October 1761, Ballindalloch Muniments, Bundle 378. Stuart's indignation was genuine enough, even though in this same letter he asked Grant to recommend him to Amherst as successor to Atkin, who had died 'last week'.
76. Ibid.
77. Laurens to Grant, Charleston, 15 November 1761, ibid.
78. Monypenny to Grant, Forbes's House, Charleston, 14 November 1761, ibid.
79. Laurens to Grant, Charleston, 15 November 1761, ibid.
80. Monypenny to Grant, Charleston, 15 November 1761, ibid.

81. McIntosh to Bull, Fort Prince George, 16 November 1761, South Carolina Commons Journal, CO 5/479, f. 125.
82. Grant to Amherst, Camp near Ninety Six, 19 November 1761, WO 34/47, ff. 116–17.
83. Ibid., f. 116. The Georgia traders' activities were well known in Charleston, probably from other sources besides Grant, by early December. See letter dated Charleston, 9 December 1761, *Royal Magazine*, February 1761, p. 104.
84. 'A Letter Signed Philolethes', 2 March 1763, *Laurens Papers*, 3, 282 and note. Corkran identified Gunninghame and McLemore as smugglers, *Cherokee Frontier*, 295. Bull to the Board of Trade (duplicate), Charleston, 23 September 1761, CO 5/377, f. 85.
85. McIntosh to Bull, Fort Prince George, 16 November 1761, South Carolina Commons Journals, CO 5/479, f. 125; Grant to Amherst, Camp near Ninety Six, 19 November 1761, WO 34/47, f. 116.
86. 'A Talk from the Little Carpenter to Mr. Mackintosh', Fort Prince George, 15 November 1761, Ballindalloch Muniments, Bundle 378
87. Ibid.
88. McIntosh to Bull, Fort Prince George, 16 November 1761, South Carolina Commons Journals, CO 5/479, f. 125.
89. Ibid.; 'A Talk From the Little Carpenter to be Sent to the Gov. & Col. Grant', Fort Prince George, 16 November 1761, Ballindalloch Muniments, Bundle 378. Copy in South Carolina Commons Journals (Thursday, 3 December 1761), CO 5/479, f. 124.
90. '[T]hey hint at Presents in the same manner as they were formerly paid for those [prisoners] who were brought down to the Fort in Winter', Grant to Amherst, Camp near Ninety Six, 19 November 1761, WO 34/47, f. 116.
91. Ibid.
92. Ibid.
93. South Carolina Commons Journals, 3 December 1761, CO 5/479, f. 124.
94. South Carolina Council Journals, 14 December 1761, CO 5/477, f. 93.
95. Ibid.
96. Ibid., f. 94.
97. Ibid., ff. 94–5.
98. Ibid., 17 December 1761, ff. 196–7.
99. Ibid.
100. Ibid., 18 December 1761, 97–9.
101. Ibid., ff. 99–100; letter from Charleston, 23 December 1761, *Royal Magazine*, Vol.6 (January–June 1762), issue for February 1762, 104.
102. South Carolina Commons Journals, Saturday 19 December 1761, CO 5/479, f. 128.
103. Ibid., Thursday, 17 December 1761.
104. Ibid., Monday, 21 December 1761, f. 128.
105. Ibid., Tuesday, 22 December 1761, f. 128.
106. Ibid., f. 129.
107. Ibid.
108. J. Russell Snapp, *John Stuart and the Struggle for Empire on the Southern Frontier*. Louisiana State University Press, Baton Rouge and London, 1996, Introduction and chs 1–6, *passim*.
109. 'A Letter Signed Philolethes', *Laurens Papers*, 3, 284.

110. Letter from Charleston, 16 December 1761, *Royal Magazine*, Vol. 6 (January –June 1762), February 1762, 104.

Epilogue: Toward Augusta

1. Timberlake, *Memoirs*, 9–11 [36–40].
2. For a full account of this embassy, see John Oliphant, 'The Cherokee Embassy to London, 1762', *Journal of Imperial and Commonwealth History*, vol. 27, no. 1, January 1999.
3. Timberlake, *Memoirs*, 30–4 [57–60].
4. Ibid., 73–4 [96–7].
5. Boone to the Board of Trade, Charleston, 28 February 1762, CO 5/377, f. 94.
6. Timberlake, *Memoirs*, 81–87 [105–9].
7. Ibid., 90 [111].
8. Ibid.
9. Ibid., 87–90 [109–11]; Corkran, *Cherokee Frontier*, 270.
10. Letter from Fort Prince George dated 13 June 1762, *Public Advertiser*, 21 August 1762.
11. Timberlake, *Memoirs*, 97–111 [117–29]
12. Fauquier to the Board of Trade, Williamsburg, 16 April, 1 May 1762, CO 5/1330, ff. 121, 123–5. For the Order see Sosin, *Whitehall and the Wilderness*, 48, and Chapter 1 above.
13. Ibid.; Timberlake, *Memoirs*, 112–3 [129–32]; Foreman, *Indians Abroad*, 65–6.
14. Ibid.
15. Board of Trade to Egremont, Whitehall, 11 December 1761 (received on 12 December), enclosing Bull to the Board of Trade, 23 September 1761 (extract) and a copy of the preliminary peace terms.
16. Egremont to Amherst, Whitehall, 12 December 1761, CO 5/214, f. 244. The letter may well have been drafted by Ellis. Cashin, *Henry Ellis*, 153.
17. Sosin, *Whitehall and the Wilderness*, 32, 47.
18. Ibid.
19. Foreman, *Indians Abroad*, 67; Timberlake, *Memoirs*, 115 [133]; *St. James's Chronicle or the British Evening Post*, 17–19 June 1762; *London Evening Post*, 17–19 June 1762.
20. Foreman, *Indians Abroad*, 68–9; Timberlake, *Memoirs*, 116–26 [134–44]; Egremont to Fauquier, Whitehall, 10 July 1762, CO 5/1345, ff. 9–10; *St. James's Chronicle*, 17–19, 19–22, 24–26 June, 3–6, 6–8, 10–10 [sic], 20–22 July 1762; *Public Advertiser*, 21, 24 June, 9, 12 July, 14 August 1762; *The Annual Register or a Vieue of the History, Politics and Literature for the Year 1762*, (5th edn (London, 1787) 92–3; 'Montgomerie, Hon. Archibald (1726–96) of Minnoch, Ary', in Sir Lewis Namier and John Brooke (eds), *History of Parliament: the House of Commons 1754–1790. Vol III: Members K-Y* (HMSO for the History of Parliament Trust, 1964) 157–8.
21. Timberlake, *Memoirs*, 126–9 [145–7]; *Public Advertiser*, 20 August 1762; *London Evening Post*, 19–21 August 1762; *Royal Magazine*, vol. VII (August 1762) 109; *Gentleman's Magazine*, August 1762, 388.
22. Boone to Egremont, Charleston, 11 November 1762 (received 4 March 1763), ibid., 1–5, enc. 'A Talk between His Excellency Thomas Boone

Esquire ... And Judds friend the Head-man of the Cherokee Nation Delivered in the Council Chamber at Charleston, Weds. 3 Nov. 1762'.

23. Stuart to Amherst, Charleston, 15 March 1763, Amherst Papers, vol. 3, microfilm Reel 2, Clements Library.
24. Thornton, *The Cherokees*, 31. See the population figures on pp. 1–2, above.
25. Ibid.; Jones, *License for Empire*, 41; De Vorsey, *Indian Boundary*, 19–23. Creek fighting strength was estimated at 3500 in 1764, Alden, *John Stuart*, 10.
26. Hatley, *Dividing Paths*, 161–5.
27. Ibid.
28. Jones, *License for Empire*, 51.
29. Milling, *Red Carolinians*, 308.
30. *South Carolina Gazette*, 2 April 1763; Hatley, *Dividing Paths*, 183.
31. Ibid.
32. De Vorsey, *Indian Boundary*, 48–58.
33. Ibid., 58; Sosin, *Whitehall and the Wilderness*, 46; Fauquier to the Board of Trade, Williamsburg, 30 November 1761, f. 91.
34. Boone to Egremont, 21 April 1763, CO 5/390, f. 10.
35. Jones, *License for Empire*, 47.
36. 'Journal of the Congress at Augusta', CO 5/65, ff. 48, 49, 53.
37. Boone's message to the Commons, 3 September 1763 (copy), enclosing the affidavit of Richard Henderson, of the parish of St. Paul in Augusta, 26 August 1763, and William Richardson to Stuart, Wraxhaws, 31 August 1763 (copy), CO 5/377, ff. 241–4.
38. Sosin, *Whitehall and the Wilderness*, 32 ff.
39. Stagg, 'Protection and Survival', Chapter IX, 460 ff., *passim*.
40. Ibid., 442.
41. Deposition of John and William Gray, n.d., William Drake, Commissioner for Indian Affairs, to Charles Pinckney, Santee, 20 July 1736; 'Extracts of Conferences held with the Cherokee Deputies transmitted by Col. Grant Sept. 3 to Sr. Jef. Amherst & by him sent to Pit in his letter of 5 October 1761'; 'Humble Representation of William Bull' to the Board of Trade, 25 May 1758, Egremont Papers, PRO 30/41/14/14-58.
42. Egremont Papers, PRO 30/41/14/ 3, 21.
43. Ellis to Egremont, Gray's Inn, 15 December 1762, Ibid., 22/240–247; [Henry Ellis], 'On the methods to prevent giving any alarm to the Indians by taking possession of Florida and Louisiana', ibid., 246–9.
44. Egremont to the Board of Trade (unsigned copy), ibid., 37–42.
45. Circular letter to the governors of Virginia, North Carolina, South Carolina and Georgia, and to John Stuart; Egremont to Amherst, 16 March 1763, Egremont Papers, PRO 30/47/14/61–6.
46. Stagg, 'Protection and Survival', 461–85.
47. Stuart to Egremont, Charleston, 5 December 1763, CO 5/65, Part 2, ff. 69–71 (Stuart had not yet heard of Egremont's death and Halifax's succession); Boone to Egremont, Charleston, 1 June 1763, CO 5/390, ff. 12–13.
48. Stuart to Egremont, Charleston, 5 December 1763, CO 5/65, Part 2, ff. 69–71; 'Journal of the Congress.', ibid, Part 3, f. 41; *Maryland Gazette*, Thursday, 15 October 1763; Alden, *John Stuart*, 182.
49. 'Journal of the Congress', CO5/65, Part 2, 49, ff. 41–8.
50. Ibid., 48–9.

51. Ibid., 49.
52. Ibid., f. 50
53. Ibid.
54. Jones, *License for Empire*, 50-1.
55. Ibid.
56. 'Journal of the Conference...', CO 5/65, Part 3, CO 5/65, f. 53.
57. Ibid., f. 53.
58. Ibid., ff. 55-9.
59. The Governors and Superintendent to the Secretary of State, Augusta, 10 November 1763, Ibid., f. 67. This is the file copy sent to Halifax as part of the Journal. Another, perhaps the original and in Stuart's hand, is at ibid., Part 2, ff. 57-9.
60. 'Journal of the Congress', CO 5/65, ff. 59-60.
61. Ibid., f. 60.
62. Ibid.
63. Ibid., f. 61.
64. Ibid., ff. 62-5.
65. Jones, *License for Empire*, 50.
66. De Vorsey, *Indian Boundary*, 125-32; Alden, *John Stuart*, 215-7. Cochrane and Price, backed by Stuart, also successfully reduced the trade in rum after Bull, frightened as always of controversy, refused to act.
67. Jones, *License for Empire*, 48-9.

Bibliography

Bibliographies and guides

Anderson, William L. and Lewis, James A. *A Guide to Cherokee Documents in Foreign Archives*. Native American Bibliographical Series, No. 4. Scarecrow Press, Methuen (New Jersey) and London, 1983. Invaluable. Calendars individually many of the British-held documents used in this study.

Kutsche, Paul. *A Guide to Cherokee Documents in the Northeastern United States*. Scarecrow Press, Methuen (New Jersey) and London, 1986.

O'Donnell, James Howlett. *Southeastern Frontiers: Europeans, Africans, and American Indians, 1513–1840. A Critical Bibliography*. Indiana University Press, Bloomington, for the Newberry Library, 1982.

Manuscript sources

Public Record Office, Kew

Colonial Office. America And West Indies (Class Co 5). Carolina, North. Carolina, South. Georgia. Virginia.
Original Correspondence. Secretary of State.
Original Correspondence. Board of Trade.
Sessional Papers.
War Office. Amherst Papers (Class WO 34)
Chatham Papers
Egremont Papers

British Library

Bouquet Papers
This is a very large collection, containing both in-letters and copies of Bouquet's missives, sometimes in French, to a wide range of recipients. The most important of these concern the Fort Duquesne expedition of 1758.
Newcastle Papers

Ballindalloch Castle, Banffshire, Scotland

Papers in the Office of Sir Ewan Macpherson-Grant (Ballindalloch Muniments)
The thousands of bundles in this private archive include virtually all of James Grant's correspondence. An indispensable calendar is available at the National Register of Archives, Quality Court, Chancery Lane, London, and at the NRA (Scotland) in Edinburgh. However, only the general contents of each bundle is described, and the relevant ones have to be worked through in detail. The owners, Mr and Mrs O. M. Russell, must be approached initially through the NRA (S).

National Register of Archives (Scotland), Edinburgh [NRA(S)]

Dalhousie Muniments GD [Gifts And Deposits] 45
Part 2 of this large collection contains a significant number of letters by John Forbes.
Murray of Murraythwaite Muniments
Ferguson of Craigdarroch Muniments

Tracy W. McGregor Library, University of Virginia Library

Headquarters Papers Of Brigadier-General John Forbes Relating To The Expedition Against Fort Duquesne In 1758
The whole collection is microfilmed on three reels and is available free on inter-library loan for in-house use only. The papers complement the Forbes Papers in the Dalhousie Muniments, in Bouquet's papers and in the *Writings of Forbes*.

William L. Clements Library, University of Michigan

William Henry Lyttelton Papers
Lyttelton's in-letters, fully filmed on three reels. A wealth of material from other governors, military officers, various agents including Samuel Wyly and Daniel Pepper, and other correspondents.
Sir Jeffrey Amherst Papers
Not nearly as useful as WO 34, but has a few items of correspondence between Amherst and Stuart, mainly about the Augusta Congress. Microfilm.

Henry E. Huntington Library, San Marino, California

Loudoun Papers
Abercromby Papers

Library of Congress, Washington DC

The Journals of Christopher French
Available for purchase on microfilm.

Wisconsin State Historical Society

Draper Manuscripts. Series ZZ (Virginia Papers)
The most important items here are the William Byrd Papers in volume 4 (4ZZ) relating to Byrd's recruiting expedition in 1758 and to his command of the Virginian forces on the Holston in 1760 and 1761. Being directed to and from persons outside South Carolina, a good number of these items do not appear in other collections.

Thomas Gilcrease Museum, Tulsa, Oklahoma

Alexander Monypenny, Order Book and Journal 1761
Photocopies of the Museum's typed transcripts. The journal, particularly, provides valuable insight into Grant's expedition up to the end of May 1761.

Published documents

Hamer, Philip M., and Rogers, George C. (eds). *The Papers of Henry Laurens Vol. Three: Jan. 1 1759–Aug. 31 1763*. University of South Carolina Press, Columbia, 1972. The most important documents here are his letter to John Etwein of 11 July 1761, and the 'Letter signed Philolethes'.

Hamilton, S. M. (ed.). *Letters to Washington and Accompanying Papers*, Volumes II and III. Boston and New York, 1899. Transcriptions of many materials relating to Cherokee affairs. A useful complement to Bouquet, Forbes and Byrd respecting the events of 1758.

Jacobs, Wilbur R. (ed.). *Indians of the Southern Colonial Frontier: The Edmond Atkin Report and Plan of 1756*. University of Nebraska Press, Lincoln, 1967. Atkin's documents reproduced in full, with a useful introduction.

James, A. P. (ed.). *The Writings of General John Forbes Relating to his Service in North America*. Collegiate Press, Menasha, Wisconsin, 1938. Contains many documents from the Loudoun and Abercromby Papers, held in the Huntington Library, San Marino, California, as well as many from the Bouquet Papers in the British Library.

Kimball, G. S. (ed.). *Correspondence of William Pitt when Secretary of State with Colonial Governors and Military and Naval Commissioners in America*, Volume II. Macmillan, New York and London, 1906.

McDowell, William L. (ed.). *Colonial Records of South Carolina. Series 2. Documents Relating to Indian Affairs 1754–1765*. University of South Carolina Press for the South Carolina Department of Archives and History, Columbia, 1970. DRIA, as this volume is referred to in footnotes, contains the 'Indian Books', the files of Indian related correspondence kept by the South Carolina Commons House of Assembly, and now in the South Carolina archives. Copies of many, but not all, of the letters in the Lyttelton Papers are here, together with many which appear nowhere else. Only a few were entered into the Commons House's Journals. Unfortunately no entries were made after the spring of 1760.

Sullivan, James et al. *The Papers of Sir William Johnson*. Volumes II, III and IX. University of the State of New York, 1922, 1921, 1939.

Tinling, Marion (ed.). *The Correspondence of the Three William Byrds of Westover, Virginia 1684–1776*, Volume II. University Press of Virginia, Charlottesville, for the Virginia Historical Society, 1977. Largely the letters of the third William Byrd relating to his diplomatic and military activities in 1756, 1758, and 1760–1. Contains many documents located in the Amherst Papers WO 34, the MS Journals of the Virginia Council, the Virginia Papers (Series ZZ), the Draper Manuscripts held by the Wisconsin State Historical Society, and Monckton's papers the Public Archives Library, Ottawa. The editor has used the 'Received Copy', the version actually sent, wherever possible, and has noted the locations of transcriptions and contemporary copies.

Williams, S. C. 'An Account of the Presbyterian Mission to the Cherokees 1757–1759', *Tennessee Historical Magazine*, 2nd. ser., vol. I (1931) 125–38. Richardson's journal with commentary.

Woodmason, C. *The Carolina Backcountry on the Eve of the Revolution*. Ed. R. J. Hooker. University of North Carolina Press, 1953. The diaries and sermon books of Rev. Charles Woodmason, itinerant Anglican priest.

Works by contemporaries

Adair, James. *The History of the American Indians, Particularly Those Nations adjoining to the Mississippi, East and West Florida, Georgia, South and North Carolina and Virginia...* Edward and Charles Dilly, London, MDCCLXXV [1775].

Hewatt, Alexander. *An Historical Account of the Rise and Progress of the Colonies of South Carolina and Georgia*, 2 volumes. Printed for Alexander Donaldson, London, 1779. Reprinted by The Reprint Co., Spartanburg, South Carolina, 1971.

Mante, Thomas. *The History of the Late War in North America and the Islands of the West Indies including the Campaigns of MDCCLXIII and MDCCLXIV against His Majesty's Indian Enemies.* London, 1772.

Philopatrios [Pseud.]. *Some Observations of the Two Campaigns against the Cherokee Indians.* Printed by Peter Timothy, Charleston, 1762. Microprint copy, Huntington Library.

Timberlake, Henry. *The Memoirs of Lieutenant Henry Timberlake.* London, 1765. See also the more recent edition, S. C. Williams (ed.), The Watuga Press, Johnson City, 1927.

Newspapers and journals

British Library

The Annual Register or a Vieue of the History, Politics and Literature for the Year 1762, 5th edn (London, 1787)
The Gentleman's Magazine
The Royal Magazine, or Gentleman's Monthly Companion
The Gazette and London Daily Advertiser
The London Chronicle
The London Evening-Post
The Public Advertiser
The St. James's Chronicle or the British Evening Post

Cambridge University Library

The South Carolina Gazette
This is the newspaper edited by Peter Timothy. Cambridge will supply the persistent with microfilm copy on inter-library loan. No relevant copies of the rival *Gazette*, which published Grant's letters, survive.

Yale University Library

The Maryland Gazette
This paper did not merely copy stories from South Carolina, but had its own correspondents, probably traders or soldiers. The microfilm can be bought from Yale, but is not available on inter-library loan.

Secondary works

Alden, John R. *John Stuart and the Southern Colonial Frontier*. University of Michigan Press, Ann Arbor, 1944.

Aquila, R. *The Iroquois Restoration: Iroquois Diplomacy and the Colonial Frontier 1701–1754*. Wayne State University Press, Detroit, Michigan, 1983.

Axtell, James. *The European and the Indian: Essays in the Ethnohistory of Colonial North America*. Oxford University Press, New York, 1981.

Bargor, B. D. *Royal South Carolina 1719–1763*. University of South Carolina Press, Columbia, 1970.

Bartley, N. V. *The Creation of Modern Georgia*. Georgia University Press, Athens, 1983.

Billings, Warren M. et al. *Colonial Virginia: A History*. KTO Press, White Plains, New York, 1986.

Billington, Ray Allen. *Westward Expansion: A History of the American Frontier*, 4th edn. Macmillan, New York, 1974.

Brown, John P. *Old Frontiers: The Story of the Cherokee Indians from Earliest Times to the Date of their Removal to the West*. Southern Publishers, Kingsport, Tennessee, 1938.

Bull, J. Kinloch. *The Oligarchs in Colonial and Revolutionary Charleston: Lieutenant Governor William Bull and his Family*. University of South Carolina Press, Columbia, 1991.

Calmes, Alan. 'The Lyttelton Expedition of 1759: Military Failures and Financial Successes'. *South Carolina Historical Magazine*, vol. 77 (1976) 10–33.

Carroll, B. R. *Historical Collections of South Carolina*. 2 vols. Harper & Bros, New York, 1836.

Cashin, Edward J. *Governor Henry Ellis and the Transformation of British North America*. University of Georgia Press, Athens and London, 1994.

Cashion, Jerry Clyde. 'North Carolina and the Cherokees: The Quest for Land on the Eve of the American Revolution'. Unpublished PhD dissertation, University of North Carolina, 1979.

Cook, Thomas H. 'Old Fort Loudoun: the first English Settlement in what is now the state of Tennessee', *Tennessee Historical Magazine*, vol. 7 (1921) 111–33.

Corkran, David H. 'The Unpleasantness at Stecoe'. *North Carolina Historical Review*, vol. 32 (1955).

Corkran, David H. *The Cherokee Frontier: Conflict and Survival 1740–1762*. University of Oklahoma Press, Norman, 1962.

Crane, Verner W. *The Southern Frontier 1670–1732*. Duke University Press, Durham, North Carolina, 1929.

De Vorsey, L. *The Indian Boundary of the Southern Colonies 1763–1775*. University of North Carolina Press, Chapel Hill, 1966.

Eccles, W. J. *France in America*. Harper & Row, New York, 1972.

Eliades, D. K. 'The Indian Policy of Colonial South Carolina 1670–1763'. Unpublished PhD dissertation, University of South Carolina, 1981.

Foreman, Carolyn Thomas. *Indians Abroad 1493–1938*. University of Oklahoma Press, Norman, 1943.

Fortescue, J. W. *A History of the British Army*, vol. 2. Macmillan, London, 1910.

Franklin, W. Neill. 'Virginia and the Cherokee Indian Trade 1753–1778', *East Tennessee Historical Society Publications*, vol. 5 (1933) 22–38.

Gearing, Fred. *Priests and Warriors: Social Structures for Cherokee Politics in the Eighteenth Century*. American Anthropological Association, Memoir 93, Menasha, 1962.

George, David P. 'Ninety-Six Decoded: Origins of a Community's Name', *South Carolina Historical Magazine*, Vol. 92 (April 1991) 69–84.

Goodwin, Gary C. *Cherokees in Transition: A Study of Changing Culture and Environment Prior to 1775*. University of Chicago Department of Geography Research Paper No. 181, Chicago, 1977.

Greene, Jack P. 'The South Carolina Quartering Dispute 1757–1758', *South Carolina Historical Magazine*, vol. 60, (1959) 193–203.

Greene, Jack P. *The Quest For Power: The Lower Houses of Assembly in the Southern Royal Colonies 1169–1776*. W.W. Norton, for the Institute of Early American History, New York, 1963 [1972 edition].

Griffith, Lucille Blanch. 'South Carolina and Fort Albama 1714–1763', *Alabama Historical Review*, vol. 12 (1959) 258–271.

Halliburton, R. *Red Over Black: Black Slavery Amongst the Cherokee Indians*. Greenwood Press, Westport, Connecticut, and London, 1977.

Hamer, P. M. 'Anglo-French Rivalry in the Cherokee Country 1754–1757'. *North Carolina Historical Review*, vol. 2 (1925) 303–22.

Hatley, Tom. *The Dividing Paths: The Cherokees and South Carolina Through the Era of Revolution*. Oxford University Press, New York, 1993.

Hinderaker, Eric. *Elusive Empires: Constructing Colonialism in the Ohio Valley 1673-1800*. Cambridge University Press, New York, 1997.

Hudson, Charles. *The Southeastern Indians*. University of Tennessee Press, Knoxville, 1976.

Jacobs, Wilbur R. *Wilderness Politics and Indian Gifts: The Northern Colonial Frontier*. University of Nebraska Press, Lincoln, 1966.

Jacobs, Wilbur R. (ed.) *The Appalachian Indian Frontier: The Edmond Atkin Report and Plan*. University of Nebraska Press, Lincoln, 1967.

Jacobs, Wilbur R. *Dispossessing the American Indian: Indians and Whites on the Colonial Frontier*. University of Oklahoma Press, Norman, 1985.

Jennings, Francis P. *The Ambiguous Iroquois Empire: The Covenant Chain Confederation of Indian Tribes with English Colonies from its Beginning to the Lancaster Treaty of 1744*. W. W. Norton, New York, 1984.

Jennings, Francis P. *Empire of Fortune*. W.W. Norton, New York, 1988.

Jones, Dorothy. *License for Empire: Colonialism by Treaty in Early America*. University of Chicago Press, Chicago and London, 1983.

Jones, J. R. *Britain and the World 1649–1815*. London, Fontana, 1980.

King, Duane H. *The Cherokee Indian Nation: A Troubled History*. University of Tennessee Press, Knoxville, 1979.

Leach, D. E. *Arms for Empire: A Military History of the British Colonies in North America 1607–1763*. Macmillan, New York and London, 1973.

McCrady, E. *History of South Carolina Under the Royal Government 1719–1775*. Macmillan, New York, 1899.

McCue, Margaret Carrere. 'Lieutenant-Colonel James Grant's Expedition Against the Cherokee Indians, 1761'. Unpublished MA thesis, University of South Carolina, 1947.

Malone, H. T. *Cherokees of the Old South: A People in Transition*. University of Georgia Press, Athens, 1956.

Meriwether, Robert L. *The Expansion of South Carolina 1729–1768*. Southern Publishing, Tennessee, Kingsport, 1940.

Merrell, James H. 'The Problem of Slavery in Cherokee Culture'. *Reviews in American History*, vol. 7 (December 1979) 509–14.

Merrell, James H. 'The Indians' New World: the Catawba Experience'. *William and Mary Quarterly*, 3rd ser., vol. 41 (1984) 537–65.

Merrell, James H. 'The Racial Education of the Catawba Indians', *Journal of Southern History*, vol. 50 (August 1984) 363–84.

Merrell, James H. '"Minding the Business of the Nation": Hagler as Catawba Leader', *Ethnohistory*, vol. 33 (1986) 56–70.

Merrell, James H. '"Their Very Bones Shall Fight": The Catawba–Iroquois Wars', in Daniel K. Richter and James H. Merrell (eds), *Beyond the covenant Chain: The Iroquois and Their Neighbours in Indian North America 1600–1800*. Syracuse University Press, Syracuse, New York, 1987, 115–33.

Merrell, James H. *The Indians' New World: Catawbas and Their Neighbours From European Contact Through The Era of Removal*. Institute of Early American History and Culture, Williamsburg, Virginia/University of North Carolina Press, 1989.

Merrell, James H. 'Some Thoughts on Colonial Historians and American Indians', *William and Mary Quarterly*, 3rd ser., vol. 46 (January 1989) 94–119.

Merrell, James H. *Into the American Woods: Negotiations on the Pennsylvania Frontier*. W.W. Norton, New York and London, 1999.

Merrens, H. R. *Colonial North Carolina in the Eighteenth Century: A Study in Historical Geography*. University of North Carolina Press, Chapel Hill, 1964.

Milling, Chapman J. *Red Carolinians*. University of North Carolina Press, Chapel Hill, 1940.

Mooney, J. *Myths of the Cherokees*. 19th Annual Report of the Bureau of American Ethnology, 1897–1898, Washington, 1905.

Moore, John Hammond. *Columbia and Richland County: A South Carolina Community 1740–1990*. University of South Carolina Press, Columbia, 1993.

Morton, Richard L. *Colonial Virginia*. 2 vols. University of North Carolina Press, Chapel Hill, 1960.

Nelson, Paul David. *General James Grant: Scottish Soldier and Governor of East Florida*. University Press of Florida, Gainesville, 1993.

Olsen, Alison. 'Coffee House Lobbying', *History Today*, vol. 41 (January 1991) 35–41.

Parker, King L. 'Anglo-American Wilderness Campaigning 1754–1764: Logistical and Tactical Developments'. Unpublished PhD dissertation, Columbia University, 1970.

Peckham, Howard H. *The Colonial Wars 1689–1762*. University of Chicago Press, Chicago and London, 1964.

Perdue, Theda. *Slavery and the Evolution of Cherokee Society 1540–1866*. University of Tennessee Press, Knoxville, 1979.

Perdue, Theda. 'Cherokee Relations with the Iroquois in the Eighteenth Century', in Daniel K. Richter and James H. Merrell (eds), *Beyond the Covenant Chain: The Iroquois and Their Neighbours in Indian North America 1600–1800*. Syracuse University Press, Syracuse, New York, 1987, 135–48.

Perdue, Theda. *Cherokee Women: Gender and Culture Change 1700–1835*. University of Nebraska Press, Lincoln, 1998.

Reid, J. P. *A Better Kind of Hatchet: Law, Trade, and Diplomacy in the Cherokee Nation During the Early Years of European Contact*. University of Pennsylvania Press, University Park and London, 1976.

Rice, Otis T. 'The Sandy Creek Expedition of 1756'. *West Virginia History*, vol. 13 (1952) 5–19.

Robinson, Walter Stitt. *The Southern Colonial Frontier 1607–1763*. University of New Mexico Press, Albuquerque, 1979.

Robinson, Walter Stitt. *James Glen: from Scottish Provost to Royal Governor of South Carolina*. Greenwood Press, Westport, Connecticut, 1996.

Rogers, George C. *The History of Georgetown County, South Carolina*. University of South Carolina Press, Columbia, 1971.

Rothrock, Mary U. 'Carolina Traders Among the Overhill Cherokees 1690–1760', *East Tennessee Historical Society's Publications*, no. 1 (1929) 21–9.

Salley, A. S. *The History of Orangeburg County, South Carolina, from its first settlement to the close of the Revolutionary War*. R.L. Berry, Orangeburg, 1898.

Shaw, Helen Louise. *British Administration of the Southern Indians*. Lancaster Press, Lancaster, Pennsylvania, 1981; reprinted by Amo Press, New York, 1981.

Silver, Timothy. *A New Face on the Countryside: Indians, Colonists and Slaves in South Atlantic Forests 1500–1800*. Studies in Environmental History, Cambridge University Press, New York, 1990.

Simmons, R. C. *The American Colonies From Settlement to Independence*. Longman, London, 1976.

Sirmans, Eugene M. *Colonial South Carolina: A Political History*. University of North Carolina Press, Chapel Hill, 1966.

Smith, Betty Anderson. 'Distribution of Eighteenth Century Cherokee Settlements', in Peter H. Wood, Gregory A. Waselkin and M. Thomas (eds), *Powhatan's Mantle: Indians in the Colonial Southeast*. University of Nebraska Press, Lincoln, 1989.

Smith, W. Roy. *South Carolina as a Royal Province 1719–1776*. Macmillan, New York, 1903; reprinted New York, 1973.

Stagg, J. E. 'Protection and Survival: Anglo-Indian Relations 1748–60 – Britain and the northern colonies'. Unpublished PhD thesis, Cambridge, 1984.

Stone, Richard G. 'Captain Paul Demere at Fort Loudon 1757–1760', *East Tennessee Historical Society's Publications*, 41 (1969) 17–32.

Thornton, Russell, with Snipp, Matthew and Breen, Nancy. *The Cherokees: A Population History*. University of Nebraska Press, Lincoln and London, 1992. Based on original and secondary sources. Offers a detailed analysis and evaluation of previous demographic works and methods, as well as its own conclusions.

Wallace, David Duncan. *History of South Carolina*, 4 vols, American Historical Society, New York, 1934.

Wallace, David Duncan. *The Life of Henry Laurens: with a Sketch of the Life of Lieutenant-Colonel John Laurens*. G.P. Putnam & Sons, The Knickerbocker Press, New York and London, 1915.

Washburn, Wilcomb E. *Handbook of North American Indians*. Vol 4: *History of Indian–White Relations*. Smithsonian Institution, Washington, 1988.

Weir, R. M. *Colonial South Carolina: A History*. KTO, Millwood, New York, 1983.

White, Richard. *The Middle Ground: Indians, Empires and Republics in the Great Lakes Region 1650–1815*. Cambridge University Press, Cambridge, 1991.

Williams, S. C. *Early Travels in the Tennessee Country 1540–1800*. Watuga Press, Johnson City, 1938

Index